T0315927

The
Territories of the
Russian Federation
2006

The **Territories** of the **Russian Federation** 2006

7th Edition

Routledge
Taylor & Francis Group

LONDON AND NEW YORK

First published 1999

Seventh Edition 2006

Published 2014
by Routledge
2 Park Square, Milton Park, Abingdon, Oxon OX14 4RN

and by Routledge
711 Third Avenue, New York, NY, 10017, USA

Routledge is an imprint of the Taylor & Francis Group, an informa business

© **2006 Routledge**

All rights reserved. No part of this book may be reprinted or reproduced or utilised in any form or by any electronic, mechanical, or other means, now known or hereafter invented, including photocopying and recording, or in any information storage or retrieval system, without permission in writing from the publishers.

Whilst every effort has been made to ensure that the information contained in this work is correct, neither the authors nor Routledge can accept any responsibility for any errors or omissions or for any consequences arising therefrom.

Product or corporate names may be trademarks or registered trademarks and are used only for identification and explanation without intent to infringe.

ISBN 978-1-85743-357-9 (hbk)
ISSN 1465-461X

Editor: Dominic Heaney

Typeset in Times New Roman

Typeset by Unwin Brothers Limited, The Gresham Press, Old Woking, Surrey

Foreword

This, the seventh edition of *The Territories of the Russian Federation*, aims to furnish a clear and comprehensive introduction to Russia's regions, without which an understanding of the world's largest country must remain opaque. Since the sixth edition of this book was published, legislation, approved in late 2004, providing for the appointment of regional governors and presidents has taken effect, replacing a system of popular suffrage that had become almost universal across the Federation by the late 1990s. By the end of 2005 the majority of regional leaders who had sought reappointment, following either the expiry of their elective mandate or their resignation to seek presidential endorsement, had retained their office, although there were several notable exceptions. The unification, in December 2005, of two regions, Perm Oblast and the Komi-Permyak Autonomous Okrug, to form Perm Krai, was expected to be followed in due course by further measures that would result in a more substantial reduction in the number of federal subjects. In the mean time, acts of violence associated with the unresolved status of the Chechen (Nokchi) Republic, or related to an apparent increase in support for militant Islamist groups across the North Caucasus, threatened to destabilize several regions within the Federation, while prospects for a settlement of the Chechen conflict remained uncertain.

All the themes apparent in the Russian Federation as a whole are reflected in its 88 constituent parts. Issues such as the balance of power between the executive and legislative branches of government, the progress of economic or judicial reforms and the relative political influence of the security organs or of companies engaged in exploiting natural resources are frequently played out in the territories as much as they are at the national level.

This book is divided into four parts. Part One is an Introduction, with an authoritative article, revised and updated for this edition, providing a context for regional politics and a description of the place of the territories in the national economy. There is also a Chronology of Russian history and politics, some fully updated economic and demographic statistics, and information on the federal administration. Part Two comprises the Territorial Surveys, the heart of the book, with individual chapters on each of the 88 federal units. The geographical and historical background, the current political situation and an economic outline are accompanied by the names and contact details of the main officials in every territory and by the dates of appointment or election of regional governors or presidents. Each chapter includes a map of the federal unit, and there are, in addition, two maps covering wider geographical areas. A Select Bibliography of books appears in Part Three. Finally, the Indexes of Part Four provide an alphabetic listing (including alternative or historical names) of the territories, and additional indexes group them according to their geographical location within the Federal Okrugs and Economic Areas into which Russia is divided.

February 2006

Acknowledgements

The editors gratefully acknowledge the co-operation, interest and advice of all who have contributed to this volume. We are also indebted to many organizations within the Russian Federation, particularly the Federal Service of State Statistics (formerly the State Committee of Statistics).

Thanks are due to the authors of the introductory article, Professor Philip Hanson of the University of Birmingham and Professor Michael J. Bradshaw of the University of Leicester. We owe special thanks to Rebecca Bomford, and are very grateful to Eugene Fleury, who originally prepared the maps included in this book.

Contents

PART THREE

Select Bibliography

PART FOUR

Indexes

Abbreviations

Acad.	Academician; Academy	ft	foot (feet)
AD	anno domini		
Adm.	Admiral	g	gram(s)
AOb	Autonomous Oblast	GDP	gross domestic product
AOk	Autonomous Okrug	Gen.	General
ASSR	Autonomous Soviet Socialist Republic	GNP	gross national product
		Gov.	Governor
Aug.	August	Govt	Government
		GRP	gross regional product
BC	before Christ		
		ha	hectares
b/d	barrels per day	hl	hectolitre(s)
C	Centigrade		
c.	circa	IBRD	International Bank for Reconstruction and Development (World Bank)
Capt.	Captain		
CIS	Commonwealth of Independent States		
		IMF	International Monetary Fund
cm	centimetre(s)	in (ins)	inch (inches)
CMEA	Council for Mutual Economic Assistance	Inc, Incorp., Incd	Incorporated
Co	Company; County		
Col	Colonel	incl.	including
Commdr	Commander	Is	Islands
Commr	Commissioner		
Corpn	Corporation	Jan.	January
CPRF	Communist Party of the Russian Federation	Jr	Junior
CPSU	Communist Party of the Soviet Union	kg	kilogram(s)
		KGB	Komitet Gosudarstvennoi Bezopasnosti (Committee for State Security)
cu	cubic		
		km	kilometre(s)
Dec.	December	kW	kilowatt(s)
Dep.	Deputy	kWh	kilowatt hours
Dr	Doctor		
		lb	pound(s)
EBRD	European Bank for Reconstruction and Development	LDPR	Liberal Democratic Party of Russia
EC	European Community	Lt, Lieut	Lieutenant
EEC	European Economic Community	Ltd	Limited
e.g.	exempli gratia (for example)		
e-mail	electronic mail	m	metre(s)
et al.	et alii (and others)	m.	million
etc.	et cetera	Maj.	Major
EU	European Union	mm	millimetre(s)
excl.	excluding	MWh	megawatt hour(s)
F	Fahrenheit		
fax	facsimile	n.a.	not available
Feb.	February	nab.	naberezhnaya (embankment, quai)
Fr	Father	NATO	North Atlantic Treaty Organization
Fri.	Friday	no.	number
FSB	Federalnaya sluzhba bezopasnosti (Federal Security Service)	Nov.	November

obl.	oblast (region)	sel.	selo (village)
Oct.	October	Sept.	September
OECD	Organisation for Economic Co-operation and Development	sq	square (in measurements)
		SS	Saints
Ok	Okrug (district)	SSR	Soviet Socialist Republic
		St	Saint
p.	page	Supt	Superintendent
p.a.	per annum (yearly)		
per.	pereulok (lane, alley)	tel.	telephone
PGT	Poselok gorodskogo tipa (Urban-type settlement)		
		UK	United Kingdom
pl.	ploshchad (square)	ul.	ulitsa (street)
PLC	Public Limited Company	UF-UR	Unity and Fatherland-United Russia
POB	Post Office Box	UN	United Nations
pos.	poselok (settlement)	UNDP	United Nations Development Programme
pr.	prospekt (avenue)		
Prof.	Professor	UNEP	United Nations Environment Programme
		USSR	Union of Soviet Socialist Republics
q.v.	quod vide (to which refer)		
		VAT	value-added tax
Rep.	Republic	Ven.	Venerable
retd	retired	viz.	videlicet (namely)
Rev.	Reverend	vol.(s)	volume(s)
RSFSR	Russian Soviet Federative Socialist Republic		
		yr	year

PART ONE
Introduction

The Territories and the Federation: An Economic Perspective

Prof. PHILIP HANSON and Prof. MICHAEL J. BRADSHAW

With effect from 1 December 2005, the Russian Federation comprised 88 regions or 'federal subjects'; the federation of 89 regions that had existed since the early 1990s, and which commentators had become used to, was being modestly reshaped. From 1 January 2007 the number of federal subjects is scheduled further to decrease, to 86. The plans involve merging autonomous okrugs (AOks) into the region in which they are located, thereby reducing the total number of administrative units. The first such merger involved the absorption of the Komi-Permyak AOk into Perm Oblast to form a new entity, Perm Krai. The second anticipated merger was to involve the absorption of the Taimyr (Dolgano-Nenets) and Evenk AOks into Krasnoyarsk Krai.

These modest changes nevertheless represented progress towards the simplification of the baroque federal structure that came into being as the Russian Federation emerged from the USSR in 1991. The 'federal subjects' were never 89 units of equal status. The status of one, the Chechen (Nokchi) Republic—Chechnya, remains, effectively, in dispute, and most socio-economic data for that republic are not reported by the Federal Service of State Statistics (formerly the State Committee of Statistics, Goskomstat). Of the others, the AOks, which are in the process of being reduced in number from 10 to seven, and the autonomous oblast (AOb—region) are, for most purposes, of lesser status than the 20 republics, krais (provinces—which increased in number from six to seven upon the formation of Perm Krai), 49 oblasts and two cities of federal status (Moscow and St Petersburg).

All but one of the AOks officially form part of an oblast or krai. The Chukot AOk (Chukotka), in the far north-east of Russia, facing the US state of Alaska, is the exception: it was taken out of Magadan Oblast in July 1992 and left as a free-standing okrug (free-standing, that is, in a purely administrative sense—in every other sense it was collapsing); the population declined by approximately one-half between 1985 and 1999, but its fortunes improved with the election of 'oligarch' Roman Abramovich as Governor in late 2000. The inappropriately named Jewish AOb, of which only 1.2% of the population defined their 'nationality' (ethnicity) as Jewish at the 2002 census, based around the town of Birobidzhan, had, likewise, been separated from Khabarovsk Krai in 1991. This means that nine of the original 11 'lesser autonomies', as they might be called, were parts of other regions (oblasts and krais), although this number was being reduced to six.

In this chapter, we refer mainly to the 78 territories (when Chechnya is excluded) that together cover the whole of Russia, whether they are autonomous republics, krais, oblasts, federal cities, an AOk (Chukotka) or the AOb. These 78 can, generically, be labelled as 'regions'. We shall not consider separately the AOks that form part of other regions. Two of them—the Khanty-Mansii AOk—Yugra and the Yamalo-Nenets AOk—should, none the less, be noted as regions of exceptional economic importance. They are located within Tyumen Oblast and are the sources of a large part of Russian petroleum and gas production. Merging these rich AOks with 'their' surrounding region would be a much more contentious affair than in other cases, because of their wealth, which is significantly greater than that of the region within which they are contained.

In May 2000 the territorial-administrative structure was modified in another way. Putin issued an edict (*ukaz*) establishing an additional level of administration: seven Federal Okrugs (districts) covering the whole country and headed by centrally appointed presidential representatives. The creation of these seven okrugs was part of a series of measures designed to curtail the autonomy of regional leaders. In September a new State Council was created to provide a means by which governors (who, together with the heads of regional parliaments, were gradually being removed from the upper house of the national legislature, the Sovet Federatsii—Federation Council) could advise the President on regional issues. The presidium of the State Council, which consists of the President and one governor from each of the seven Federal Okrugs, rotates every six months. In January 2002 a new session of the Sovet Federatsii opened, with a reformed composition, comprising the full-time appointees of both regional leaders and chairmen of regional legislative assemblies. Governors were no longer to be members *ex officio* and, in practice, regional representatives were not necessarily close allies of their territory's governor.

In the remainder of this essay we shall: first, describe the evolving status of the Russian federal territories and their relations with the central Government; then, review the differences in the levels of economic development and the production structures they inherited from the Soviet period; next, discuss the different economic trajectories that various regions have followed since 1991; then, examine the differences in economic conditions between them and their greatly differing investment potential; and, finally, offer some thoughts about the likely longer-term evolution of these enormously different territorial economies.

THE FEDERALIZATION OF RUSSIA

In Soviet times Russia was a nominal federation within a nominal federation that was, in fact, a unitary state. The diverse patchwork of 15 Union Republics (Soviet Socialist Republics—SSRs), some of them sub-divided into autonomous republics and other administrative territories, was managed by the apparatus of the Communist Party of the Soviet Union (CPSU). The party's officials formed a clear hierarchy, with appointment from above; the territorial divisions were merely decorative. Part of that decoration consisted in assigning the names of particular national groups to areas historically associated with them. In general, this Soviet legacy has been preserved in the existing administrative divisions within the Russian Federation. The labels can, however, be grossly misleading. Many nominally ethnically defined territories are more in the nature of heritage sites. Thus, Evenks constituted 21.5% of the population of the Evenk AOk in 2002, while Khants comprised 1.2% and Mansi 0.7% of the inhabitants of the Khanty-Mansii AOk. Even at the level of republics, ethnic Russians are often in the majority in what are nominally ethnic-minority territories: for example, they accounted for 76.6% of the population in Kareliya, 64.5% in Adygeya, 60.8% in Mordoviya, 60.1% in the Udmurt Republic and 59.6% in Komi in 2002.

The results of the census that took place in October 2002 were thought likely to demonstrate a change in the relative importance of the so-called titular nationalities in such regions. In many instances, the actions of republican governments had served to favour the titular group at the expense of others, resulting in out-migration by non-titular groups. In addition, the population of traditionally Muslim ethnic groups in many territories in the Volga, Urals and Southern Federal Okrugs districts registered relatively high birth rates compared with those of ethnic Russians in the region. However, there were concerns about the validity of the census results, and the census did not request information on religious affiliation, owing to historical reasons, as much as to a desire to avoid causing offence.

When the USSR disintegrated into 15 states there was some discussion of reshaping Russia's internal administrative boundaries into units of comparable population size, without ethnic labels, although nothing was implemented. One consequence of this inheritance is that the 78 main territories or regions vary enormously in population size—from around 53,800 in the Chukot AOk to some 10.4m. in Moscow City, according to the 2002 census. The territories also vary enormously in levels of economic development, a matter that is dealt with in the next section.

Boundaries within independent Russia may have changed very little since the Soviet era, but the formal status of several territories has been amended since 1991. While Russia was still part of the USSR, Boris Yeltsin (Russian leader from 1990 and President in 1991–99) notoriously advised the local leaderships throughout the USSR to 'grab as much sovereignty as you can'. He was engaged in doing just that for the Russian Federation, and the remark no doubt seemed appropriate. The 1990–91 'parade of sovereignties', however, did not stop at the level of Russia and the 14 SSRs. Autonomous republics (then known as Autonomous Soviet Socialist Republics—ASSRs) sought to become Union Republics, while several autonomous oblasts became autonomous republics. In 1992–95 several oblasts and krais considered declaring themselves to be republics (within Russia), because the powers of republics were, in some ways, greater.

More precisely, it was members of the regions' political élite who initiated such claims. The extent of popular support for autonomist assertiveness varies greatly. In some republics, such as Tatarstan, it is strong, at least among ethnic Tatars. In others, a common attitude is that living in an autonomous republic merely means paying more to support a more elaborate and costly government—which is routinely assumed to be corrupt. On the whole, the most assertive republics have been those that are comparatively strong economically.

The Chechen (Nokchi) Republic, Chechnya, has been the main exception. Although a poor, mountainous region, its inhabitants fought Russian invaders throughout much of the 19th century, and from the last decade of the 20th century they seized the opportunity to express their dissatisfaction once more. The 'first' Chechen war (1994–96) ended, effectively, with a retreat by the federal authorities. The 'second', which commenced in late 1999, led to the federal Government securing troubled and uncertain control over Chechen territory north of the guerrillas' mountain strongholds. International pressure on the Russian Government to halt what it presented as its 'anti-terrorism' activity in Chechnya declined substantially after the large-scale suicide attacks by militant Islamists in the USA on 11 September 2001. Putin made much of the fact that both Russia and the USA had been targeted by terrorists, in a reference to bombings in Moscow and elsewhere, which had been attributed to Chechen rebels. In October 2002 a Chechen-led hostage crisis at a Moscow theatre only added to Putin's determination to confront what he regarded as a terrorist threat, rather than a civil conflict, despite the Government's questionable handling of the incident (as a result of which, together with the kidnappers, at least 129 hostages were killed, mostly by an incapacitating gas). In 2003 the federal

Government attempted to convince its own citizens and the wider world that 'normalization' was under way. On 5 October the federal Government's ally, Akhmad haji Kadyrov, officially received 87.7% of the votes cast, with a rate of participation by the electorate of 82.6%, in a republican presidential election from which his most credible challengers had withdrawn or been excluded. Major international organizations, such as the Council of Europe, declined to recognize the election as free and fair, and did not send monitors, and there were media reports of widespread irregularities. Kadyrov's assassination, in May 2004, showed that no lasting stabilization had been achieved. In September 331 people, according to official figures, including 186 children, were killed, following the seizure, by armed militants, of a school in Beslan, North Osetiya—Alaniya, in an attack that shocked not only Russia but the wider world. Again, Russian security forces were subject to criticism. President Putin used the occasion to announce a radical, and arguably unconstitutional, change: central authority would be made more direct by ending the election of governors, who would, henceforth, be appointed by the federal author-ities. Putin signed legislation to this end, following its approval by the two chambers of the federal legislature, in December 2004. This measure had been under consideration for several years; the attack at Beslan merely provided a pretext for introducing it. Fighting in Chechnya continued and, particularly after the school seizure, fears increased of a more general disorder in the whole region of the North Caucasus, as political assassinations and small-scale bomb attacks became increas-ingly frequent in several republics in the region, notably Dagestan and Ingushetiya. A large-scale assault in October 2005 on government buildings in Nalchik, the capital of the Kabardino-Balkar Republic, suggested these fears were well-founded. Although the attack was defeated, it appeared that many of the attackers were not Chechens but local Islamist radicals.

In the 1990s a jostling of regions for autonomy, or even independence, had become possible with the collapse of the communist monopoly on power. The regional élite was often little changed in terms of personnel (one study in the mid-1990s found that about two-thirds of the regional political élite were former members of the communist-era regional nomenklatura). The chain of command from Moscow, however, had been broken as early as 1988, when Mikhail Gorbachev (the last Soviet leader, 1985–91) introduced the local election of regional leaders, in place of their appointment from above. This opened the way for the local party chiefs of the old order (or, often, their deputies) to transform their party positions into post-communist power.

From the beginning of the post-communist Russian state, therefore, there was a shifting struggle, both between the regions and the centre, and between the regions themselves, over who was to have power, and at how high a level. It was further complicated by a struggle between different areas of government, notably the executive and legislative branches. Friction over budgets and other matters is a part of everyday political life in any federation and, indeed, in any state with different levels of government. What was exceptional in 1990s Russia was that a new state was being constructed. The rules of the political game were still to be established in 1992, a situation that persisted, to some extent, even in 2006. Insofar as the federal territories and the centre are concerned, the bargaining was described by some as a process of 'federalization', the making of a real federation from the smallest of bases. There are other Russians of influence, however, who do not even concede that Russia should be a federation, and who argue for the construction of a unitary state. This

6

view was being reasserted under the Putin presidency, even before the imposition of appointed, rather than elected governors (see above).

In March 1992, three months after Russia's emergence as an independent state, three treaties (sometimes known collectively as the Federation Treaty) were signed between the federal leadership, on the one hand, and, on the other, separately, the republics, krais, oblasts and autonomous okrugs. Two republics refused to sign: Tatarstan, on the middle Volga; and what was then the Checheno-Ingush ASSR, in the North Caucasus. (Later Ingushetiya was hived off as a separate republic and the cities of Moscow and St Petersburg were granted the status of federal units.) These treaties set out three areas of competence: those that were exclusively federal; those that were shared; and those that were exclusively sub-federal.

The powers of the federal centre were predictable. They included: defence; weapons production; foreign policy; the adoption, amendment and enforcement of federal laws; the establishment of federal legislative, executive and judicial bodies; the determination of internal boundaries; citizenship issues; the operation of the federal budget, the central bank and the money supply; and energy, transport and communications policies. The list of shared powers was long, and the treaties contained little guidance about just how these powers would be distributed. Exclusively sub-national powers were merely whatever was left over. Relations between regional and sub-regional (local) government were left for later legislation and, in many ways, remain legally unclear. For instance, there were no clear rules governing budgetary relations between regions and municipalities or rural districts. In 2003 the Kozak Commission on regional and local government structure (headed by Dmitrii Kozak, the First Deputy Head of the Presidential Administration, who was appointed as the Presidential Representative in the Southern Federal Okrug in September 2004) made recommendations for a clearer delimitation of powers and responsibilities of the different levels of government, and some of these recommendations are being implemented.

Insofar as federal-territorial relations were concerned, the treaties of March 1992 left three important unresolved problems: the non-participation of two republics; the large and ill-defined area of shared powers; and language that appeared (although contradicted elsewhere in the text) to give republics more control than other regions over natural resources on their territories. These problems were compounded by two other circumstances. There was very little to guarantee that devolved responsibilities would be supported by devolved tax-raising powers—that is, the powers to set tax rates and tax bases. Moreover, the judicial system, in practice, was unsuited to act as an arbiter between the centre and the regions when disagreement over the interpretation of these agreements occurred.

The new Russian Constitution approved in late 1993 superseded the federal treaties. This specified that where the federal treaties disagreed with the Constitution, the latter had priority. Moreover, the federal Constitution had precedence, in any conflicts, over sub-national constitutions or their equivalent. The new federal Constitution gave the President of the Russian Federation exceptionally strong powers. These were used to ensure that, for the next three years (approximately), regional governors were appointed and subject to dismissal by the President. That, however, did not apply to the republics, where presidents were locally elected. It was only in 1996–97 that the executive heads of all the territories became formally answerable to their electorates rather than to the federal President—a situation that prevailed until 2004.

Meanwhile, the Federation negotiated a series of so-called power-sharing treaties with individual territories. This began in February 1994 with Tatarstan, and had extended to more than one-half of the regions by late 1998. At that time the First Deputy Head of the Presidential Administration, Oleg Sysoyev, spoke publicly of plans to discontinue the practice and, eventually, to reorder uniformly federal-territorial relations. The power-sharing treaties were anomalous, often allowing conflicting provisions in the federal and regional constitutions to co-exist. A number of the treaties also included special arrangements on the retention of larger-than-normal shares of taxes collected within the borders of the territory concerned. This applied to Bashkortostan, Kareliya, Sakha (Yakutiya) and Tatarstan—all republics and all comparatively strong economically (Sakha—Yakutiya, for instance, accounts for almost all of Russia's diamond-mining). Finally, these budget deals were, typically, not published.

'Asymmetric federalism' would be a generous description of the network of central-territorial relations that emerged. None the less, many observers concluded that these arrangements probably helped as interim measures to hold Russia together. For much of the 1990s the centre was weak and divided, with the President and parliament often in conflict, and successive governments unable to implement key parts of their agendas (notably in tax collection). Consequently, all the territories, not just the favoured, strong republics, had considerable leeway. In practice, even in 1993–97, regional governors often defied the centre and acted as though they were more beholden to the local élite than to a President who could, in theory, dismiss them. Thus, for example, Yevgenii Nazdratenko, in the Maritime (Primorskii) Krai on the Pacific coast ran a corrupt regime, while defying the centre's efforts to remove him, and was re-elected in December 1999 with a sizeable majority, largely owing to his ability to discredit the opposition and his control over the local media. Nazdratenko was eventually removed from the governorship in 2001, but the strength of such local power bases was demonstrated by the fact that he was subsequently offered a federal post with ministerial status.

Until the 1998 financial crisis four developments had tended to stabilize central-territorial political relations. First, the instigation of federal military action in Chechnya in December 1994, although ill-managed, costly in human life and unsuccessful in its immediate aim, acted as a deterrent to less determined and less advantageously located secessionists elsewhere. Second, the development of the Sovet Federatsii as a body representing the territories facilitated accommodation between the centre and the periphery. Third, the eight associations of territories (based on the 11 Economic Areas) had, throughout 1997, begun to emerge as regular channels for informal policy consultation between the central Government and representatives of the regions, and had begun to supplement the Sovet Federatsii as an institutionalized communications channel. Fourth, the Constitutional Court was beginning to act somewhat more independently in rulings over conflicts regarding the distribution of powers. The financial crisis undermined some of this progress. It brought to the fore an underlying problem: the centre's dwindling ability to provide economic help to weaker territories and to use economic levers to achieve some consistency in the implementation of economic policy across Russia. The crisis also revealed that many of Russia's poorest regions were simply being excluded from the country's new market economy, a fact that isolated them from the immediate impact of the crisis, but threatened the cohesion of Russia.

The measures introduced by Putin in May 2000 were designed to strengthen the central Government's control over its federal agencies in the regions and to ensure regional compliance with federal legislation. Unlike his predecessor, Putin was prepared to move openly and boldly against concentrations of power that limited his own authority. With the advantage of a more compliant parliament and a background in the security service, he was prepared to attack determinedly both regional governors and business tycoons who attempted to influence politics at the federal level. Whereas Yeltsin had relied on negotiations that played region against region, Putin sought directly to limit regional political authority. He was assisted in this by the recovery of the Russian economy: the central Government was better resourced and, therefore, better able to fulfil its responsibilities. In the past, the poverty of the federal agencies often meant that they had to turn to regional presidents and governors for financial support, which made them pliable and more sympathetic to regional interests.

Thus far, the presidential representatives in the seven Federal Okrugs have proved largely ineffective. They lack a clear mandate and the President appears unwilling to give them the necessary political power and financial resources to carry out the tasks that they have set themselves. Each representative has to deal with a distinct set of problems and has approached the job somewhat differently. Some have received a hostile reception. The Presidential Representative in the Urals, Col-Gen. Petr Latyshev, for example, encountered difficulties with the Governor of Sverdlovsk Oblast, Eduard Rossel. The circumstances surrounding the resignation of Maritime Krai Governor Nazdratenko, following an extended energy crisis in the region, and the subsequent gubernatorial election, also proved a major embarrassment for the first Presidential Representative in the Far East, Lt-Gen. Konstantin Pulikovskii (based, significantly, in Khabarovsk city, rather than Vladivostok, the capital of Maritime Krai), who was unable to control Nazdratenko. He was eventually eased out of the governorship, but only by means of what was, apparently, a negotiated deal with the centre (see above). Sergei Darkin (who was alleged to have connections with Nazdratenko) won the election to succeed him as governor, standing against a candidate supported by Pulikovskii. In general, the efforts by the presidential representatives to increase their powers and gain access to additional resources have been thwarted, not only by the resistance of the regional leaders, many of whom refused to take them seriously, but also by the power of federal ministries. Agencies of the federal Government report to the Chairman of the Government (Prime Minister) and not, in any direct sense, to the President. These agencies have resisted efforts by the presidential administration's territorial representatives to exercise control over regional branches of federal ministries. Moreover, the economic ministries have not established branches at the federal okrug level; the only agencies to have done so are concerned with law and order. In his November 2005 reshuffle, President Putin replaced Sergei Kiriyenko, the Presidential Representative in the Volga Federal Okrug, with Aleksandr Konovalov, the former prosecutor of Bash-kortostan, and in the Far East Konstantin Pulikovskii was replaced by Kamil Iskhakov, the former head of the city administration of Kazan, in Tatarstan. Some commentators interpreted these changes as an indication that the roles of the presidential representatives to the Federal Okrugs were being downgraded, given that a greater degree of control over the regions had been established by the federal, and particularly the presidential, authorities.

Russia's ongoing recentralization of power is not necessarily the result of the creation of the Federal Okrugs and the appointment of presidential representatives. Changes in fiscal legislation and a shift in the distribution of revenue between the centre and the regions, in favour of the federal authorities, mean that the central Government has increasing control over state expenditure (see below). The removal of governors from the Sovet Federatsii has reduced their influence in national politics and divested them of their immunity from prosecution. The centre reasserted its power to appoint regional heads of police and the Procuracy and, in 2004, the regional governors. Initially, Putin reappointed incumbents as their terms expired, suggesting a limited ability, or a limited will, to exercise his new powers. In March 2005 he used his additional powers for the first time, declining to nominate the incumbent Governors of Saratov and Tula Oblasts. In the same month Putin dismissed the Governor of the Koryak AOk, representing the first instance in which he had formally and explicitly used this power. The resignation of Valerii Kokov as President of the Kabardino-Balkar Republic, in September 2005, officially on grounds of ill health, was also widely believed to have been influenced, at least in part, by pressure from the federal authorities. These actions served to give a credible warning to regional leaders that they should not contradict the federal President's wishes. Meanwhile, the re-investment of natural-resource sector profits by Moscow-based, large-scale companies, and their consequent acquisition of a wide range of other businesses across the Federation, has, in several cases, disrupted what had been comfortable relationships between regional political leaders and regional entrepreneurs. Indeed, by 2002 governors and presidents of republics were already judged less frequently to be among the most influential people in Russia.

ECONOMIC DIFFERENTIATION

Russian regional inequality in Soviet times is impossible to assess, chiefly because such data as there were on rouble incomes and outputs concealed differences in availability that, in a geographically huge, shortage economy, were very large indeed. It was well known that the largest cities had priority in the allocation of consumer goods. Many everyday items that were widely available in Moscow were completely unobtainable in many lesser cities and small towns. Then, as now, barter and subsistence food production were predominant in rural areas, and were poorly accounted for in statistical reporting.

It is, nevertheless, clear that in 1992 the new Russian state had inherited an exceptionally uneven array of regional development levels. Underdeveloped, rural territories had little in common with the very big cities such as Moscow, St Petersburg, Yekaterinburg, Nizhnii Novgorod and Samara. In 1991 both Dagestan and Tyva, for example, had rural populations of more than 45% of the total (this was still the case in the 2002 census), while, at the other end of the scale (omitting the far northern districts and the two cities of federal status), Kemerovo's rural population comprised only 13% of the total and Samara's 19%. (The Russian average was 26% in 1989 and 27% in 2002.) In a country where poverty was concentrated in rural areas these differences dictated large inequalities in average real incomes across the regions.

Later in the 1990s, as local food-price controls waned and the measurement of regional inequalities became a little less problematic, it was clear that differences in territorial, per-head, real output and personal incomes were very large indeed. They were also becoming larger over time. In 1998 per-head gross regional product

(GRP—which approximates to regional gross domestic product—GDP) was 19 times higher in petroleum-rich Tyumen Oblast than in Ingushetiya; by 2002 the GRP of Tyumen Oblast was more than 23 times higher than that of Ingushetiya. In mid-2002 the average money income in Moscow City, divided by the cost of the 'subsistence minimum' basket of goods at local prices, was more than eight times the equivalent measure for Tyva. This was substantially greater than the range from poorest to richest region in the European Union of 15 (EU15), using the EU's second-tier definition of 'region' (in which the average population size happens to be very close to that for Russian regions—1.8m.). The Moscow–Tyva difference is probably overstated by this measure, because uncounted subsistence food production will play a larger role in Tyva. Nevertheless, even if one guesses at a 'true' ratio of 6:1, the range is still enormous.

A more comprehensive measure of dispersion among regional average real incomes, the co-efficient of variation, shows a clear, rapid increase throughout the 1990s. In 1992 it was 0.31. In 1998 it was 0.56, although the economic recovery that followed the rouble devaluation of that year seemed to lessen substantially this dispersion, bringing the indicator down to 0.40 by mid-1999, before edging up slightly, to 0.42, by mid-2002. Even this degree of inequality stands in marked contrast to that of developed countries: the comparable figure for the 50 US states plus the District of Columbia in 2001 was 0.15. In 2003 the differences in GRP per head were huge: if no adjustment is made for differences in price level, the Moscow City figure was nearly four-and-a-half times the Russian average, that for the oil- and gas-rich region of Tyumen was nearly seven times the average, while at the other end of the scale the figure for Dagestan was only 39% of the national average, and that for Ingushetiya only 19%. Even if one allows for consumer prices in Moscow or Tyumen being of the order of two-and-a-half times those recorded in Dagestan or Ingushetiya, the 'real' difference between richest and poorest is larger in Russia than it is in the enlarged (from May 2004) 25-member EU (despite the fact that, in 2002, income per head in London, the capital of the United Kingdom and the wealthiest region in the EU, was about 10 times that of the poorest region in Poland).

There are very few countries that exhibit sharper regional economic inequalities than Russia. One is the People's Republic of China, across the regions of which the coefficient of variation of GDP per head was 0.83 in 1999. It is clear that in Russia the regions' economic fortunes diverged rapidly from the end of communist rule. This suggests that there is a large capacity for inter-regional discord under the new economic order, and one that may, despite some fluctuation, increase in the long term. The growing concentration of state resources within the federal Government in Moscow makes it all the more important for the Government to create a mechanism to redistribute wealth from richer to poorer regions. The sum of federal transfers to sub-national budgets has indeed increased, but, at 4.5% of GDP in the first half of 2005, transfers remained modest, relative to national income. (In 1998 the equivalent figure for the USA, with 50 less unevenly developed states, was 2.9%. In the late 1990s the figure for Argentina, with 24 primary administrative sub-divisions demonstrating extremely uneven development, was about 6%.)

THE PROCESSES OF CHANGE AND THE ROLE OF THE CENTRE

Insofar as a territory's economic fortunes are concerned, the fundamental measure must be the standard of living of its inhabitants. The real-income measures that can be made for contemporary Russia are full of problems: neither the data on money incomes nor the data on regional price levels are of good quality, and one cannot assume that these defects produce a bias that is uniform across regions. Regions with particularly large informal economies, such as Kaliningrad Oblast, are doing better than the official figures suggest. Nevertheless, the regions that are doing particularly well or particularly badly are probably reasonably well identified by the official statistics. To put these differences in perspective, it should be said that post-communist economic adaptation in Russia as a whole has taken the form of collapse. In 2003 measured national income (GDP) was about 73% of the 1989 level. Only one region, Moscow City, has shown all the outward signs of economic success; and even in Moscow a large proportion of the population has been left behind. However, a small number of other regions have adapted comparatively well; typically, these are territories that began to show real growth in output in 1997, well above the slight improvement of 1.4% recorded for Russian GDP as a whole.

Analyses of inter-regional differences in average real incomes suggest that two kinds of territory fared better than the Russian average: those with particularly strong reserves of exploitable petroleum, natural gas, metals and hydroelectric power (such as Tyumen Oblast and Irkutsk Oblast); and a small number of regions that contain emerging commercial and financial 'hubs' (Moscow and St Petersburg Cities; and Nizhnii Novgorod, Samara and Sverdlovsk Oblasts). St Petersburg apart, maritime 'gateway' territories, such as Kaliningrad (on the Baltic), Krasnodar (Black Sea) and the Maritime Krai (Pacific), have fared far less well than might have been expected. The reasons for this are not clear, but each has had, for most of the post-communist period, a traditionalist, even xenophobic, leadership. In addition, Maritime Krai has suffered for reasons common to the Russian Far East as a whole (on which, more below). A study by the Russian Ministry of Economic Development and Trade confirmed this analysis. It suggested that the number of regions enjoying an 'above average' level of economic development increased from 20 in 1998 to 25 in 2000. Of these 25 regions, 17 were characterized as resource-processing, two (Moscow and St Petersburg) as financial-economic centres, and the remainder (including Belgorod Oblast, Moscow Oblast, Samara Oblast and Tatarstan) as industrial centres. This list reflects the regional consequences, post-1998, of high resource prices, which are of benefit to resource-exporting regions, and of a devalued rouble, which increased the costs of imports and provided import-substitution benefits for the major industrial regions.

Those regions where economic adaptation has been more uniformly gloomy are, not to put too fine a point upon it, all the rest. They fall into two main categories: the strongly rural and agricultural regions; and what might be called 'typical Russian regions', mainly industrial, but without the particular attributes that have favoured the emerging hub and natural-resource regions or the industries that have been able to respond to domestic market opportunities post-1998. The former have suffered from a lack of farm restructuring and a massive deterioration in agricultural prices relative to all other prices; the latter have been victims of the lack of competitiveness of Russian industry and have failed to develop new activities on any scale. The natural-resource and the hub regions have in common an engagement with the outside world, either as generators of exports to the West or as magnets for foreign business and for trading in imports, or both.

The reasons why these particular hub regions have emerged are harder to determine. Econometric studies suggest that small business, the development of which has been generally very weak, has grown rather better in regions with large urban populations and, therefore, large and concentrated domestic markets, other things being equal. It also seems the case that those regions that have a positive attitude towards economic reform, in addition to a well-educated population, have the highest level of new-enterprise formation. A study of regional economic performance by Moscow-based investment firm ATON Capital concluded that the regions delivering 'quality growth' in 1999–2002 included those that benefited from: natural-resource wealth; a large urban population; and/or a large services sector. It appears highly plausible that the development of financial and other services, stunted during the Soviet era, and of new lines of economic activity generally, would be easier in very large cities. In these very large communities a wide range of skills and lines of production are available. This must facilitate the recombining of capital and labour resources into new activities, as well as providing a large market for those activities, and explains why those same hub regions seem to be leading the way in the development of 'new economy' activities, relating, for example, to mobile telecommunications and the internet.

It may be the case that the advantage of being a hub region is more durable than that of being a natural-resource region. Energy and raw-materials reserves become depleted and their prices fluctuate. The slide in petroleum and natural gas prices in 1996–99 and again, briefly, between late 2001 and early 2002, made a difference to the regional rankings. More recently, natural-resource-rich regions have again been in the ascendant, but there is no guarantee that this will last. In addition, it is in petroleum, natural gas, gold, aluminium and diamonds that the Russian élite is most determined to maintain control of what it views as the serious earners. In many cases it is concerned simply to make private fortunes out of these assets, regardless of the long-term development of the business. Seeking Western partners, with a view to long-term development, has been the exception rather than the rule. In June 2003 the finalization of a joint venture between BP (formerly British Petroleum—of the United Kingdom) and the Tyumen Oil Company (TNK), creating TNK-BP, suggested that this pattern might be changing, but in 2004–05 President Putin and some influential individuals in the Presidential Administration made their mistrust of foreign capital clear. In October 2005 the Ministry of Natural Resources published a list of five major deposits of petroleum, natural gas, gold, and copper to which companies controlled by foreign interests would not be allowed access, on the grounds that these were resources of 'strategic importance' for Russia. These restrictions were less than had been originally proposed and were expected to slow, rather than prevent, the development and fuller exploitation of natural-resource deposits in Siberia. Meanwhile, in 2003–05 the state's investigation of the Yukos Oil Company, and its former Chief Executive, Mikhail Khodorkovskii, weakened business confidence—both foreign and Russian—in the natural-resource sector, amid concerns that the state intended to take a greater role.

It is clear that Russia's economic recovery in 1999–2005 (when GDP growth averaged around 6% per year) has been associated with some moderation of inter-regional inequality, probably because the massive devaluation of the rouble enabled moribund industries like engineering, building materials and food-processing, which dominate many ordinary Russian regions, to revive as producers of import substitutes. However, the continuing real appreciation of the rouble may well undermine those gains and again lead to greater regional differentiation, as a relatively small number of regions enjoy sustained economic recovery, while the vast majority of the remainder remain depressed. Russia's politicians are increasingly concerned about the development gap between Moscow and the rest of Russia, but outside Moscow there is also a huge gap between the winners in Russia's new economy and the losers from the old.

One other factor has been of great importance for the territories of Russia's Far North and Far East. This is the erosion of the enormous subsidies to transport, energy and food supplies that had supported their development in the Soviet era. Most of that development would not have occurred in a market economy; now that a market economy is being established, these regions have experienced an exceptionally severe decline. One reaction was substantial out-migration from those areas during the 1990s and early 2000s, and the Russian Government received financial assistance from the World Bank to support further out-migration from the Far North and the Far East. Between 1989 and 2002 the population of Magadan Oblast declined by 53% and that of the Chukot AOk by 67%. The net result is that the economically active are leaving behind a welfare-dependent population in regions that the federal Government is no longer inclined to support, a stark reminder of the human consequences of the collapse of Soviet socialism.

These, then, are (in very crude summary) the factors that lie behind the sharp divergence of regional fortunes. It is doubtful whether differences in policies among regional leaders have made much difference to the outcome. The economic structure inherited from the past, including population size and the presence or absence of major conurbations and natural-resource industries, seem to have been far more important, as have basic geographical characteristics, such as accessibility and remoteness. A few regional leaders, such as Boris Nemtsov in Nizhnii Novgorod (1991–97) and Mikhail Prusak in Novgorod (1995–), gained reputations as serious reformers, but such cases are rare, and even they worked with the grain of their region's inheritance. Governors who were overtly hostile to foreign business activity and economic restructuring, as in Krasnodar and Maritime Krais, were probably capable of making matters worse, although they were usually at odds with the mayors of their major cities. The latter, like most governors, tended to be pragmatists who saw little personal benefit in making special efforts to block change.

By the end of the Yeltsin era an impasse had been reached. Regional politicians still looked to the centre and lobbied institutions in Moscow, but there was little expectation that the central Government would do much to help a region deal with its most pressing problems. Meanwhile, the centre and regions competed to obtain revenue from the same sources (under tax-sharing arrangements), which led both to damagingly high nominal rates of tax and to collusion between regional governments and local businesses to conceal resources from the central budget—a process aided by the use of barter and money surrogates. At the same time, the centre had devolved some major responsibilities for public provision, notably welfare and housing, to sub-national levels, without making available the means to pay for them. It was estimated that in 1998 such 'unfunded mandates' amounted to at least 5% of GDP—an amount that should, in international accounting practice, have been added to the officially reported government deficit.

Putin changed things radically. He may not have succeeded in resolving the complex issue of centre-regional financial relations, but he was certainly prepared to tackle it directly. In 2000 sub-national government revenue before transfers from the federal budget was equivalent to 13.0% of GDP, and transfers added 1.4% of GDP to this figure. In 2003 the corresponding figures were 11.3% and 3.2%. Thus, the regions (and the local governments below them) were receiving a similar proportion of a national total that was almost one-fifth larger, but were receiving less of it directly, and more at the discretion of the central Government. In the first three quarters of 2005, although federal transfers to sub-national budgets had increased as a share of GDP, total budgetary spending had tilted in favour of the centre: the federal budget was equivalent to 16.6% of GDP, while the sum of regional and sub-regional budgets totalled just over 13%. This still allowed an absolute increase in sub-national budget spending, given the growth of the economy. However, if the economy slowed and profits declined, then the regions would begin to come under financial pressure. By removing the influence of the governors from the federal policy-making process, and by increasing their reliance on funds channelled through the federal Government, Putin was strengthening central control by stealth. If the Yeltsin era witnessed a shift in centre-regional relations that favoured the regions, the Putin presidency appeared to be heralding a reassertion of central influence. By 2005, at least, this had been achieved without open conflict; most governors remained supportive of the President, and it appeared that the reintroduction of presidentially appointed governors had further strengthened this tendency.

However, other developments had an ambiguous effect on presidential power. From 1999 the expansion of large, Moscow-based firms into the regions both disrupted 'crony' relations between regional politicians and regional-level business magnates, and offered the possibility of new alliances. Many governors sought to build alliances with large-scale Russian enterprises, and in 2002 a World Bank study confirmed that the concentration of market power in a small number of firms was much greater at the regional than the national level. However, the relationship between a particular region and the dominant company varies. A further World Bank study, published in 2004 and dealing with the period 1996–2000, found that regional administrations in 25 regions could be judged to have been 'captured' by business interests—some of them the business interests of state-owned or state-controlled firms. This meant that significant preferential treatment had been given to these firms, to the detriment of the functioning of other firms. Among the 'captured regions' was Moscow City, where the business group associated with Mayor Yurii Luzhkov had special influence. At the same time, the development of businesses with activities spanning several regions was large. In 2004 the periodical *Ekspert* (Expert) concluded that 70% of the turnover of Russia's 400 largest firms (by sales) was attributed to 'inter-regional firms'. In the 2000–01 cycle of gubernatorial elections, large-scale businesses sought to ensure the election of governors who would promote their interests, as did the federal Government. In the gubernatorial election held in Krasnoyarsk Krai in September 2002, both leading candidates were supported by rival large firms. The most prominent cases of business executives becoming governors were those of the Chukot, Evenk and Taimyr AOks. In other regions there were close relationships between governors and corporations, for example, between the state-controlled gas monopoly, Gazprom, and Yurii Neyelov in the Yamalo-Nenets AOk. However, in a number of other regions businesses supported losing candidates. For example, in the Nenets AOk elements associated with the petroleum company LUKoil tried, and failed, to oust the incumbent, Vladimir Butov (although he was later prohibited by the federal Supreme Court from contesting election to a further term of office, following the expiry of his mandate in early 2005).

Another form of special business link between a firm and a region was to be seen in the so-called domestic 'offshore' zones—regions where special tax exemptions were given to companies registering there. Tax claims issued by the federal authorities against Yukos in 2004 were prompted by its use of trading companies based in such zones, in order to reduce its own tax payments. The legality of these arrangements had not been clearly established, and Yukos was just one of a great number of companies that were exploiting such arrangements.

INVESTMENT POTENTIAL

Throughout 1998 investment in Russia declined even more rapidly than did output. The country's capital stock diminished, although the decline could not be measured with any confidence. Domestic investment recovered, increasing strongly in 1999–2003, and profits from natural-resource exports at last began to be channelled in significant quantities into internal investment, rather than placed off shore. Although this investment was heavily concentrated in the natural-resource sectors, there was some expansion into other sectors.

Foreign direct investment (FDI) should also have helped to support production capacity, but it continued to languish. Accurate statistics on FDI are difficult to come by. In 2003 the Federal Service of State Statistics estimated total FDI stock in Russia to be US $36,600m. According to the same source, in 2004 total FDI was $9,400m., which would put the total capital stock at $46,000m. Between January and September 2005 an additional $6,600m. of FDI was attracted to Russia, an increase of 16%, compared with the first three quarters of 2004. Thus, by the end of 2005 total FDI stock would be expected to be well over $50,000m. However, the presence of a number of well-known tax havens among the top 10 investors in Russia suggests that much of this 'foreign' investment is actually returning 'flight' capital. This is not a bad thing, but it does suggest that many of the major multinational corporations have yet to invest in Russia's economic recovery. Furthermore, from an international perspective, these figures are small for an economy of Russia's size. Despite its modest total, this FDI, establishing or expanding joint ventures and wholly foreign-owned firms, has a special role in channelling the flow of investment to different Russian regions. The regional distribution of FDI reflects the perceived economic potential of activities in each region, allowing for the barriers to foreigners gaining significant control in those activities. In turn, FDI influences regional outcomes: it must usually have beneficial effects on a region's output.

In practice, FDI has been heavily concentrated in Moscow City, although that dominance is dwindling quite significantly. During 2003 Moscow City accounted for 36.6% of FDI in Russia, well below its peak level of 76.9% in 1997. The surrounding Moscow Oblast accounted for a further 10.4% of FDI in 2003. Such a concentration on the capital city and its surrounding region is not unusual for FDI in former communist countries. Some of it was recorded in Moscow only because head offices of large companies are often based there; insofar as the resource inflow goes through that head office to provincial production, the real concentration of FDI resources on the metropolis will be somewhat less. None the less, there remain many Russian regions that have received little or no foreign investment. According to the official figures, the 10 leading regions for foreign investment in 1995–2002 received, on average, over 80% of all inward FDI; of this, around one-half went to Moscow City and the rest was distributed in small amounts around an array of regions, which changed from year to year. Moscow Oblast, St Petersburg City, Tyumen Oblast and Samara Oblast feature with some regularity and prominence. It is clear, however, that, in a number of second-tier regions, a particular investment project in a particular year can push that region, a little fortuitously, into a leading ranking.

Sakhalin Oblast is the most notable case, home to two very large offshore petroleum and gas projects involving the Anglo-Dutch company Royal Dutch/Shell, and a US company, ExxonMobil, which are being developed under production-sharing agreements. In 2003 Sakhalin Oblast accounted for 29.1% of total FDI in Russia. In the period following the financial crisis of 1998 the regional pattern of foreign investment moved away from the resource regions and favoured regions involved in import-substitution manufacturing. It is also noteworthy that, despite the political complexion of certain of these territories, the major port regions: St Petersburg and Leningrad Oblast; Krasnodar Krai and Rostov Oblast; and Maritime Krai, consistently appear in the top 10. This pattern reflects the impact of rouble devaluation on the cost of imported consumer goods and the failure of the resource sector to capture substantial amounts of investment; the latter is partly the result of problems in reforming Russia's production-sharing legislation, and partly owing to the reluctance, thus far, of large-scale businesses to loosen their control over major hard-currency-earning assets. The profile of Krasnodar Krai was also raised as a result of the construction of a petroleum-export pipeline from Tengiz, Kazakhstan, to the port of Novorossiisk, on the Black Sea, which opened in 2001.

Whether the pattern of foreign investment corresponds to the potential of different Russian territories is not clear. Western investors can be assumed to know what they are doing, but one of the things they are forced to do is to take into account the obstacles placed in their way, often by regional administrations. There are, for instance, a number of natural-resource developments from which, as noted earlier, foreign business has been more or less excluded. There are also some regions, such as Archangel Oblast, where Russian interests, assisted by the local political élite, have effectively acted to exclude investors. *Ekspert* publishes an annual ranking of regional investment risk and potential. The top five regions in 2004/05, in terms of investment potential were, in order: Moscow City; St Petersburg City; Moscow Oblast; the Khanty-Mansii AOk; and Sverdlovsk Oblast. Moscow City was placed ninth in terms of security from investment risks, while St Petersburg City was considered the least risky place to invest in, suggesting a change in Russia's investment landscape. Sakhalin Oblast, ranked third in terms of total FDI, was ranked only 75th in this regard by *Ekspert*. A review of research on the investment potential of the regions of Russia reveals a consensus on the top 10 or so regions (those that account for the vast majority of FDI), meaning that the majority of Russian regions are missing out on the potential modernizing impact of foreign investment.

PROSPECTS

Output in Russia declined between 1989 and 1998, with a brief halt in 1997. Thereafter, GDP recovered, rising by a total of about 46%, in real terms, in the seven subsequent years. Putin hoped to increase GDP two-fold within a decade (2001–10, through average annual growth of 7.2%), although few economists considered this growth rate to be sustainable in the medium term. Many analysts regard the massive devaluation of the rouble in 1998 and the unrelated subsequent strengthening of world petroleum prices as generating an upturn that could only be sustained if basic structural reforms were undertaken—not merely legislated, as was the case in 2001–02, but also implemented in everyday practice. Some continued growth, but at a slower rate (of, say, 3%–5% per year) seemed more likely, while pervasive government intervention continues to hinder the competitive process. Studies by the World Bank and OECD have suggested that between 3% and 5%, out of the overall growth rate of 7%, was the result of the direct and indirect benefits of high petroleum prices. Thus, if petroleum prices declined, the real effectiveness of Russia's economic reforms would rapidly be revealed. One factor in favour of effective reform was Russia's attempt to join the World Trade Organization (WTO). Members of the WTO were insisting on further liberalization that would open the Russian financial services, telecommunications and energy sectors to Western business, introducing more competition to the system. Putin and a section of the Russian business élite had apparently chosen to pursue WTO membership on such terms.

Whatever the outcome for Russia in the medium term, the fortunes of individual regions will continue to differ enormously. Sustained convergence of regional living standards requires a strengthening of market institutions, to facilitate the establishment of new business in low-wage areas and the freer movement of people to high-wage areas. Even that, however, although desirable in itself, may not be sufficient to prevent inter-regional inequalities from increasing. Russia's regions differ so markedly in natural-resource endowments, infrastructure, location and human capital, that agglomeration in a number of comparatively successful places may well be stronger than the forces making for convergence. In late 2004 a Ministry of Regional Development was created and in June 2005 a concept document was released, presenting a new strategy for regional development in Russia. Rather than attempting to promote economic growth across all of Russia's regions, this strategy proposed to focus assistance on 10 'propulsive' regions. The basis for determining these regions was not clear by late 2005, but they would not be resource regions. Instead, the resource regions were to provide the revenue to support development in the propulsive regions. This strategy forms part of a wider trend towards state direction of the economy, although it may ultimately be the case that it is not implemented.

Putin's evident desire to impose greater central control could help bring about economic change. Regional governments have played a key role in preventing structural change by supporting favoured large enterprises and helping to generate barter and money-surrogate transactions. All other things being equal, the weakening of regional governments should aid economic adjustment. There are, however, two reasons for being cautious about this scenario. First, the power of regional networks of politicians and businessmen may be such that the introduction of the Federal Okrugs and other measures designed to give the centre more leverage may, in practice, make very little difference. Second, even if regional power is reduced, there is no guarantee that a strengthened federal centre will put an end to corrupt and ineffective government. Russia's problem may be not so much that regional government works poorly, but that all levels of government work poorly.

Chronology of Russia

c. 878: Kievan Rus, the first unified state of the Eastern Slavs, was founded, with Kiev (Kyiv—now in Ukraine) as its capital.

c. 988: Vladimir I—'the Great', ruler of Kievan Rus, converted to Orthodox Christianity.

1237–40: The Rus principalities were invaded and conquered by the Mongol Tatars.

1462–1505: Reign of Ivan III of Muscovy (Moscow), who consolidated the independent Rus domains into a centralized state.

1480: Renunciation of Tatar suzerainty.

1533–84: Reign of Ivan IV—'the Terrible', who began the eastern expansion of Russian territory.

1547: Ivan IV was crowned 'Tsar of Muscovy and all Russia'.

1552: Subjugation of the Khanate of Kazan.

1556: Subjugation of the Khanate of Astrakhan.

1581: The Russian adventurer, Yermak Timofeyev, led an expedition to Siberia, pioneering Russian expansion beyond the Ural Mountains.

1645: A Russian settlement was established on the Sea of Okhotsk, on the coast of eastern Asia.

1654: Eastern and central Ukraine came under Muscovite rule as a result of the Treaty of Pereyaslavl.

1679: Russian pioneers reached the Kamchatka Peninsula and the Pacific Ocean.

1682–1725: Reign of Peter (Petr) I—'the Great', who established Russia as a European Power, expanded its Empire, and modernized the civil and military institutions of the state.

1703: St Petersburg was founded at the mouth of the River Neva, in north-west Russia.

1721: The Treaty of Nystad with Sweden ended the Great Northern War and brought Estonia and Livonia (now Latvia and parts of Estonia) under Russian rule. Peter I, who was declared the 'Tsar of all the Russias', proclaimed the Russian Empire.

1728: The Treaty of Kyakhta with China secured the Russian annexation of Transbaikal.

1762–96: Reign of Catherine (Yekaterina) II—'the Great'.

1774: As a result of the Treaty of Kuçuk Kainavci with the Turks, Russia gained a port on the Black Sea.

1783: Annexation of the Khanate of Crimea.

1801–25: Reign of Alexander (Aleksandr) I.

1809: Finland became a possession of the Russian Crown.

1812: The French, under Napoleon I, invaded Russia.

1825: On the death of Alexander I, a group of young officers, the 'Decembrists', attempted to seize power; the attempted *coup d'état* was suppressed by troops loyal to the new Tsar, Nicholas (Nikolai) I, who reigned until 1855.

1853–56: The Crimean War was fought, in which the United Kingdom and France aided Turkey against Russia.

1855–81: Reign of Alexander II, who introduced economic and legal reforms.

1859: The Russian conquest of the Caucasus was completed.

1860: Acquisition of provinces on the Sea of Japan from China and the establishment of Vladivostok.

1861: Emancipation of the serfs.

1864: Final defeat of the Circassian peoples and the confirmation of Russian hegemony in the Caucasus.

1867: The North American territory of Alaska was sold to the USA for US $7m.

1875: Acquisition of Sakhalin from Japan in exchange for the Kurile Islands.

1876: Subjugation of the last of the Central Asian khanates.

1881–94: Reign of Alexander III, who acceded following the assassination of his father and re-established autocratic principles of government.

1891: Construction of the Trans-Siberian Railway was begun.

1894–1917: Reign of Nicholas II, the last Tsar.

1898: The All-Russian Social Democratic Labour Party (RSDLP), a Marxist party, was founded, five years later dividing into 'Bolsheviks' (led by Lenin—Vladimir Ulyanov) and 'Mensheviks'.

1904–05: Russia was defeated in the Russo–Japanese War.

22 January 1905: Some 150 demonstrators were killed by the Tsar's troops, in what came to be known as 'Bloody Sunday'.

17 October 1905: Strikes and demonstrations in the capital, St Petersburg, and other cities forced the Tsar to introduce limited political reforms, including the holding of elections to a Duma (parliament).

January 1912: The Bolsheviks formally established a separate party, the RSDLP (Bolsheviks).

1 August 1914: Russia entered the First World War against Austria-Hungary, Germany and the Ottoman Empire (the Central Powers).

2 March (New Style: 15 March) 1917: Abdication of Tsar Nicholas II after demonstrations and strikes in Petrograd (as St Petersburg was renamed in 1914); a Provisional Government, headed by Prince Georgii Lvov, took power.

9 July (22 July) 1917: In response to widespread public disorder, Prince Lvov resigned; he was replaced as Prime Minister by Aleksandr Kerenskii, a moderate socialist.

25 October (7 November) 1917: The Bolsheviks, led by Lenin, overthrew the Provisional Government; the Russian Soviet Federative Socialist Republic (RSFSR or Russian Federation) was proclaimed.

6 January (19 January) 1918: The Constituent Assembly, which had been elected in November 1917, was dissolved on Lenin's orders. A civil war between the Bolshevik Red Army and various anti-Communist leaders (the 'Whites'), who received support from German and from Entente or Allied forces, was by now under way and lasted until 1921.

14 February (1 February) 1918: Adoption of the Gregorian Calendar by the Russian civil authorities.

3 March 1918: Treaty of Brest-Litovsk: the Bolsheviks ceded large areas of western territory to Germany, including the Baltic regions, and recognized the independence of Finland and Ukraine.

6–8 March 1918: The RSDLP (Bolsheviks) was renamed the Russian Communist Party (Bolsheviks)—RCP (B).

9 March 1918: The capital of Russia was moved from Petrograd (renamed Leningrad in 1924) to Moscow.

10 July 1918: The first Constitution of the RSFSR was adopted by the Fifth All-Russian Congress of Soviets.

18 July 1918: Tsar Nicholas II and his family were murdered in Yekaterinburg (Sverdlovsk, 1924–91) by Bolshevik troops.

11 November 1918: The Allied Armistice with Germany (which was denied its gains at Brest-Litovsk) ended the First World War.

March 1921: As the civil war ended, the harsh policy of 'War Communism' was replaced by the New Economic Policy (NEP), which allowed peasants and traders some economic freedom.

18 March 1921: A rebellion by Russian sailors in the island garrison of Kronstadt (near St Petersburg) was suppressed by the Red Army.

3 April 1922: Stalin (Iosif Dzhugashvili) was elected General Secretary of the RCP (B).

30 December 1922: The Union of Soviet Socialist Republics (USSR) was formed by the RSFSR, the Transcaucasian Soviet Federative Socialist Republic (TSFSR), the Ukrainian SSR (Soviet Socialist Republic), the Belarusian SSR, and the Central Asian states of the Khorezm People's Socialist Republic and the People's Soviet Republic of Bukhara.

6 July 1923: Promulgation of the first Constitution of the USSR (the Constitution was ratified by the Second All-Union Congress of Soviets in January 1924).

21 January 1924: Death of Lenin.

October 1927: Expulsion of Trotskii (Lev Bronstein) and other opponents of Stalin from the Communist Party.

1928: The NEP was abandoned; beginning of the First Five-Year Plan and forced collectivization of agriculture, which resulted in widespread famine, particularly in Ukraine.

November 1933: Recognition of the USSR by the USA.

18 September 1934: The USSR was admitted to the League of Nations.

1 December 1934: Sergei Kirov, a leading member of the Political Bureau (Politburo) of the Communist Party, was shot and killed in Leningrad; following the shooting, Stalin initiated a new campaign of repression.

26 September 1936: Nikolai Yezhov was appointed head of the security police, the People's Commissariat for Internal Affairs (NKVD); a series of mass arrests and executions, which came to be known as the 'Great Purge' or the 'Yezhovshchina', began. Yezhov was dismissed in November 1938, before himself being sentenced to death.

25 November 1936: The anti-Comintern (Third Communist International—established in 1919) Pact was signed between imperial Japan and Nazi Germany.

5 December 1936: The second Constitution of the USSR (the 'Stalin' Constitution) was adopted; two new Union Republics (the Kyrgyz and Kazakh SSRs) were created, and the TSFSR was dissolved into the Georgian, Armenian and Azerbaijani SSRs. The decade was also dominated by a number of ruthless political purges.

March 1938: Nikolai Bukharin, Aleksei Rykov and other prominent Bolsheviks were sentenced to death at the Moscow 'Show' Trials.

23 August 1939: Signing of the Treaty of Non-Aggression with Germany (the Nazi-Soviet Pact), including the 'Secret Protocols', which sanctioned territorial gains for the USSR.

17 September 1939: Soviet forces invaded eastern Poland.

28 September 1939: The Treaty on Friendship and Existing Borders was signed by Germany and the USSR, by which the two powers agreed that the USSR should annex Lithuania.

30 November 1939: The USSR invaded Finland.

14 December 1939: The USSR was expelled from the League of Nations.

June 1940: The Baltic states and Bessarabia (now mostly in the Republic of Moldova) were annexed by the USSR.

22 June 1941: Germany invaded the USSR.

2 February 1943: German forces surrendered at Stalingrad (now Volgograd), marking the first reverse for the German Army.

1944: In a consolidation of domestic authority, Stalin ordered a number of mass deportations of populations from the North Caucasus and Crimea. Tannu-Tuva (Tyva), a Russian protectorate from 1914, was formally incorporated into the USSR (as part of the RSFSR).

8 May 1945: German forces surrendered to the USSR in Berlin, and Germany subsequently capitulated; most of Eastern and Central Europe had come under Soviet control.

26 June 1945: The USSR, the USA, the United Kingdom, China and 46 other countries, including the Belarusian and Ukrainian SSRs, signed the Charter of the United Nations (UN).

8 August 1945: The USSR declared war on Japan and occupied Sakhalin and the Kurile Islands.

25 January 1949: The Council for Mutual Economic Assistance (CMEA or Comecon) was established, as an economic alliance between the USSR and its Eastern European allies.

14 July 1949: The USSR exploded its first atomic bomb.

5 March 1953: Death of Stalin; he was replaced by a collective leadership, which included Georgii Malenkov and Nikita Khrushchev.

September 1953: Khrushchev was elected First Secretary of the Central Committee of the Communist Party of the Soviet Union (CPSU).

14 May 1955: The Warsaw Treaty of Friendship, Co-operation and Mutual Assistance was signed by the USSR and its Eastern European satellites, establishing a military alliance known as the Warsaw Treaty Organization (or the Warsaw Pact).

14–25 February 1956: At the 20th Party Congress, Khrushchev denounced Stalin in the 'secret speech'.

4 November 1956: Soviet forces invaded Hungary to overthrow Imre Nagy's reformist Government.

June 1957: Malenkov, Vyacheslav Molotov and Lazar Kaganovich (the so-called 'Anti-Party' group) were expelled from the CPSU leadership after attempting to depose Khrushchev.

March 1958: Khrushchev consolidated his position in the leadership by being elected Chairman of the Council of Ministers (premier), while retaining the office of CPSU First Secretary.

October 1961: Stalin's body was removed from its place of honour in the mausoleum in Red Square, in Moscow.

18–28 October 1962: The discovery of Soviet nuclear missiles in Cuba by the USA led to the 'Cuban Missile Crisis'; tension eased when Khrushchev announced the withdrawal of the missiles, following a US blockade of the island.

13–14 October 1964: Khrushchev was deposed from the leadership of the CPSU and the USSR and replaced as First Secretary by Leonid Brezhnev and as premier by Aleksei Kosygin.

20–21 August 1968: Soviet and other Warsaw Pact forces invaded Czechoslovakia to overthrow the reformist Government of Alexander Dubček.

May 1972: The US President, Richard Nixon, visited Moscow, thus marking a relaxation in US-Soviet relations, a process which came to be known as *détente*.

16 June 1977: Brezhnev became Chairman of the Presidium of the Supreme Soviet (titular head of state).

7 October 1977: The third Constitution of the USSR was adopted.

24 December 1979: Soviet forces invaded Afghanistan (troops were withdrawn between July 1986 and February 1989).

10 November 1982: Death of Brezhnev; Yurii Andropov, former head of the Committee for State Security (KGB), succeeded him as party leader.

9 February 1984: Death of Andropov; Konstantin Chernenko succeeded him as General Secretary.

10 March 1985: Death of Chernenko; he was succeeded as General Secretary by Mikhail Gorbachev.

24 February–6 March 1986: At the 27th Congress of the CPSU, Gorbachev proposed radical economic and political reforms and 'new thinking' in foreign policy; emergence of the policy of *glasnost* (openness).

26 April 1986: An explosion occurred at a nuclear reactor in Chernobyl (Chornobyl), Ukraine, which resulted in discharges of radioactive material.

January 1987: At a meeting of the CPSU Central Committee, Gorbachev proposed plans for the restructuring of the economy and some democratization of local government and the CPSU (*perestroika*).

21 October 1987: Boris Yeltsin, the First Secretary of the Moscow City Party Committee in 1985, resigned from the Politburo.

1 October 1988: Andrei Gromyko resigned as Chairman of the Presidium of the Supreme Soviet, to be replaced by Gorbachev.

1 December 1988: The all-Union Supreme Soviet approved constitutional amendments creating a new legislative system, consisting of the Congress of People's

Deputies and a full-time Supreme Soviet (a number of wide-ranging reforms, including partly free elections, had been agreed by the Party earlier in the year).

25 March 1989: Multi-party elections to the newly established legislature, the Congress of People's Deputies, took place.

25 May 1989: The Congress of People's Deputies convened for the first time; Gorbachev was elected to the new post of Chairman of the USSR Supreme Soviet (executive President).

27 May 1989: Congress elected an all-Union Supreme Soviet, which would act as a full-time legislature, in which only a few reformers managed to secure seats.

4 February 1990: Some 150,000 people joined a pro-reform march in the centre of Moscow. Three days later the CPSU Central Committee approved draft proposals to abolish Article 6 of the Constitution, which had guaranteed the CPSU's monopoly of power.

4 March 1990: Elections took place to the local and republican legislatures of the Russian Federation; reformists made substantial gains in the larger cities, notably Moscow and Leningrad.

15 March 1990: The all-Union legislature approved the establishment of the post of President of the USSR and elected Mikhail Gorbachev to that office.

29 May 1990: Boris Yeltsin was elected as Chairman of the Supreme Soviet of the Russian Federation. On 12 June Congress adopted a declaration of Russian sovereignty.

3 September 1990: Boris Yeltsin announced a 500-day programme of economic reform to the Supreme Soviet of the Russian Federation.

October 1990: Legislation allowing the existence of other political parties, apart from the CPSU, was adopted by the all-Union Supreme Soviet. It also approved a reform programme designed to establish a market economy.

17 March 1991: In an all-Union referendum on the issue of the future state of the USSR, some 75% of participants approved Gorbachev's concept of a 'renewed federation' (several republics did not participate).

12 June 1991: Yeltsin was elected President of the Russian Federation in direct elections, with Aleksandr Rutskoi as Vice-President; residents of Leningrad voted to change the city's name back to St Petersburg.

1 July 1991: The USSR and the other member countries of the Warsaw Pact signed a protocol, formalizing the dissolution of the alliance.

18–21 August 1991: An attempted *coup d'état*, led by a 'hardline' State Committee for the State of Emergency in the USSR (SCSE), was frustrated by popular and institutional opposition, with Yeltsin prominent in the successful campaign to reinstate Gorbachev.

24 August 1991: Gorbachev resigned as General Secretary of the CPSU, nationalized the party's property, demanded the dissolution of the Central Committee and banned party cells in the Armed Forces, the KGB and the police. The Supreme Soviet of Ukraine adopted a declaration of independence, pending approval by referendum on 1 December (90% of the participating voters were to approve the decision). On the following day Gorbachev established an interim government.

6 September 1991: The newly formed State Council, which comprised the supreme officials of the Union Republics, recognized the independence of Estonia, Latvia and

Lithuania. (By the end of the year all of the other Union Republics had declared their independence from the USSR.)

27 September 1991: Ivan Silayev, the reformist leader of the interim Government in Russia, was promoted to the position of Soviet Prime Minister.

21 October 1991: The first session of the newly established all-Union Supreme Soviet was attended by delegates of the Russia and six other republics.

27 October 1991: An election to the presidency of the self-proclaimed 'Chechen Republic' (Chechnya) was won by Gen. Dzhokhar Dudayev.

November 1991: President Yeltsin announced the formation of a new Russian Government, with himself as Chairman (Prime Minister).

8 December 1991: The leaders of the Russian Federation, Belarus and Ukraine, meeting at Belovezhskaya Pushcha, Belarus, agreed to form a Commonwealth of Independent States (CIS) to replace the USSR, as stated in the so-called Minsk Agreement.

16 December 1991: Kazakhstan declared its independence, following a decision by it and the four other Central Asian republics to join a Commonwealth.

21 December 1991: At a meeting in Almaty, Kazakhstan, the leaders of 11 former Union Republics of the USSR signed a protocol on the formation of the new CIS.

25 December 1991: Mikhail Gorbachev formally resigned as President of the USSR, thereby confirming the effective dissolution of the Union.

30 December 1991: The 11 members of the CIS agreed, in Minsk, Belarus, to establish a joint command for armed forces (this arrangement was formally ended in 1993); use of nuclear weapons was to be under the control of the Russian Federation's President, after consultation with other Commonwealth leaders and the agreement of the presidents of Belarus, Kazakhstan and Ukraine.

2 January 1992: A radical economic reform programme was introduced in Russia.

31 March 1992: The leaders of the Russian administrative regions and the mayors of Moscow and St Petersburg signed the Russian Federation Treaty; representatives from the 'Chechen Republic' and Tatarstan did not participate.

June 1992: Ingushetiya (which had hitherto formed part of the Checheno-Ingush ASSR) was recognized as a separate republic within the Russian Federation.

9 December 1992: The Congress rejected Yeltsin's nomination of a supporter of radical economic reform, Yegor Gaidar, as Prime Minister (Gaidar had been serving as premier, in an acting capacity, since mid-June); Yeltsin subsequently appointed Viktor Chernomyrdin to the post.

11 March 1993: Congress granted itself the right to suspend any presidential decrees that contravened the Constitution, pending a ruling by the Constitutional Court.

20 March 1993: Following the rejection by Congress of his proposal to hold a referendum on the issue of the respective powers of the presidency and the legislature, Yeltsin announced his intention to rule Russia by decree until such a referendum could take place.

25 April 1993: In a referendum organized by President Yeltsin, in order to resolve the increasing conflict between the executive and the legislature, 57.4% of the electorate endorsed the President and 70.6% voted in favour of early parliamentary elections.

31 August 1993: The heads of administration from 58 constituent parts of the Russian Federation and 45 heads of regional legislative bodies approved Yeltsin's proposal for the establishment of a Sovet Federatsii (Federation Council), to represent the interests of the regions, which convened in mid-September.

21 September 1993: Yeltsin issued a decree 'On Gradual Constitutional Reform' (Decree 1,400), which suspended the powers of the legislature with immediate effect and scheduled elections to a new bicameral legislature, the Federalnoye Sobraniye (Federal Assembly). An emergency session of the Supreme Soviet appointed Rutskoi acting President, although the Constitutional Court ruled against this.

26 September 1993: Some 10,000 demonstrators attended a rally outside the White House, the seat of the Supreme Soviet, in Moscow, in support of the legislators.

28 September 1993: An unarmed police officer was killed in disturbances in the centre of Moscow, as a crowd of several thousand supporters of Ruslan Khasbulatov (the parliamentary Chairman and one of Yeltsin's leading opponents) and Rutskoi attempted to break through the police cordon around the White House.

3 October 1993: Negotiations between the Government and parliament broke down. A state of emergency was declared in Moscow after a group of anti-Yeltsin demonstrators stormed the office of the Mayor of Moscow and the Ostankino television building. Rutskoi was formally dismissed.

4 October 1993: The White House was shelled by government forces and severely damaged by fire, and over 140 people were killed. Later that day Khasbulatov and Rutskoi surrendered and the perpetrators of the violence were arrested.

12 December 1993: A proposed new Constitution was approved by 58.4% of participating voters in a referendum. On the same day elections to the new Federalnoye Sobraniye (Federal Assembly—comprising the Sovet Federatsii and the Gosudarstvennaya Duma—State Duma) were held, producing an unexpected number of votes (22.8% of the total) for Vladimir Zhirinovskii's nationalist Liberal Democratic Party of Russia (LPDR) and for the Communist Party (12.4%).

February 1994: The Gosudarstvennaya Duma granted an amnesty to the members of the SCSE of the 1991 coup attempt and to the organizers of the parliamentary resistance of September–October 1993.

30 July 1994: Against a background of armed raids by rebel Chechens, Yeltsin declared his support for an 'Interim Council' in Chechnya. The Council, headed by Umar Avturkhanov, had proclaimed itself the rightful Government of Chechnya, in opposition to the administration of President Dudayev, which, within two weeks, ordered mobilization in Chechnya.

3 September 1994: Armed conflict broke out in Argun, east of Groznyi, the capital of Chechnya, between supporters of Dudayev and opposition troops.

11 December 1994: Following the collapse of peace negotiations, Yeltsin ordered 40,000 ground troops to restore order in Chechnya.

19 January 1995: After a bitterly fought resistance, Dudayev fled Groznyi and established his headquarters outside the city.

March 1995: The Russian Government installed a 'Government of National Revival' in Chechnya, chaired by Salambek Khadzhiyev; this existed alongside the Interim Council, by this time largely discredited, but was replaced in November by a new Government, under Doku Zavgayev.

14 June 1995: The militant Chechen leader, Shamil Basayev, took over 1,000 people hostage in a hospital in Budennovsk (Stavropol Krai). After a few days, to secure the release of the captives, the Prime Minister, Chernomyrdin, intervened in the negotiations and agreed to resume peace talks with the Chechen rebels. More than 100 people died during the hostage-taking, and, particularly, during the operations to end the siege.

21 June 1995: A vote of 'no confidence' in the Government was overwhelmingly approved by the Gosudarstvennaya Duma.

12 July 1995: An impeachment motion against the President was defeated, largely owing to the fact that Yeltsin was hospitalized at the time, having suffered a heart attack.

30 July 1995: Opposition to the continuing war in Chechnya prompted a military accord on the gradual disarmament of the Chechen rebels, in return for the partial withdrawal of federal troops from Chechnya; it remained in effect until October.

17 December 1995: In elections to the Gosudarstvennaya Duma, in which an estimated 64.4% of eligible voters participated, the Communist Party of the Russian Federation (CPRF) achieved the greatest success, winning 22.7% of the votes cast; the LDPR won 11.2% of the votes, Our Home is Russia (an electoral bloc headed by Viktor Chernomyrdin) 10.1% and Yabloko (headed by the liberal, Grigorii Yavlinskii) 6.9%.

9 January 1996: Chechen rebels, led by Salman Raduyev, held some 2,000 civilians captive in the town of Kizlyar, Dagestan. Some hostages were later released, while others were taken in convoy to the nearby village of Pervomaiskoye. The village was bombarded for several days by federal air and ground troops, resulting in the release of the captives at the expense of many casualties.

21 April 1996: Dzhokhar Dudayev was killed in a Russian missile attack. He was succeeded by his erstwhile Deputy, Zemlikhan Yandarbiyev.

16 June 1996: Eleven candidates contested the presidential election; Yeltsin secured the greatest number of votes (35%), followed by the leader of the CPRF, Gennadii Zyuganov (32%); Lt-Gen. (retd) Aleksandr Lebed won an unexpectedly high level of support, with 15% of the votes cast, and was later appointed to the Government.

3 July 1996: Amid increasing speculation about his health, Boris Yeltsin won the second round of voting in the presidential election, with 53.8% of the votes cast. Yeltsin was inaugurated as President on 9 August.

31 August 1996: Following a successful attack by Chechen forces on Groznyi, Lebed negotiated a cease-fire agreement (the Khasavyurt Accords) with the rebel chief of staff, Col Khalid 'Aslan' Maskhadov; the basic principles of the agreement included postponing a solution to the issue of Chechen sovereignty until 2001. Despite the peace deal, Lebed was dismissed in mid-October.

1 January 1997: Maskhadov was elected as President of the Chechen Republic (which subsequently renamed itself 'the Chechen Republic of Ichkeriya'), defeating Basayev.

2 April 1997: A Treaty of Union was signed by the Presidents of Russia and Belarus, without consultation with their respective legislatures; the following month a Charter of the Union of Belarus and Russia was concluded, committing the two countries to closer integration.

November 1997: During a visit by President Yeltsin to the People's Republic of China, it was agreed to end a long-running border dispute and allow for the implementation of a 1991 accord demarcating the entire 4,300-km frontier.

27 March 1998: Following the dismissal of Chernomyrdin and his Government a few days before, Sergei Kiriyenko, hitherto Minister of Fuel and Energy, was nominated as premier; a new Government was gradually appointed over the following month. Kiriyenko was confirmed as premier by the Gosudarstvennaya Duma on 24 April, his nomination having been rejected twice earlier in the month.

17 August 1998: In response to an escalating financial crisis, and in a complete reversal of its monetary policies, the Government announced a series of emergency measures, which included the effective devaluation of the rouble.

21 August 1998: The Gosudarstvennaya Duma reconvened for an extraordinary plenary session to debate the financial and economic crisis in Russia; a resolution was passed urging the voluntary resignation of President Yeltsin. Two days later President Yeltsin dismissed the Government and reappointed Chernomyrdin premier.

11 September 1998: Following the Gosudarstvennaya Duma's second conclusive rejection of Chernomyrdin's nomination as Prime Minister, the Minister of Foreign Affairs, Yevgenii Primakov, was confirmed as premier.

5 November 1998: The Constitutional Court ruled that Boris Yeltsin was ineligible to seek a third presidential term in 2000.

24 March 1999: Russia condemned airstrikes by the North Atlantic Treaty Organization (NATO) against Yugoslav targets, initiated in response to the repression of ethnic Albanians in the Serbian province of Kosovo and Metohija (Kosovo), and suspended relations with the Alliance.

16 April 1999: The Duma voted overwhelmingly in favour of the admission of the Federal Republic of Yugoslavia (now Serbia and Montenegro) to the Union of Russia and Belarus. Political leaders assessed the measure to be of solely symbolic significance.

12 May 1999: The dismissal of Primakov and his Government was effected by Yeltsin, who appointed Sergei Stepashin, hitherto First Deputy Prime Minister and Minister of the Interior, as acting premier; he was approved by the Gosudarstvennaya Duma one week later.

12 June 1999: Russian troops entered Kosovo, ahead of NATO forces, following the capitulation of Serb forces three days earlier. International negotiations took place throughout the month on the role to be undertaken in the region by Russian peace-keeping forces.

7 August 1999: Armed Chechen guerrillas invaded neighbouring Dagestan and seized control of two villages. Federal troops retaliated and claimed, by the end of the month, to have quelled the rebel action.

9 August 1999: Stepashin was dismissed by Yeltsin, and replaced as premier by Vladimir Putin, hitherto the Secretary of the Security Council and head of the Federal Security Service (FSB).

9 and 13 September 1999: Two bomb attacks, which targeted apartment blocks in Moscow, killing almost 200 people, were attributed by the federal authorities to Chechen rebels. In August a bomb explosion at a Moscow shopping centre had injured more than 30 people, and further bombings in southern Russian, against both civilian and military targets, took place in mid-September.

23 September 1999: Russia initiated airstrikes against Chechnya, officially in retaliation for the bombings, and as part of a declared 'anti-terrorism' campaign. Federal forces instigated full-scale military operations in Chechnya at the beginning of November, and in December a ground offensive commenced against the republic's capital, Groznyi.

19 December 1999: In elections to the Gosudarstvennaya Duma, the CPRF secured the most seats, with 113. Unity, formed by 31 leaders of Russia's regions, obtained 72 seats, and the Fatherland-All Russia bloc obtained 67. The pro-market Union of Rightist Forces, led by Sergei Kiriyenko, obtained 29 seats, Yabloko took 21, and the Zhirinovskii bloc (contesting the election in place of the LDPR) won 17. Some 62% of the electorate participated.

31 December 1999: Yeltsin unexpectedly resigned as President; Putin assumed the role in an acting capacity.

26 March 2000: Putin achieved a clear victory in the first round of the presidential election, with 52.9% of the votes cast. Gennadii Zyuganov was the second-placed candidate, with 29.2% of the votes cast.

5 May 2000: Putin decreed that, henceforth, Chechnya was to come under direct federal, rather than direct presidential, rule. Maskhadov was no longer to be recognized as President of the Republic, and on 19 June a new administrative leader for Chechnya, Akhmad haji Kadyrov, was inaugurated.

7 May 2000: Vladimir Putin was inaugurated as President of the Russian Federation. He subsequently relinquished the post of premier and formed a new Government headed by the former First Deputy Prime Minister, Mikhail Kasyanov.

13 May 2000: The President issued a decree dividing Russia's 89 constituent regions and republics between seven federal districts (okrugs). Each district was to come under the control of a presidential envoy, who was to oversee local regions' compliance with federal legislation. Of the new presidential envoys, five were senior officers of the security services or the military.

31 May 2000: Three pieces of legislation, proposed by Putin to extend the powers of the President and curtail those of the regional governors, were passed by the Gosudarstvennaya Duma. The first proposed that regional governors should lose their seats in the Sovet Federatsii, and be replaced by representatives elected from regional legislatures; following its ratification by the Sovet Federatsii in July, all existing Council members were to be replaced by the beginning of 2002. The second bill accorded the President the right to dismiss regional governors, and the third allowed governors to remove from office elected officials who were subordinate to them.

23 November 2000: The State Council, a body comprising the President and the territorial governors and formed as part of the ongoing reform of the Sovet Federatsii, convened for the first time.

22 January 2001: Putin signed a decree transferring control of operations in Chechnya from the Ministry of Defence to the FSB.

12 July 2001: New conditions for the registration of political organizations were introduced, which were intended to facilitate the consolidation of national parties.

October 2001: Following the commencement of US-led military action against targets of the Taliban regime, and the al-Qa'ida militant Islamist organization, in Afghanistan, on 7 October, Russia provided military intelligence, and allowed the coalition access to its airspace. Russia also increased logistical and military support to the anti-Taliban forces of the United Islamic Front for the Salvation of Afghanistan (the 'Northern Alliance').

1 December 2001: The founding congress of the Unity and Fatherland-United Russia (UF-UR) party, uniting two hitherto separate centrist movements, Fatherland-All Russia and Unity, took place.

16 January 2002: A new session of the Sovet Federatsii opened; for the first time, the Council comprised the full-time appointees of both regional governors and the chairmen of regional legislative assemblies.

25 April 2002: Federal sources reported that the rebel Islamist leader, al-Khattab, who had led a faction in the war in Chechnya, had been killed, a report that was subsequently confirmed by rebel sources.

9 May 2002: During Victory Day processions in Kaspiisk, Dagestan, 45 people were killed, and more than 130 others injured as the result of a bomb attack attributed to Chechen militants.

24 May 2002: Putin and the US President, George W. Bush, signed an agreement, in accordance with which Russia and the USA were each to reduce their stocks of strategic nuclear warheads by more than one-half over a period of 10 years. This development followed an announcement by the USA in late 2001 that it was to withdraw from the Anti-Ballistic Missiles (ABM) Treaty, signed between the USA and the USSR in 1972, with effect from June 2002. On 13 June Russia withdrew from the second Strategic Arms Reduction Treaty (START 2), which had been superseded by the new nuclear arms reduction agreement.

28 May 2002: The new NATO-Russia Council, which made Russia a full partner of NATO in discussions on a number of issues, including counter-terrorism, non-proliferation and emergency planning, was inaugurated at a NATO conference in Rome, Italy.

19 August 2002: In the single largest loss of life since the recommencement of military operations in Chechnya in 1999, some 118 federal troops were killed when rebels shot down a military helicopter.

6 October 2002: Following months of escalating tension between Georgia and Russia, the latter accusing Georgia of allowing Chechen rebels to operate from bases within its territory, the two countries agreed to undertake joint patrols of their common border.

23 October 2002: Some 50 heavily armed Chechen rebels took more than 700 people hostage in a Moscow theatre, demanding the immediate withdrawal of federal troops from Chechnya. On 26 October élite Russian troops stormed the theatre, killing the rebels in an operation that also resulted in the deaths of some 129 hostages, according to official figures. It rapidly emerged that the vast majority of these deaths had resulted from the use of an incapacitating gas by the federal troops.

7 November 2002: In a move that was generally regarded as a promotion, Stanislav Ilyasov, hitherto Chairman of the Government of Chechnya, was appointed to the federal Government as Minister without Portfolio, responsible for the Social and Economic Development of Chechnya. Capt (retd) Mikhail Babich was appointed as the new premier of Chechnya; Babich resigned in January 2003 and was replaced in the following month by Anatolii Popov, hitherto the Deputy Chairman of the State Commission for the Reconstruction of Chechnya.

27 December 2002: At least 83 people died, and more than 150 others were injured, when suicide bombers detonated bombs in two vehicles stationed outside the headquarters of the Chechen republican Government in Groznyi.

11 March 2003: Putin removed Valentina Matviyenko from her post as Deputy Chairman of the Government, responsible for Social Affairs, appointing her as Presidential Representative in the North-Western Federal District, based in St Petersburg. Several presidential decrees issued on the same day provided for a reorganization of the federal security agencies, as a result of which the powers of the FSB were expanded.

23 March 2003: A referendum was held in Chechnya on the draft republican constitution, which described the region as an integral part of the Russian Federation. According to the official results, some 88.4% of the electorate participated in the plebiscite, of whom 96.0% voted in favour. Two further questions, on the method of electing the president and the parliament of the republic, were also approved, receiving the support of 95.4% and 96.1% of the votes cast, respectively.

12 May 2003: At least 59 people were killed when suicide bombers attacked offices of the Chechen Government in Znamenskoye, in the north of the republic. Two days later another suicide bombing in Chechnya, at a religious festival attended by Kadyrov, resulted in at least 14 deaths.

16 June 2003: Vladimir Yakovlev, hitherto Governor of St Petersburg, was appointed to the federal Government as a Deputy Chairman, with particular responsibility for housing and utilities.

21 June 2003: An interim legislative body in Chechnya, the State Council, was inaugurated.

6 July 2003: Fifteen people were killed as the result of a suicide bombing, attributed to Chechen militants, at a music festival outside Moscow.

1 September 2003: The overall command for military operations in Chechnya was transferred from the FSB to the Ministry of Internal Affairs. Moreover, the Minister of Internal Affairs, Boris Gryzlov, stated that such operations were no longer regarded as having an 'anti-terrorist' character, but were rather, henceforth, to form part of an 'operation to protect law and constitutional order'.

5 October 2003: At a second round of voting, Matviyenko was elected as Governor of St Petersburg, having received the support of Putin. On the same day Kadyrov was elected as President of Chechnya, with 88% of the votes cast, according to official figures. However, many observers were critical of the conduct of voting in Chechnya, citing a heightened military presence at polling stations, and noting that several of Kadyrov's principal rivals had withdrawn, or been obliged to withdraw, their candidacies.

26 October 2003: Mikhail Khodorkovskii, the Chief Executive of Yukos Oil Co, and a prominent supporter of the pro-market URF and the liberal Yabloko party, was arrested and detained, reportedly following his failure to attend a court hearing at which various charges of fraudulent practice by the company were being investigated. Khodorkovskii, who was the third senior executive of the company to be arrested since July, was subsequently charged with tax evasion and fraud. He was sentenced to nine years' imprisonment, having been found guilty on six charges, including tax evasion and embezzlement, in May 2005.

7 December 2003: Gosudarstvennaya Duma elections were dominated by UF-UR, which won 226 of the 450 seats. The CPRF secured 53 seats, the LDPR 38, and the recently formed Motherland electoral bloc received 37. Yabloko and the URF failed to obtain the 5% of votes necessary to obtain representation on the basis of federal party lists, and their legislative representation was much reduced, to only four and three seats, respectively. Turn-out was relatively low, at 55.75% .

9 December 2003: Six people were killed when a bomb exploded in Moscow, outside a hotel located close to the Kremlin; the intended target was thought to have been the Gosudarstvennaya Duma building and the attack was widely attributed to female Chechen suicide bombers (often referred to as 'black widows'). Four days earlier a bomb attack had targeted a passenger train in Stavropol Krai, killing some 45 people and injuring about 170.

29 December 2003: Boris Gryzlov, who had resigned his ministerial portfolio, was elected Chairman of the Gosudarstvennaya Duma.

6 February 2004: An explosion on the Moscow metro attributed to Chechen militants killed at least 39 people.

24 February 2004: Putin dismissed the Government of Mikhail Kasyanov. Mikhail Fradkov, former representative to the EU, was subsequently appointed Prime Minister of the new Government, in which the number of ministries was reduced from 30 to 17.

14 March 2004: Vladimir Putin was overwhelmingly re-elected as President, receiving 71.31% of votes cast. His closest rival, Nikolai Kharitonov of the CPRF, received 13.69%. A total of 64.39% of registered voters participated in the election. Notably, both the CPRF and LDPR declined to nominate leading members of their parties as candidates, in both cases presenting relatively obscure figures.

16 March 2004: Sergei Abramov was appointed as Prime Minister of Chechnya, following the resignation of Popov for reasons of ill health.

9 May 2004: Chechen President Akhmad Kadyrov was killed in a bombing in Groznyi.

21–22 June 2004: A series of raids on Ministry of Internal Affairs targets in Ingushetiya, variously attributed to Chechen, Ingush and international militants, left 97 people dead.

24 August 2004: Two passenger planes, both flying from Moscow's Domodedovo airport, crashed within minutes of each other, killing all 89 people on board. Both crashes were attributed to suicide bombers.

29 August 2004: The presidential elections in Chechnya was won by Maj-Gen. Alu Alkhanov, who was perceived to be the favoured candidate of the federal authorities. Council of Europe observers described the elections as undemocratic.

31 August 2004: An explosion outside a Moscow Metro station, reportedly caused by a suicide bomber, killed 10 people.

1 September 2004: Armed militants occupied a school in Beslan, North Osetiya— Alaniya, on the first day of the school year, taking up to 1,500 parents, teachers and children hostage. After two days of largely fruitless negotiations, on 3 September members of the special forces stormed the school. More than 330 hostages, including 186 children, died during the course of the siege, according to official figures.

13 September 2004: Putin announced plans for political reform, including the appointment by the federal President of regional governors, and the introduction of a system of fully proportional representation for Gosudarstvennaya Duma elections.

13 October 2004: The Gosudarstvennaya Duma voted in favour of overturning a law that had hitherto prevented members of the Government holding membership of political parties.

12 December 2004: Putin signed legislation providing for the appointment of regional governors, subject to the approval of regional legislatures.

22 December 2004: Putin approved legislation increasing the minimum membership of a political party to 50,000 (compared with the previous minimum of 10,000 that had been introduced in 2001) in order for it to be allowed to register and to participate in elections.

8 March 2005: The Russian military announced that Maskhadov had been killed during a special operation in the settlement of Tolstoi-Yurt, north of the Chechen capital Groznyi; Maskhadov was succeeded as leader of the rebel 'State Defence Committee" by Abdul-Khalim Sadulayev.

26 August 2005: It was reported that Sadulayev had appointed a new rebel Chechen 'Government', following his implementation of personnel changes to representations of the separatists internationally; the 'Government' was notable for its inclusion of Basayev as 'First Deputy Prime Minister'; Basayev had been distanced from the rebel 'authorities' following the theatre siege in Moscow in late 2002.

13 October 2005: Some 100 militants staged a series of co-ordinated attacks against government, police, and commercial buildings across Nalchik, the capital of the Kabardino-Balkar Republic, in the North Caucasus. According to official figures, at least 130 people were killed in the ensuing clashes, including more than 90 militants. Basayev claimed responsibility for the organization of the attacks, although it was unclear whether the principal insurgents were associated with a local Islamist group, Yarmuk, with a broader 'Caucasus Front' associated with Basayev and Sadulayev, or with both groups.

14 November 2005: President Putin implemented a minor governmental reorganization. Dmitrii Medvedev, hitherto Head of the Presidential Administration was appointed as First Deputy Chairman of the Government; he was to retain his position as Chairman of the Board of Directors of the state-controlled natural gas utility and producer, Gazprom. Sergei Ivanov, hitherto Minister of Defence, was additionally appointed as a Deputy Chairman of the Government.

27 November 2005: Elections were held to a new bicameral legislature in Chechnya, in which an absolute majority of seats were obtained by UF-UR.

Statistics

MAJOR DEMOGRAPHIC AND ECONOMIC INDICATORS

	Area ('000 sq km)	Population at 2002 census ('000)	Population density, 2002 census (per sq km)	Average annual change in population, 1989–2002 (%)[1]	Life expectancy at birth, 2003
Central Federal Okrug	650.7	38,000.7	58.4	−0.01	65.81
Moscow City	1.0	10,382.8	10,382.8	1.13	69.64
Belgorod Oblast . . .	27.1	1,511.6	55.8	0.68	68.26
Bryansk Oblast . .	34.9	1,378.9	39.5	−0.46	64.62
Ivanovo Oblast . . .	21.8	1,148.3	52.7	−0.86	62.42
Kaluga Oblast . . .	29.9	1,041.6	34.8	−0.16	64.56
Kostroma Oblast . . .	60.1	736.6	12.3	−0.62	62.39
Kursk Oblast	29.8	1,235.1	41.4	−0.56	65.35
Lipetsk Oblast . . .	24.1	1,213.5	50.4	−0.10	65.85
Moscow Oblast[3] . . .	46.0	6,618.5	143.9	−0.02	65.26
Orel Oblast	24.7	860.3	34.8	−0.23	65.23
Ryazan Oblast . . .	39.6	1,227.9	31.0	−0.68	63.91
Smolensk Oblast . . .	49.8	1,049.6	21.1	−0.69	62.34
Tambov Oblast . . .	34.3	1,178.4	34.4	−0.83	65.47
Tula Oblast	25.7	1,675.8	65.2	−0.76	63.03
Tver Oblast	84.1	1,471.5	17.5	−0.88	61.53
Vladimir Oblast . . .	29.0	1,524.0	52.6	−0.57	63.18
Voronezh Oblast . . .	52.4	2,378.8	45.4	−0.26	66.19
Yaroslavl Oblast . . .	36.4	1,367.4	37.6	−0.52	63.46
North-Western Federal Okrug	1,677.9	13,974.5	8.3	−0.62	63.43
St Petersburg City . .	0.6	4,669.4	8,191.9	−0.48	66.49
Republic of Kareliya . .	172.4	716.3	4.2	−0.70	60.81
Republic of Komi . .	415.9	1,018.7	2.4	−1.48	61.67
Archangel Oblast	587.4	1,336.5	2.3	−1.17	62.11
Nenets AOk . .	176.7	41.5	0.2	−1.98	58.87
Kaliningrad Oblast . .	15.1	955.3	63.3	0.67	61.68
Leningrad Oblast[4] . .	85.3	1,669.2	19.6	0.07	61.74
Murmansk Oblast . .	144.9	892.5	6.2	−1.92	63.20
Novgorod Oblast . . .	55.3	694.4	12.6	−0.56	60.34
Pskov Oblast	55.3	760.8	13.8	−0.76	60.86
Vologda Oblast . . .	145.7	1,269.6	8.7	−0.44	62.47

[1] According to 1989 and 2002 census results.
[3] Moscow Oblast excludes Moscow City.
[4] Leningrad Oblast excludes St Petersburg City.

Gross regional product (GRP), 2002 (m. roubles)	GRP per head, 2002 (roubles)	Rate of un-employment, 2003 (%)	Inflation rate, 2003 (%)[2]	Foreign investment, 2003 (US $m.)	
3,227,843.4	84,941.8	5.4	11.7	15,664.3	**Central Federal Okrug**
1,999,995.3	192,626.7	1.3	10.4	13,886.9	Moscow City
65,702.0	43,464.6	8.2	12.0	23.3	Belgorod Oblast
41,327.6	29,970.5	7.3	12.9	6.4	Bryansk Oblast
29,467.1	25,660.9	6.5	14.7	0.3	Ivanovo Oblast
40,213.4	38,605.8	6.2	14.3	27.4	Kaluga Oblast
27,574.8	37,433.2	6.3	13.5	49.0	Kostroma Oblast
46,690.5	37,803.3	8.6	16.2	8.8	Kursk Oblast
71,108.1	58,597.6	4.4	13.4	12.6	Lipetsk Oblast
370,816.8	56,027.0	4.3	11.7	1,258.0	Moscow Oblast[3]
38,837.0	45,145.5	7.8	12.2	12.1	Orel Oblast
54,711.2	44,556.4	8.3	14.9	45.8	Ryazan Oblast
47,000.5	44,780.5	10.9	12.9	33.6	Smolensk Oblast
39,211.2	33,273.7	9.1	10.5	3.5	Tambov Oblast
67,891.9	40,514.1	5.3	16.7	27.5	Tula Oblast
58,775.7	39,943.8	6.6	12.8	4.9	Tver Oblast
53,294.9	34,970.6	10.1	15.3	85.2	Vladimir Oblast
88,151.6	37,057.1	8.1	11.7	29.6	Voronezh Oblast
87,073.3	63,678.1	5.7	11.9	149.4	Yaroslavl Oblast
					North-Western Federal
937,245.2	67,068.4	7.0	13.2	1,877.4	**Okrug**
367,804.1	78,907.3	4.1	12.2	695.8	St Petersburg City
41,605.6	58,085.6	8.5	12.9	34.7	Republic of Kareliya
93,153.2	91,445.5	11.9	18.0	89.9	Republic of Komi
84,681.0	63,358.4	9.9	12.7	234.3	Archangel Oblast
16,739.6	402,917.2	8.6	12.7	171.1	Nenets AOk
41,095.6	43,019.4	7.5	17.5	55.9	Kaliningrad Oblast
101,774.7	60,972.0	8.7	13.0	239.7	Leningrad Oblast[4]
68,005.9	76,194.2	10.0	13.9	21.6	Murmansk Oblast
31,858.2	45,881.7	5.0	14.4	212.8	Novgorod Oblast
24,630.2	32,373.7	8.1	12.7	6.2	Pskov Oblast
82,636.7	65,090.4	4.8	13.1	286.6	Vologda Oblast

[2] Percentage change in the Consumer Price Index, Dec.–Dec.

MAJOR DEMOGRAPHIC AND ECONOMIC INDICATORS (CONTINUED)

	Area ('000 sq km)	Population at 2002 census ('000)	Population density, 2002 census (per sq km)	Average annual change in population, 1989–2002 (%)[1]	Life expectancy at birth, 2003
Southern Federal Okrug	589.2	22,907.1	38.9	0.80	67.49
Republic of Adygeya .	7.6	447.1	58.8	0.25	67.51
Chechen (Nokchi) Rep. .	n.a.	1,103.7	n.a.	1.55[3]	69.06
Republic of Dagestan .	50.3	2,576.5	51.2	2.66	72.33
Republic of Ingushetiya .	n.a.	467.3	n.a.	1.55[3]	75.13
Kabardino-Balkar Rep. .	12.5	901.5	72.1	1.30	68.70
Republic of Kalmykiya .	75.9	292.4	3.9	−7.1	66.18
Karachai-Cherkess Rep. .	14.1	439.5	31.2	0.43	68.10
Republic of North Osetiya—Alaniya . .	8.0	710.3	88.8	0.84	68.47
Krasnodar Krai . . .	76.0	5,125.2	67.4	0.75	67.33
Stavropol Krai . . .	66.5	2,735.1	41.1	0.91	67.14
Astrakhan Oblast . . .	44.1	1,005.3	22.8	0.11	65.36
Rostov Oblast	100.8	4,404.0	43.7	0.19	66.47
Volgograd Oblast . .	113.9	2,699.2	23.7	0.30	66.43
Volga Federal Okrug .	1,038.0	31,154.7	30.0	−0.14	65.29
Rep. of Bashkortostan .	143.6	4,104.3	28.6	0.29	66.39
Chuvash Republic . .	18.3	1,313.7	71.8	−0.13	66.09
Republic of Marii-El . .	23.2	728.0	31.4	−0.21	63.99
Republic of Mordoviya .	26.2	888.8	33.9	−0.59	66.28
Republic of Tatarstan .	68.0	3,779.3	55.6	0.27	67.84
Udmurt Republic . . .	42.1	1,570.3	37.3	−0.16	64.34
Kirov Oblast . . .	120.8	1,503.5	12.4	−0.86	63.71
Nizhnii Novgorod Oblast	76.9	3,524.0	45.8	−0.43	64.03
Orenburg Oblast . . .	124.0	2,179.6	17.6	0.02	65.35
Penza Oblast	43.2	1,452.9	33.6	−0.26	65.67
Perm Oblast[8] . . .	160.6	2,819.4	17.6	−0.66	62.31
Komi-Permyak AOk[8] .	32.9	136.1	4.1	−1.09	56.73
Samara Oblast . . .	53.6	3,239.7	60.4	−0.05	65.59
Saratov Oblast . . .	100.2	2,668.3	26.6	−0.04	65.46
Ulyanovsk Oblast . .	37.3	1,382.8	37.1	−0.07	65.25
Urals Federal Okrug	1,788.9	12,373.9	6.9	−0.08	64.79
Chelyabinsk Oblast . .	87.9	3,603.3	41.0	−0.02	64.78
Kurgan Oblast . . .	71.0	1,019.5	14.4	−0.57	63.87
Sverdlovsk Oblast . .	194.8	4,486.2	23.0	−0.34	63.97
Tyumen Oblast . . .	1,435.2	3,264.8	2.3	0.39	66.07
Khanty-Mansii AOk— Yugra	523.1	1,432.8	2.7	0.81	67.36
Yamalo-Nenets AOk .	750.3	507.0	0.7	0.17	66.74

[1] According to 1989 and 2002 census results.
[3] Combined figure for the Chechen (Nokchi) Republic and the Republic of Ingushetiya (as the former Checheno-Ingush ASSR).
[8] On 1 Dec. 2005 Perm Oblast and the Komi-Permyak AOk merged to form Perm Krai.

Gross regional product (GRP), 2002 (m. roubles)	GRP per head, 2002 (roubles)	Rate of un-employment, 2003 (%)	Inflation rate, 2003 (%)[2]	Foreign investment, 2003 (US $m.)	
743,172.7	32,442.8	15.3	10.8	665.8	**Southern Federal Okrug**
8,403.5	18,795.2	15.8	13.2	2.1	Republic of Adygeya
n.a.	n.a.	70.9	n.a.	n.a.	Chechen (Nokchi) Rep.
42,443.9	16,473.3	20.1	9.5	0.1[4]	Republic of Dagestan
3,842.1	8,222.0	53.1	13.9	n.a.	Republic of Ingushetiya
23,518.8	26,088.7	22.0	8.9	0.2[5]	Kabardino-Balkar Rep.
13,476.2	46,086.7	17.9	10.1	1.6[6]	Republic of Kalmykiya
10,539.2	23,981.6	19.0	9.4	0.0[7]	Karachai-Cherkess Rep.
16,757.3	23,592.7	10.1	7.8	n.a.	Republic of North Osetiya—Alaniya
234,503.7	45,754.8	10.1	10.7	325.7	Krasnodar Krai
85,482.3	31,253.4	10.3	12.9	13.8	Stavropol Krai
44,807.2	44,572.0	10.1	14.1	56.1	Astrakhan Oblast
147,157.5	33,414.4	12.3	12.2	223.5	Rostov Oblast
112,241.0	41,582.7	10.9	10.0	44.6	Volgograd Oblast
1,627,179.9	52,229.0	7.6	12.2	944.7	**Volga Federal Okrug**
214,822.2	52,340.3	8.2	11.1	40.2	Rep. of Bashkortostan
39,845.7	30,329.7	8.6	13.3	4.0	Chuvash Republic
18,887.6	25,945.3	12.2	12.1	4.4	Republic of Marii-El
24,332.4	27,377.7	7.4	9.0	23.2	Republic of Mordoviya
261,843.9	69,284.3	6.7	12.4	176.1	Republic of Tatarstan
83,139.7	52,944.6	6.7	12.5	21.6	Udmurt Republic
53,738.3	35,741.4	7.4	13.3	2.1	Kirov Oblast
196,901.4	55,874.0	6.1	15.3	124.2	Nizhnii Novgorod Oblast
102,995.0	47,255.1	11.3	10.1	60.0	Orenburg Oblast
44,860.3	30,875.5	9.1	9.9	0.3	Penza Oblast
194,355.1	68,934.4	6.9	14.6	35.9	Perm Oblast[8]
2,905.7	21,353.5	10.9	14.1	1.5	Komi-Permyak AOk[8]
238,056.4	73,480.2	4.4	12.7	414.3	Samara Oblast
104,666.2	39,225.7	10.5	10.2	14.9	Saratov Oblast
48,735.7	35,243.9	7.4	14.6	23.5	Ulyanovsk Oblast
1,421,572.4	114,884.5	7.5	10.3	5,561.8	**Urals Federal Okrug**
183,386.3	50,893.4	5.9	10.6	1,029.8	Chelyabinsk Oblast
32,081.1	31,466.5	9.6	11.4	0.4	Kurgan Oblast
246,059.5	54,847.9	7.6	11.2	1,314.6	Sverdlovsk Oblast
960,045.5	294,055.8	8.3	10.7	3,216.9	Tyumen Oblast
581,777.0	406,037.2	9.4	14.2	3,143.6	Khanty-Mansii AOk—Yugra
279,355.6	550,990.7	5.5	9.3	58.2	Yamalo-Nenets AOk

[2] Percentage change in the Consumer Price Index, Dec.–Dec.
[4] 1998 figure.
[5] 2000 figure.
[6] 1995 figure.
[7] 2001 figure.

MAJOR DEMOGRAPHIC AND ECONOMIC INDICATORS (CONTINUED)

	Area ('000 sq km)	Population at 2002 census ('000)	Population density, 2002 census (per sq km)	Average annual change in population, 1989–2002 (%)[1]	Life expectancy at birth, 2003
Siberian Federal Okrug	5,114.8	20,062.9	3.9	−0.35	63.17
Republic of Altai . . .	92.6	202.9	2.2	0.44	60.24
Republic of Buryatiya .	351.3	981.2	2.8	−0.41	61.25
Republic of Khakasiya .	61.9	546.1	8.8	−0.27	60.75
Republic of Tyva . . .	170.5	305.5	1.8	0.05	54.31
Altai Krai	169.1	2,607.4	15.4	−0.07	66.05
Krasnoyarsk Krai . .	2,339.7	2,966.0	1.3	−0.18	63.03
Evenk AOk . . .	767.6	17.7	0.0	−2.36	60.83
Taimyr (Dolgano-Nenets) AOk . .	862.1	39.8	0.1	−2.42	61.42
Chita Oblast	431.5	1,155.3	2.7	−1.25	60.24
Aga-Buryat AOk .	19.0	72.2	3.8	−0.49	62.89
Irkutsk Oblast	767.9	2,581.7	3.4	−0.65	60.68
Ust-Orda Buryat AOk	22.4	135.3	6.0	−0.05	60.70
Kemerovo Oblast . . .	95.5	2,899.1	30.4	−0.65	61.86
Novosibirsk Oblast . .	178.2	2,692.3	15.1	−0.23	65.83
Omsk Oblast	139.7	2,079.2	14.9	−0.22	66.01
Tomsk Oblast	316.9	1,046.0	3.3	0.31	64.44
Far Eastern Federal Okrug	6,215.9	6,692.9	1.1	−1.25	62.42
Republic of Sakha (Yakutiya)	3,103.2	949.3	0.3	−1.04	63.96
Khabarovsk Krai . . .	788.6	1,436.6	1.8	−0.78	61.85
Maritime (Primorskii) Krai	165.9	2,071.2	12.5	−0.63	63.07
Amur Oblast	363.7	902.8	2.5	−1.09	61.26
Kamchatka Oblast . .	472.3	358.8	0.8	−1.97	63.00
Koryak AOk . . .	301.5	25.2	0.1	−3.36	53.32
Magadan Oblast . . .	461.4	182.7	0.4	−5.39	63.03
Sakhalin Oblast . . .	87.1	546.7	6.3	−1.89	61.44
Jewish AOb	36.0	190.9	5.3	−0.82	60.80
Chukot AOk	737.7	53.8	0.1	−7.77	59.10
Russian Federation . .	17,075.4	145,166.7	8.5	−0.09	65.07

[1] According to 1989 and 2002 census results.

Source: Federal Service of State Statistics, Moscow.

Gross regional product (GRP), 2002 (m. roubles)	GRP per head, 2002 (roubles)	Rate of un-employment, 2003 (%)	Inflation rate, 2003 (%)[2]	Foreign investment, 2003 (US $m.)	
1,029,430.4	51,310.1	11.7	12.8	2,138.0	**Siberian Federal Okrug**
6,349.4	31,286.0	10.2	13.5	0.1[3]	Republic of Altai
39,065.5	39,812.5	16.8	14.2	1.2	Republic of Buryatiya
24,509.9	44,884.0	10.5	11.4	0.0[4]	Republic of Khakasiya
6,749.3	22,091.9	20.7	11.6	0.4[3]	Republic of Tyva
75,629.8	29,005.5	12.1	12.8	2.0	Altai Krai
235,988.7	79,563.5	11.2	18.4	208.9	Krasnoyarsk Krai
870.1	21,869.5	5.0	12.0	n.a.	Evenk AOk
2,863.4	161,801.4	6.9	9.0	0.1	Taimyr (Dolgano-Nenets) AOk
45,053.4	38,995.6	15.3	13.3	0.1	Chita Oblast
1,634.7	22,637.2	12.9	8.8	n.a.	Aga-Buryat AOk
149,613.2	57,951.3	11.7	13.6	111.2	Irkutsk Oblast
3,794.8	28,041.7	10.9	12.2	0.0[3]	Ust-Orda Buryat AOk
144,610.9	49,880.6	9.7	11.8	39.4	Kemerovo Oblast
130,009.6	48,290.3	11.0	11.5	9.2	Novosibirsk Oblast
90,933.0	43,734.2	9.5	10.9	1,716.8	Omsk Oblast
80,918.5	77,357.1	13.7	14.4	49.1	Tomsk Oblast
485,323.4	72,513.5	8.4	12.8	2,846.8	**Far Eastern Federal Okrug**
114,897.1	121,036.0	9.4	11.8	596.7	Republic of Sakha (Yakutiya)
101,584.9	70,713.5	6.1	15.3	27.4	Khabarovsk Krai
100,976.1	48,752.2	7.9	12.8	62.7	Maritime (Primorskii) Krai
46,606.4	51,621.8	10.1	15.5	16.1	Amur Oblast
25,365.7	70,701.3	11.4	10.2	52.8	Kamchatka Oblast
3,605.6	143,323.9	13.6	10.0	2.2	Koryak AOk
20,960.0	114,707.3	10.2	11.9	7.5	Magadan Oblast
56,389.7	103,146.5	9.1	11.8	2,083.1	Sakhalin Oblast
6,649.2	34,828.1	6.5	14.5	0.5	Jewish AOb
11,894.3	220,985.1	4.8	17.0	n.a.	Chukot AOk
9,471,767.4	65,247.5	8.6	12.0	29,698.9	**Russian Federation**

[2] Percentage change in the Consumer Price Index, Dec.–Dec.

[3] 2000 figure.

[4] 2002 figure.

RUSSIAN CURRENCY AND EXCHANGE RATES

Monetary Units

  100 kopeks = 1 Russian rouble (rubl or ruble).

Sterling, Dollar and Euro Equivalents (30 November 2005)

  £1 sterling = 49.619 roubles;
  US $1 = 28.731 roubles;
  €1 = 33.814 roubles;
  1,000 roubles = £20.15 = $34.81 = €29.57.

Average Exchange Rate (roubles per US dollar)

  2002   31.3485
  2003   30.6920
  2004   28.8137

RUSSIAN INFLATION

The annual increase in consumer prices in the Russian Federation as a whole, according to official figures, for the year to December was:

  2002   15.1%
  2003   12.0%
  2004   11.7%

The Government of the Russian Federation

According to the Constitution of December 1993, the Russian Federation is a democratic, federative, multi-ethnic republic, in which state power is divided between the executive, the legislature and the judiciary, which are independent of one another. The President, who wields considerable executive authority, is elected for a term of four years by universal direct suffrage. The President appoints the Chairman (Prime Minister) of the Government, but the cabinet must be approved by the legislature. Supreme legislative power is vested in a bicameral Federalnoye Sobraniye (Federal Assembly).

For much of the 1990s and the first half of the 2000s the Russian Federation comprised 89 federal territorial units. Following the formation of Perm Krai by the merger of Perm Oblast with the Komi-Permyak Autonomous Okrug, which took effect from 1 December 2005, the number of federal subjects was reduced to 88, comprising 21 republics, seven krais (provinces), 48 oblasts (regions), two cities of federal status, one autonomous oblast and nine autonomous okrugs (districts). Autonomous republics, autonomous okrugs and the autonomous oblast are ethnically defined, while krais, oblasts and the cities of federal status are defined on territorial grounds. The total number of territories was expected to be further reduced, to 86, with effect from 1 January 2007, following the proposed merger of Krasnoyarsk Krai with the Evenk and Taimyr (Dolgano-Nenets) Autonomous Okrugs, while several other mergers, principally of several of the remaining autonomous okrugs with the territories within which they were contained, were envisaged. The status of the federal subjects had begun to be regularized by the Federation Treaty of 31 March 1992, which, *inter alia* provided for the transformation of four former nominally autonomous oblasts into republics (the remaining 16 republics having formerly held the status of Autonomous Soviet Socialist Republic—ASSR). The autonomous okrugs remained under the jurisdiction of the krai or oblast within which they were located (a situation that largely continued thereafter) but were additionally granted the status of federal units in their own right. The former republic of Checheno-Ingushetiya was divided into two republics in June 1992, by the formal recognition of a republic of Ingushetiya. Moscow and St Petersburg subsequently assumed the status of cities of federal status.

The republics each have their own governments and ministries; in many cases there is also a republican president. Under the terms of the 1992 treaties, republics were granted far wider-reaching powers than the other federal units, specifically over the use of natural resources and land. The remaining federal units are governed by a local administration, the head or governor of which is the highest official in the territory, and a representative assembly. Governors are able to veto regional legislation, although their vetoes may be overridden by a two-thirds' parliamentary majority. The federal legislature, which created the post of governor in August 1991, intended that the official be elected by popular vote. The federal President, Boris Yeltsin, however, secured an agreement that the governors be appointed. In many regions conflict subsequently arose between the executive and legislative bodies, as the presidential appointees encountered much resistance from the communist-dominated assemblies. In those cases where a vote of 'no confidence' was passed in the governor, elections were permitted. (This occurred in eight territories in April 1993.) Following Yeltsin's dissolution of the Russian legislature in September 1993, and parliament's violent resistance, it was announced that all heads of administration of federal subjects would, henceforth, be appointed and dismissed by presidential decree. In response to increasing pressure, however, this ruling was relaxed in December 1995, when gubernatorial elections were held in 12 territories, and from the second half of the 1990s elected governors became the norm across the Federation, as initial terms of office expired. Additionally, from 1995 agreement of bilateral treaties to delineate powers between the federal Government and the regional authorities became increasingly commonplace, leading to concerns that the country was being transformed from a constitution-based to a treaty-based federation.

Vladimir Putin, who was elected as President in March 2000, announced his intention to introduce a regime of what he termed 'vertical power'. One of Putin's earliest actions as elected President was to group the federal subjects into seven Federal Okrugs, each of which was headed by a plenipotentiary representative of the President. These Federal Okrugs co-existed alongside the existing 11 economic areas; the latter, however, had limited political significance. A series of presidential decrees in 2000–01 ruled that laws specific to certain regions were unconstitutional and must be amended. The republics, which had the greatest degree of autonomy to lose under the new arrangements, were most severely affected; by April 2002 some 28 of the 42 power-sharing treaties signed between the regional and federal authorities had been annulled, and many of those which remained had been amended, in order to bring regional legislation into conformity with the federal norm, as had the constitutions of several Republics. However, Putin made no use of presidential decrees to appoint or dismiss regional governors during his first term of office (2000–04).

In December 2004 the federal legislature approved proposals, initially presented by President Putin, in accordance with which governors of all federal subjects would henceforth be appointed by the federal authorities, subject to approval by regional legislatures; the election of a Governor in the Nenets Autonomous Okrug, in February 2005, was expected to represent the final such poll. During the course of 2005 the appointment of governors became widespread, sometimes occurring when an incumbent regional leader's mandate expired, but also taking place when a leader requested an expression of confidence from the federal President. During that year only a small number of incumbent leaders were not returned to office as a result of these procedures.

Presidential Representative in the Central Federal Okrug: Lt-Gen. GEORGII S. POLTAVCHENKO (appointed 18 May 2000), 103132 Moscow, Nikolskii per. 6; tel. (495) 206-12-76; e-mail malakhov_dm@gov.ru; internet www.cfopolpred.ru.

Presidential Representative in the Far Eastern Federal Okrug: KAMIL SH. ISKHAKOV (appointed 14 November 2005), 680030 Khabarovsk, ul. Sheronova 22; tel. (4212) 31-39-78; fax (4212) 31-38-04; internet www.dfo.ru.

Presidential Representative in the North-Western Federal Okrug: ILYA I. KLEBANOV (appointed 1 November 2003), 193015 St Petersburg, ul. Shpalernaya 47; tel. (812) 346-20-09; fax (812) 326-64-84.

Presidential Representative in the Siberian Federal Okrug: ANATOLII V. KVASHNIN (appointed 9 September 2004), 630091 Novosibirsk, ul. Derzhavina

18/120; tel. (3832) 20-17-56; fax (3832) 20-13-90; e-mail sibokrug@online.sinor.ru; internet www.sfo.nsk.su.

Presidential Representative in the Southern Federal Okrug: DMITRII N. KOZAK (appointed 13 September 2004), 344006 Rostov-on-Don, ul. B. Sadovaya 73; tel. (8632) 44-16-16; fax (8632) 40-39-40; e-mail polpred@polpred-ug.donpac.ru.

Presidential Representative in the Urals Federal Okrug: Col-Gen. PETR M. LATYSHEV (appointed 18 May 2000), 620031 Sverdlovsk obl., Yekaterinburg, pl. Oktyabrskaya 3; tel. (3432) 77-18-96; e-mail support@uralfo.ru; internet www uralfo.ru.

Presidential Representative in the Volga Federal Okrug: ALEKSANDR V. KONO-VALOV (appointed 14 November 2005), 603082 Nizhnii Novgorod, Kreml, kor. 1; tel. (8312) 31-46-07; fax (8312) 31-47-51; internet www.pfo.ru.

HEAD OF STATE

President of the Russian Federation: VLADIMIR V. PUTIN (elected 26 March 2000; re-elected 14 March 2004; inaugurated 7 May 2004).

PRESIDENTIAL ADMINISTRATION

Office of the President: 103132 Moscow, Staraya pl. 4; tel. (495) 925-35-81; fax (495) 206-07-66; e-mail president@gov.ru; internet www.kremlin.ru.

THE GOVERNMENT
(January 2006)

Chairman (Prime Minister): MIKHAIL YE. FRADKOV.

First Deputy Chairman: DMITRII A. MEDVEDEV.

Deputy Chairman, Minister of Defence: SERGEI B. IVANOV.

Deputy Chairman: ALEKSANDR D. ZHUKOV.

Head of the Government Staff, Minister: SERGEI YE. NARYSHKIN.

Minister of Agriculture: ALEKSEI V. GORDEYEV.

Minister of Civil Defence, Emergencies and Clean-up Operations: Col-Gen. SERGEI K. SHOIGU.

Minister of Culture and the Mass Media: ALEKSANDR S. SOKOLOV.

Minister of Economic Development and Trade: GERMAN O. GREF.

Minister of Education and Science: ANDREI A. FURSENKO.

Minister of Finance: ALEKSEI L. KUDRIN.

Minister of Foreign Affairs: SERGEI V. LAVROV.

Minister of Health and Social Development: MIKHAIL YU. ZURABOV.

Minister of Industry and Energy: VIKTOR B. KHRISTENKO.

Minister of Information and Communications Technologies: LEONID D. REIMAN.

Minister of Internal Affairs: Col-Gen. RASHID G. NURGALIYEV.

Minister of Justice: YURII YA. CHAIKA.

Minister of Natural Resources: YURII P. TRUTNEV.

Minister of Regional Development: VLADIMIR A. YAKOVLEV.

Minister of Transport: IGOR YE. LEVITIN.

MINISTRIES

Office of the Government: 103274 Moscow, Krasnopresnenskaya nab. 2; tel. (495) 205-57-35; fax (495) 205-42-19; internet www.government.ru.

Ministry of Agriculture: 107139 Moscow, Orlikov per. 1/11; tel. (495) 207-83-86; fax (495) 207-95-80; e-mail info@mcx.ru; internet www.mcx.ru.

Ministry of Civil Defence, Emergencies and Clean-up Operations: 109012 Moscow, Teatralnyi proyezd 3; tel. (495) 926-39-01; fax (495) 923-57-45; e-mail info@mchs.gov.ru; internet www.mchs.gov.ru.

Ministry of Culture and the Mass Media: 103074 Moscow, Kitaigorodskii proyezd 7; tel. (495) 925-11-95; fax (495) 928-17-91; e-mail root@mincult.isf.ru; internet www.mincultrf.ru.

Ministry of Defence: 105175 Moscow, ul. Myasnitskaya 37; tel. (495) 293-38-54; fax (495) 296-84-36; internet www.mil.ru.

Ministry of Economic Development and Trade: 125818 Moscow, ul. Tverskaya-Yamskaya 1/3; tel. (495) 200-03-53; e-mail presscenter@economy.gov.ru; internet www.economy.gov.ru.

Ministry of Education and Science: 113833 Moscow, ul. Lyusinovskaya 51; tel. (495) 237-61-55; fax (495) 237-83-81; e-mail mail@ministry.ru; internet www.ed.gov.ru.

Ministry of Finance: 103097 Moscow, ul. Ilinka 9; tel. (495) 298-91-01; fax (495) 925-08-89; internet www.minfin.ru.

Ministry of Foreign Affairs: 119200 Moscow, Smolenskaya-Sennaya pl. 32/34; tel. (495) 244-16-06; fax (495) 230-21-30; e-mail ministry@mid.ru; internet www.mid.ru.

Ministry of Health and Social Development: 101431 Moscow, ul. Neglinnaya 25; tel. (495) 927-28-48; fax (495) 928-58-15; e-mail press-center@minzdrav-rf.ru; internet www.minzdrav-rf.ru.

Ministry of Industry and Energy: 125889 Moscow, pl. Miusskaya 3, POB 47; tel. (495) 972-70-51; fax (495) 229-55-49; e-mail info@mpnt.gov.ru; internet www.mte.gov.ru.

Ministry of Information and Communications Technologies: 103375 Moscow, ul. Tverskaya 7; tel. (495) 292-71-44; fax (495) 292-74-55; internet www.minsvyaz.ru.

Ministry of Internal Affairs: 117049 Moscow, ul. Zhitnaya 16; tel. (495) 237-75-85; fax (495) 293-59-98; e-mail uimvd@mvdinform.ru; internet www.mvdinform.ru.

Ministry of Justice: 109830 Moscow, ul. Vorontsovo Pole 4A; tel. (495) 206-05-54; fax (495) 916-29-03; internet www.minjust.ru.

Ministry of Natural Resources: 123812 Moscow, ul. B. Gruzinskaya 4/6; tel. (495) 254-48-00; fax (495) 254-43-10; e-mail admin@mnr.gov.ru; internet www.mnr.gov.ru.

Ministry of Regional Development: 103051 Moscow, ul. Sadovaya-Samotechnaya 10/23/1; tel. (495) 200-25-65; fax (495) 299-38-41; e-mail info@minregion.ru; internet www.minregion.ru.

Ministry of Transport: 109012 Moscow, ul. Rozhdestvenka 1/1; tel. (495) 926-10-00; fax (495) 200-33-56; e-mail mcc@morflot.ru; internet www.mintrans.ru.

FEDERALNOYE SOBRANIYE

The Federalnoye Sobraniye (Federal Assembly) is the bicameral federal parliament. Its upper chamber, the Sovet Federatsii (Federation Council), comprises 176 deputies, two appointed from each of the federal units, representing the executive and legislative branches of power in each territory. The lower chamber is the Gosudarstvennaya Duma (State Duma), with 450 deputies elected for a four-year term (the last general election was held on 7 December 2003).

Chairman of the Sovet Federatsii: SERGEI M. MIRONOV, 103426 Moscow, ul. B. Dmitrovka 26; tel. (495) 203-90-74; fax (495) 203-46-17; e-mail post_sf@gov.ru; internet www.council.gov.ru.

Chairman of the Gosudarstvennaya Duma: BORIS V. GRYZLOV, 103265 Moscow, Okhotnyi ryad 1; tel. (495) 292-83-10; fax (495) 292-94-64; e-mail www@duma.ru; internet www.duma.ru.

THE STATE COUNCIL

The State Council is a consultative body, established in September 2000, and intended to improve co-ordination between federal and regional government, and to strengthen federal control in the regions. The membership of the Council comprises the leaders of the 88 federal subjects and the President of the Russian Federation, who chairs the Council. The President appoints a presidium, comprising seven-members of the Council, who serve for a period of six months.

PART TWO
Territorial Surveys

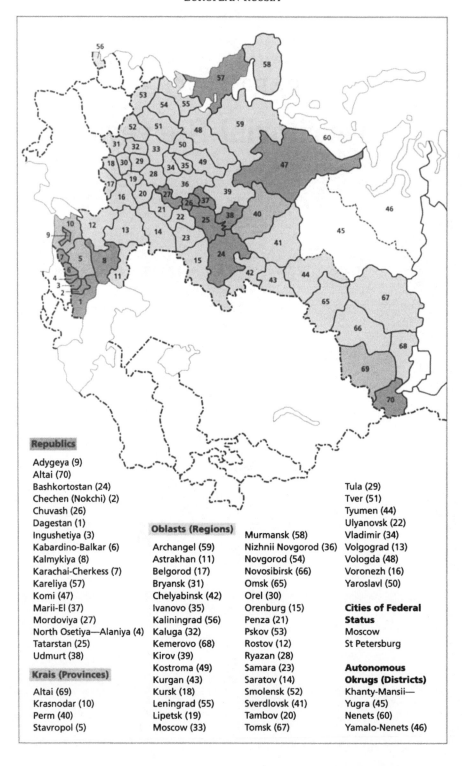

Republics

Adygeya (9)
Altai (70)
Bashkortostan (24)
Chechen (Nokchi) (2)
Chuvash (26)
Dagestan (1)
Ingushetiya (3)
Kabardino-Balkar (6)
Kalmykiya (8)
Karachai-Cherkess (7)
Kareliya (57)
Komi (47)
Marii-El (37)
Mordoviya (27)
North Osetiya—Alaniya (4)
Tatarstan (25)
Udmurt (38)

Krais (Provinces)

Altai (69)
Krasnodar (10)
Perm (40)
Stavropol (5)

Oblasts (Regions)

Archangel (59)
Astrakhan (11)
Belgorod (17)
Bryansk (31)
Chelyabinsk (42)
Ivanovo (35)
Kaliningrad (56)
Kaluga (32)
Kemerovo (68)
Kirov (39)
Kostroma (49)
Kurgan (43)
Kursk (18)
Leningrad (55)
Lipetsk (19)
Moscow (33)

Murmansk (58)
Nizhnii Novgorod (36)
Novgorod (54)
Novosibirsk (66)
Omsk (65)
Orel (30)
Orenburg (15)
Penza (21)
Pskov (53)
Rostov (12)
Ryazan (28)
Samara (23)
Saratov (14)
Smolensk (52)
Sverdlovsk (41)
Tambov (20)
Tomsk (67)

Tula (29)
Tver (51)
Tyumen (44)
Ulyanovsk (22)
Vladimir (34)
Volgograd (13)
Vologda (48)
Voronezh (16)
Yaroslavl (50)

Cities of Federal Status

Moscow
St Petersburg

Autonomous Okrugs (Districts)

Khanty-Mansii—Yugra (45)
Nenets (60)
Yamalo-Nenets (46)

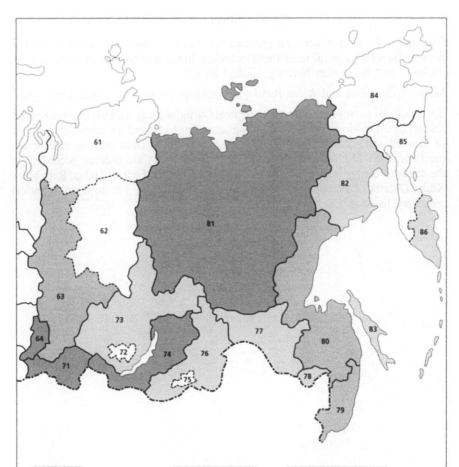

Republics
Buryatiya (74)
Khakasiya (64)
Tyva (71)
Sakha (Yakutiya) (81)

Krais (Provinces)
Khabarovsk (80)
Krasnoyarsk (63)
Maritime (Primorskii) (79)

Oblasts (Regions)
Amur (77)
Chita (76)
Irkutsk (73)
Kamchatka (86)
Magadan (82)
Sakhalin (83)

Autonomous Oblast
Jewish (78)

**Autonomous
Okrugs (Districts)**
Aga-Buryat (75)
Chukot (84)
Evenk (62)
Koryak (85)
Taimyr (Dolgano-Nenets) (61)
Ust-Orda Buryat (72)

Notes

The maps distinguish between international borders (dots and dashes), borders between separate federal units (bold unbroken lines) and borders of units that are formally part of another territory (dashed lines).

Maps of European and Asian Russia are included on the two preceding pages.

The territorial surveys are ordered by Federal Okrug, starting with the Central Federal Okrug, based in Moscow, and continuing according to the order conventionally used in Russian statistical publications, which broadly runs from west to east across the Federation. Within each Federal Okrug the surveys are ordered according to the status of the territory concerned, as follows: Cities of Federal Status; Republics; Krais; Oblasts; Autonomous Oblast; Autonomous Okrugs. Territories of identical status are listed in English alphabetical order.

CENTRAL FEDERAL OKRUG

Moscow City

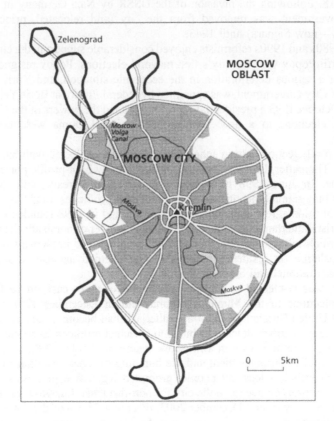

Moscow (Moskva) is located in the west of European Russia, on the River Moskva, which crosses the city from the north-west to the south-east. It is connected to the Volga river system by the Moscow–Volga Canal. Moscow is included in the Central Federal Okrug and the Central Economic Area. The city's total area is 994 sq km (384 sq miles). Moscow is the largest city in the Russian Federation and had a total population of 10.4m., according to the census of 9–16 October 2002, and a population density of 10,382.8 per sq km. The area administrated as the federal city comprises both the city of Moscow (which itself had a population of 10.1m., according to preliminary results of the census) and Zelenograd, to the north-west, with a population of 215,900. In 2002 some 84.8% of the city's population were ethnically Russian, 2.4% Ukrainian, 1.6% Tatar, 1.2% Armenian, 0.9% Azeri and 0.8% Jewish. Moscow City is included in the time zone GMT+3.

History

Moscow city was founded in about 1147. In 1325 it became the seat of the Eastern Orthodox Metropolitan of Rus (from 1589–1721 and after 1917 the Patriarch of Moscow and all Rus) and the steadily expanding Muscovite state became the foundation for the Russian Empire. The centre of tsarist government was moved to St Petersburg in 1712. Moscow was restored as the Russian and Soviet capital in March 1918. Following the invasion of the USSR by Nazi Germany in 1941, the Soviet Government was removed from the city (and relocated, principally, to Kuibyshev—now Samara) until 1943.

In the 1980s and 1990s reformists enjoyed considerable support in the city. In June 1991 Gavriil Popov won the city's first mayoral elections. Popov resigned in June 1992, after a serious deterioration in the economic situation, and Yurii Luzhkov, head of the City Government, was appointed by federal President Boris Yeltsin in his place. In October 1993 a presidential decree suspended the powers of the City Soviet (Council); elections to a new 35-member Municipal Duma were held on 12 December.

In a mayoral election held in June 1996 Luzhkov was elected with 89.7% of the votes cast. Thereafter, Luzhkov became an increasingly high-profile political figure nation-wide. In June 1998 he signed a power-sharing treaty with the federal authorities that granted the city taxation and budget privileges. Luzhkov concluded a number of trade agreements with other regions, and in 1998 founded the nation-wide, centrist Fatherland movement. Following a number of bomb attacks in the city in 1999, which killed over 200 people, the city authorities implemented yet more firmly legislation on residence permits already deemed unconstitutional by the federal Constitutional and Supreme Courts.

Luzhkov was re-elected as Mayor, with 69.9% of votes cast, on 19 December 1999. In elections to the Municipal Duma held in December 2001 Unity and Fatherland-United Russia (UF-UR—as Fatherland had become) secured the largest number of seats. Further attacks attributed to Chechen militants in the city in 2002–04, including an armed siege in a Moscow theatre in October 2002, as a result of which at least 129 hostages died, and the bombing of a subway train in February 2004, which killed at least 39 people, prompted legislative proposals to further increase restrictions on access to the city for non-residents. Luzhkov was elected to a third term as Mayor on 7 December 2003, receiving 75.5% of the votes cast. The rate of participation by the electorate was 56.7%. In elections to the Municipal Duma, held on 4 December 2005, UF-UR won a sizeable majority, having received some 47% of votes cast. The Communist Party of the Russian Federation won over 16%, while the liberal Yabloko party took around 11%. The nationalist Motherland party was banned from participating in the elections following a decision, upheld by the Supreme Court, that one of its television advertisements incited inter-ethnic strife.

Economy

In 2002 the city of Moscow's gross regional product amounted to 1,999,995.3m. roubles, equivalent to 192,626.7 roubles per head. There are nine railway termini in the city and 11 electrified radial lines. The metro system includes 11 lines and 170 stations and extends for 276 km; a suburban light railway extension opened in late 2003. The entire public-transport system carries around 6.5m. passengers per day. Moscow's waterways connect with the Baltic, White, Caspian and Black Seas. There are also four airports on the city's territory.

Moscow's industry consists primarily of mechanical engineering, metal-working, electricity production, production of chemicals and petrochemicals, petroleum-refining and food-processing. Industry employed around 11.6% of the city's working population in 2003 (in contrast to the 0.1% engaged in agriculture) and generated 453,354m. roubles, a figure surpassed in the Russian Federation only by the Khanty-Mansii Autonomous Okrug—AOk (and therefore Tyumen Oblast, which incorporates the AOk), which has the majority of natural gas and petroleum deposits in the Federation. The Moskvich Inc. Automobile Plant, in which the City Government held a controlling stake from 1998, is one of Moscow's principal companies. There are also significant defence-sector industries in the city. In 2002 some 14.0% of the working population of Moscow City were engaged in the construction sector. The services sector (which employed 18.9% of the work-force in 2000) is also an important contributor to the city's economy. As the Russian capital, the city is the site of a large number of government offices, as well as the centre for major business and financial companies. Tourism is another important service industry.

In 2003 the economically active population of the city stood at 4.39m., and the proportion of the labour force that was unemployed, at 1.3%, was the lowest in the Russian Federation. Those in employment earned, on average, 8,611.6 roubles per month, one of the highest rates in the Federation. The 2003 budget recorded a deficit of 17,084.0m. roubles. In 2003 international trade amounted to a value of US $29,644.9m. in exports and $19,736.1m. in imports, by far the highest level of any federal subject. Capital investment in the city represents around one-10th of that in Russia as a whole. In 2002 some 6,438 enterprises and organizations involving foreign capital, representing some 46.6% of the total in Russia, were situated in Moscow City and the surrounding Moscow Oblast. Of these 1,004 were joint ventures with the People's Republic of China (representing a marked increase in Chinese involvement in the city's economy compared with previous years), 569 were joint ventures with partners from the USA, 518 had German partners, 379 British, 179 Ukrainian and 176 Belarusian. Total foreign investment in the city amounted to $13,886.9m. in 2003. At the end of 2003 there were 190,900 small businesses registered in the city, more than twice the number recorded in any other federal subject.

Directory

Mayor and Prime Minister of the City Government: YURII M. LUZHKOV (appointed 6 June 1992, elected 16 June 1996, re-elected 19 December 1999 and 7 December 2003), 125032 Moscow, ul. Tverskaya 13; tel. (495) 777-77-77; fax (495) 232-18-74; e-mail mayor@mos.ru; internet www.mos.ru.

Chairman of the Municipal Duma: VLADIMIR M. PLATONOV, 127994 Moscow, ul. Petrovka 22; tel. (495) 692-15-96; fax (495) 921-92-02; e-mail spravka@duma.mos .ru; internet duma.mos.ru.

Representation of Moscow City in the Russian Federation: Moscow.

Belgorod Oblast

Belgorod Oblast is situated in the south-west of the Central Russian Highlands. It forms part of the Central Federal Okrug and the Central Chernozem Economic Area. The Oblast lies on the international border with Ukraine, with the Oblasts of Kursk to the north and Voronezh to the east. Its main rivers are the Severnii Donets, the Vorskla and the Oskol. The territory occupies 27,100 sq km (10,460 sq miles). According to the census of 9–16 October 2002, Belgorod Oblast had a total population of 1,511,620, giving a population density of 55.8 per sq km. Some 65.2% of the population inhabited urban areas at that time. Some 92.9% of the Oblast's inhabitants were ethnically Russian, and 3.8% were Ukrainian. The Oblast's administrative centre is at Belgorod, which had 337,600 inhabitants in October 2002, according to provisional census results. A further major city is Staryi Oskol (216,000). Belgorod Oblast is included in the time zone GMT+3.

History

Belgorod was established as a bishopric during the early days of Orthodox Christianity. The region was part of Lithuania until 1503, when it was annexed by the Muscovite state. The new city of Belgorod was founded in 1593. On 12 July 1943, north-east of the city, the Red Army defeated the Germans in the largest single tank battle in history, the most vital action in the wider, so-called Kursk offensive. Belgorod Oblast was formally established on 6 January 1954.

In October 1993 President Boris Yeltsin dismissed the region's Governor, Viktor Berestovoi, and arranged for elections to a new Regional Duma to be held. The communists enjoyed a majority in this body, too, and there was constant conflict with the administration headed by Yeltsin's appointee, Yevgenii Savchenko, who, however, also enjoyed popular support. The Oblast was one of 12 areas in the Federation to be permitted gubernatorial elections in December 1995, when Savchenko was duly elected. He was re-elected in May 1999 and again in May 2003, when he stood as an independent candidate. In elections to the regional legislature, held on 16 October 2005, the pro-Government Unity and Fatherland-United Russia won 53.0% of votes cast.

Economy

In 2002 Belgorod Oblast's gross regional product amounted to 65,702.0m. roubles, or 43,464.6 roubles per head. The main industrial centres in the territory are situated at Belgorod and Shebekino. At the end of 2002 there were 695 km of railway lines and 6,545 km of paved roads on the Oblast's territory.

Belgorod Oblast's principal crops are grain, sugar beet, sunflower seeds and essential-oil plants. Horticulture, animal husbandry and bee-keeping are also important. In 2003 agriculture engaged 20.3% of the labour force and generated 23,903m. roubles. The Oblast has substantial reserves of bauxite, iron ore and apatites. Its main industries are ore-mining (iron ores), the production of electricity, mechanical engineering, metal-working, chemicals, the manufacture of building materials and food-processing. Industry employed 20.9% of the work-force in 2003 and generated 80,588m. roubles.

The economically active population in Belgorod Oblast numbered 712,000 in 2003, when 8.2% of the region's labour force were unemployed. The average monthly salary in that year was 4,468.6 roubles, and there was a budgetary deficit of 849.5m. roubles. Export trade totalled US $713.6m., while import trade amounted to $927.5m. Foreign investment in the Oblast totalled $23.3m. in 2003. At the end of 2003 there were 8,200 small businesses in the Oblast.

Directory

Head of the Regional Administration (Governor): YEVGENII S. SAVCHENKO (appointed 18 December 1993, elected 17 December 1995, re-elected 30 May 1999 and 25 May 2003), 308005 Belgorod, pl. Revolyutsii 4; tel. (472) 222-42-47; fax (472) 222-33-43; e-mail admin@regadm.bel.ru; internet beladm.bel.ru.

Chairman of the Regional Duma: ANATOLII YA. ZELIKOV, 308005 Belgorod, pl. Revolyutsii 4; tel. (472) 232-24-37; fax (472) 227-65-88; e-mail duma@bel.ru; internet duma.bel.ru.

Chief Representative of Belgorod Oblast in the Russian Federation: ALEKSANDR G. MATSEPURO, 117152 Moscow, Zagorodnoye shosse 5/21; tel. (495) 952-59-30; fax (495) 952-28-36; e-mail moscow@bel.ru.

Head of Belgorod City Administration: VASILII N. POTRYASAYEV, 308800 Belgorod, ul. Lenina 38; tel. (472) 227-72-06.

Bryansk Oblast

Bryansk Oblast is situated in the Central Russian Highlands and is in the Central Federal Okrug and the Central Economic Area. It has international borders to the west (Belarus) and south (Ukraine), and domestic borders with Kursk and Orel Oblasts to the east, Kaluga to the north-east and Smolensk to the north-west. Bryansk's main river is the Desna, a tributary of the Dnepr (Dnieper). The Oblast occupies 34,900 sq km (13,480 sq miles). According to the census of 9–16 October 2002, the region had a total population of 1,378,941, giving a population density of 39.5 per sq km. Some 68.4% of the population inhabited urban areas. 96.3% of the population were ethnically Russian; 1.5% were Ukrainian. Bryansk, with a population of 431,600, according to provisional census results, is the Oblast's administrative centre. Bryansk Oblast is included in the time zone GMT+3.

History

The city of Bryansk (first mentioned in 1146) was part of the independent principality of Novgorod-Seversk until 1356. It was an early Orthodox Christian bishopric. The Muscovite state acquired the city from Lithuania in the 16th century. In the early 17th century the city figured in the insurrections associated with the pretenders to the tsarist throne known as the 'false Dmitriis'. Generally, it was a loyal garrison town. Bryansk Oblast was founded on 5 July 1944.

Bryansk was one of eight federal territories permitted gubernatorial elections in December 1992. The incumbent (appointed in December 1991), Vladimir Barabanov, was defeated by the communist-backed candidate, Yurii Lodkin. During the constitutional crisis of September–October 1993 Lodkin was dismissed and the Soviet disbanded, and an oblast Duma formed. After a series of short-lived (and non-communist) governors: Vladimir Karpov (September 1993–August 1995); Barabanov (August 1995–May 1996); and Aleksandr Semernev (June–December 1996), Lodkin was elected Governor in December 1996. A power-sharing agreement was signed between the oblast and federal authorities in July 1997. Lodkin was re-elected in December 2000, although he obtained only 29% of the votes cast. Prior to gubernatorial elections scheduled for 5 December 2004 the oblast court prohibited Lodkin's candidacy, on the grounds that he had breached several campaign rules. Nikolai Denin, the candidate of the pro-Government Unity and Fatherland–United Russia (UF–UR), and hitherto a member of the Gosudarstvennaya Duma (State Duma), obtained the largest share of the votes cast (44.8%); Denin and Yevgenii Zelenko, of the pro-market Union of Rightist Forces, who obtained 12.5% of the votes cast, proceeded to a second round of voting. Lodkin had called for his supporters to vote against all candidates, and some 20.5% of those taking part in the election did so. In concurrent elections to the Regional Duma, 14 of the 30 deputies elected were representatives of UF–UR. In the 'run-off' election held on 19 December, Denin was elected Governor, receiving 77.8% of the votes cast.

Economy

Bryansk Oblast is one of the Russian Federation's major industrial regions. The territory's gross regional product was 41,327.6m. roubles in 2002, equivalent to 29,970.5 roubles per head. Its main industrial centres are at Bryansk and Klintsy. At the end of 2002 there were 1,010 km of railway track on its territory, and 6,406 km of paved roads.

The Oblast's agriculture, which employed 15.5% of its work-force and generated 13,897m. roubles in 2003, consists mainly of grain, sugar beet and potato production, and animal husbandry. Around one-half of the territory's area is used for agricultural purposes. The Oblast's main industries are mechanical engineering, food-processing, electrical energy, the manufacture of building materials and timber-working. Industry employed 20.0% of the work-force in 2003 and generated 28,180m. roubles.

In 2003 the economically active population of Bryansk Oblast numbered 660,000, and 7.3% of the region's labour force were unemployed. The average monthly wage was 3,316.0 roubles. There was a regional government budgetary deficit of 211.9m. roubles in 2003. In that year international trade comprised US $99.7m. of exports and $427.7m. of imports. Foreign investment amounted to $6.4m. At the end of 2003 there were 3,200 small businesses registered in the region.

Directory

Head of the Regional Administration (Governor): NIKOLAI V. DENIN (elected 19 December 2004), 241002 Bryansk, pr. Lenina 33; tel. (483) 266-26-11; fax (483) 241-38-95; e-mail gubernator@bryanskobl.ru; internet www.bryanskobl.ru.

Chairman of the Regional Duma: STEPAN N. PONASOV, 241000 Bryansk, pl. K. Marksa 2; tel. (483) 243-36-91; fax (483) 274-31-95; e-mail main@duma.bryansk .ru; internet duma.bryansk.ru.

Chief Representative of Bryansk Oblast in the Russian Federation: ANDREI R. IVANOV, 127025 Moscow, ul. Novyi Arbat 19; tel. and fax (495) 203-50-52.

Head of Bryansk City Administration (Mayor): VALERII POLYAKOV, 241002 Bryansk, pr. Lenina 35; tel. (483) 274-30-13; fax (483) 274-47-30; e-mail postmaster@comimm.bryansk.su.

Ivanovo Oblast

Ivanovo Oblast is situated in the central part of the Eastern European Plain. It forms part of the Central Federal Okrug and the Central Economic Area. It is surrounded by the Oblasts of Kostroma (to the north), Nizhnii Novgorod (east), Vladimir (south) and Yaroslavl (north-west). Its main river is the Volga. The Oblast covers 21,800 sq km (9,230 sq miles). According to the census of 9–16 October 2002, the Oblast's population numbered 1,148,329, giving a population density of 52.7 per sq km. Some 82.7% of the population inhabited urban areas. 93.7% of the population were ethnically Russian; 0.9% were Ukrainian. The Oblast's administrative centre, Ivanovo, had a population of 432,200 at that time, according to provisional census results. Ivanovo Oblast is included in the time zone GMT+3.

History

A village of Ivanovo was first mentioned in 1561. The city of Ivanovo (initially Ivanovo-Voznesensk) was founded in 1871. It was an important centre of anti-government activity during the strikes of 1883 and 1885 and in the 1905 Revolution. Ivanovo Oblast was founded on 20 July 1918.

Moderate candidates were successful in the gubernatorial and regional legislative elections held in 1996, when Vladislav Tikhomirov was elected as Governor. In December 2000 the Communist Party of the Russian Federation (CPRF) candidate, Vladimir Tikhonov, was elected as Governor. In July 2004 Tikhonov was elected as leader of a breakaway, left-wing, faction of the CPRF. (However, attempts by the faction to form a separate party proved unsuccessful, as it was unable to form the requisite number of regional branches across the Federation.) A campaign led by members of the local branch of the pro-Government Unity and Fatherland-United Russia (UF-UR) party, in mid-2005, to encourage federal President Vladimir Putin to dismiss Tikhonov, resulted in the representation of the UF-UR in the regional Legislative Assembly splitting into two separate factions. Tikhonov's administration was also affected by allegations of improprieties in road-construction projects. In advance of the expiry of Tikhonov's mandate later in the year, he was not nominated

www.europaworld.com

to serve a further term under the recently introduced system providing for the appointment of regional governors. Instead, on 22 November the regional legislature approved the nomination of Mikhail Men, hitherto Deputy Mayor of Moscow, as the new Governor; Men took up office on 27 December. Meanwhile, at regional legislative elections held on 4 December, UF-UR was the most successful party, winning 32.1% of the votes cast, according to preliminary results; the nationalist Liberal Democratic Party of Russia was placed second, with 13.0%, while each of the Communist Party of the Russian Federation and the nationalist Motherland party obtained more than 10% of the votes cast.

Economy

In 2002 Ivanovo Oblast's gross regional product totalled 29,467.1m. roubles, equivalent to 25,660.9 roubles per head. The region's main industrial centres include Ivanovo, Shuya and Vichuga. There are well-developed rail, road and river transport networks in the region and an international airport. At the end of 2002 there were 345 km of railways and 3,551 km of paved roads on the Oblast's territory.

Ivanovo Oblast was the historic centre of Russia's cotton-milling industry. Flax production was still an important agricultural activity in the region in the 2000s, as were grain and vegetable production and animal husbandry. However, agriculture employed just 7.7% of the work-force in 2003, when the sector generated 6,179m. roubles. The region's main industries are light manufacturing (especially textiles), electrical energy, mechanical engineering and metal-working, food-processing and handicrafts (especially lacquerware). Some 32.1% of the working population were engaged in the sector, which generated 26,897m. roubles in 2003.

The territory's economically active population amounted to 590,000 in 2003, when 6.5% of the labour force were unemployed. The average wage was 3,524.6 roubles per month in 2003, the lowest level of any federal subject in the Central Federal Okrug. In 2003 the budget recorded a deficit of 71.5m. roubles. External trade amounted to US $100.5m. in exports and $144.9m. in imports. Foreign investment amounted to just $0.3m. in 2003. At the end of 2003 there were 5,700 small businesses registered in the region.

Directory

Head of the Regional Administration (Governor): MIKHAIL A. MEN (appointment confirmed 22 November 2005, assumed office 27 December), 153002 Ivanovo, ul. Baturina 5; tel. (493) 241-77-05; fax (493) 241-92-31; e-mail aio@adminet.ivanovo .ru; internet ivadm.ivanovo.ru.

Chairman of the Legislative Assembly: VLADIMIR S. GRISHIN, 153000 Ivanovo, ul. Pushkina 9; tel. (493) 241-60-68; fax (493) 241-14-96; e-mail zsio@gov.ivanovo.ru; internet www.zsio.ru.

Chief Representative of Ivanovo Oblast in the Russian Federation: ALEKSANDR D. KULIKOV, 127025 Moscow, ul. Novyi Arbat 19; tel. (495) 203-41-34; fax (495) 203-93-45.

Head of Ivanovo City Administration: ALEKSANDR FOMIN, 153001 Ivanovo, pl. Revolyutsii 6; tel. (493) 232-70-20; fax (493) 241-25-12; internet www.ivgoradm.ru.

Kaluga Oblast

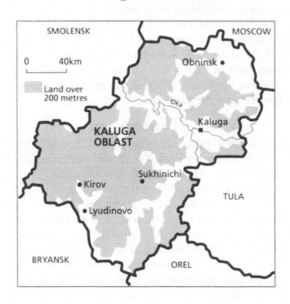

Kaluga Oblast is situated in the central part of the Eastern European Plain. It forms part of the Central Federal Okrug and the Central Economic Area. Tula and Orel Oblasts lie to the south-east, Bryansk to the south-west, Moscow Oblast to the north-east and Smolensk to the north-west. It occupies 29,900 sq km (11,540 sq miles). According to the census of 9–16 October 2002, the Oblast's population totalled 1,041,641, giving a population density of 34.8 per sq km. Some 74.8% of the population inhabited urban areas. 93.5% of the population were ethnically Russian, and 2.2% were Ukrainian. The administrative centre is at Kaluga, a river-port on the Oka river, which had a population of 335,100, according to provisional census results. Other major cities in the Oblast include Obninsk (105,800), the site of the world's first nuclear power station. Kaluga Oblast is included in the time zone GMT+3.

History

The city of Kaluga, first mentioned in the letters of a Lithuanian prince, Olgerd, in 1371, was founded as a Muscovite outpost. The region was the scene of an army mutiny in 1905 and was seized by Bolshevik troops at the end of 1917. Kaluga Oblast was founded on 5 July 1944.

Communist-affiliated managers of industrial and agricultural bodies dominated the new representative body, the Legislative Assembly, elected in March 1994. Valerii Sudarenkov, the Governor from November 1996, had previously been the Deputy Chairman of the Government (Prime Minister) of the Uzbek SSR (Uzbekistan). Sudarenkov did not stand for re-election in November 2000; his former deputy, Anatolii Artamonov, was elected to succeed him, with 56.7% of the votes cast. Artamonov was re-elected for a second term on 14 March 2004, receiving 66.9% of votes cast. At elections to the regional Legislative Assembly, held on 14

November 2004, the pro-Government Unity and Fatherland-United Russia obtained a far greater share of support than any other party, with 41.0% of the votes cast. In July 2005 Artamonov announced his premature resignation, in order to seek a further term as an appointed Governor. Artamonov was duly nominated to serve a further term of office, which was confirmed by vote of the regional legislature on 26 July.

Economy

In 2002 gross regional product in Kaluga Oblast totalled 40,213.4m. roubles, equivalent to 38,605.8 roubles per head. Apart from Kaluga, the region's main industrial centres are at Lyudinovo, Kirov and Maloyaroslavets. At the end of 2002 there were 872 km of railway track in the Oblast, and 5,136 km of paved roads.

Certain areas of the Oblast contain fertile black earth (*chernozem*). Agriculture employed 10.9% of the work-force and generated 9,395m. roubles in 2003. The Oblast's main industries are mechanical engineering, food-processing, timber and timber-processing, and wood-working. The industrial sector employed 25.1% of the working population in 2003 and generated 43,760m. roubles.

The territory's economically active population totalled 553,000 in 2003, when 6.2% of the labour force were unemployed. The average monthly wage in Kaluga Oblast was 4,489.3 roubles in 2003. There was a budgetary deficit of 71.5m. roubles. In that year export trade amounted to a value of US \$128.3m.; imports amounted to \$228.0m. Total foreign investment amounted to \$27.4m. in 2003. At the end of that year there were 5,600 small businesses registered in the region.

Directory

Head of the Regional Administration (Governor): ANATOLII D. ARTAMONOV (elected 12 November 2000, re-elected 14 March 2004; appointment confirmed 26 July 2005), 248661 Kaluga, pl. Staryi Torg 2; tel. (484) 256-23-57; fax (484) 253-13-09; e-mail contact@admobl.kaluga.su; internet www.artamonovad.ru.

Chairman of the Legislative Assembly: PAVEL F. KAMENSKII, 248600 Kaluga, pl. Staryi Torg 2; tel. (484) 256-21-89; fax (484) 259-15-63; internet www .admoblkaluga.ru/New_SERVER/VLAST/Zaksobr/default.htm.

Chief Representative of Kaluga Oblast in the Russian Federation: VLADIMIR V. POTEMKIN, 119002 Moscow, per. Glazovskii 8; tel. (495) 241-66-36; fax (495) 229-98-05; e-mail kaluga@orc.ru.

Head of Kaluga City Administration: M. A. AKIMOV, 248600 Kaluga, ul. Lenina 93; tel. (484) 256-26-46; fax (484) 224-41-78; e-mail pressa@kaluga-gov.ru; internet www.kaluga-gov.ru.

Kostroma Oblast

Kostroma Oblast is situated in the central part of the Eastern European Plain. It forms part of the Central Federal Okrug and the Central Economic Area. It is bordered by Vologda Oblast to the north, Kirov Oblast to the east, Nizhnii Novgorod and Ivanovo Oblasts to the south and Yaroslavl Oblast to the west. Its main rivers include the Volga, the Kostroma, the Unzha and the Vetluga. The total area of Kostroma Oblast is 60,100 sq km (23,200 sq miles), almost three-quarters of which is forested. According to the census of 9–16 October 2002, the region had a total population of 736,641 and a population density of 12.3 per sq km. Some 67.4% of the population inhabited urban areas. 95.6% of the population were ethnically Russian; 1.1% were Ukrainian. The Oblast's administrative centre is at Kostroma, a river-port situated on both banks of the Volga, which is a popular tourist resort of the 'Golden Ring' and had 279,400 inhabitants, according to provisional census results. Kostroma Oblast is included in the time zone GMT+3.

History

The city of Kostroma was founded in the 12th century and became the base of the Gudunov family, as well as, later, an important centre for the Romanovs (Mikhail Romanov was proclaimed tsar in the Ipatiyevskii Monastery here in 1613). The city became an industrial centre from the mid-18th century. Kostroma Oblast was formed on 13 August 1944. The region remained loyal to the communist nomenklatura in the 1990s—its oblast Soviet supported the federal parliament in its 1993 defiance of the Russian President, Boris Yeltsin, and was replaced by a new representative body, the Duma, in 1994. The Communist Party of the Russian Federation (CPRF) was the predominant party in this body, and the CPRF candidate, Viktor Shershunov, was elected Governor in December 1996. Shershunov was re-elected to serve a further term of office in December 2000. In April 2005 federal President Vladimir Putin nominated Shershunov to serve a further term of office; this nomination was duly confirmed by vote of the regional Duma on 11 May.

Economy

In 2002 gross regional product in Kostroma Oblast amounted to 27,574.8m. roubles, or 37,433.2 roubles per head. The Oblast's main industrial centres are at Kostroma, Sharya, Galich and Manturovo. At the end of 2002 there were 640 km of railways in the Oblast and 5,590 km of paved roads. There were 985 km of navigable waterways in 1998.

Agriculture in Kostroma Oblast, which employed 9.3% of the work-force and generated 7,971m. roubles in 2003, consists mainly of the production of grain, flax (the region is one of Russia's major producers of linen) and vegetables, and animal husbandry. Adverse weather conditions in mid-2003 caused severe disruption to the regional harvest. Electricity generation comprised 31.3% of total industrial production in Kostroma Oblast in 2002; around four-fifths of electrical energy produced in the region is exported. The other main industries in the region are light manufacturing, wood-working, mechanical engineering, food- and timber-processing and handicrafts (especially jewellery). Some 26.6% of the Oblast's working population was engaged in industry in 2003, when the sector generated 22,600m. roubles.

The economically active population numbered 376,000 in 2003, when 6.3% of the labour force of the region were unemployed. The average wage in the Oblast was 3,869.3 roubles per month. There was a budgetary deficit of some 888.7m. roubles. External trade comprised US $93.5m. of exports and $55.8m. of imports. Foreign investment totalled $49.0m. At the end of 2003 there were 2,900 small businesses registered in the Oblast.

Directory

Head of the Regional Administration (Governor): VIKTOR A. SHERSHUNOV (elected 22 December 1996, re-elected 24 December 2000; appointment confirmed 11 May 2005), 156001 Kostroma, ul. Dzerzhinskogo 15; tel. (494) 231-34-72; fax (494) 231-33-95; e-mail shershunov@kos-obl.kmtn.ru; internet www.region .kostroma.net.

Chairman of the Regional Duma: VALERII P. IZHITSKII, 156000 Kostroma, Sovetskaya pl. 2; tel. (494) 231-62-52; fax (494) 231-21-73; e-mail info@kosoblduma.ru; internet www.kosoblduma.ru.

Chief Representative of Kostroma Oblast in the Russian Federation: VASILII M. DUMA, 127025 Moscow, ul. Novyi Arbat 19/1811; tel. (495) 203-80-87; fax (495) 203-41-69.

Head of Kostroma City Administration: IRINA V. PEREVERZEVA, 156000 Kostroma, pl. Sovetskaya 1; tel. (494) 231-44-40; fax (494) 231-39-32.

Kursk Oblast

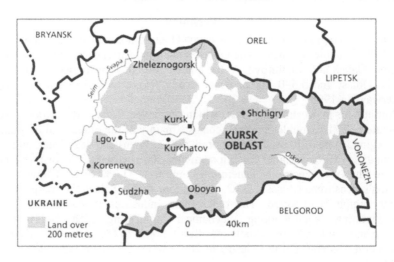

Kursk Oblast is situated within the Central Russian Highlands. It forms part of the Central Federal Okrug and the Central Chernozem Economic Area. An international boundary with Ukraine lies to the south-west, with the neighbouring Oblasts within Russia comprising Bryansk in the north-west, Orel and Lipetsk in the north, Voronezh in the east and Belgorod in the south. Its main river is the Seim. The Oblast occupies 29,800 sq km (11,500 sq miles). According to the census of 9–16 October 2002, the Oblast had a total population of 1,235,091, giving a population density of 41.4 per sq km. Some 61.2% of the population inhabited urban areas. 95.9% of the population were ethnically Russian; 1.7% were Ukrainian. The Oblast's administrative centre is at Kursk, with 412,600 inhabitants, according to provisional census results. Kursk Oblast is included in the time zone GMT+3.

History

The city of Kursk, one of the oldest in Russia, was founded in 1032, destroyed by the Tatars in 1240 and fortified as a Muscovite outpost in the 16th century. The region was the scene of an army mutiny in 1905 and, in 1943, of a decisive battle against German forces during the Second World War. Kursk Oblast was formed on 13 July 1934.

The Communist Party of the Russian Federation (CPRF) dominated the regional Duma elected in 1994, and its successors, elected in 1996 and 2001. The former federal Vice-President, Aleksandr Rutskoi, a noted opponent of liberal reforms, was elected Governor in October 1996. However, he was prevented from contesting the gubernatorial election of October–November 2005 owing to a legal technicality, and the CPRF candidate, Aleksandr Mikhailov, was elected as Governor, defeating the candidate most supportive of the federal Government, Viktor Surzhikov, a former Federal Security Service (FSB) general. In early 2005 Mikhailov resigned from the CPRF and announced his affiliation to the pro-Government Unity and Fatherland-United Russia party. Shortly afterwards, federal President Vladimir Putin nominated Mikhailov to serve a further term of office as Governor; this nomination was confirmed by vote of the regional Duma on 22 February. In June, following a steep increase (of some 500%–600%) in prices charged for communal services in the Oblast, regular demonstrations demanding the resignation of Mikhailov, on occasion attracting several hundred people, were held in Kursk. In August the regional authorities imposed severe restrictions on public gatherings, apparently in excess of measures permitted by federal legislation.

Economy

Kursk Oblast's gross regional product stood at 46,690.5m. roubles in 2002, equivalent to 37,803.3 roubles per head. Its main industrial centres are at Kursk and Zheleznogorsk. At the end of 2002 there were 1,063 km of railway lines and 6,144 km of paved roads on the Oblast's territory.

The region's agriculture, which employed 22.7% of the working population and generated 19,113m. roubles in 2003, consists mainly of sugar beet and grain production, horticulture and animal husbandry. The territory contains a major iron-ore basin, with significant deposits of Kursk magnetic anomaly. Kursk Oblast's main industries are the production of electricity, production and enrichment of iron ores, mechanical engineering, chemicals and petrochemicals, ferrous metallurgy and food-processing. Some 18.7% of the work-force were engaged in industry in 2003, when the sector generated 50,527m. roubles.

The economically active population in Kursk Oblast numbered 604,000 in 2003, when 8.6% of the labour force were unemployed. The average monthly wage in the region was 3,973.7 roubles in that year. There was a budgetary deficit of 119.8m. roubles. In 2003 external trade comprised US $133.9m. in imports and $182.3m in exports. Foreign investment in 2003 amounted to $8.8m. At the end of 2003 some 3,700 small businesses were registered in the Oblast.

Directory

Head of the Regional Administration (Governor): ALEKSANDR N. MIKHAILOV (elected 5 November 2000; appointment confirmed 22 February 2005), 305002 Kursk, Krasnaya pl., Dom Sovetov; tel. (471) 222-62-62; fax (471) 256-65-73; e-mail glava@region.kursk.ru; internet www.region.kursk.ru.

Chairman of the Regional Duma: ALEKSANDR N. ANPILOV, 305001 Kursk, ul. S. Perovskoi 24; tel. (471) 256-09-91; fax (471) 256-20-06; e-mail oblduma@kursknet .ru; internet oblduma.kursknet.ru.

Chief Representative of Kursk Oblast in the Russian Federation: SERGEI M. KLUSHIN, 127025 Moscow, ul. Novyi Arbat 19/1052–56; tel. (495) 203-53-14; fax (495) 202-53-14.

Head of Kursk City Administration: VIKTOR P. SURZHIKOV, 305000 Kursk, ul. Lenina 1; tel. (471) 255-47-01; fax (471) 222-43-16; e-mail gorod@kurskadmin.ru; internet www.kurskadmin.ru.

Lipetsk Oblast

Lipetsk Oblast is situated within the Central Russian Highlands, some 508 km (315 m) south-east of Moscow. It forms part of the Central Federal Okrug and the Central Chernozem Economic Area. It is bordered by Voronezh and Kursk to the south, Orel to the west, Tula to the north-west, Ryazan to the north and Tambov to the east. Its main rivers are the Don and the Voronezh. The Oblast occupies 24,100 sq km (9,300 sq miles). According to the census of 9–16 October 2002, the Oblast had a total population of 1,213,499, and a population density of 50.4 per sq km. Some 64.3% of the Oblast's population inhabited urban areas. 95.8% of the population were ethnically Russian; 1.1% were Ukrainian. Its administrative centre is at Lipetsk, with a population of 506,000, according to provisional census results. The Oblast's second largest city is one of the oldest in Russia, Yelets (116,700). Lipetsk Oblast is included in the time zone GMT+3.

History

Lipetsk city was founded in the 13th century. In the late tsarist and Soviet periods the region became increasingly industrialized. Lipetsk Oblast was formed on 6 January 1954. In April 1993, when Lipetsk was one of eight territorial units permitted to hold gubernatorial elections, a left-wing candidate, Mikhail Narolin, was duly elected. In September 1993 both the oblast Soviet (Council) and Narolin denounced the Russian President's dissolution of the federal parliament. In April 1998 the Chairman of the regional legislature, Oleg Korolev, who was supported, primarily, by the Communist Party of the Russian Federation (CPRF), but also by the local branch of the liberal party, Yabloko, won an overwhelming victory (with some 79.5% of the votes cast) in the gubernatorial election, overwhelmingly defeating Narolin, who was regarded as the pro-Government candidate. In the election to the federal presidency of March 2000, Lipetsk Oblast awarded the CPRF candidate, Gennadii Zyuganov, a higher proportion of the votes (47.4%) than did any other federal subject. Korolev, who was now regarded as the candidate supported by the federal Government, was re-elected on 14 April 2002, with 73% of the votes cast, after his principal rival withdrew his candidacy. In May 2005 federal President Vladimir Putin nominated Korolev to serve a further term of office; the regional legislature approved this nomination on 28 May.

Economy

In 2002 Lipetsk Oblast's gross regional product totalled 71,108.1m. roubles, or 58,597.6 roubles per head. Its main industrial centres are at Lipetsk, Yelets, Dankov and Gryazi. At the end of 2002 there were 746 km of railway lines and 5,196 km of paved roads on the Oblast's territory. In mid-2005 Governor Korolev cited insufficiencies in the Oblast's transport and energy infrastructures as factors that significantly inhibited economic growth in the region.

The region's agriculture consists mainly of animal husbandry and the production of grain, sugar beet and sunflower seeds. In 2003 agriculture employed 14.5% of the work-force and generated 16,552m. roubles. In mid-2005, following concerns about outbreaks of avian influenza in other regions of Russia, the Lipetsk Oblast administration prohibited, initially for a period of three months, all imports of poultry and eggs from outside of the Oblast, a measure which was interpreted in some quarters as representing a form of protectionism not justified by the circumstances. The Oblast's main industries are ferrous metallurgy (which comprised 61.8% of the region's total industrial output in 2002), mechanical engineering, metal-working and food-processing. Novolipetsk MetKom (New Lipetsk Metallurgical Group), based in the region, is one of the country's major industrial companies. In 2003 the industrial sector employed 23.0% of the region's working population and generated 121,859m. roubles.

The economically active population totalled 608,000 in 2003, when 4.4% of the labour force were unemployed. Those in employment earned, on average, 4,394.8 roubles per month. In December 2003 a 'minimum consumer basket' purchased in Lipetsk was found to be the lowest-priced in any federal subject. In that year the regional budget recorded a surplus of 154.8m. roubles. In 2003 exports amounted to US $1,650.1m. and imports were worth $282.7m. Foreign investment amounted to $12.6m. At the end of 2003 there were 5,600 small businesses registered in the Oblast.

Directory

Head of the Regional Administration (Governor): OLEG P. KOROLEV (elected 12 April 1998, re-elected 14 April 2002; appointment confirmed 28 May 2005), 398014 Lipetsk, Sobornaya pl. 1; tel. (474) 277-65-96; fax (474) 272-24-26; e-mail office@ admlr.lipetsk.ru; internet www.admlr.lipetsk.ru.

Chairman of the Regional Council of Deputies: ANATOLII I. SAVENKOV, 398014 Lipetsk, Sobornaya pl. 1; tel. (474) 274-35-08; fax (474) 272-24-15; e-mail 48sov00@lipadm.lipetsk.ru; internet sovet.lipetsk.ru.

Chief Representative of Lipetsk Oblast in the Russian Federation: PAVEL A. GUCHEK, 111024 Moscow, ul. Aviyamotornaya 49/1; tel. and fax (495) 918-03-90.

Head of Lipetsk City Administration (Mayor): MIKHAIL V. GULEVSKII, 398001 Lipetsk, ul. Sovetskaya 5; tel. (474) 277-65-24; fax (474) 274-44-30; internet www .lipetskcity.ru.

Moscow Oblast

Moscow Oblast is situated in the centre of the Eastern European Plain, forming part of the Central Federal Okrug and the Central Economic Area. Moscow is surrounded by seven other oblasts: Tver and Yaroslavl to the north, Vladimir and Ryazan to the east, Tula and Kaluga to the south-west and Smolensk to the west. Moscow City is enclosed by the Oblast. The main rivers are the Moskva and the Oka. The Oblast covers 47,000 sq km (18,147 sq miles). According to the census of 9–16 October 2002, the Oblast had a population of 6,618,538 and a population density of 143.9 per sq km. 79.3% of the population inhabited urban areas. 91.0% of the population were ethnically Russian, 2.2% were Ukrainian and 0.8% Tatar. The Oblast's administrative centre is Moscow City. There are several cities with a population of over 100,000, including Podolsk (181,500), Mytishchi (159,200), Lyubertsy (156,900), Kolomna (150,100), Balashikha (148,200), Elektrostal (146,100), Korolev (143,100), Khimki (141,300), Odintsovo (134,700), Serpukhov (131,200), Orekhovo-Zuyevo (122,300), Noginsk (118,000), Sergiyev-Posad (formerly Zagorsk—113,800) and Shchelkovo (113,700). Sergiyev-Posad is an important centre of Russian Orthodoxy, containing Russia's foremost monastery and two medieval cathedrals. Moscow Oblast is included in the time zone GMT+3.

History

The city of Moscow was established in the mid-12th century and became the centre of a burgeoning Muscovite state. The region, an important trade route between the Baltic and Black or Caspian Seas, became industrialized in the early 18th century, with the development of the textiles industry. The region and the city of Moscow were captured by the troops of Emperor Napoleon I of France in 1812, but the invaders were forced to retreat later that year. German invaders reached the Moscow region (which had been formed as Moscow Oblast on 14 January 1929) in 1941, although by early 1942 the German forces had been driven from the Oblast's territory. Otherwise, since 1918 the region and the city have benefited from Moscow being the Soviet, and the Russian, capital.

Col-Gen. Boris Gromov, a former member of the State Duma and a Deputy Minister of Defence, was elected as governor following two rounds of polling in December 1999–January 2000; he was re-elected to the position on 7 December 2003, with 85.5% of the valid votes cast; the rate of participation by the electorate was 51.9%.

Economy

In 2002 Moscow Oblast's gross regional product amounted to 370,816.8m. roubles, or 56,027.0 roubles per head. The main industrial centres are at Podolsk, Lyubertsy, Kolomna, Mytishchi, Odintsovo, Noginsk, Serpukhov, Orekhovo-Zuyevo and Shchelkovo. At the end of 2002 there were 2,703 km of railways and 16,408 km of paved roads in the Oblast. In mid-2003 the regional Government announced proposals for the construction of the first toll motorway in Russia.

Moscow Oblast's agriculture, which employed 6.6% of the region's work-force and generated 39,958m. roubles in 2003, consists mainly of the production of vegetables and animal husbandry. The Oblast's industry, in which some 22.8% of the working population were engaged in 2003, mainly comprises heavy industry. The region's major industries are mechanical engineering, radio electronics, chemicals, light manufacturing, textiles, ferrous and non-ferrous metallurgy, metal-working, the manufacture of building materials, wood-working and handicrafts. The region's military-industrial complex is also important. Industrial output was worth 310,830m. roubles in 2003, one of the highest levels recorded in any federal subject.

The economically active population of the Oblast was 3,527,000 in 2003, when 4.3% of the labour force were unemployed. The average monthly wage was 6,071.2 roubles. In the same year there was a regional budgetary deficit of 6,308.6m. roubles. In 2003 external trade comprised US $1,814.4m. in exports and $4,646.5m. in imports. Total foreign investment in Moscow Oblast amounted to $1,258.0m. At the end of 2003 there were 37,400 small businesses registered in the Oblast.

Directory

Governor: BORIS V. GROMOV (elected 9 January 2000; re-elected 7 December 2003), 103070 Moscow, pl. Staraya 6; tel. (495) 923-24-13; fax (495) 206-61-23; e-mail amo@mosreg.ru; internet www.mosreg.ru.

Chairman of the Regional Duma: VIKTOR A. AKSKAKOV, 103070 Moscow, pl. Staraya 6; tel. (495) 924-81-53; fax (495) 925-17-46; e-mail info@mosoblduma.ru; internet www.mosoblduma.ru.

Chief Representative of Moscow Oblast in the Russian Federation: NIKOLAI P CHURKIN, 103070 Moscow, pl. Staraya 6; tel. (495) 206-66-13.

Orel Oblast

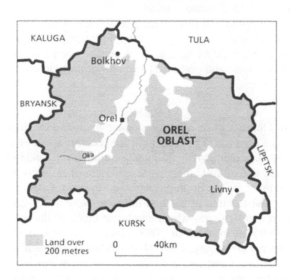

Orel Oblast is situated in the central part of the Eastern European Plain, in the Central Russian Highlands. The Oblast forms part of the Central Federal Okrug and the Central Economic Area. It is surrounded by five other oblasts: Kursk (to the south), Bryansk (west), Kaluga (north-west), Tula (north-east) and Lipetsk (east). The Oblast's major river is the Oka. Orel Oblast covers some 24,700 sq km (9,530 sq miles). According to the census of 9–16 October 2002, the total population of the Oblast was 860,262 and the population density was 34.8 per sq km. Some 63.5% of the inhabitants of the region lived in urban areas. 95.3% of the population were ethnically Russian; 1.3% were Ukrainian. The Oblast's administrative centre is at Orel, which had 333,600 inhabitants, according to provisional census results. Orel Oblast is included in the time zone GMT+3.

History

Orel was founded as a fortress in 1566. In the 1860s it served as a place of exile for Polish insurgents and was later a detention centre for prisoners on their way to exile in Siberia. Orel Oblast was formed on 27 September 1937. The region was permitted gubernatorial elections in April 1993, which were won by Yegor Stroyev. A 50-seat Regional Duma, elected in March 1994, was dominated by the Communist Party of the Russian Federation (CPRF). Despite the loyalty to the federal President, Boris Yeltsin, shown by Stroyev (who was, additionally, the speaker of the upper house of the federal parliament, the Federalnoye Sobraniye—Federation Council—in 1996–2001) as head of the regional administration, the greatest show of support in the presidential election of 1996 was for Gennadii Zyuganov, the CPRF candidate, who was a native of the region. Stroyev was re-elected Governor, with more than 97% of the votes cast, in October 1997, and was elected to a further term of office in October 2001, when he obtained 91.5% of the votes cast. In the regional legislative elections held in March 2002 the CPRF retained just three seats. In March 2003 Stroyev was elected to the Supreme Council of the pro-Government Unity and Fatherland-United

Russia party. In April 2005 federal president Vladimir Putin nominated Stroyev to serve a further term of office; this nomination was confirmed by the regional legislature on 23 April.

Economy

Orel Oblast's gross regional product amounted to 38,837.0m. roubles in 2002, equivalent to 45,145.5 roubles per head. The principal industrial centres in the region are at Orel, Livny and Mtsensk. Orel lies on the Moscow–Simferopol (Crimea, Ukraine) highway and is an important railway junction. At the end of 2002 there were 595 km of railway track in the Oblast and 4,144 km of paved roads.

Orel Oblast is an important agricultural trade centre. In 2003 around 19.9% of the economically active population were engaged in agriculture. Agricultural production, which amounted to 13,289m. roubles in 2003, consists mainly of the cultivation of grain and sugar beet. There are some 17.5m. cu m of timber reserves in the Oblast and a major source of iron ore, at Novoyaltinskoye. However, this and reserves of other minerals in the region have generally not been exploited to their full potential. The industrial sector employed around 21.8% of the economically active population in 2003 and generated 23,209m. roubles. The Oblast's main industries are mechanical engineering, metal-working, the production of building materials and food-processing.

The region's economically active population numbered 440,000 in 2003, when 7.8% of the labour force were unemployed. Those in employment earned an average of 3,563.5 roubles per month. There was a budgetary surplus of 250.3m. roubles. In that year external trade amounted to a value of US $387.7m. in exports and $355.3m. in imports. Total foreign investment in Orel Oblast amounted to $12.1m. in 2003. At the end of that year some 2,600 small businesses were registered in the Oblast.

Directory

Head of the Regional Administration (Governor): YEGOR S. STROYEV (elected 11 April 1993, re-elected 26 October 1997 and 29 October 2001; appointment confirmed 23 April 2005), 302021 Orel, pl. Lenina 1; tel. (486) 241-63-13; fax (486) 241-25-30; e-mail post@adm.orel.ru; internet www.adm.orel.ru.

Chairman of the Regional Council of People's Deputies: NIKOLAI A. VOLODIN, 302021 Orel, pl. Lenina 1; tel. (486) 241-58-53; fax (486) 241-60-22.

Chief Representative of Orel Oblast in the Russian Federation: MARINA G. ROGACHEVA, 109240 Moscow, ul. Goncharnaya 12/3; tel. (495) 915-85-51; fax (495) 915-86-14.

Head of Orel City Administration (Mayor): VASILII I. UVAROV, 302000 Orel, Proletarskaya gora 1; tel. (486) 243-33-12; fax (486) 226-39-44.

Ryazan Oblast

Ryazan Oblast is situated in the central part of the Eastern European Plain and forms part of the Central Federal Okrug and the Central Economic Area. The region neighbours the Oblasts of Moscow (to the north-west), Vladimir (north), Nizhnii Novgorod (north-east), Penza (south-east), Tambov and Lipetsk (south) and Tula (west), and the Republic of Mordoviya lies to the east. The Oblast occupies 39,600 sq km (15,290 sq miles). According to the census of 9–16 October 2002, the population of Ryazan Oblast totalled 1,227,910, giving a population density of 31.0 per sq km. Some 68.9% of the population inhabited urban areas. 94.6% of the population were ethnically Russian; 1.0% were Ukrainian. The Oblast's principal city is Ryazan, with a population of 521,700, according to provisional census results. Ryazan Oblast is included in the time zone GMT+3.

History

Ryazan city was an early Orthodox Christian bishopric. The Oblast was formed on 26 September 1937. In the mid-1990s the Communist Party of the Russian Federation (CPRF) dominated the Regional Duma. In October 1996 the incumbent Governor (appointed in January 1994), Gennadii Merkulov, was removed by the federal Government; the candidate of the People's Patriotic Union of Russia (PPUR—led by Gennadii Zyuganov, also the leader of the CPRF), Vyacheslav Lyubimov, was the successful candidate in the gubernatorial election held in December. Lyubimov was re-elected as Governor in December 2000, as the candidate of the CPRF, supported by the PPUR and the centrist Unity grouping. At gubernatorial elections held in March 2004, Lyubimov, who was widely perceived to have lost the support of the oblast branch of the CPRF, failed to qualify for the second round of voting. Instead, the former Commander-General of the Air Force (who had recently been elected to the State Duma as a member of the nationalist Motherland electoral bloc), Georgii Shpak, was elected Governor on 29 March, receiving 53.65% of the votes cast. In March 2005, prior to the holding of elections to the regional Duma, Shpak announced that he had left Motherland and joined the pro-Government Unity and Fatherland-United Russia (UF-UR) party. At these elections UF-UR emerged as the most successful party, with around 22.2% of the votes cast, according to preliminary results, with the CPRF placed second, with 15.2%, ahead of Motherland, with 13.0%. (The relatively poor performance of UF-UR was, in part, attributable to a schism in the regional organization of the party in late 2004.)

Economy

In 2002 Ryazan Oblast's gross regional product amounted to 54,711.2m. roubles, or 44,556.4 roubles per head. The Oblast's industrial centres are at Ryazan, Skopin and Kasimov. At the end of 2002 there were 974 km of railways and 6,784 km of paved roads in the region.

The Oblast's warm, moist climate is conducive to agriculture, which consists mainly of production of grain, vegetables, fruit, potatoes and sugar beet, and animal husbandry, and employed 13.4% of the work-force in 2003. Total agricultural production amounted to a value of 12,211m. roubles in that year. There are substantial reserves of timber, brown coal and peat in the region. The Oblast's main industries are mechanical engineering, metal-working, the generation of electrical energy, petroleum-processing, the production of building materials, light manufacturing and food-processing. In 2003 some 24.9% of the working population were engaged in industry, which generated a total of 59,341m. roubles.

The economically active population numbered 605,000 in 2003, when 8.3% of the labour force were unemployed. In that year those in employment earned, on average, 4,028.1 roubles per month. The budget showed a surplus of 175.0m. roubles in 2003, and foreign investment in the region totalled US $45.8m, compared with just $900,000 in the previous year. In 2003 external trade amounted to a value of $667.1m. in exports and $263.3m. in imports. At the end of that year some 7,300 small businesses were registered in the Oblast.

Directory

Head of the Regional Administration (Governor): Georgii I. Shpak (elected 29 March 2004), 390000 Ryazan, ul. Lenina 30; tel. (491) 227-21-25; fax (491) 244-25-68; e-mail korn@adm1.ryazan.su; internet www.gov.ryazan.ru.

Chairman of the Regional Duma: Vladimir K. Sidorov, 390000 Ryazan, ul. Pochtovaya 50/57; tel. (491) 225-58-48; fax (491) 221-64-22; e-mail post@duma.ryazan.ru; internet www.duma.ryazan.net.

Chief Representative of Ryazan Oblast in the Russian Federation: Ileksei Khon, 123610 Moscow, Krasnopresnenskaya nab. 12/1220; tel. (495) 967-09-33.

Head of Ryazan City Administration (Mayor): Aleksandr Kukushkin, 390000 Ryazan, ul. Radishcheva 28; tel. (491) 277-34-02; fax (491) 224-05-70; e-mail glava@cityadmin.ryazan.ru.

Smolensk Oblast

Smolensk Oblast is situated in the central part of the Eastern European Plain on the upper reaches of the Dnepr (Dnieper). It forms part of the Central Federal Okrug and the Central Economic Area. An international boundary with Belarus lies to the south-west, while the Oblasts of Pskov and Tver lie to the north, Moscow to the north-east and Kaluga and Bryansk to the south-east. The Oblast covers an area of 49,800 sq km (19,220 sq miles). According to the census of 9–16 October 2002, the population numbered 1,049,574, giving a population density of 21.1 per sq km. 70.8% of the region's inhabitants lived in urban areas. 93.4% of the population were ethnically Russian, 1.7% were Ukrainian, and 1.5% were Belarusian. The Oblast's administrative centre is at Smolensk, a river-port on the Dnepr, with 325,500 inhabitants, according to provisional census results. Smolensk Oblast is included in the time zone GMT+3.

History

Smolensk city was first documented in 863, as the chief settlement of the Krivichi, a Slavic tribe. It became an Orthodox Christian bishopric in 1128. It achieved prosperity during the 14th and 15th centuries as it was situated on one of the Hanseatic trade routes. Smolensk was the site of a major battle in 1812, between the Russian imperial army and the forces of Emperor Napoleon I of France. Smolensk Oblast was formed on 27 September 1937.

The region was a centre of support for the Communist Party of the Russian Federation (CPRF) for much of the 1990s. In the gubernatorial election of 1998, the CPRF candidate and Mayor of Smolensk, Aleksandr Prokhorov, defeated the incumbent, Anatolii Glushenkov. Support for the CPRF declined significantly in the regional legislative elections held in May 2002. In the same month Viktor Maslov, a general in the Federal Security Service, was elected as the new Governor, receiving 41.6% of the votes cast, narrowly defeating Prokhorov. Maslov's campaign had concentrated on issues of law and order and concern about, in particular, organized crime, which was subsequently heightened following the assassination of Vladimir Prokhorov, the First Deputy Governor, in early August. In June 2005 federal President Vladimir Putin nominated Maslov to serve a further term of office; this nomination was unanimously approved by the Regional Duma on 24 June.

Economy

In 2002 Smolensk Oblast's gross regional product amounted to 47,000.5m. roubles, or 44,780.5 roubles per head. Its major industrial centres are at Smolensk, Safonovo and Vyazma. At the end of 2002 there were 1,159 km of railway lines and 8,882 km of paved roads in the Oblast.

Agriculture in Smolensk Oblast, which employed 12.1% of the work-force and generated 9,319m. roubles in 2003, mainly consists of animal husbandry, bee-keeping, and the production of flax, potatoes, fruit and vegetables, grain, sugar beet and sunflower seeds. The Oblast's main industries are mechanical engineering (in particular the production of automobiles), metal-working, chemicals and petrochemicals, food-processing and electrical-energy production. In 2003 some 23.3% of the work-force were engaged in industry. Total industrial production in that year amounted to a value of 48,467m. roubles.

The region's economically active population numbered 551,000 in 2003, when 10.9% of the labour force were unemployed—the highest level in the Central Federal Okrug. The average monthly wage in the Oblast was 4,173.3 roubles. The 2003 budget showed a deficit of 150.0m. roubles. The value of external trade in that year amounted to US \$467.5m. in exports and \$171.9m. in imports. Total foreign investment in the region amounted to \$33.6m. At the end of 2003 there were 2,600 small businesses registered in the Oblast.

Directory

Head of the Regional Administration (Governor): VIKTOR N. MASLOV (elected 19 May 2002; appointment confirmed 24 June 2005), 214008 Smolensk, pl. Lenina 1; tel. (481) 238-66-11; fax (481) 223-68-51; e-mail maslov@admin.smolensk.ru; internet admin.smolensk.ru.

Chairman of the Regional Duma: VLADIMIR I. ANISIMOV, 214008 Smolensk, pl. Lenina 1; tel. (481) 238-67-00; fax (481) 238-71-85; e-mail duma@admin.smolensk .ru; internet admin.smolensk.ru/~duma.

Chief Representative of Smolensk Oblast in the Russian Federation: ALEKSEI V. MESHKICHEV, 123610 Moscow, Krasnopresnenskaya nab. 12/3.

Head of Smolensk City Administration: VLADISLAV N. KHALETSKII, 214000 Smolensk, ul. Oktyabrskoi Revolyutsii 1/2; tel. and fax (481) 038-06-02; e-mail smol@ admin.smolensk.ru; internet www.admcity.smolensk.ru.

Tambov Oblast

Tambov Oblast is situated in the central part of the Oka-Don plain. It forms part of the Central Federal Okrug and the Central Chernozem Economic Area. Penza and Saratov Oblasts lie to the east, Voronezh to the south, Lipetsk to the west and Ryazan to the north. Its major rivers are the Tsna and the Vorona. Its territory occupies 34,300 sq km (13,240 sq miles). According to the census of 9–16 October 2002, its population was 1,178,443, giving a population density of 34.4 per sq km. At that time, 57.2% of the population inhabited urban areas. 96.5% of the population were ethnically Russian; 0.9% were Ukrainian. The administrative centre is at Tambov, which had a population of 294,300, according to provisional census results. Tambov Oblast is included in the time zone GMT+3.

History

Tambov city was founded in 1636 as a Muscovite fort. The region was the scene of an army mutiny during the anti-tsarist uprising of 1905, and came under Bolshevik control immediately after the October Revolution in 1917. Numerous peasant revolts against the Bolsheviks, which were brutally suppressed by forces led by Marshal Mikhail Tukachevskii, took place in the region in the early 1920s. Tambov Oblast was formed on 27 September 1937. The dissolution of the oblast Soviet in October 1993, and its replacement by a Regional Duma, did not ease tensions between the communist-led assembly and the regional administration. Having appointed Oleg Betin as Governor in March 1995, President Boris Yeltsin permitted a gubernatorial election in Tambov in December of that year. However, Betin lost to the Communist Party of the Russian Federation candidate, Aleksandr Ryabov, and was instead appointed as presidential representative to the region. Betin was elected Governor in December 1999, with the support of two centrist movements that subsequently merged, Fatherland and Unity. On 7 December 2003 Betin was re-elected, receiving over 75% of the votes cast. Although his term was not due to expire until 2008, in mid-2005 Betin requested that the federal President, Vladimir Putin, who had assumed the power to nominate regional governors in late 2004, demonstrate his confidence in Betin's leadership. Putin subsequently nominated Betin to serve a further term of office, and this nomination was unanimously approved by the Regional Duma on 13 July. The pro-Government Unity and Fatherland-United Russia party obtained the largest share of the votes (some 40%, according to provisional results) cast at elections to the Regional Duma on 18 December.

Economy

In 2002 Tambov Oblast's gross regional product amounted to 39,211.2m. roubles, equivalent to 33,273.7 roubles per head. The region's industrial centres are at Tambov, Michurinsk and Morshansk. It is situated on the ancient trading routes from the centre of Russia to the lower Volga and Central Asia, and contains several major road and rail routes. At the end of 2002 there were 735 km of railway lines and 5,475 km of paved roads in the region.

The Oblast's agriculture, which employed some 25.9% of the work-force in 2003 consists mainly of the production of grain, sugar beet, sunflower seeds and potatoes. Total agricultural output was worth 16,853m. roubles in that year. The principal industries in the Oblast are mechanical engineering, metal-working, chemicals and petrochemicals, the production of electrical energy, light manufacturing and food-processing. In 2003 industry employed 18.2% of the working population and generated 21,278m. roubles.

The economically active population stood at 574,000 in 2003, when 9.1% of the labour force were unemployed. In 2003 the average monthly wage in the Oblast was just 3,303.6 roubles, although living costs in the region were also found to be among the lowest in the Federation in late 2003. There was a budgetary surplus of 77.5m. roubles in that year. In 2003 the value of external trade amounted to US $52.9m. in exports and $98.7m. in imports; foreign investment in the Oblast stood at $3.5m. At the end of 2003 some 3,100 small businesses were registered in the region.

Directory

Head of the Regional Administration (Governor): OLEG I. BETIN (elected December 1999, re-elected 7 December 2003; appointment confirmed 13 July 2005), 392017 Tambov, ul. Internatsionalnaya 14; tel. (475) 272-10-61; fax (475) 272-25-18; e-mail post@regadm.tambov.ru; internet www.regadm.tambov.ru.

Chairman of the Regional Duma: VLADIMIR N. KAREV, 392017 Tambov, ul. Internatsionalnaya 14; tel. (475) 271-23-70; fax (475) 271-07-72; internet www .regadm.tambov.ru/duma.

Chief Representative of Tambov Oblast in the Russian Federation: VALERII I. YEVDOKIMOV, 127025 Moscow, ul. Novyi Arbat 19.

Head of Tambov City Administration (Mayor): ALEKSEI YU. ILIN, 392000 Tambov, ul. Kommunalnaya 6; tel. (475) 272-20-30; fax (475) 272-47-71; e-mail cvc_t@rambler.ru; internet www.cityadm.tambov.ru.

Tula Oblast

Tula Oblast is situated in the central part of the Eastern European Plain in the northern section of the Central Russian Highlands. It forms part of the Central Federal Okrug and the Central Economic Area and is bordered by Ryazan to the east, Lipetsk to the south-east, Orel to the south-west, Kaluga to the north-west and Moscow Oblast to the north. Tula Oblast covers 25,700 sq km (9,920 sq miles). According to the census of 9–16 October 2002, it had a total population of 1,675,758 and a population density of 65.2 per sq km. 81.6% of the Oblast's population inhabited urban areas. 95.2% of the population were ethnically Russian; 1.3% were Ukrainian. The Oblast's administrative centre is at Tula, with a population of 472,300, according to provisional census results. Its second largest city is Novomoskovsk (with 134,000 inhabitants). Tula Oblast is included in the time zone GMT+3.

History

The city of Tula was founded in the 12th century. It became an important economic centre in 1712, with the construction of the Imperial Small Arms Factory. Tula Oblast was founded on 26 September 1937.

On 7 October 1993 the Tula Regional Soviet refused to disband itself, but was subsequently dissolved and replaced by a Regional Duma. The Communist Party of the Russian Federation (CPRF) remained the most widely supported party in the Oblast throughout the 1990s. The Oblast had a high-profile CPRF Governor, following the election in March 1997 of Vasilii Starodubtsev (who had been a participant in the attempted coup organized against the Soviet leader, Mikhail Gorbachev, in Moscow in August 1991).

Gubernatorial elections, held in April 2001, aroused widespread controversy. On 22 April Starodubtsev received over 71% of the votes cast in the second round of voting, for which his opponent, Viktor Sokolovskii, had refused to campaign. (Sokolovskii had been placed third in the first round of elections, but the second-placed candidate, Andrei Samoshin, subsequently withdrew his candidacy, citing his dissatisfaction with the conduct of the electoral commission.) Further controversy was aroused by the decision that the votes of the approximately 100,000 overseas Russian citizens resident in Israel at the State Duma elections held in December 2003 would be assigned to Tula Oblast, where they comprised nearly one-quarter of registered voters. In contrast to previous Duma elections, on this occasion the CPRF finished in fourth place in the Oblast, behind the option to vote against all candidates, while the pro-Government Unity and Fatherland-United Russia finished in first place.

On 30 March 2005 the Regional Duma voted in favour of President Putin's nomination of Vyacheslav Dudka, hitherto chief engineer at a state instrument-making company, to replace Starodubtsev as Governor. Starodubtsev thereby became the second Governor to be removed from office, following Dmitrii Ayatskov of Saratov Oblast, as a result of the new system of gubernatorial appointments.

Economy

In 2002 Tula Oblast's gross regional product amounted to 67,891.9m. roubles, or 40,514.1 roubles per head. Its important industrial centres are at Tula, Novo-moskovsk and Shchekino. At the end of 2002 there were 1,064 km of railway lines and 5,134 km of paved roads in the Oblast.

Around 73.7% of the Oblast's territory is used for agricultural purposes. Agri-culture, which engaged 9.2% of the work-force and generated 15,284m. roubles in 2003, consists primarily of the production of grain, potatoes, fruit and vegetables, and sugar beet, as well as animal husbandry. The Oblast's main industries are mechanical engineering, metal-working, chemicals and petrochemicals, ferrous metallurgy, food-processing, the production of brown coal (lignite) and the gen-eration of electricity. Industry employed 27.2% of the work-force and generated 88,125m. roubles in 2003. Ferrous metallurgy, mechanical engineering and metal-working dominated exports in the region.

The economically active population in the Oblast numbered 812,000 in 2003, when 5.3% of the labour force were unemployed. The average monthly wage was 4,205.5 roubles. The 2003 budget showed a deficit of 1,477.9m. roubles. In 2003 external trade comprised US \$969.1m. of exports and \$215.7m. of imports. Total foreign investment amounted to \$27.5m. in that year. At the end of 2003 some 6,400 small businesses were registered in the Oblast.

Directory

Head of the Regional Administration (Governor): VYACHESLAV DUDKA (appoint-ment confirmed 30 March 2005), 300600 Tula, pl. Lenina 2; tel. (487) 227-84-36; fax (487) 220-63-26; e-mail admin@region.tula.ru; internet www.region.tula.ru.

Chairman of the Regional Duma: OLEG TATARINOV, 300600 Tula, pl. Lenina 2; tel. (487) 220-50-24; fax (487) 236-47-66; e-mail oblduma@duma.tula.ru.

Chief Representative of Tula Oblast in the Russian Federation: ISMAIL I. BARATOV, 127030 Moscow, Veskovskii per. 2; tel. (495) 978-14-56; fax (495) 978-06-43.

Head of Tula City Administration (Mayor): ALBERT UKOLOV, Tula; tel. (487) 227-80-85.

Tver Oblast

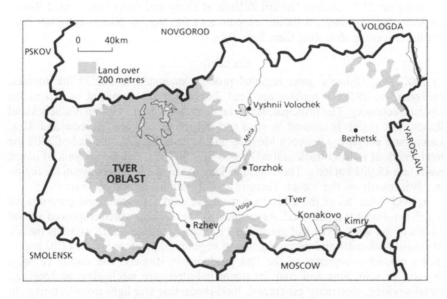

Tver Oblast is situated in the central part of the Eastern European Plain. It forms part of the Central Federal Okrug and the Central Economic Area. Moscow and Smolensk Oblasts lie to the south, Pskov to the west, Novgorod and Vologda to the north and Yaroslavl to the east. The major rivers in the region are the Volga, which rises within its territory, the Mologa and the Tvertsa. The western part of the territory is mountainous. The Oblast occupies 84,100 sq km (32,460 sq miles). According to the census of 9–16 October 2002, the Oblast had a total of 1,471,459 inhabitants, and a population density of 17.5 per sq km; some 73.1% of the population inhabited urban areas. 92.5% of the population were ethnically Russian, 1.5% were Ukrainian, and 1.0% were Kareliyan. The administrative centre is at Tver (Kalinin, 1931–90), a river-port, which had a population of 409,400, according to provisional census results. Tver Oblast is included in the time zone GMT+3.

History
Tver was founded as a fort in 1135 and its princes rivalled those of Moscow in the 14th and 15th centuries. The Oblast was formed in January 1935. In October 1993 the Regional Soviet refused to disband itself, but was subsequently obliged to comply with the directives of the federal authorities and a new body, the Legislative Assembly, was elected the following year. This was dominated by members of the Communist Party of the Russian Federation (CPRF) and was obstructive of executive action. At a gubernatorial election, held in December 1995, the incumbent, Vladimir Suslov, was defeated by Vladimir Platov, a member of the CPRF. In June 1996 the region was granted greater autonomy, with the signing of a power-sharing treaty between the regional and federal authorities. Platov, by then one of the founders of the Unity electoral bloc, was re-elected in January 2000. In September 2003 criminal charges of abuse of office were formally issued against Platov, relating to the apparent disappearance of 463m. roubles from oblast funds in 2002.

In the first round of gubernatorial elections, held on 7 December 2003, Platov was the third-placed candidate, obtaining just 12.0% of the votes cast. In a second round of voting on 21 December Dmitrii Zelenin of Unity and Fatherland-United Russia (as Unity had become), a former executive of the Norilsk Nickel company, was elected Governor, defeating Gen. Igor Zubov.

Economy

In 2002 Tver Oblast's gross regional product amounted to 58,775.7m. roubles, equivalent to 39,943.8 roubles per head. Industry is the dominant branch of the Oblast's economy. The principal industrial centres are Tver, Vyshnii Volochek and Rzhev. The region is crossed by road and rail routes between Moscow and Rīga, Latvia, and a highway between Moscow and St Petersburg. At the end of 2002 the total length of railway track in the Oblast was 1,807 km, and the network of paved roads was 15,002 km long. There were 924 km of navigable waterways in the region in 1998, mainly on the Volga. There is an international airport at Tver.

Around 2.4m. ha of the Oblast's territory is used for agricultural purposes, of which two-thirds is arable land. Agriculture in Tver Oblast, which employed around 13.0% of the work-force and generated 11,111m. roubles in 2003, consists mainly of animal husbandry and the production of vegetables, potatoes and flax (the region grows around one-quarter of the flax produced in Russia). The region contains deposits of peat, lime and coal. Its major industries are mechanical engineering, metal-working, electricity generation, food-processing and light manufacturing. In 2003 industry employed 24.1% of the work-force and generated 55,140m. roubles.

The region's economically active population numbered 767,000 in 2003, when 6.6% of the labour force were unemployed. The average wage amounted to 4,267.9 roubles per month. The 2003 regional budget recorded a deficit of 157.7m. roubles. In that year external trade amounted to a value of US $129.0m. in exports and $154.9m. in imports. Total foreign investment in the Oblast amounted to $4.9m. in 2003. At the end of 2003 some 7,000 small businesses were registered in the Oblast.

Directory

Head of the Regional Administration (Governor): DMITRII ZELENIN (elected 21 December 2003), 170000 Tver, ul. Sovetskaya 44; tel. (482) 235-37-77; fax (482) 242-55-08; e-mail tradm@tversa.ru; internet www.region.tver.ru.

Chairman of the Legislative Assembly: MARK ZH. KHASAINOV, 170000 Tver, ul. Sovetskaya 33; tel. (482) 232-10-11; fax (482) 248-10-15; e-mail zsto@tdn.ru; internet www.zsto.ru.

Chief Representative of Tver Oblast in the Russian Federation: (vacant), 103246 Moscow, ul. B. Dmitrovka 26; tel. (495) 926-65-19; fax (495) 292-14-85.

Head of Tver City Administration (Mayor): OLEG S. LEBEDEV, 170640 Tver, ul. Sovetskaya 11; tel. (482) 233-01-31; fax (482) 242-59-39; e-mail info@www.tver.ru; internet www.tver.ru.

Vladimir Oblast

Vladimir Oblast is situated in the central part of the Eastern European Plain. It forms part of the Central Federal Okrug and the Central Economic Area. It borders the Oblasts of Ryazan and Moscow to the south-west, Yaroslavl and Ivanovo to the north and Nizhnii Novgorod to the east. The Oblast's main rivers are the Oka and its tributary, the Klyazma. Over one-half of its territory is forested. It occupies 29,000 sq km (11,200 sq miles). According to the census of 9–16 October 2002, the region had a total population of 1,523,990, giving a population density of 52.6 per sq km; some 79.7% of the population inhabited urban areas. 94.7% of the population were ethnically Russian; 1.1% were Ukrainian. The Oblast's administrative centre is at Vladimir, which had a population of 316,300, according to provisional census results. Other major cities are Kovrov (155,600) and Murom (126,800). Vladimir Oblast is included in the time zone GMT+3.

History

Founded in 1108 as a frontier fortress by Prince Vladimir Monomakh, after the disintegration of Kyivan (Kievan) Rus, Vladimir city was the seat of the principality of Vladimir-Suzdal and an early Orthodox Christian bishopric. Vladimir fell under the rule of Muscovy in 1364 and declined in importance from the 15th century, being supplanted by Moscow as the seat of the Russian Orthodox patriarch, although Vladimir was chosen for the coronations of several Muscovite princes. Vladimir Oblast was formed on 14 August 1944.

The Communist Party of the Russian Federation (CPRF) secured the election of Nikolai Vinogradov, former Chairman of the regional Legislative Assembly, to the post of Governor in late 1996. A new oblast flag was adopted in April 1999 that, notably, incorporated the Soviet symbol of a hammer and sickle. Vinogradov was re-elected Governor in December 2000, with some 66% of the votes cast, defeating Yurii Glasov, who had held the post in 1991–96. In February 2005 federal President Vladimir Putin nominated Vinogradov to serve a further term of office; on 18 February the regional Legislative Assembly overwhelmingly approved this nomination. At elections to the regional legislature, held on 20 March, the pro-Government Unity and Fatherland-United Russia party obtained the greatest share of the votes cast, with 20.5%, slightly more than the CPRF, who received 20.3%. Some 17.9% of votes were cast 'against all candidates', a greater share of the vote than was received by any other party.

Economy

Vladimir Oblast's gross regional product in 2002 totalled 53,294.9m. roubles, or 34,970.6 roubles per head. The Oblast's main industrial centres are at Vladimir, Kovrov, Murom, Aleksandrov, Kolchugino and Gus-Khrustalnyi. At the end of 2002 there were 934 km of railway track and 5,538 km of paved roads on its territory.

Agriculture in the region, which employed 8.0% of the work-force and generated 12,128m. roubles in 2003, consists mainly of animal husbandry, vegetable production and horticulture. Vladimir is rich in peat deposits and timber reserves, but relies on imports for around 70% of its energy supplies. The Oblast's main industries are mechanical engineering, metal-working, food-processing, the production of electrical energy, light manufacturing, chemicals, glass-making and handicrafts. Industry employed 35.7% of the work-force and generated 64,132m. roubles in 2003.

Vladimir Oblast's economically active population numbered 824,000 in 2003, when 10.1% of the labour force were unemployed. The average monthly wage in the Oblast was 4,024.6 roubles. In 2003 there was a regional budgetary deficit of 307.9m. roubles. In that year external trade constituted US $205.0m. in exports and $230.5m. in imports; total foreign investment amounted to $85.2m. At the end of 2003 some 7,100 small businesses were registered in the Oblast.

Directory

Head of the Regional Administration (Governor): NIKOLAI V. VINOGRADOV (elected 8 December 1996, re-elected 10 December 2000; appointment confirmed 18 February 2005), 600000 Vladimir, pr. Oktyabrskii 21; tel. (492) 233-15-52; fax (492) 225-34-45; e-mail post@avo.ru; internet avo.ru.

Chairman of the Legislative Assembly: ANATOLII V. BOBROV, 600000 Vladimir, Oktyabrskaya pr. 21; tel. (492) 232-66-53; fax (492) 223-08-06; e-mail zsvo@zsvo .ru; internet www.zsvo.ru.

Chief Representative of Vladimir Oblast in the Russian Federation: (vacant), Moscow; tel. (495) 299-66-49.

Head of Vladimir City Administration: ALEKSANDR P. RYBAKOV, 600000 Vladimir, ul. Gorkogo 36; tel. (492) 223-28-17; fax (492) 223-85-54; e-mail mayor@ vladimir-city.ru; internet www.vladimir-city.ru.

Voronezh Oblast

Voronezh Oblast is situated in the centre of the Eastern European Plain on the middle reaches of the Volga. It forms part of the Central Federal Okrug and the Central Chernozem Economic Area. There is a short border with Ukraine in the south. Belgorod and Kursk lie to the west, Lipetsk and Tambov to the north, Saratov to the north-east, Volgograd to the east and Rostov to the south-east. The west of the territory is situated within the Central Russian Highlands and the east in the Oka-Don lowlands. Its main rivers are the Don, the Khoper and the Bityug. The Oblast occupies 52,400 sq km (20,230 sq miles). According to the census of 9–16 October 2002, the total population was 2,378,803, and the population density 45.4 per sq km. Some 61.9% of the population lived in urban areas. 94.1% of the population were ethnically Russian; 3.1% were Ukrainian. The region's administrative centre is at Voronezh, which had a population of 848,700, according to provisional census results. Voronezh Oblast is included in the time zone GMT+3.

History

Voronezh city was founded in 1586 as a fortress. Tsar Petr (Peter—'the Great') founded the first units of what became the imperial Russian Navy in Voronezh in 1696. The centre of a fertile region, the city began to industrialize in the tsarist period. Voronezh Oblast was formed in June 1934.

In the immediate post-Soviet years the region was largely supportive of the Communist Party of the Russian Federation (CPRF). Ivan Shabonov, a member of that party, was elected Governor in December 1996. At the gubernatorial election held in December 2000 Shabonov was defeated by Vladimir Kulakov, a general in the Federal Security Service (FSB). At the regional legislative election held in March 2001 the level of CPRF representation was reduced from 23 seats to five. In elections to the Gosudarstvennaya Duma (State Duma—lower chamber of the federal legislature) in December 2003 the Oblast recorded the lowest level of support for the pro-Government Unity and Fatherland-United Russia (UF-UR) of any federal subject. At a gubernatorial election held on 14 March 2004 Kulakov was re-elected, receiving

52.5% of votes cast. At elections to the regional legislature, held on 20 March 2005, UF-UR obtained the largest share of the votes cast (29.1%); the nationalist Motherland party were placed second, with 21.0%.

Economy

In 2002 Voronezh Oblast's gross regional product amounted to 88,151.6m. roubles, equivalent to 37,057.1 roubles per head. The important industrial centres in the Oblast are at Voronezh, Borisoglebsk and Rossosh. In 2002 the territory contained some 1,160 km of railway track and 9,152 km of paved roads. The road network includes sections of major routes, including the Moscow–Rostov and Moscow–Astrakhan highways. There are some 640 km of navigable waterways.

Around 90% of the Oblast's territory is used for agricultural purposes. In 2003 agriculture employed 20.4% of the work-force and generated 29,419m. roubles. The Oblast's agriculture consists mainly of the production of grain, sugar beet, sunflower seeds, potatoes and vegetables. Animal husbandry is also important. The main industries are mechanical engineering, metal-working, chemicals and petrochemicals, the production of electricity, the manufacture of building materials and food-processing. In 2003 industry employed 19.6% of the work-force and generated 66,563m. roubles.

The Oblast's economically active population numbered 1,122,000 in 2003, when 8.1% of the labour force were unemployed. In 2003 the Oblast's average monthly wage was 3,549.1 roubles. There was a budgetary deficit of 1,397.2m. roubles in 2003. In that year the value of external trade amounted to US $309.8m. in exports and $337.2m. in imports. Foreign investment amounted to $29.6m. in 2003. At the end of 2003 some 14,600 small businesses were registered in the region.

Directory

Head of the Regional Administration (Governor): VLADIMIR G. KULAKOV (elected 24 December 2000, re-elected 14 March 2004), 394018 Voronezh, pl. Lenina 1; tel. (473) 255-27-37; fax (473) 253-28-02; e-mail serzh@comch.ru; internet admin.vrn .ru.

Chairman of the Regional Duma: VLADIMIR KLYUCHNIKOV, 394018 Voronezh, ul. Kirova 2; tel. (473) 252-21-03; fax (473) 252-09-22; e-mail voblduma@inbox.ru.

Chief Representative of Voronezh Oblast in the Russian Federation: ALEKSANDR I. FIRSOV, 125047 Moscow, ul. 2-aya Tverskaya-Yamskaya 26; tel. (495) 250-98-55; fax (495) 299-90-27.

Head of Voronezh City Administration (Mayor): BORIS M. SKRYNNIKOV, 394067 Voronezh, ul. Plekhanovskaya 10; tel. (473) 255-34-20; fax (473) 255-47-16; e-mail admin@city.vrn.ru.

Yaroslavl Oblast

Yaroslavl Oblast is situated in the central part of the Eastern European Plain. It forms part of the Central Federal Okrug and the Central Economic Area. The region borders the Oblasts of: Ivanovo to the south-east, Vladimir and Moscow to the south, Tver to the west; Vologda to the north and Kostroma to the east. There is a large reservoir at Rybinsk, formed in 1941, following the completion of a dam and a hydroelectric power plant nearby. (However, proposals to drain the reservoir were announced in the mid-1990s.) The Volga river flows through the region. The Oblast covers 36,400 sq km (14,050 sq miles). According to the census of 9–16 October 2002, the Oblast's total population was 1,367,398, and the population density 37.6 per sq km. 80.9% of the population inhabited urban areas. 95.2% of the population were ethnically Russian; 1.0% were Ukrainian. The Oblast's administrative centre is at Yaroslavl, which had a population of 613,200, according to provisional census results. The second largest city in the Oblast is Rybinsk (known as Andropov in 1984–92, with 222,800). Yaroslavl Oblast is included in the time zone GMT+3.

History

Yaroslavl city is reputed to be the oldest town on the River Volga, having been founded c. 1024. The region was acquired by the Muscovite state during the reign of Ivan III (1462–1505) and the city briefly served as the capital when Moscow was captured by Polish and Lithuanian invaders in 1610. Yaroslavl Oblast was formed in March 1936. In the 1990s the region developed a liberal and diverse political climate. In December 1995 the federal President, Boris Yeltsin, permitted his appointed Governor, Anatolii Lisitsyn, to contest a direct election for the post, which he won.

He was re-elected for a further term on 19 December 1999. Lisitsyn, who was supported by the pro-Government Unity and Fatherland-United Russia (UF-UR) party, was re-elected for the second time on 7 December 2003, receiving 75.2% of the votes cast. The rate of participation by the electorate was 59.0%. At elections to the regional Duma held on 14 March 2005 UF-UR were the most successful group, obtaining 21 of a total of 72 contested seats; the second largest grouping elected was that of the nationalist Motherland party, with 14.

Economy

In 2002 Yaroslavl Oblast's gross regional product amounted to 87,073.3m. roubles, equivalent to 63,678.1 roubles per head—the highest level in the Central Federal Okrug, after Moscow City. The major industrial centres in the region are at Yaroslavl, Rybinsk, and Pereslavl-Zalesskii. There are river-ports at Yaroslavl, Rybinsk and Uglich. The total length of railway track in the Oblast amounted to 650 km at the end of 2002. The Oblast lies on the Moscow–Yaroslavl–Archangel and Yaroslavl–Kostroma highways. There were 6,253 km of paved roads in the region, and around 800 km of navigable waterways.

The climate and soil quality in the region is not favourable to agriculture. Agricultural activity, which employed 9.0% of the work-force and generated 10,438m. roubles in 2003, consists primarily of the production of vegetables, fruit and flax and of animal husbandry. The main industries are mechanical engineering (particularly the manufacture of aircraft engines), chemicals and petrochemicals, petroleum-refining, peat production, the production of electricity and food-processing. In 2003 industry employed 29.4% of the work-force and generated 78,404m. roubles.

The Oblast's economically active population numbered 737,000 in 2003, when the region had an unemployment rate of 5.7%. The average wage was 4,952.1 roubles per month. In 2003 there was a regional budgetary deficit of 1,079.6m. roubles. In that year total foreign investment in the region amounted to US $49.4m., and external trade comprised $410.9m. in exports and $276.5m. in imports. At the end of 2003 there were 8,400 small businesses registered in the Oblast.

Directory

Governor: ANATOLII I. LISITSYN (appointed 10 September 1992, elected 17 December 1995, re-elected 19 December 1999 and 7 December 2003), 150000 Yarovslavl, pl. Sovetskaya 3; tel. (485) 272-81-28; fax (485) 232-84-14; internet www.adm.yar.ru.

Chairman of the Regional Duma: ANDREI G. KRUTIKOV, 150000 Yaroslavl, pl. Sovetskaya 5; tel. (485) 272-89-35; fax (485) 272-76-45; e-mail dumpress@region .adm.yar.ru; internet www.adm.yar.ru/duma/index.asp.

Chief Representative of Yaroslavl Oblast in the Russian Federation: OLEG N. RASSADKIN, 127025 Moscow, ul. Novyi Arbat 19/1932; tel. (495) 203-62-21.

Head of Yaroslavl City Administration (Mayor): VIKTOR V. VOLONCHUNAS, 150000 Yaroslavl, ul. Andropova 6; tel. (485) 230-46-41; fax (485) 230-52-79; e-mail ird@gw.city.yar.ru; internet www.city.yar.ru.

NORTH-WESTERN FEDERAL OKRUG

St Petersburg City

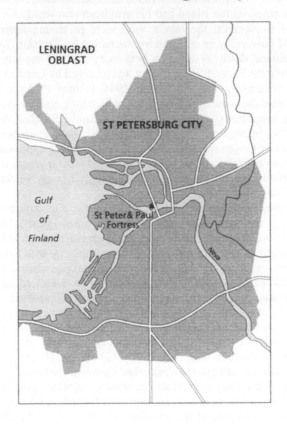

St Petersburg (Sankt-Peterburg) is a seaport at the mouth of the River Neva, which drains into the easternmost part of the Gulf of Finland (part of the Baltic Sea). St Petersburg is included in the North-Western Federal Okrug and the North-Western Economic Area. The city's territory, including a total of 42 islands in the Neva delta, occupies an area of 570 sq km (220 sq miles—making it the smallest of Russia's federal subjects), of which its waterways comprise around 10%. There are more than 580 bridges in the city and surrounding area, including 22 drawbridges. According to the census of 9–16 October 2002, the population of the city was 4,661,219, with a population density of 7,768.3 per sq km. 84.7% of the population were ethnically

Russian, 1.9% Ukrainian, 1.2% Belarusian, 0.8% Jewish and 0.8% Tatar. St Petersburg is included in the time zone GMT+3.

History

St Petersburg was founded by Tsar Peter—Petr I ('the Great') in 1703, as a 'window on the West', and was the Russian capital from 1712 until 1918. At the beginning of the First World War, in 1914, the city was renamed Petrograd. Following the fall of the Tsar and the Bolshevik Revolution in 1917, the Russian capital was moved back to Moscow. A revolt at the naval base of Kronstadt, west of mainland Petrograd, in March 1921 presented one of the most serious challenges to the nascent Bolshevik authorities, as the island had hitherto been renowned as a stronghold of support for the Bolsheviks; the rebels, who were protesting against the steady centralization of powers, were quashed by troops led by Trotskii (Lev Bronstein), and several thousand deaths resulted on both sides. In 1924 the city was renamed Leningrad. During the Second World War it was besieged by German troops for 870 days, between November 1941 and January 1944. In June 1991 the citizens of the city voted to restore the name of St Petersburg, which took effect from October. Also in June 1991 a supporter of economic reform, Anatolii Sobchak, was elected as Governor. In 1994–96 the future federal President, Vladimir Putin, was First Deputy Governor of the city Government. On 24 April 1996 Sobchak approved a draft treaty on the delimitation of powers between municipal and federal organs of government. In May 1996 another liberal, the hitherto First Deputy Mayor, Vladimir Yakovlev, was elected as Mayor, defeating Sobchak.

In the mid-1990s the reformist Yabloko bloc was the dominant political force in the city, although the party went into opposition following the December 1998 municipal legislative elections. Meanwhile, in September 1998 the federal President, Boris Yeltsin, approved the administrative merger of the city with Leningrad Oblast, although there was no indication when, or if, the unification (which would be subject to a referendum) would actually occur. Yakovlev was re-elected as Mayor on 14 May 2000, obtaining 72.7% of the votes cast, having secured the support of the Communist Party of the Russian Federation and nationalist elements.

At the municipal legislative election held in December 2002 some 38 of the 50 incumbent deputies were re-elected to the regional Assembly, although the rate of participation in the election was only 29.4% (31 of the 50 deputies in the new Assembly held no party allegiance). Yakovlev's political position appeared to have been weakened by the formation of an opposition majority in the new legislature (despite the defection to a new faction, known as United St Petersburg, of several deputies elected as members of the pro-Government Unity and Fatherland-United Russia—UF-UR party), and, in particular, by the appointment of a close ally of Putin (who was generally regarded as an opponent of Yakovlev) and a former ambassador, Valentina Matviyenko, as Presidential Representative to the North-Western Federal Okrug in mid-March. On 16 June, Putin appointed Yakovlev as a Deputy Chairman of the federal Government, with special responsibility for housing and the reform of utility services; he was thereby obliged to resign as Mayor. In mid-June Matviyenko announced her candidacy for the forthcoming mayoral elections; she received the support of Putin to an extent that was unprecedented for a candidate to a post of regional leadership. In addition, Matviyenko was supported by the pro-market Union of Rightist Forces, Yabloko, UF-UR, and the Communist Party of the Russian Federation, and she also received the backing of Yakovlev. In the first round of polling, on 21 September, Matviyenko received 48.7% of votes cast. In the 'run-off' election, held on 5 October, Matviyenko was elected Governor, receiving 63.2% of the votes cast, defeating Anna Markova, Yakovlev's former Deputy Governor. The rate of participation in both rounds was less than 30%.

Economy

In 2002 St Petersburg's gross regional product amounted to 367,804.1m. roubles, or 78,907.3 roubles per head.

Industry in St Petersburg, which employed around 20.1% of its work-force in 2003 (compared with the 0.6% engaged in agriculture), consists mainly of mechanical engineering, metal-working and food-processing. Other important areas are ferrous and non-ferrous metallurgy, electricity generation, manufacture of chemicals and petrochemicals, rubber production, light manufacturing, the manufacture of building materials, timber-processing and printing. There is also a significant defence-sector industry. Total industrial production in the city amounted to a value of 293,506m. roubles in 2003. The city is also an important centre for service industries, such as tourism, financial services and leisure activities.

The economically active population of St Petersburg amounted to 2.48m. in 2003, when 4.1% of the work-force were unemployed, the second lowest rate in Russia, after Moscow City. In 2003 the average monthly wage in St Petersburg was 6,467.5 roubles, somewhat higher than the national average. The city budget in 2003 showed a deficit of 1,092.5m. roubles. The city is an important centre of trade: in 2003 external trade comprised some US $2,832.2m. in exports and $5,825.7m. in imports, although this was equivalent to only around 17.7% of the value of Muscovite trade in that year. In 2003 foreign investment in St Petersburg amounted to just $695.8m., compared with the $13,886.9m. attracted by Moscow City. At the end of 2003 there were some 89,900 small businesses registered in the city, less than one-half the number recorded in Moscow City.

Directory

Mayor (Governor and Premier of the City Government): VALENTINA I. MAT-VIYENKO (elected 5 October 2003), 191060 St Petersburg, Smolnyi; tel. (812) 276-45-01; fax (812) 276-18-27; e-mail gov@gov.spb.ru; internet www.gov.spb.ru.

Chairman of the Legislative Assembly: VADIM A. TYULPANOV, 190107 St Petersburg, Isaakiyevskaya pl. 6; tel. (812) 319-99-31; fax (812) 319-90-01; e-mail vtulpanov@assembly.spb.ru; internet www.assembly.spb.ru.

Chief Representative of St Petersburg in the Russian Federation: VITALII M. AZAROV, 123001 Moscow, ul. Spiridonovka 20/1; tel. (495) 290-43-64; fax (495) 203-50-60.

Republic of Kareliya

The Republic of Kareliya is situated in the north-west of Russia, on the edge of the Eastern European Plain. The Republic forms part of the North-Western Federal Okrug and the Northern Economic Area. It is bordered by Finland to the west and by the oblasts of: Murmansk to the north and, beyond the White Sea, to the north-east; Archangel to the east; Vologda to the south-east; and Leningrad to the south. Kareliya contains some 83,000 km (51,540 miles) of waterways, including its major rivers, the Kem and the Vyg, and its numerous lakes (the Ladoga and the Onega being the largest and second largest lakes in Europe, respectively). A canal system 225 km long, the White Sea Canal, connects the Kareliyan port of Belomorsk to St Petersburg. One-half of Kareliya's territory is forested and much of the area on the White Sea coast is marshland. Kareliya occupies an area of 172,400 sq km (66,560 sq miles). According to the census of 9–16 October 2002, the Republic had a total population of 716,281, and a population density of 4.2 per sq km. Some 75.0% of the Republic's population inhabited urban areas. 76.6% of the population were ethnically Russian, 9.2% Kareliyan, 5.2% Belarusian, 2.7% Ukrainian and 2.0% Finnish. The dominant religion among Kareliyans, and in the Republic as a whole, is Orthodox Christianity. The Kareliyan language consists of three dialects of Finnish (Livvi, Karjala and Lyydiki), which are all strongly influenced by Russian. In 1989, however, more than one-half of the ethnically Kareliyan population spoke

Russian as their first language. The capital of Kareliya is at Petrozavodsk, with a population of 266,200, according to provisional results of the 2002 census. Kareliya is included in the time zone GMT+3.

History

Kareliya was an independent, Finnish-dominated state in medieval times. In common with much of present-day Finland, in the 16th century the area came under Swedish hegemony, before being annexed by Russia in 1721. A Kareliyan Labour Commune was formed on 8 June 1920 and became an autonomous republic within the Russian Federation (in the USSR) in July 1923. A Karelo-Finnish SSR (Union Republic), including territory annexed from Finland, was created in 1940. However, part of its territory was ceded to the Russian Federation in 1946; in 1956 Kareliya subsequently resumed the status of an ASSR within the Russian Federation.

The Republic declared sovereignty on 9 August 1990; a republican Constitution was adopted in January 1994. In April elections took place to a new bicameral legislature, the Legislative Assembly (comprising a Chamber of the Republic and a Chamber of Representatives). On 17 May 1998 the hitherto premier, Viktor Stepanov, was narrowly defeated in the second round of direct elections to the premiership (Head of the Republic) by the Mayor of Petrozavodsk, Sergei Katanandov. In December 2001 Stepanov (who had hitherto been widely regarded as the most popular potential challenger to the incumbent premier in the forthcoming elections) was appointed as the Republic's representative to the Federation Council, the upper chamber of the Russian Federal Assembly. Katanandov was re-elected on 28 April 2002, receiving 54% of the votes cast. Non-partisan candidates were elected to a majority of seats in the concurrent legislative elections. With effect from these elections, the republican legislature was reconstituted on a unicameral basis, with the abolition of the Chamber of Representatives.

Economy

The economy of Kareliya is largely based on its timber industry. In 2002 its gross regional product was 41,605.6m. roubles, equivalent to 58,085.6 roubles per head. Its major industrial centres include those at Petrozavodsk, Sortavala and Kem. At the end of 2002 there were 2,105 km of railway lines and 6,674 km of paved roads in the Republic. In the mid-1990s Russia's first privately operated railway was constructed on Kareliya's territory. The Republic is at an important strategic point on Russia's roadways, linking the industrially developed regions of Russia with the major northern port of Murmansk. Kareliya's main port is at Petrozavodsk.

Kareliya's agriculture employed just 4.3% of the work-force in 2003 and generated 2,558m. roubles. The Republic ranks among the leading producers of rosin and turpentine in the Russian Federation. The Republic also has important mineral reserves. Kareliya's main industries, apart from the processing of forestry products, are food-processing, ferrous metallurgy, the production of electrical energy, and the extraction of iron ore and muscovite (mica). Industry engaged some 25.7% of the Republic's labour force in 2003 and generated 38,848m. roubles. The Republic's major enterprise, the Segezha Pulp and Paper Mill (Segezhabumprom), is one of the world's largest pulp and paper manufacturers. In 2002 forestry and the processing of forestry products comprised 45.2% of the territory's industrial production.

The economically active population totalled 399,000 in 2003, when 8.5% of the labour force were unemployed. The average monthly wage in the Republic was

5,692.0 roubles. The republican budget recorded a deficit of 679.5m. roubles in 2003. In that year exports from the Republic were worth US $639.1m., and the value of imports was $180.5m. Foreign investment in Kareliya in 2003 amounted to $34.7m. At the end of 2003 there were 4,000 small businesses registered in the Republic.

Directory

Chairman of the Government (Head of the Republic): SERGEI L. KATANANDOV (elected 17 May 1998, re-elected 28 April 2002), 185028 Kareliya, Petrozavodsk, pr. Lenina 19; tel. (8142) 76-41-41; fax (8142) 76-41-48; e-mail government@karelia .ru; internet www.gov.karelia.ru.

Chairman of the Legislative Assembly: NIKOLAI I. LEVIN, 185610 Kareliya, Petrozavodsk, ul. Kuibysheva 5; tel. (8142) 78-02-95; fax (8142) 78-28-27; e-mail inbox@zsrk.onego.ru; internet www.karelia-zs.ru.

Chief Representative of the Republic of Kareliya in the Russian Federation: ANATOLII A. MARKOV, 101934 Moscow, per. Arkhangelskii 1/555; tel. (495) 207-87-24; fax (495) 208-03-18; e-mail kareliap@rambler.ru.

Head of Petrozavodsk City Administration (Mayor): VIKTOR N. MASLYAKOV, 185620 Kareliya, Petrozavodsk, pr. Lenina 2/501; tel. (8142) 78-35-70; fax (8142) 78-47-53; e-mail admcity@karelia.ru; internet www.petrozavodsk-mo.ru.

Republic of Komi

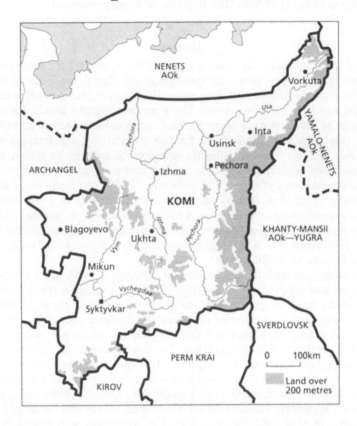

The Republic of Komi is situated in the north-east of European Russia. It forms part of the North-Western Federal Okrug and the Northern Economic Area. Mountains of the Northern, Circumpolar and Polar Urals occupy the eastern part of the Republic. Its major rivers are the Pechora, the Vychegda and the Mezen. Komi is bordered to the north and west by Archangel Oblast (including the Nenets Autonomous Okrug—AOk), and to the east by Tyumen Oblast (including the Khanty-Mansii AOk—Yugra and the Yamalo-Nenets AOk). To the south Komi borders Kirov Oblast, Perm Krai and Sverdlovsk Oblast. Some 90% of its territory is taiga (forested marshland), while the extreme north-east of the Republic lies within the Arctic tundra zone. The Republic occupies an area of 415,900 sq km (160,580 sq miles). According to the census of 9–16 October 2002, it had a population of 1,018,674, and a population density of 2.4 per sq km. Some 75.3% of the population lived in urban areas. 59.6% of the population were ethnically Russian, 25.2% Komi (including 1.2% of the total who stated their ethnicity as Komi-Izhemets), 6.1% Ukrainian, 1.5% Tatar, 1.5% Belarusian and 0.9% German. The predominant religion in the region is Orthodox Christianity, although among the Komi this faith is combined with strong animist traditions. The language of the Komi population, spoken as a native tongue by some 74%, belongs to the Finnic branch of the Uralo-

Altaic family. Komi's capital is at Syktyvkar, which had a population of 230,000, according to the provisional results of the 2002 census. The Republic's second largest city is Ukhta (103,500). The Republic of Komi is included in the time zone GMT+3.

History

The Komi (known historically as the Zyryans or the Permyaks) are descended from inhabitants of the river basins of the Volga, the Kama, the Pechora and the Vychegda. From the 12th century Russian settlers began to inhabit territory along the Vychegda, and later the Vym, rivers. The Vym subsequently acquired a strategic significance as the main route along which Russian colonists advanced to Siberia, and Ust-Sysolsk (now Syktyvkar), the territory's oldest city, was founded in 1586. The number of Slavs increased after the territory was annexed by Russia in 1478. The region soon acquired importance as the centre of mining and metallurgy, following the discovery of copper and silver ores. In 1697 petroleum was discovered in the territory; the first refinery was built in the territory in 1745. The Komi exploited important trade routes between Archangel and Siberia, trading in fish, furs and game animals, while coal, timber, iron ore and paper became significant prior to the 1917 revolutions. The Komi Autonomous Oblast was established on 22 August 1921 and became an ASSR in 1931.

The territory declared its sovereignty on 30 August 1990. A new republican Constitution was adopted on 17 February 1994, establishing a quasi-presidential premier at the head of government and a State Council as the legislature. The Republic repudiated its declaration of sovereignty in September 2001, following a ruling by the federal Supreme Court that over one-half of the provision's declarations were in contravention of federal law. The republican presidential election, held on 16 December, was won by Vladimir Torlopov, hitherto Chairman of the republican legislature, who narrowly defeated the incumbent, Yurii Spiridonov. Torlopov, an ethnic Komi, received the support of the liberal Yabloko party, whereas Spiridonov's supporters included the pro-Government Unity and Fatherland-United Russia party. In May 2002 Torlopov signed an agreement with federal President Vladimir Putin annulling a power-sharing treaty signed by the federal and republican authorities in March 1996. A new State Council, elected in March 2003, was reportedly dominated by representatives of business interests, particularly the energy industry.

Economy

The Republic of Komi is Russia's second largest fuel and energy base. Apart from a wealth of natural resources, it is strategically placed close to many of Russia's major industrial centres and has a well-developed transport network. In 2002 gross regional product in the Republic amounted to 93,153.2m. roubles, equivalent to 91,445.5 roubles per head—one of the highest figures in Russia. Komi's major industrial centres are at Syktyvkar, Ukhta and Sosnogorsk. At the end of 2002 the Republic contained 1,692 km of railway lines and 5,447 km of paved roads. In September 2002 Russia's first privately constructed railway line was opened by the domestic metals producer SUAL Holding, providing access to the Middle-Timan bauxite reserves.

Komi's agriculture, which employed just 3.6% of the work-force and generated 4,109m. roubles in 2003, consists principally of animal husbandry, especially reindeer-breeding. Ore-mining was developing from the mid-1990s: the Republic contained the country's largest reserves of bauxite, titanium, manganese and chromium ore, and also has significant reserves of petroleum and natural gas. Total industrial production, which was based on the production and processing of petroleum and natural gas, the production of coal and electrical energy, and the processing of forestry products, was worth 71,156m. roubles in 2003, when the sector employed 22.3% of the work-force. The Republic contains the Vorga-shorskaya coal mine, the largest in Europe.

In 2003 the economically active population numbered 607,000, and 11.9% of the labour force were unemployed. In 2003 the average monthly wage in the Republic was relatively high, at 7,884.2 roubles. The budgetary deficit amounted to some 942.6m. roubles. In 2003 external trade comprised US $1,284.5m. in exports and $173.8m. in imports. Foreign investment in Komi was substantial in the late 1990s, amounting to $218.1m. in 1998, although the level of investment had declined to $89.9m. by 2003. From the mid-1990s a number of joint ventures were established in Komi, and important foreign investors included the Finnish company Fortum Oil and Gas Oy, which established SeverTEK, a joint venture with LUKoil, the principal natural resources company operating in the Republic. In March 2002 the South African company Anglo-American purchased a majority stake in the Republic's leading paper manufacturer, Syktyvkar Forest Enterprise. At the end of 2003 there were 3,600 small businesses registered in the Republic.

Directory

Chairman of the Government (Head of the Republic): VLADIMIR A. TORLOPOV (elected 16 December 2001), 167000 Komi, Syktyvkar, ul. Kommunisticheskaya 9; tel. (8212) 28-51-05; fax (8212) 21-43-84; e-mail glava@rkomi.ru; internet www .rkomi.ru.

Chairman of the State Council: IVAN YE. KULAKOV, 167000 Komi, Syktyvkar, ul. Kommunisticheskaya 8; tel. (8212) 28-55-08; fax (8212) 42-44-90; internet www .rkomi.ru/gossov/gossovet/gs_rk.html.

Chief Representative of the Republic of Komi in the Russian Federation: STEPAN V. IGNATOV, 123367 Moscow, Volokolamskoye shosse 62; tel. (495) 490-44-33; fax (495) 490-51-57.

Head of Syktyvkar City Administration: SERGEI M. KATUNIN, 167000 Komi, Syktyvkar, ul. Babushkina 22; tel. (8212) 29-44-71; fax (8212) 24-17-23; e-mail katunin@syktyvkar.komi.com; internet www.syktyvkar.komi.com.

Archangel Oblast

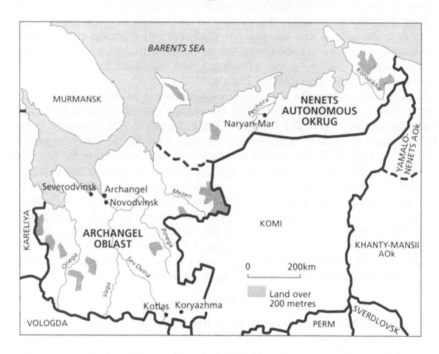

Archangel Oblast is situated in the north of the Eastern European Plain. It lies on the White, Barents and Kara Seas (parts of the Arctic Ocean) and includes the northern archipelago of Zemlya Frantsa-Iosifa and the Novaya Zemlya islands. The Oblast forms part of the North-Western Federal Okrug and the Northern Economic Area. In the north-east the Nenets Autonomous Okrug (AOk), a constituent part of the Oblast, runs eastwards along the coast to end in a short border with the Yamalo-Nenets AOk (within Tyumen Oblast). The Republic of Komi lies to the east of the Oblast. Kirov and Vologda Oblasts form the southern border and the Republic of Kareliya lies to the west. North-west, across the White Sea, lie the Kola Peninsula and Murmansk Oblast, while to the north there is access to the Barents Sea. The Oblast contains several large rivers (including the Onega, the Severnaya Dvina and the Pechora) and some 2,500 lakes. Some two-fifths of its entire area is forested and almost one-quarter classed as reindeer pasture. The Oblast occupies an area of 587,400 sq km (226,800 sq miles). It spans three climatic zones—arctic, sub-arctic and continental. According to the census of 9–16 October 2002, the Oblast's total population was 1,336,539 and its population density stood at 2.3 per sq km; some 74.8% of the population lived in urban areas. 94.2% of the population were ethnically Russian, 2.1% were Ukrainian and 0.8% were Belarusian. Archangel Oblast's administrative centre is at Archangel (Arkhangelsk), which had 355,500 inhabitants, according to provisional census results. The Oblast's second city is Severodvinsk (201,500). Archangel Oblast is included in the time zone GMT+3.

History

The city of Archangel was founded in the 16th century, to further Muscovite trade. It was the first Russian seaport and the country's main one until the building of St Petersburg in 1703. The port played a major role in the attack by the Entente fleet (British and French navies) against the Red Army in 1918, and was an important route for supplies from the Allied Powers during the Second World War. Archangel Oblast was founded on 23 September 1937.

On 13 October 1993 the Archangel Regional Soviet transferred its responsibilities to the Regional Administration. Communist candidates initially formed the largest single group elected to the Regional Assembly of Deputies, although supporters of the federal Government and liberal reformists also enjoyed some support in the cities. In February 1996 the regional Governor appointed in September 1991, Pavel Balakshin, was dismissed, following the opening of a judicial enquiry into alleged corrupt practices. His successor, Anatolii Yefremov (appointed in March 1996), was confirmed as Governor by his popular election to the post in December 1997, and by his re-election in December 2000.

Yefremov contested a third term in the gubernatorial election on 14 March 2004. His perceived main rival, State Duma deputy Vladimir Krupchak, had withdrawn his candidacy on 2 March (allegedly in response to pressure from the federal Government). In the event, however, Yefremov was defeated in the 'run-off' election, held on 28 March, by dairy owner Nikolai Kiselev, who received 75.1% of the votes cast.

Economy

All figures in this survey incorporate data for the Nenets AOk, which is also treated separately. Archangel Oblast's gross regional product totalled 84,681.0m. roubles in 2002, equivalent to 63,358.4 roubles per head. The Oblast's main industrial centres are at Archangel, Severodvinsk, Novodvinsk and, in the south-east, Kotlas. At the end of 2002 there were 1,764 km of railways and 7,345 km of paved roads on the Oblast's territory. Its main ports are Archangel, Onega, Mezen and, in the Nenets AOk, Naryan-Mar.

The Oblast's agriculture, which employed just 5.2% of the labour force and generated 5,418m. roubles in 2003, consists mainly of potato and vegetable production, animal husbandry (livestock and reindeer) and hunting. The Oblast's industry, which employed 26.7% of the working population and generated 74,965m. roubles in 2003, is based on timber and timber-processing and wood-working (which accounted for 44.5% of industrial production in 2002). Other important areas of industry are the extraction of minerals (in particular, bauxite), petroleum and natural gas, electrical energy, mechanical engineering and metal-working, and the processing of fish products. Diamonds are also mined in the Oblast, although repeated licensing problems and legal disputes have inhibited the growth of the sector.

The Oblast's economically active population amounted to 763,000 in 2003, when 9.9% of the region's labour force were unemployed. The average monthly wage was 6,242.6m. roubles. In 2003 the Oblast recorded a budgetary deficit of 500.9m. roubles. External trade in that year comprised $754.0m. in exports and $115.6m. in imports. Total foreign investment amounted to $234.3m. in 2003. At the end of 2003 there were 4,600 small businesses registered in the Oblast.

Directory

Head of the Regional Administration (Governor): NIKOLAI I. KISELEV (elected 28 March 2004), 163061 Archangel, pr. Troitskii 49; tel. (8182) 65-30-41; fax (8182) 64-85-97; internet www.arkhadm.gov.ru.

Chairman of the Regional Assembly of Deputies: VITALII S. FORTYGIN, 163061 Archangel, pl. Lenina 1; tel. (8182) 64-66-81; fax (8182) 64-66-30; e-mail ac@aosd .ru.

Chief Representative of Archangel Oblast in the Russian Federation: IGOR T. ZOLOYEV, 163000 Moscow, ul. M. Dmitrovka 3/10/222; tel. (495) 299-74-86; fax (495) 209-45-94; e-mail arxpred@rambler.ru.

Head of Archangel City Administration (Mayor): ALEKSANDR DONSKOI, 163061 Archangel, pl. Lenina 5; tel. (8182) 65-64-84; fax (8182) 65-20-71; e-mail mail@ arhcity.ru; internet www.arhcity.ru.

Kaliningrad Oblast

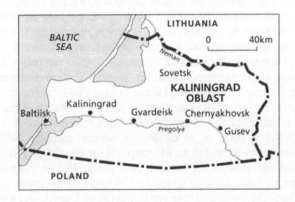

Kaliningrad Oblast forms the westernmost part of the Russian Federation, being an exclave separated from the rest of the country by Lithuania (which borders it to the north and east) and Belarus. Poland lies to the south. The Oblast falls within the North-Western Federal Okrug and is sometimes included in the North-Western Economic Area. The city of Kaliningrad is sited at the mouth of the River Pregolya, where it flows into the Vistula Lagoon, an inlet of the Baltic Sea. The other main river is the Neman. The Oblast occupies 15,100 sq km (5,830 sq miles), of which 13,300 sq km are dry land, the rest of its territory comprising the freshwater Curonian Lagoon, in the north-east, and the Vistula Lagoon. The coastline is 140 km (87 miles) long. According to the census of 9–16 October 2002, it had a total population of 955,281 and its population density was 63.2 per sq km. Some 77.7% of the population inhabited urban areas. 82.4% of the population were ethnically Russian, 5.3% Belarusian, 4.9% Ukrainian, 1.5% Lithuanian, 0.9% Armenian and 0.9% German. The Oblast's administrative centre is at Kaliningrad, which had a population of 430,300, according to provisional census results. The Oblast is included in the time zone GMT+2.

History

The city of Kaliningrad was founded in 1255, as Königsberg, during German expansion eastwards. The chief city of East Prussia, it was the original royal capital of the Hohenzollerns (from 1871 the German emperors). After the Second World War it was annexed by the USSR and received its current name (1945). Most of the German population was deported and the city almost completely destroyed and rebuilt. On 7 April 1946 the region became an administrative-political unit of the Russian Federation.

In mid-1993 Kaliningrad Oblast requested the status of a republic, a petition refused by the federal authorities. On 15 October the Regional Soviet was disbanded by the head of the regional Administration for failing to support the state presidency's struggle against the federal parliament. A regional Duma was later formed. In January 1996 Yurii Matochkin was one of the first oblast governors to sign a power-sharing agreement with the federal Government. Leonid Gorbenko, an independent candidate, was elected Governor in October.

In 1998 a proposal that the region be awarded the status of an autonomous Russian Baltic republic was submitted to the Sovet Federatsii (Federation Council). However, Gorbenko opposed plans for greater autonomy, instead supporting the growth of closer ties with Belarus. In gubernatorial elections held in November 2000, Gorbenko was defeated by Adm. Vladimir Yegorov, the former Commander of the Baltic Fleet. Yegorov was regarded as an ally of the federal President Vladimir Putin, and was elected largely on the basis of his anti-corruption campaign. In 2002, as the European Union (EU) prepared to admit several Eastern European countries, including neighbouring Lithuania and Poland in May 2004, the status of Kaliningrad became an increasing source of contention; in particular, Russia initially objected to proposals that residents of Kaliningrad would require visas to travel to metropolitan Russia. In November 2002, at an EU-Russia summit meeting, held in Brussels, Belgium, Russia finally agreed to an EU proposal for simplified visa arrangements; the new regulations took effect from 1 July 2003. In late August 2005 Putin nominated Georgii Boos, hitherto a Deputy Chairman of the lower chamber of the federal legislature, the Gosudarstvennaya Duma (State Duma), and a member of the pro-Government Unity and Fatherland-United Russia party, to replace Yegorov as Governor. On 16 September the regional Duma voted to confirm Boos's nomination, which took effect from 19 November, following the expiry of Yegorov's term of office.

Economy

Kaliningrad Oblast is noted for containing more than 90% of the world's reserves of amber. Within Russia it also became noted for its reputedly flourishing parallel ('black') market, despite the establishment of a 'free trade zone' in the Oblast in 1991, with federal officials suggesting in 1999 that the region had become a major transhipment point for illegal drugs. Kaliningrad also suffers from a military and industrial legacy of severe pollution. In 2002 its official gross regional product totalled 41,095.6m. roubles, or 43,019.4 roubles per head. Its main industrial centres are at Kaliningrad, Gusev and Sovetsk. There are rail services to Lithuania and Poland, and there were 618 km of railways on the Oblast's territory at the end of 2002. At that time Kaliningrad Oblast's road network consisted of 4,600 km of paved roads. Its main ports are at Kaliningrad and Baltiisk.

Kaliningrad Oblast's agricultural sector, which employed 10.2% of its work-force and generated 5,810m. roubles in 2003, consists mainly of animal husbandry, including fur farming, and vegetable growing and fishing. The Oblast has substantial reserves of petroleum (around 275m. metric tons), more than 2,500m. cu m in peat deposits and 50m. tons of coal. The industrial sector employed 18.9% of its working population and generated 34,872m. roubles in 2003. The region's main industries are mechanical engineering and metal-working, the processing of fishing and forestry products, electrical energy, and the production and processing of amber. In 2002 some 745,000 tons of petroleum were extracted. A plant to construct German BMW automobiles for the Russian market opened in 1999. The continuing strategic geopolitical situation of Kaliningrad Oblast meant that demilitarization proceeded at a much slower pace than it did elsewhere in the former USSR; in 1998 there were still around 200,000 members of military units in the Oblast. The coastal town of Svetlogorsk (formerly Rauschen) is an important tourist resort.

The economically active population numbered 502,000 in 2003, when some 7.5% of the labour force were unemployed, compared with 15.4% in 2000. The average monthly wage was 4,743.3 roubles in 2003. The 2003 regional budget recorded a deficit of 394.8m. roubles. In the mid-2000s the region experienced severe problems related to the prevalence of organized crime and ill-health, with the rate of HIV infection a particular source of concern. Concern was also expressed at the additional expenses resulting from new requirements for documentation for the transit of goods between Kaliningrad and metropolitan Russia introduced in 2003 (see above); some reports suggested that transhipment costs for some goods had increased by as much as 25%. Foreign investment totalled US $55.9m. in 2003, when export trade amounted to $470.7m., and imports were worth $2,097.8m. At the end of 2003 there were 5,600 small businesses registered in the Oblast.

Directory

Head of the Regional Administration (Governor): GEORGII V. BOOS (appointment confirmed 16 September 2005; assumed office 19 November), 236007 Kaliningrad, ul. D. Donskogo 1; tel. (401) 259-90-01; fax (401) 246-38-62; internet www.gov .kaliningrad.ru.

Chairman of the Regional Duma: VLADIMIR A. NIKITIN, 236000 Kaliningrad, ul. Kirova 17; tel. (401) 222-84-39; fax (401) 222-84-82; e-mail nikitin@duma .kaliningrad.org; internet duma.kaliningrad.org.

Chief Representative of Kaliningrad Oblast in the Russian Federation: YEVGENII I. IZOTOV, 123242 Moscow, ul. M. Krasnaya Presnya 7; tel. (495) 258-44-01; fax (495) 292-12-87; e-mail rngs@online.ru.

Head of Kaliningrad City Administration (Mayor): YURII A. SAVENKO, 236040 Kaliningrad, ul. Pobedy 1; tel. (401) 221-14-82; fax (401) 221-16-77; e-mail cityhall@klgd.ru; internet www.klgd.ru.

Leningrad Oblast

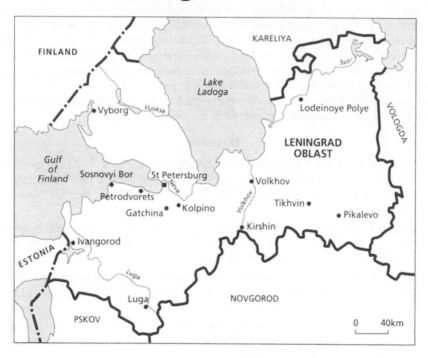

Leningrad Oblast is situated in the north-west of the Eastern European Plain. It lies on the Gulf of Finland, an inlet of the Baltic Sea, and forms part of the North-Western Federal Okrug and the North-Western Economic Area. The Republic of Kareliya lies to the north and the oblasts of Vologda to the east and Novgorod and Pskov to the south. There is an international border with Estonia to the west and with Finland to the north-west. Two-thirds of the Oblast are forested. The Oblast occupies 85,300 sq km (32,935 sq miles). According to the census of 9–16 October 2002, its total population was 1,669,205, giving a population density of 19.6 per sq km, and some 66.4% of the population of the Oblast inhabited urban areas. Some 89.6% of the population were ethnically Russian, 2.5% Ukrainian and 1.6% Belarusian. The administrative centre is St Petersburg, which does not itself comprise part of the Oblast. The largest city within the Oblast is Gatchina (with an estimated population of 82,200 at 1 January 2002). Leningrad Oblast is included in the time zone GMT+3.

History

The city of St Petersburg (known as Petrograd in 1914–24 and Leningrad until 1991) was built in 1703. Leningrad Oblast, which was formed on 1 August 1927, was heavily industrialized during the Soviet period, particularly during 1926–40. The region did not change its name when the city reverted to the name of St Petersburg in October 1991.

Gubernatorial elections, held in late 1996, were won by an independent candidate, Vladimir Gustov. On 24 September 1998 the federal President, Boris Yeltsin, approved a proposal to merge the Oblast with St Petersburg city. Gustov resigned to take up the position of a Deputy Chairman in the federal Government in September 1998, and his replacement, Valerii Serdyukov, confirmed his position on 5 September 1999, by securing 30% of the votes cast in an election contested by 16 candidates. A power-sharing agreement signed by the federal and regional authorities in 1996 was annulled in April 2002. In February 2003 the regional legislature approved an extension to the gubernatorial term of office from four to five years, to take effect from the forthcoming elections. Serdyukov was re-elected Governor on 21 September 2003, receiving 56.8% of the votes cast. Less than 30% of the electorate participated in the elections.

Economy

Leningrad Oblast's gross regional product amounted to 101,774.7m. roubles in 2002, equivalent to 60,972.0 roubles per head. A new port opened at Primorsk in December 2001, as part of Russia's Baltic Pipeline System, to facilitate the transportation of petroleum. In 2005 it was announced that a further port under construction, at Ust-Luga, was eventually to form part of a special economic zone intended to attract foreign investment. In 2002 the region contained 2,829 km of railway track (of which 1,352 km were electrified in 1999) and 10,579 km of paved roads.

The Oblast's agricultural sector employed 11.1% of the working population and generated 23,279m. roubles in 2003. The region's timber reserves are estimated to cover 6.1m. ha. Its major industries are the processing of forestry and agricultural products, petroleum-refining and the production of electrical energy. In 2003 the industrial sector employed 25.6% of the Oblast's work-force, and generated 127,445m. roubles.

The economically active population numbered 873,000 in 2003, when 8.7% of the labour force were unemployed. The average monthly wage was 5,466.1 roubles in 2003. In that year the budget showed a deficit of 875.2m. roubles. In 2003 external trade comprised US $2,920.5m. in exports and $1,390.5m. in imports. Foreign investment amounted to $239.7m. in that year. At the end of 2003 there were 12,200 small businesses registered in the Oblast.

Directory

Head of the Regional Administration (Governor): VALERII P. SERDYUKOV (elected 5 September 1999, re-elected 21 September 2003), 193311 St Petersburg, Suvorovskii pr. 67; tel. (812) 274-35-63; fax (812) 274-67-33; internet www.lenobl.ru.

Chairman of the Regional Legislative Assembly: KIRILL V. POLYAKOV, 193311 St Petersburg, Suvorovskii pr. 67; tel. (812) 274-68-73; fax (812) 274-85-39; e-mail mail@lenoblzaks.ru; internet www.lenoblzaks.ru.

Chief Representative of Leningrad Oblast in the Russian Federation: ALEKSEI I. AKULOV, 119019 Moscow, ul. Novyi Arbat 15/1/1604; tel. (495) 291-33-55; e-mail plorf@mail.ru.

Murmansk Oblast

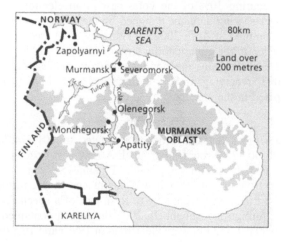

Murmansk Oblast occupies the Kola Peninsula, neighbouring the Barents Sea to the north and the White Sea to the south-east. It forms part of the North-Western Federal Okrug and the Northern Economic Area. There are international borders with Norway and Finland to the west; the Russian federal subject of Kareliya lies to the south. Much of the territory lies within the Arctic Circle. The Oblast covers 144,900 sq km (55,930 sq miles). The climate is severe and changeable, influenced by cold fronts from the Arctic and warm, moist weather from the Atlantic. According to the census of 9–16 October 2002, the population of Murmansk Oblast was 892,534 and the population density 6.2 per sq km. Some 92.2% of the population inhabited urban areas. 85.2% of the population were ethnically Russian, 6.4% Ukrainian, 2.3% Belarusian and 0.9% Tatar. Its administrative centre is at Murmansk, with a population of 336,700, according to provisional census results. Murmansk Oblast is included in the time zone GMT+3.

History

The city of Romanov-on-Murman was founded in 1916. After the Bolshevik Revolution of 1917 (following which the city was renamed Murmansk), the region was a centre of anti-communist resistance until a peace treaty was signed with the Soviet Government on 13 March 1920. Murmansk Oblast was formed on 28 May 1938. The development of industry in the region, particularly after the Second World War, resulted in a steady increase in population until the late 1950s. Yurii Yevdokimov, a candidate favoured by the former Chairman of the National Security Council, Gen. (retd) Aleksandr Lebed, was elected in the Oblast's first direct poll to the governorship, held in November 1996. A power-sharing agreement was signed between the federal and regional authorities in November 1997. On 26 March 2000 Yevdokimov was re-elected Governor. On 14 March 2004 Yevdomikov was re-elected for a third term with 77.0% of the votes cast.

Economy

In 2002 Murmansk Oblast's gross regional product stood at 68,005.9m. roubles, or 76,194.2 roubles per head. The Oblast's principal industrial centres are at Murmansk, Zapolyarnyi and Apatity. At the end of 2002 there were 891 km of railway track in the region and 2,472 km of paved roads. The port at Murmansk is Russia's sole all-weather Northern port, through which some 12m. metric tons of cargo pass every year. This is also the base for the world's only nuclear ice-breaker fleet, the Northern Fleet. There is an international airport at Murmansk.

The Oblast's agricultural sector, which employed just 1.7% of the work-force and generated 1,322m. roubles in 2003, consists mainly of fishing (the region produces 45% of the country's fish supplies), animal husbandry (livestock and reindeer) and vegetable production. The territory is rich in natural resources, including phosphates, iron ore and rare and non-ferrous metals. In 1985 the Shtokmanovsk gas-condensate deposit, the world's largest, was opened on the continental shelf of the Barents Sea. The region produces all of Russia's apatites, over 40% of its nickel, some 14% of its refined copper and about 11% of its concentrates of iron. In 2003 industry engaged 25.3% of the work-force and generated 70,851m. roubles. The major industries are the production and enrichment of ores and ferrous metals, ore-mining, ferrous metallurgy, chemicals and petrochemicals, the production of electricity and food-processing. In 1999 LUKoil, the domestic petroleum producer, signed an agreement which made Murmansk a base for exploration of the Barents Sea, in association with the natural gas producer, Gazprom. In 2002 LUKoil, in association with Tyumen Oil Co (TNK—now TNK-BP), Sibneft and Yukos, announced that they were to develop a deep-sea petroleum terminal in Murmansk and connecting pipelines, at a projected cost of some US \$4,500m., in an attempt to increase exports. In 2004 Gazprom announced plans to establish a specialized company and a liquefying plant in Murmansk by the end of the year, with the intention of increasing exports of liquefied natural gas, particularly to the USA.

In 2003 the region's economically active population numbered some 572,000. Unemployment declined from the late 1990s, from 21.1% of the labour force in 1998, to 10.0% in 2003. In 2003 the average monthly wage in the Oblast was some 8,645.5 roubles, one of the highest in the Federation. The budget recorded a deficit of 1,276.2m. roubles. The Oblast's major exports are non-ferrous metals, fish products and apatite concentrate. In 2003 exports amounted to US \$709.6m., and imports were worth \$177.0m. Foreign investment totalled \$21.6m. At the end of 2003 there were 4,600 small businesses registered in the Oblast.

Directory

Head of the Regional Administration (Governor): YURII A. YEVDOKIMOV (elected November 1996, re-elected 26 March 2000 and 14 March 2004), 183006 Murmansk, pr. Lenina 75; tel. (8152) 48-62-01; fax (8152) 47-65-40; e-mail evdokimov@ murman.ru; internet gov.murman.ru.

Chairman of the Regional Duma: PAVEL A. SAZHINOV, 183016 Murmansk, ul. S. Perovskoi 2; tel. (8152) 45-36-72; fax (8152) 45-97-79; e-mail murduma@com.mels .ru; internet 2004.murman.ru/power/legislature/index.shtml.

Chief Representative of Murmansk Oblast in the Russian Federation: RENAT I. KARCHAA, 103851 Moscow, ul. B. Nikitskaya 12; tel. (495) 229-69-77; fax (495) 229-53-51.

Head of Murmansk City Administration (Mayor): MIKHAIL I. SAVCHENKO, 183006 Murmansk, pr. Lenina 75; tel. (8152) 45-81-60; fax (8152) 45-93-62.

Novgorod Oblast

Novgorod Oblast is situated in the north-west of the Eastern European Plain, some 500 km north-west of Moscow and 180 km south of St Petersburg. It forms part of the North-Western Federal Okrug and the North-Western Economic Area. Tver Oblast lies to the south-east, Pskov Oblast to the south-west and Leningrad and Vologda Oblasts to the north. Just over two-fifths of its territory is forested. The Oblast covers an area of 55,300 sq km (21,350 sq miles). According to the census of 9–16 October 2002, the population of the Oblast was 694,355 and its population density was 12.5 per sq km. 69.9% of the population lived in urban areas. 93.9% of the population were ethnically Russian, 1.5% were Ukrainian and 0.8% were Belarusian. The region's administrative centre is at Velikii (Great) Novgorod (also known simply as Novgorod), which lies on the River Volkhov, some 6 km from Lake Ilmen (the city had a population of some 217,200, according to provisional census results). Novgorod Oblast is located in the time zone GMT+3.

History

One of the oldest Russian cities, Velikii Novgorod remained a powerful principality after the dissolution of Kyivan (Kievan) Rus. In 1478 Ivan III ('the Great'), prince of Muscovy and the first Tsar of All Russia, destroyed the Republic of Novgorod, a polity sometimes used as evidence for the rather spurious claim of a democratic tradition in Russia. The wealth and importance of the city, based on trade, declined after the foundation of St Petersburg in the early 18th century. Novgorod Oblast was formed on 5 July 1944.

In the mid-1990s the region displayed a relatively high level of support for reformists and centrists. The Oblast was permitted gubernatorial elections in December 1995, which were won by the pro-Yeltsin incumbent appointed in October 1991, Mikhail Prusak. Prusak was re-elected for a further term of office on 5 September 1999, with approximately 90% of the votes cast. He combined demands for regional governors to be appointed rather than elected, and even for the end of direct elections to the federal presidency, with support for the purported (historical)

'Novgorod model' of federalism, property rights and subsidiarity. (When appointed Governors became the norm, from late 2004, Prusak was, however, critical of aspects of the system of nomination and approval of appointees, calling for an eventual restoration of the process of electing regional leaders, as well as for an extension in the term of office of the federal President from four to seven years.) Prusak was re-elected Governor on 7 September 2003, receiving 78.7% of the votes cast.

Economy

In 2002 Novgorod Oblast's gross regional product amounted to 31,858.2m. roubles, equivalent to 45,881.7 roubles per head. The Oblast's major industrial centres are at Velikii Novgorod and Staraya Russa (a resort town famous for its mineral and radon springs). The major Moscow–St Petersburg road and rail routes pass through the region. At the end of 2002 there were 1,145 km of railways and 8,760 km of paved roads on the Oblast's territory.

The region's agriculture, which employed just 9.2% of the work-force and generated 6,324m. roubles in 2003, consists mainly of flax production and animal husbandry. Its major natural resource is timber: in the late 1990s some 2.5m. cu m were produced annually. The region's major industries include mechanical engineering and metal-working, chemicals and petrochemicals, wood-working, the processing of forestry and agricultural products, and electricity production. The industrial sector employed 26.5% of the working population in 2003, and generated 36,098m. roubles. Velikii Novgorod is an important tourist destination, attracting around 1m. visitors annually.

The economically active population totalled 371,000 in 2003, when 5.0% of the labour force were unemployed. Those in employment earned an average wage of 4,393.4 roubles per month. In that year the regional budget showed a deficit of 408.2m. roubles and the external trade of the Oblast comprised US $428.7m. in exports and $227.2m. in imports. In 2003 total foreign investment in the region amounted to some $212.8m. At the end of 2003 there were 2,600 small businesses registered in the Oblast.

Directory

Head of the Regional Administration (Governor): MIKHAIL M. PRUSAK (appointed 24 October 1991, elected 17 December 1995, re-elected 5 September 1999 and 7 September 2003), 173005 Novgorod obl., Velikii Novgorod, Sofiiskaya pl. 1; tel. (8162) 27-47-79; fax (8162) 13-13-30; e-mail infoserv@niac.natm.ru; internet region.adm.nov.ru.

Chairman of the Regional Duma: ANATOLII A. BOITSEV, 173005 Novgorod obl., Velikii Novgorod, Sofiiskaya pl. 1; tel. (8162) 27-47-79; fax (8162) 13-25-14; internet duma.niac.ru.

Chief Representative of Novogorod Oblast in the Russian Federation: VLADIMIR N. PODOPRIGORA, 127006 Moscow, ul. M. Dmitrovka 3/219–220; fax (495) 299-40-04.

Head of Velikii Novgorod City Administration (Mayor): NIKOLAI I. GRAZHDANKIN, 173007 Novgorod obl., Velikii Novgorod, ul. B. Vasilyevskaya 4; tel. (81622) 77-25-40; fax (8162) 13-25-99; e-mail mayor@adm.nov.ru; internet www.adm.nov.ru.

Pskov Oblast

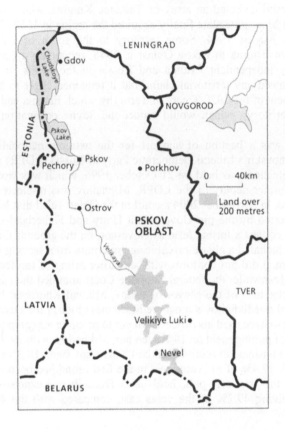

Pskov Oblast is situated on the Eastern European Plain. The Oblast forms part of the North-Western Federal Okrug and the North-Western Economic Area. It has international borders with Belarus to the south and Latvia and Estonia to the west. (By the mid-2000s there had still been no formal ratification of the border delimitations with Estonia or Latvia.) There are borders with the oblasts of: Smolensk in the south-east; Tver and Novgorod in the east; and Leningrad in the north-east. Around two-fifths of the Oblast's territory are forested. On its border with Estonia lie the Pskov (Pihkva) and Chudskoye (Peipsi) lakes. Pskov Oblast covers an area of 55,300 sq km (21,350 sq miles). According to the census of 9–16 October 2002, the population numbered 760,810 and the population density was 13.8 per sq km; some 66.1% of inhabitants lived in urban areas. Some 94.3% of the territory's inhabitants were ethnically Russian, 1.6% were Ukrainian and 1.3% were Belarusian. The Oblast's administrative centre is at Pskov, which had a population of 202,700 in October 2002, according to provisional census results. The second largest city is Velikiye Luki (105,000). Pskov Oblast is included in the time zone GMT+3.

History

Pskov city was founded in 903, and in 1242 was the area in which Muscovite Prince Aleksandr Nevskii defeated an army of Teutonic Knights, who sought to expand eastwards. The Muscovite state finally acquired the region in 1510. The Oblast was created on 23 August 1944. Some territory to the south of Lake Pskov was transferred from Estonia to Pskov Oblast in 1945, remaining a cause for dispute between newly independent Estonia and Russia in the 1990s. In 1995 Estonia formally renounced any territorial claim, but it remained eager to secure Russian acknowledgement of the 1920 Treaty of Tartu (by which Estonia had been awarded the disputed territory), which would render the Soviet occupation of the Baltic republic illegal.

The Oblast was a bastion of support for the extreme nationalist policies of Vladimir Zhirinovskii's Liberal Democratic Party of Russia (LDPR) in the 1990s; a gubernatorial election was held on 21 October 1996, which was won by Yevgenii Mikhailov, a former deputy of the LDPR. Mikhailov was re-elected Governor in November 2000. In November 2004 a court in the Oblast ruled that Mikhailov (who was now supported by the pro-Government Unity and Fatherland-United Russia) was eligible to contest a further term as Governor, on the grounds that the Oblast's charter (which included a clause prohibiting governors from serving more than two consecutive terms) did not conform with an earlier ruling of the federal Constitutional Court. Meanwhile, the federal Supreme Court annulled the candidacy in the gubernatorial elections of the Mayor of Pskov, Mikhail Khoronen (who had been widely regarded as Mikhailov's most credible competitor in the elections), after he had been found to have used his office as Mayor to promote his campaign. Following the first round of polling, held on 14 November, Mikhailov, with 29.7% of the votes cast, and a local business executive, Mikhail Kuznetsov (with 18.3%), progressed to a second round; 17.4% of the votes cast in the first round had been cast against all candidates. In the 'run-off' poll, held on 5 December, Kuznetsov was elected Governor, receiving 49.2% of the votes cast, compared with the 41.7% won by Mikhailov.

Economy

In 2002 Pskov Oblast's gross regional product amounted to 24,630.2m. roubles, equivalent to 32,373.7 roubles per head—the lowest figure in the North-Western Federal Okrug. The Oblast's principal industrial centres are at Pskov and Velikiye Luki. At the end of 2002 there were 1,092 km of railway track in the region and 9,975 km of paved roads. There is an international airport at Pskov.

Agricultural activity, which employed 16.5% of the work-force and generated 6,811m. roubles in 2003, consists mainly of animal husbandry and the production of flax. A major project to improve the agricultural infrastructure of the region was implemented in the mid-1990s. Fishing is an important source of income in the north of the territory. The region's major industries are the production of electricity, mechanical engineering and metal-working, and food-processing. Industry employed 19.6% of the working population in 2003, and generated 18,296m. roubles.

Pskov Oblast's economically active population numbered 375,000 in 2003, when 8.1% of the labour force were unemployed. Those in employment earned, on average, 3,762.0 roubles per month, reflecting Pskov's status as one of the poorer areas of the Russian Federation. There was a budgetary deficit of 519.8m. roubles.

In that year external trade amounted to a value of just US $146.5m. in exports and $208.6m. in imports, while foreign investment in the region totalled just $6.2m. At the end of 2003 some 4,600 small businesses were registered in the Oblast.

Directory

Head of the Regional Administration (Governor): MIKHAIL V. KUZNETSOV (elected 5 December 2004), 180001 Pskov, ul. Nekrasova 23; tel. (8122) 16-92-89; fax (8122) 16-03-90; e-mail glava@obladmin.pskov.ru; internet www.pskov.ru.

Chairman of the Regional Assembly of Deputies: BORIS G. POLOZOV, 180001 Pskov, ul. Nekrasova 23; tel. (8122) 16-24-44; fax (8122) 16-00-51; internet www .pskov.ru/ru/authority/obl_sobranie.

Chief Representative of Pskov Oblast in the Russian Federation: IGOR P. NOVOSELOV, 109013 Moscow, ul. Nikolskaya 10/2; tel. (495) 928-84-43; fax (495) 928-07-95.

Head of Pskov City Administration (Mayor): MIKHAIL YA. KHORONEN, 180000 Pskov, ul. Nekrasova 22; tel. (8122) 16-26-67; internet gorodpskov.ru.

Vologda Oblast

Vologda Oblast is situated in the north-west of the Eastern European Plain. It forms part of the North-Western Federal Okrug and the Northern Economic Area. It has a short border, in the north-west, with the Republic of Kareliya, which includes the southern tip of Lake Onega. Onega also forms the northern end of a border with Leningrad Oblast, which lies to the west of Vologda. Novgorod Oblast lies to the south-west and Tver, Yaroslavl and Kostroma Oblasts to the south. Kirov Oblast lies to the east and Archangel Oblast to the north. Vologda Oblast occupies 145,700 sq km (56,250 sq miles). According to the census of 9–16 October 2002, the Oblast's population totalled 1,269,568 and the population density was 8.7 per sq km. 69.0% of the total population inhabited urban areas. 96.6% of the population were ethnically Russian; 1.0% were Ukrainian. The Oblast's administrative centre is at Vologda, which had a population of 292,800, according to provisional census results. Its largest major city is Cherepovets (312,200). Vologda Oblast is included in the time zone GMT+3.

History

Vologda province was annexed by the state of Muscovy in the 14th century. Vologda Oblast was formed on 23 September 1937. In October 1991 the recently elected Russian President, Boris Yeltsin, appointed a new head of administration of Vologda Oblast, Nikolai Podgornov. In mid-1993 the Vologda Oblast declared itself a republic, but failed to be acknowledged as such by the federal authorities. On 13 October the Regional Soviet transferred its responsibilities to the Regional Administration and elections were later held to a Legislative Assembly. In 1995 ballots implemented the Statutes of Vologda Oblast, according to which the region's Governor would lead the executive. There was a high level of support for the nationalist Liberal Democratic Party of Russia, particularly in rural areas, for much of the 1990s. In June 1996 Boris Yeltsin dismissed Podgornov, who was subsequently arrested and imprisoned on charges of corruption. His successor, Vyacheslav Pozgalev, won 80% of the votes cast in a direct election in late 1996, and was re-elected for further terms of office on 19 December 1999 and 7 December 2003, on both occasions obtaining over 80% of the votes cast. In March 2003 Pozgalev was elected to the Supreme Council of the pro-Government Unity and Fatherland-United Russia party.

Economy

In 2002 Vologda Oblast's gross regional product amounted to 82,636.7m. roubles, equivalent to 65,090.4 roubles per head. Its main industrial centres are at Vologda and Cherepovets. At the end of 2002 there were 772 km of railway track in use on its territory, as well as 11,944 km of paved roads. There are some 1,800 km of navigable waterways, including part of the Volga–Baltic route network.

Agriculture in Vologda Oblast, which employed 8.7% of the work-force and generated 12,939m. roubles in 2003, consists mainly of animal husbandry and production of flax and vegetables. Its main industries are ferrous metallurgy; the region produces around one-fifth of each of Russia's iron, rolled stock and steel, as well as significant quantities of textiles and chemicals, including, notably, mineral fertilizers. In 2003 the industrial sector engaged 29.6% of the region's working population and generated 137,102m. roubles. Severstal, the largest privately owned steel manufacturer in Russia (which purchased the US company, Rouge Steel, in 2003), based in Cherepovets, is one of the major employers in the Oblast.

The Oblast's economically active population numbered 655,000 in 2003, when the rate of unemployment was 4.8%. Those in employment earned, on average, 5,497.5 roubles per month. The 2003 budget showed a surplus of 101.8m. roubles. In 2003 export trade constituted US $1,524.1m. in exports and $195.4m. in imports; total foreign investment in the Oblast in that year amounted to $286.6m., compared with $31.6m. in the previous year. At the end of 2003 some 6,300 small businesses were registered in the Oblast.

Directory

Governor: VYACHESLAV YE. POZGALEV (appointed 3 June 1996, elected 6 October 1996, re-elected 19 December 1999 and 7 December 2003), 160035 Vologda, ul. Gertsena 2; tel. (8172) 72-07-64; fax (8172) 25-15-54; e-mail governor@vologda-oblast.ru; internet www.vologda-oblast.ru.

Chairman of the Legislative Assembly: NIKOLAI V. TIKHOMIROV, 160035 Vologda, ul. Pushkinskaya 25; tel. (8172) 72-02-60; fax (8172) 25-11-33; e-mail zsvo@vologda.ru; internet www.zs.gos35.ru.

Chief Representative of Vologda Oblast in the Russian Federation: VLADIMIR S. SMIRNOV, 119034 Moscow, Starokonyushennyi per. 4/5; tel. (495) 201-58-58; fax (495) 201-55-24.

Head of Vologda City Administration (Mayor): ALEKSEI S. YAKUNICHEV, 160035 Vologda, ul. Kamennyi most 4; tel. (8172) 72-02-42; fax (8172) 72-25-29; e-mail adm.gor@vologda.ru.

Nenets Autonomous Okrug

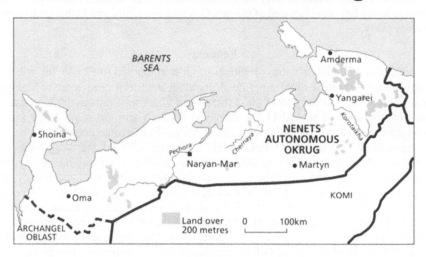

The Nenets Autonomous Okrug (AOk) is part of Archangel Oblast and, hence, the North-Western Federal Okrug and the Northern Economic Area. It is situated in the north-east of European Russia, its coastline lying, from west to east, on the White, Barents and Kara Seas, parts of the Arctic Ocean. Most of the territory lies within the Arctic Circle. Archangel proper lies to the south-west, but most of the Nenets southern border is with the Republic of Komi. At its eastern extremity the district touches the Yamalo-Nenets AOk (part of Tyumen Oblast) and, stretching away to the north-east, the island of Novaya Zemlya, which forms a part of Archangel Oblast proper. The major river is the Pechora, which drains into the Pechora Gulf of the Barents Sea north of Naryan-Mar. The territory occupies an area of 176,700 sq km. According to the census of 9–16 October 2002, the total population of the Nenets AOk was 41,546, giving a population density of 0.2 per sq km. Around 63.1% of the population inhabited urban areas. Some 62.4% of the population were ethnically Russian, 18.7% Nenets, 10.9% Komi, 3.2% Ukrainian and 1.0% Belarusian. The language spoken by the Nenets belongs to the Samoyedic group of Uralian languages, which is part of the Uralo-Altaic linguistic group. The district capital is at Naryan-Mar, which had an estimated population of 18,600, according to provisional results of the 2002 census. The Nenets AOk is included in the time zone GMT+3.

History

The Nenets were traditionally concerned with herding and breeding reindeer. A Samoyedic people, they are believed to have broken away from other Finno-Ugrian groups in around 3000 BC and migrated east where, in around 200 BC, they began to mix with Turkish-Altaic people. By the early 17th century AD their territory had come entirely under the control of the Muscovite state. The Russians established forts in the region, from which they collected fur tax.

The Nenets National Okrug was formed on 15 July 1929, and was reconstituted as a nominally Autonomous Okrug in 1977. During the Soviet period, collectivization of the Nenets' economic activity, and the exploitation of petroleum and natural gas (which increased markedly from the mid-1960s) resulted in mass migration of ethnic Russians to the region.

In March 1994 the federal President, Boris Yeltsin, suspended a resolution by the District Administration ordering a referendum to be held on the territory of the AOk, concerning the status of the district within the Russian Federation. Despite the President's move, however, the district maintained its style of the 'Nenets Republic'. A district Assembly of Deputies replaced the old legislature, and election results in the mid-1990s indicated continued disaffection with federal policies—there was strong support for the nationalist Liberal Democratic Party of Russia. The December 1996 election to head the district administration was won by an independent candidate and businessman, Vladimir Butov, who was re-elected on 14 January 2001, with some 68% of the votes cast. In June 2002 a warrant was issued for the arrest of Butov on charges of abuse of office, in particular with regard to his dismissal of three successive district prosecutors. Although the warrant was subsequently cancelled, a further federal arrest warrant against Butov was issued in July 2003, after he had allegedly assaulted a police officer in St Petersburg. Butov also attracted criticism for his reputedly authoritarian style. A prominent source of opposition to Butov was believed to be the petroleum company LUKoil, which objected to the preferential treatment granted in the AOk to the Nenets Oil Company (NNK), which Butov controlled. On 14 January 2005 the federal Supreme Court ruled that Butov was not permitted to seek a further term in office at the forthcoming gubernatorial election, and his candidacy was annulled. In the second round of voting, held on 6 February, Aleksei Barinov, a former federal inspector for the Nenets AOk, defeated Igor Koshin, a member of the district legislature, to be elected Governor, receiving 48.45% of votes cast. Some 20% of votes were cast 'against all candidates'. (The candidate supported by the pro-government Unity and Fatherland-United Russia party, Aleksandr Shmakov, had been eliminated in the first round after being placed fourth.) This election was expected to be the final such election in any federal subject following the announcement by federal President Vladimir Putin in late 2004 that, henceforth, regional governors and presidents were to be appointed by the federal authorities.

Economy

In 2002 the Nenets AOk's gross regional product amounted to 16,739.6m. roubles, equivalent to 402,917.2 roubles per head, one of the highest figures in the Federation. At the end of 2002 the AOk contained 174 km of paved roads. The AOk's major ports are Naryan-Mar and Amderma.

The territory's agriculture, which in 2003 employed 8.0% of the work-force and produced goods to a value of 264m. roubles, consists mainly of reindeer-breeding (around two-thirds of its territory are reindeer pasture), fishing, hunting and fur farming. There are substantial reserves of petroleum, natural gas and gas condensate. In 1997 Exxon Arkhangelsk, an affiliate of Exxon of the USA (now ExxonMobil), purchased a 50% stake in the development of oilfields in Timan-Pechora, although it was forced to withdraw after problems with tender arrangements. Petroleum deposits in the region were developed only slowly, although a new sea terminal for petroleum transportation was opened at Varandei in 2000. The initial annual capacity of this terminal, which was constructed by LUKoil and which was to be served by its fleet of ice-breaking tankers, was over 1m. metric tons. The issuing of unpaid back-tax demands equivalent to around US $1.46m. against the regional subsidiary of LUKoil, Naryanmarneftegaz, in mid-2005 was regarded as liable to result in the launch of a criminal investigation against the senior executives of the company. Meanwhile, the US company, ConocoPhillips, announced its intention to invest $500m. in a joint-venture in the region in association with Naryanmarneftegaz. Other sectors of the district's industry included the processing of agricultural products and the generation of electricity. Industry employed 21.8% of the AOk's work-force in 2003, and produced output worth 19,157m. roubles.

The economically active population in the territory numbered 25,000 in 2003, when 8.6% of the labour force were unemployed, compared with 20.0% in 1999. In 2003 the average monthly wage was 15,918.3 roubles, one of the highest levels of any federal subject. The AOk government budget recorded a deficit of 6.9m. roubles in 2003, when external trade comprised US $181.2m. in exports and $27.5m. in imports. In 2003 foreign investment totalled $171.1m. At the end of that year there were around 100 small businesses registered in the AOk.

Directory

Head of the District Administration: ALEKSEI V. BARINOV (elected 6 February 2005), 164700 Archangel obl., Nenets AOk, Naryan-Mar, ul. Smidovicha 20; tel. (47833) 4-21-13; fax (81853) 4-22-69.

Chairman of the Deputies' Assembly: VITALINA F. GLAZUNOVA, 164700 Archangel obl., Nenets AOk, Naryan-Mar, ul. Smidovicha 20; tel. (81853) 4-21-59; fax (81853) 4-20-11; e-mail pred@atnet.ru.

Representation of the Nenets Autonomous Okrug in Archangel Oblast: Archangel.

Chief Representative of the Nenets Autonomous Okrug in the Russian Federation: TATYANA A. MALYSHEVA, 127025 Moscow, ul. Novyi Arbat 19/1120; tel. (495) 203-90-39; fax (495) 203-91-74; e-mail neninter@atnet.ru.

Head of Naryan-Mar City Administration (Mayor): LEONID SABLIN, 164700 Archangel obl., Nenets AOk, Naryan-Mar, ul. Lenina 12; tel. (81853) 2-21-53; fax (495) 253-51-00.

SOUTHERN FEDERAL OKRUG

Republic of Adygeya

The Republic of Adygeya is situated in the foothills of the Greater Caucasus, a land-locked region in the basin of the Kuban river, surrounded by Krasnodar Krai. The Republic is in the Southern Federal Okrug and the North Caucasus Economic Area. The Republic is characterized by open grassland and fertile soil. The Republic covers 7,600 sq km (2,930 sq miles). According to the census of 9–16 October 2002, it had 447,109 inhabitants and a population density of 58.8 per sq km; 53.8% of the population of the Republic were urban. 64.5% of the population were ethnically Russian, 24.2% were Adyge (Lower Circassian or Kiakh), 3.4% Armenian, 2.0% Ukrainian and 0.8% Kurdish. Almost all of the Adyge population speak the national tongue, Adyge—part of the Abkhazo-Adyge group of Caucasian languages—as their native language, although most also speak Russian. The dominant religion in Adygeya, owing to the preponderance of ethnic Russians, is Orthodox Christianity, but the traditional religion of the Adyges is Islam. The administrative centre of Adygeya is the only large city, Maikop, which had a total of 162,400 inhabitants in October 2002, according to provisional census results. The Republic is included in the time zone GMT+3.

History

The Adyges were traditionally renowned for their unrivalled horsemanship and marksmanship. They emerged as a distinct Circassian ethnic group in the 13th century, when they inhabited much of the area between the Don river and the Caucasus, and the Black Sea and the Stavropol plateau. They were conquered by the Mongol Empire in the 13th century. In the 1550s the Adyges entered into an alliance with the Russian Empire, as protection against the Tatar Khanate of Crimea and against Turkic groups such as the Karachai, the Kumyks and the Nogai, which had retreated into the Caucasus from the Mongol forces of Temujin (Chinghiz or Ghengis Khan). Russian settlers subsequently moved into the Don and Kuban regions, causing unrest among the Adyges and other Circassian peoples, many of whom supported the Ottoman Empire against Russia in the Crimean War of 1853–56. The Circassians were finally defeated by the Russians in 1864. Most were forced either to emigrate or to move to the plains that were under Russian control. A Kuban-Black Sea Soviet Republic was established in 1918, but the region was soon occupied by anti-communist forces ('Whites'). Eventually the Red Army prevailed. The Adyge Autonomous Oblast was established on 27 July 1922. From August 1922 until August 1928 it was known as the Adyge (Circassian) Autonomous Oblast. The Oblast was ruled from Stavropol until it was included in Krasnodar Krai, which was constituted in 1937.

From the mid-1980s, the Adyge Khase Movement, which demanded the formation of a national legislative council, was formed. Adygeya officially declared its sovereignty on 28 June 1991; an inter-parliamentary council was subsequently formed between Adygeya and the other Circassian federal subjects (Kabardino-Balkariya and Karachayevo-Cherkessiya). A Constitution, which formally provided for the recognition of Adygeya as a republic, separate from the surrounding Krai, was adopted on 10 March 1995, confirming a decision of the Supreme Soviet of the RSFSR of 3 June 1991. The new Constitution provided for the institution of a bicameral legislature, the Khase (State Council), comprising a Council of Representatives (the upper chamber) and a Council of the Republic.

In an election held on 13 January 2002 the republican President Aslan Dzharimov was conclusively defeated, receiving only around 10% of the votes cast; he was succeeded by Khazrat Sovmen, the owner of a gold-mining co-operative. Some 10,000 people took part in a demonstration in Maikop in April 2005 to protest against apparent plans to reunite Adygeya with Krasnodar Krai, although the authorities of both entities denied that any such reunification was proposed. In mid-May Sovmen issued a decree dissolving the Khase (the first time that a regional Governor or President had issued such a decree in post-Soviet Russia), apparently after the legislature had approved budgetary legislation that contradicted federal norms (some reports, however, suggested that the dissolution followed the scheduling of a vote of 'no confidence' in Sovmen). Following a meeting between Sovmen and the Presidential Representative in the Southern Federal Okrug, Dmitrii Kozak, Sovmen annulled the decree, and the Khase was restored later in the month.

Economy

In 2002 the gross regional product of Adygeya was 8,403.5m. roubles, or 18,795.2 roubles per head. In 2002 there were 148 km of railway track and 1,570 km of paved roads in Adygeya.

Agricultural production consists mainly of animal husbandry, grain, sunflowers, sugar beet, tobacco and vegetables, cucurbit (gourds and melons) cultivation and viniculture, and is one of Russia's principal centres for the production of grape wine. Agriculture employed 17.4% of the work-force and generated 2,520m. roubles in 2003. There is some extraction of natural gas. Food-processing typically accounts for almost one-half of industrial production. Timber-processing, mechanical engineering and metal-working are also significant. Adygeya lies along the routes of the Blue Stream pipeline, completed in 2002, which delivers gas to Turkey, and planned petroleum pipelines from the Transcaucasus and Dagestan to the Black Sea ports of Novorossiisk and Tuapse (both in Krasnodar Krai). In 2003 industry engaged 17.3% of the work-force and generated 3,619m. roubles.

In 2003 the economically active population numbered 189,000, and some 15.8% of the labour force were unemployed. The average monthly wage was 3,317.5 roubles. In 2003 there was a budgetary deficit of 21.4m. roubles. In that year external trade amounted to US $61.6m. in exports and $8.6m. of in imports. Exports consisted mainly of food products, machine-tools and petroleum and chemical products. There was relatively little foreign investment in the Republic: in 2003 it amounted to just $2.1m. At the end of 2003 there were 2,400 small businesses registered in Adygeya.

Directory

President: KHAZRAT M. SOVMEN (elected 13 January 2002), 352700 Adygeya, Maikop, ul. Zhukovskogo 22; tel. (87722) 7-19-01; fax (87722) 2-59-58; internet www.adygheya.ru.

Prime Minister: ASFAR P. KHAGUR, 352700 Adygeya, Maikop, ul. Pionerskaya 199; tel. (8772) 57-02-22; fax (87722) 2-59-58; internet www.adygheya.ru/ispol.html.

Chairman of the Council of Representatives of the Khase (State Council): TATYANA M. PETROVA, 385000 Adygeya, Maikop, ul. Zhukovskogo 22; tel. (8772) 52-12-61; e-mail apparat@parlament.adygheya.ru; internet www.gshra.ru/sp.

Chairman of the Council of the Republic of the Khase (State Council): MUKHARBII KH. TKHARKAKHOV, 385000 Adygeya, Maikop, ul. Zhukovskogo 22; tel. (8772) 52-19-02; fax (8772) 52-19-04; e-mail apparat@parlament.adygheya.ru; internet www.gshra.ru/sr.

Chief Representative of the Republic of Adygeya in the Russian Federation: ALEKSANDR YE. SHINDER, 115184 Moscow, per. Staryi Tolmachevskii 6; tel. (495) 230-30-01; fax (495) 230-07-48.

Head of Maikop City Administration: NIKOLAI M. PIVOVAROV, 352700 Adygeya, Maikop, ul. Krasnooktyabrskaya 21; tel. (87722) 2-27-61; fax (87722) 2-63-19; e-mail priemn@admins.maykop.ru; internet www.admins.maykop.ru.

Chechen (Nokchi) Republic

The Chechen (Nokchi) Republic is located on the northern slopes of the Caucasus. It forms part of the Southern Federal Okrug and the North Caucasus Economic Area. To the east, the Republic abuts into Dagestan. Stavropol Krai lies to the north-west and North Osetiya—Alaniya and Ingushetiya lie to the west. There is an international boundary with Georgia to the south-west. The exact delimitation of much of the western boundary remained uncertain, awaiting final agreement between the Chechen and Ingush authorities on the division of the territory of the former Checheno-Ingush ASSR. The Republic comprises lowlands along the principal waterway, the River Terek, and around the capital, Groznyi, in the north; mixed fields, pastures and forests in the Chechen plain; and high mountains and glaciers in the south. The former Checheno-Ingush ASSR had an area of some 19,300 sq km (7,450 sq miles), most of which subsequently became the Chechen Republic. According to the census of 9–16 October 2002, the Republic had a population of 1,103,686, of whom 34.5% lived in urban areas. 93.5% of the Republic's population were Chechen, 3.7% ethnically Russian and 0.8% Kumyk. The Chechens, who refer to themselves as Nokchi, are closely related to the Ingush (both of whom are known collectively as Vainakhs). They are Sunni Muslims, and their language is one of the Nakh dialects of the Caucasian linguistic family. Founded as Groznyi in 1818, the capital had a population of 223,000 in 2002, according to provisional census results, compared with a total of 405,000 in 1989. The Republic is included in the time zone GMT+3.

History

In the 18th century the Russian, Ottoman and Persian (Iranian) Empires fought for control of the Caucasus region. The Chechens violently resisted the Russian forces with the uprising of Sheikh Mansur in 1785 and throughout the Caucasian War of

1817–64. Chechnya was finally conquered by Russia in 1858 after the resistance led by Imam Shamil (an ethnic Avar) ended. In 1865 many Chechens were exiled to the Ottoman Empire. Subsequently, ethnic Russians began to settle in the lowlands, particularly after petroleum reserves were discovered around Groznyi in 1893. Upon the dissolution of the Mountain (Gorskaya) People's Republic in 1922, Chechen and Ingush Autonomous Oblasts were established; they merged in 1934 and became the Checheno-Ingush ASSR in 1936. This was dissolved in 1944, when both peoples were deported en masse to Central Asia and Siberia. On 9 January 1957 the ASSR was reconstituted, but with limited provisions made for the restoration of property to the dispossessed.

During 1991 an All-National Congress of the Chechen People seized effective power in the Checheno-Ingush ASSR and agreed the division of the territory with Ingush leaders. Exact borders were to be decided by future negotiation, but by far the largest proportion of the territory was to constitute a Chechen Republic (Chechnya). Elections to the presidency of this new polity, which claimed independence from Russia, were held on 27 October, and were won by Gen. Dzhokhar Dudayev. In 1993 the territory refused to participate in the Russian general election and rejected the new federal Constitution. Against a background of armed raids by rebel Chechens, at the end of July 1994 Yeltsin declared his support for an 'Interim Council' in Chechnya. The Council, headed by Umar Avturkhanov, had proclaimed itself the rightful Government of Chechnya, in opposition to the administration of Dudayev, which, within two weeks, ordered mobilization in Chechnya. By early September armed conflict had broken out between the two groups. On 11 December, following the collapse of peace negotiations, federal President Boris Yeltsin ordered the invasion of Chechnya by some 40,000 ground troops. By January 1995 the federal forces had taken control of Groznyi, including the presidential palace, although fierce resistance continued throughout the Republic. In an effort to end hostilities, Yeltsin signed an accord with the Chechen premier granting the Republic special status. In March the federal authorities installed a 'Government of National Revival' in Chechnya, chaired by Salambek Khadzhiyev. In April more than 100 civilians were reported to have been killed by federal troops in a so-called 'cleansing' operation (*zachistka*) in the village of Samashki. In June the federal premier, Viktor Chernomyrdin, intervened in negotiations to end a siege by militants associated with the rebel Chechen leader, Shamil Basayev, who took hostage around 1,000 people in a hospital in Budennovsk, Stavropol Krai. (More than 100 people were killed during the siege.) In July opposition to the continuing conflict prompted an accord on the gradual disarmament of the Chechen rebels, in return for the partial withdrawal of federal troops from Chechnya; it remained in effect until October. In November a new Chechen Government loyal to the federal authorities, headed by Doku Zavgayev, was appointed. A further large-scale hostage-taking incident conducted by Chechen militants took place in Kizlyar, Dagestan, in January 1996, increasing demands across Russia for the Government to find a settlement to the Chechen conflict; other incidences of hostage-taking attributed to supporters of Chechen independence took place in Chechnya, in other regions of Russia and, less frequently, internationally during the late 1990s and early 2000s.

On 21 April 1996 Dudayev was killed in a Russian missile attack; he was succeeded by Zelimkhan Yandarbiyev, who concluded a cease-fire agreement with Yeltsin on 27 May. The truce, which took effect from 1 June, ended following Yeltsin's re-election as President in July. In August Chechen rebel forces led a successful assault on Groznyi, prompting the negotiation of a cease-fire by Lt-Gen. Aleksandr Lebed, the recently appointed Secretary of the Security Council. An agreement, the Khasavyurt Accords, was signed in Dagestan on 31 August. The proposed peace settlement incorporated a moratorium on discussion of Chechnya's status for five years. An agreement on the withdrawal of all federal troops by January 1997 was signed in November 1996, signalling the end of a war that had claimed up to 100,000 lives. A formal Treaty of Peace and Principles of Relations was signed on 12 May 1997 and ratified by the Chechen Parliament the following day.

On 1 January 1997 a presidential election was held in the Republic (which subsequently renamed itself 'the Chechen Republic of Ichkeriya'), at which Khalid 'Aslan' Maskhadov, a former Chechen rebel chief of staff, obtained 64.8% of the votes cast, defeating Basayev. Basayev, none the less, served as Maskhadov's First Deputy Prime Minister for several months in 1997, being re-appointed to that position for a period of six months in 1998. During 1998 two incidents drew attention to the disorderly state of Chechen society: Valentin Vlasov, the federal presidential representative in Chechnya, was kidnapped in May and held hostage for six months; later in the year four engineers from the United Kingdom and New Zealand were captured, and subsequently killed. By the end of the year Groznyi was no longer secure for the Government and Maskhadov was mainly based on the outskirts of the city.

The resurgence of Chechen nationalism in the 1990s was accompanied by a renaissance for Islam. In 1997 the republican authorities announced their intention to introduce Islamic *Shari'a* law over a three-year period from 1999, in contravention of the federal Constitution. Hostilities between armed groupings in Gudermes in July 1998 resulted in the outlawing in the Republic of oppositionist Islamist groups, which the federal authorities referred to as members of the austere Wahhabi Islamic sect. In August–September 1999 Islamist factions associated with Basayev launched a series of attacks on Dagestan from Chechnya, with the aim of protecting and extending the jurisdiction of a 'separate Islamic territory' in Dagestan, over which rebels had obtained control in the previous year. (The territory was returned to federal rule in mid-September.) A series of bomb explosions in August and September in Moscow, Dagestan and Volgodonsk (Rostov Oblast), including two that destroyed entire apartment blocks, officially attributed by the Government to Chechen separatists, killed almost 300 people, prompting the redeployment of federal armed forces in the Republic from late September; the recently appointed federal premier, Vladimir Putin, presented the deployment as an 'anti-terrorist operation'. The federal regime declined requests from Maskhadov for the negotiation of a settlement, stating that it recognized only the Moscow-based State Council of the Chechen Republic, which had been formed by former members of the republican legislature.

In February 2000 federal forces took control of Groznyi and proceeded to destroy much of the city; many republican and federal administrative bodies were relocated to Gudermes. Akhmad haji Kadyrov, a former senior mufti and a former ally of Maskhadov, was inaugurated as the Head of the Republican Administration (directly responsible to the federal presidency, to which Putin had recently been elected) on 20 June. In October it was announced that all Chechen ministries and government departments were to be relocated from Gudermes to Groznyi, with effect from November.

In January 2001 Putin transferred control of military operations in Chechnya from the Ministry of Defence to the Federal Security Service (FSB), which was to strengthen its presence in the region. The majority of defence ministry troops in the region were to be withdrawn, leaving a 15,000-strong infantry division and 7,000 interior ministry troops. Stanislav Ilyasov, a former Governor of Stavropol Krai, was appointed as Chechen premier. Despite claims that federal military operations had effectively ended, guerrilla attacks showed no sign of abating, and concern escalated among international human rights organizations about the conduct of federal troops; in 2001–02 the discovery of a number of mass graves, containing severely mutilated corpses, prompted outrage.

In late September 2001, encountering increasing demands for a political solution to the Chechen conflict, Putin announced a 72-hour amnesty. Only a negligible quantity of weapons were surrendered and the first official, direct negotiations to take place since the renewal of hostilities in 1999 resulted in no substantive agreement. Rebel activity increased markedly during the first half of 2002; although the political authority of Maskhadov, who remained in hiding, had dwindled, his military leadership of what was known as the State Defence Committee (to a senior position on which Basayev was reportedly appointed in July) became increasingly prominent as a focus for resistance to federal troops. In August federal forces experienced their single largest loss of life since the commencement of operations in 1999, when rebels shot down a military helicopter, killing 118 troops. In September Chechen rebels staged incursions into Ingushetiya; at least 17 deaths were reported in fighting near the village of Galashki.

On 23–26 October 2002 over 40 heavily armed rebels, who described themselves as a 'suicide battalion', held captive more than 800 people in a Moscow theatre and demanded the withdrawal of federal troops from Chechnya. The siege ended when élite federal forces stormed the theatre, having filled the building with an incapacitating gas. The rebels were killed and it subsequently emerged that at least 129 hostages had died, in almost all cases owing to the toxic effects of the gas. Although Maskhadov issued a statement condemning the rebels' use of terrorist methods, Akhmed Zakayev, Maskhadov's deputy premier, was arrested in Denmark on the orders of the federal Government. (In early November Basayev announced that groups linked to him had perpetrated the hostage-taking in Moscow, and stated that Maskhadov had not known of the incident.) However, Denmark formally rejected demands for Zakayev's extradition, and he was released; he subsequently took up residence in the United Kingdom, which granted him asylum in November 2003.

In mid-November 2002 Ilyasov was removed from his position as Prime Minister of Chechnya and appointed to the federal Government as Minister without Portfolio, with responsibility for the development of Chechnya. Ilyasov was succeeded as republican premier by Capt. (retd) Mikhail Babich, who had previously held senior positions in the regional administrations of Ivanovo and Moscow Oblasts. In late November Ilyasov announced that a referendum on a new draft Chechen constitution was to be held in March 2003. In late December at least 83 people were killed, and more than 150 others injured, when suicide bombers detonated bombs in two vehicles stationed outside the headquarters of the republican Government in Groznyi. (Basayev subsequently claimed responsibility for the attack.) By late December 2002 federal losses during the campaign, according to official figures, were put at 4,572 dead and 15,549 wounded, although Chechen estimates were considerably higher. (It was also estimated that more than 14,000 rebel fighters had been killed since September 1999.) In late January 2003 Babich resigned as premier. On 10 February Anatolii Popov, the hitherto deputy chairman of the state commission for the reconstruction of Chechnya, was appointed in his place.

The referendum on the draft constitution for Chechnya, describing the republic (referred to as the Chechen—Nokchi Republic) as both a sovereign entity, with its own citizenship, and as an integral part of the Russian Federation proceeded, as scheduled, on 23 March 2003, despite concerns that the instability of the Republic would prevent the poll from being free and fair. The draft constitution also provided for the holding of fresh elections to a strengthened republican presidency and legislature. According to the official results, some 88.4% of the electorate participated in the plebiscite, of whom 96.0% supported the draft constitution. Two further questions, on the method of electing the republican president and parliament, were supported by 95.4% and 96.1% of participants, respectively. However, independent observers challenged the results, reporting that the rate of participation by the electorate had been much lower than officially reported. (According to official results, an identical number of valid votes had been cast in response to all three questions, while it was reported that the total number of votes cast had, in fact, been in excess of the registered electorate.)

Political violence continued to dominate Chechen affairs; in early April 2003 at least 22 people were killed in two separate incidents when their vehicles detonated landmines. In early May 2003 at least 59 people were killed when suicide bombers attacked government offices in the northern city of Znamenskoye. Two days later another suicide bombing at a religious festival attended by Kadyrov resulted in at least 14 deaths, although Kadyrov escaped unhurt; Basayev claimed responsibility for the organization of both attacks. On 21 June Kadyrov inaugurated an interim legislative body, the 42-member State Council, comprising the head of, and an appointed representative of, each administrative district. In early July Putin announced that presidential elections in Chechnya were to be held on 5 October.

From 1 September 2003 control of military operations in Chechnya was assumed by the federal Ministry of Internal Affairs from the FSB; it was announced that such operations were no longer regarded as having an 'anti-terrorist' character but were, rather, to form part of an 'operation to protect law and constitutional order'. Meanwhile, campaigning for the presidential elections commenced; however, the withdrawal of Aslanbek Aslakhanov, a representative of the Republic in the State Duma, and the debarring of business executive Malik Saidullayev effectively removed any major challenges to Kadyrov's candidacy. On 5 October Kadyrov was elected President, receiving 87.7% of votes cast, according to official figures. Participation in the polls was reported to be 82.6%. Kadyrov subsequently reappointed Popov as premier, although he was replaced on 16 March 2004 by Sergei Abramov, hitherto an official in the audit chamber of the State Duma, owing to Popov's ill health.

A raid into Dagestan on 15 December 2003, in which border guards were killed and hostages taken, was attributed to Chechen militants. On 13 February 2004 Yandarbiyev was killed by a car bomb in Qatar. Two Russian citizens, widely reputed to be secret service agents, were subsequently tried for the murder by a Qatari court; on 30 June they were both sentenced to life imprisonment; however, they were returned to Russia to serve out their sentences in December, and in early 2005 it was reported that they were no longer being held in detention.

An explosion in Groznyi on 9 May 2004, at a commemoration to mark 'Victory Day', resulted in the deaths of several senior officials, including Kadyrov and Khusain Isayev, the head of the republican legislature. (Basayev subsequently claimed responsibility for the bombing.) Abramov assumed presidential responsibilities in an acting capacity, pending elections, while Ramzan Kadyrov, the son of the assassinated President and the leader of the presidential security service (referred to as the *Kadyrovtsi*, and believed to number some 3,000), which was widely believed to have been implicated in several unexplained 'disappearances', was appointed as First Deputy Prime Minister. Chechen militants were widely suspected of involvement in a series of raids on interior ministry targets in the neighbouring republic of Ingushetiya, which took place in June. A presidential election was held on 29 August, when Maj-Gen. Alu Alkhanov, an officer in the republican interior ministry troops, and the favoured candidate of the federal Government, was victorious, receiving some 73.5% of votes cast, according to official figures. The rate of participation was reported to be 85.2%. Council of Europe observers criticized the elections as undemocratic. Suggestions that the political process had become more stable appeared to be inaccurate; there were several incidents in Moscow, including the destruction of two passenger planes, apparently by suicide bombers, in which around 100 people were killed, in the days preceding and following Alkhanov's election. (Meanwhile, proposed elections to the republican legislature were postponed.) The taking of hostages at a school in Beslan, North Osetiya—Alaniya in early September, which some sources attributed to Chechen elements, and as a result of which more than 330 people were killed, further illustrated the potentially destabilizing effect on the North Caucasus region of the unresolved status of the Chechen Republic. (In 2004–05 there was a marked increase in militant activity, including bombings and assassination of police and state officials, in several republics of the North Caucasus, including Dagestan, Ingushetiya and the Kabardino-Balkar Republic.) Alkhanov subsequently reappointed Abramov as republican Prime Minister, and in mid-October Ramzan Kadyrov was made an adviser on security to the recently appointed Presidential Representative in the Southern Federal Okrug, Dmitrii Kozak, while retaining his existing positions within Chechnya. In late 2004 it was announced that the republican authorities were to sign a power-sharing treaty with the federal Government, but in June 2005 it was announced that the signature of such a treaty had been postponed indefinitely. Meanwhile, in April 2005 Alkhanov announced that he had joined the pro-Government Unity and Fatherland-United Russia party (UF-UR). In mid-July the repeatedly delayed elections to a new, bicameral, Chechen legislature, were scheduled for 27 November.

Meanwhile, in February 2005 Maskhadov announced that he had ordered separatist fighters to observe a unilateral one-month cease-fire, describing the move as a 'goodwill gesture' towards the Russian authorities (reports were varied as to the success of the order). On 8 March, however, Russian media reported that Maskhadov had been killed during a special operation by FSB forces in the village of Tolstoi-Yurt, north of Groznyi, although the exact circumstances of his death remained uncertain. Footage of what appeared to be Maskhadov's corpse was broadcast on national television later that day. The federal authorities subsequently refused to return Maskhadov's body to his relatives, or to identify the location of his burial, stating that such measures were prohibited by anti-terrorist legislation. (Maskhadov's family subsequently appealed to the European Court of Human Rights for the release of his body.) Maskhadov was replaced as leader of the State Defence Committee by his chosen successor, Abdul-Khalim Sadulayev; Sadulayev, like Maskhadov before him, announced his willingness to enter into negotiations with the federal authorities in order to restore peace to Chechnya, but, in the absence of such negotiations maintained that the use of force was legitimate. In early May a senior rebel commander, Doku Umarov, stated that Chechen militants would launch large-scale military operations in other regions of Russia before the end of the year; later in the month Sadulayev announced the appointment of new military commanders to what were described as various sectors of the 'Caucasus Front'. None the less, in an interview with an international radio station in June, Sadulayev condemned attacks against civilians and hostage-taking, but emphasized that his fighters would seek to inflict maximum damage against Russian military targets. Later in the month, however, Sadulayev issued a decree naming Umarov as vice president of the rebel leadership, and issued a statement to the effect that the expulsion of Russian forces from Chechnya would not constitute an end to the conflict, as the Chechens would be obligated to take vengeance against those he termed 'unbelievers' for their actions in Chechnya. In mid-July at least 15 people were killed following the detonation of a car bomb in Znamenskoye. In mid-August Sadulayev dismissed the rebel Chechen 'parliament-in-exile' and a network of 'ambassadors', which he collectively accused of financial malpractice and incompetence; he also appointed a new rebel 'Government' at the end of the month, to which, notably, Basayev was appointed as 'First Deputy Prime Minister', while Zakayev was appointed to represent the rebel authorities internationally. In early September Basayev was interviewed by a US television station, and stated that he accepted his designation as a 'terrorist', but that he regarded his use of violence as justified. (Basayev claimed responsibility for the organization of a co-ordinated series of attacks against law-enforcement bodies in Nalchik, the Kabardino-Balkar Republic, in which at least 130 people were reported to have been killed, in October.)

Tensions between Chechens and the most numerous ethnic group in neighbouring Dagestan, the Avars, were also heightened on several occasions from the first half of 2005 as a result of security forces associated with the Chechen authorities (most notably those answerable to Ramzan Kadyrov) making incursions into Dagestan, apparently in response to Chechen rebels taking refuge in the neighbouring Republic. Relations with Dagestan were further strained after 11 villagers were abducted during a 'cleansing' operation in the eastern village of Borozdinovskaya in early June; some 400 people, principally ethnic Avars, subsequently fled to Dagestan and remained there for several weeks; the operation was condemned by both the Chechen and federal authorities, and Alkhanov subsequently dismissed the administrator of the district in which the village was located. A number of clashes in Chechnya were also reported between members of the *Kadyrovtsi* and federal forces.

In October the trial commenced of four men arrested at the house in Tolstoi-Yurt where Maskhadov was killed. The charges against them included unlawful possession of weapons and membership of an illegal armed group. It was thought that the testimony of the defendants, who included Maskhadov's nephew, Viskhan Khadzhimuradov, would substantiate claims by Russian officials that Maskhadov was, in fact, shot by his bodyguards at his own request, in order to avoid capture and trial. (In December the four associates of Maskhadov were sentenced to between six and 15 years' imprisonment.)

On 27 November 2005 elections were held in the Republic to a new, bicameral legislature, comprising the 18-seat Council of the Republic (the upper chamber) and the 40-seat People's Assembly (the lower chamber). While the federal Government cited the ballot as evidence that normality was returning to Chechnya, both national and international human rights groups described the poll as a sham, as no candidates advocating Chechen independence were allowed to stand. Voter turnout was alleged to be around 60%, well above the 25% needed to validate the election, but international observers expressed doubt that the vote was free and fair. As predicted, the majority of deputies in the new parliament (33 out of 58) were from UF-UR, while the Communist Party of the Russian Federation, the pro-market Union of Rightist Forces, the Eurasian Union also obtained representation, as did 14 deputies with no party affiliation. Thus the position of Kadyrov, a member of UF-UR and widely perceived as *de facto* leader of the Chechen Government, was consolidated; furthermore, Kadyrov at this time held the position of acting premier, following the injury of Abramov in a automobile accident earlier in the month.

Economy

Prior to the outbreak of armed hostilities in the region in 1994, Groznyi was the principal industrial centre in Chechnya. At the end of 2002 there were 304 km of railways and 3,057 km of paved roads in the Republic. Its agriculture consisted mainly of horticulture, production of grain and sugar beet, and animal husbandry. Its main industrial activities were production of petroleum and petrochemicals, petroleum-refining, power engineering, manufacture of machinery and the processing of forestry and agricultural products. Conflict in 1994–96, and again from 1999, seriously damaged the economic infrastructure and disrupted both agricultural and industrial activity. A significant asset that could be sabotaged by, or displaced because of violence was one of Russia's major petroleum pipelines that crossed Chechnya: in the event of stability, transit fees from Caspian hydrocarbons could be a major source of revenue for the Republic. In mid-1999 the Chechen section of a petroleum pipeline from Baku, Azerbaijan, to Novorossiisk (Krasnodar Krai), was closed, owing to the lack of security in the region. However, attempts were being made to restore industry in the Republic; a sugar refinery and a brickworks were in operation there in 2001, and several new businesses opened thereafter. The principal petroleum company operating the Republic in the early 2000s was Grozneftegaz, which was 51%-owned by Rosneft, and 49% by the republican Government. Output of petroleum in 2002 was estimated at approximately 1.5m. metric tons. A new polypropylene-fabric factory was constructed in Groznyi in 2002. In 2003 the economically active population numbered 378,000, compared with 218,000 in the previous year. In 2003 the rate of unemployment was 70.9%, compared with 58.8% in 2002. The average monthly wage was 3,807.8 roubles in 2003. In 2003 the republican budget recorded a deficit of 1,071.8m. roubles. In 2002 exports from the Republic amounted to US $11.9m. In November 2002 it was reported that the federal budget for 2003 was to allocate some 3,500m. roubles to the Republic, under a programme that aimed to promote economic and social recovery.

Directory

President and Head of the Administration: Maj-Gen. ALU D. ALKHANOV (elected 29 August 2004), 364000 Chechen (Nokchi) Rep., Groznyi, ul. Garazhnaya 10A; tel. (8712) 22-24-80; e-mail info@chechnya.gov.ru; internet www.chechnya.gov.ru.

Chairman of the Republican Government (Prime Minister): SERGEI B. ABRAMOV, 364000 Chechen (Nokchi) Rep., Groznyi, ul. Garazhnaya 10A; tel. (8712) 22-00-01.

Chairman of the Council of the Republic: AKHMARHADZHI GAZIKHANOV, 364000 Chechen (Nokchi) Rep., Groznyi, ul. Garazhnaya 10A.

Chairman of the People's Assembly: DUKBAKHA ABDURAKHMANOV, 364000 Chechen (Nokchi) Rep., Groznyi, ul. Garazhnaya 10A.

Chief Representative of the Chechen (Nokchi) Republic in the Russian Federation: ZIYAD M. SABSADI, 127025 Moscow, ul. Novyi Arbat 19/1804; tel. (495) 203-63-47; fax (495) 203-63-52.

Head of Groznyi City Administration (Mayor): MOVSAR TEMIRBAYEV, 364000 Chechen (Nokchi) Rep., Groznyi; tel. (8712) 22-01-42.

Republic of Dagestan

The Republic of Dagestan is situated in the North Caucasus on the Caspian Sea. Dagestan forms part of the Southern Federal Okrug and the North Caucasus Economic Area. It has international borders with Azerbaijan to the south and Georgia to the south-west. The Chechen (Nokchi) Republic and Stavropol Krai lie to the west and Kalmykiya to the north. Its largest rivers are the Terek and the Sulak. It occupies 50,300 sq km (19,420 sq miles). Its Caspian Sea coastline, to the east, is 530 km long. The north of the Republic is flat, while in the south are the foothills and peaks of the Greater Caucasus. The Republic's lowest-lying area is the Caspian lowlands, at 28 m (92 feet) below sea level, while its highest peak is over 4,000 m high. The climate in its mountainous areas is continental and dry, while in coastal areas it is subtropical, with strong winds. According to the census of 9–16 October 2002, Dagestan had a population of 2,576,531, and a population density of 51.2 per sq km; 42.9% of the Republic's population inhabited urban areas. 29.4% of the population described themselves as ethnically Avar (including 0.8% of the total population who described themselves as Andiyets), 16.5% as Dargin, 14.2% as Kumyk, 13.1% as Lezgin, 5.4% as Lak, 4.7% as ethnically Russian, 4.3% as Azeri, 4.3% as Tabasaran, 3.4% as Chechen, 1.5% as Nogai, 0.9% as Rutul and 0.9% as Agul. Dagestan's capital is at Makhachkala, which had 466,800 inhabitants in October 2002, according to provisional census results. The city lies on the Caspian

Sea and is the Republic's main port. Other major cities are Khasavyurt (122,000) and Derbent (100,800). The Republic of Dagestan is included in the time zone GMT+3.

History

Dagestan formally came under Russian rule in 1723, when the various Muslim khanates on its territory were annexed from Persia (Iran). The Dagestani peoples conducted a series of rebellions against Russian control, including the Murid Uprising of 1828–59, before Russian control could be established. A Dagestan ASSR was established on 20 January 1920.

The Republic of Dagestan acceded to the Federation Treaty in March 1992 and officially declared its sovereignty in May 1993. The Republic voted against the new federal Constitution in December and adopted a new republican Constitution on 26 July 1994. On 21 March 1996 the powers of the Dagestani State Council, the supreme executive body, which comprised a representative of each of the 14 largest ethnic groups in the Republic, were prolonged by a further two years. When this extra term had elapsed, the republican legislature convened as a Constituent Assembly and, on 26 June 1998, confirmed Magomedali Magomedov as the Chairman of the State Council, a position he had held since the inauguration of the Council, on 26 July 1994. Parliamentary elections for a new People's Assembly were held on 7 March 1999, concurrently with a referendum to decide whether to institute an executive presidency in Dagestan; the proposal was rejected for a third time. Constitutional changes, approved in March 1998, permitted Magomedov to serve a further term and removed the nationality requirements for senior republican positions; this was thought liable to unsettle the balance of power between the ethnic groups in the Republic.

Concern was expressed at a growth in support for militant Islamist groups in Dagestan from the late 1990s. In February 1998 Islamist militants seized three villages in Buinaksk district as 'a separate Islamic territory'. In May a group of 200–300 fighters belonging to the Union of Russian Muslims, a political party represented in the republican parliament and led by Nadirshakh Khachilayev, the brother of the head of the ethnic Lak community in Dagestan, occupied a government building in Makhachkala; simultaneously, 2,000 demonstrators gathered in the main city square to demand the resignation of the republican Government. (Khachilayev was assassinated in August 2003.) There was also reported to be evidence of close ties between militant groups in Dagestan and those operating abroad, particularly in Arab countries. In 1996–97 Ayman al-Zawahiri, the leader of the militant Egyptian Islamic Jihad and a close ally of the Saudi-born leader of the Islamist al-Qa'ida (Base) organization, Osama bin Laden, was imprisoned for six months in Dagestan, having been found guilty of entering Russia illegally.

Chechen militants, aided by Dagestani militant Islamists, invaded Dagestan on 2 August 1999 and again on 5 September; fighting ceased on 16 September, when federal troops additionally regained control over the villages seized by rebels in February 1998. Later in September 1999, when the recommencement of military operations by federal troops in Chechnya appeared imminent, crowds of demonstrators prevented a planned meeting in Khasavyurt between Magomedov, as the *de facto* representative of the federal Government, and the President of the 'Chechen Republic of Ichkeriya', Khalid 'Aslan' Maskhadov; it was reported that the demonstrators objected to any negotiations taking place with the Chechen authorities, whom they held responsible for the increasing lawlessness, and in particular the widespread incidence of hostage-taking, in Dagestan in 1996–99, including, most notoriously, an incident in January 1996, when some 2,000 hostages had been seized in the town of Kizlyar. Indeed, such was the hostility towards the rebel Chechen movement in Dagestan that the federal authorities agreed to a request from officials of the Dagestani Government that no refugees from Chechnya be accommodated in Dagestan. In late September 1999, following the recommencement of military operations in Chechnya, an explosion in Buinaksk, outside accommodation used by federal troops, killed about 60 people. Subsequently a number of explosions in Dagestan were attributed to supporters of Chechen separatism, including a bombing on 9 May 2002 in Kaspiisk, when 45 people were killed.

On 25 June 2002 the Constituent Assembly voted by an overwhelming majority for Magomedov to be permitted to serve a third term as Chairman of the State Council. In March 2003 Magomedov was duly re-elected to that post. On 10 July a new republican Constitution, which implemented wide-ranging reforms to the structure of government, was approved; it came into effect later in the month. Notably, a directly elected Presidency was to be established, to replace the State Council, with effect from the expiry of the latter's mandate in 2006. (The potential consequences of these decisions on inter-ethnic relations in the Republic remained a topic of debate, and remained controversial after the federal President, Vladimir Putin, announced that regional leaders would be appointed, rather than elected, in late 2004.) Meanwhile, it was reported that at least eight parliamentary deputies had been assassinated in Dagestan in 1992–2003. In late August 2003 the republican Minister for National Policy, Information and Foreign Affairs, Magomedsalikh Gusayev, was killed when a bomb was detonated by his car; Gusayev had played a particularly prominent role in combating Islamist militancy in Dagestan. (His successor, Zagir Arukhov, was assassinated in May 2005, in a bombing apparently co-ordinated by the Islamist Shariat Dzhamaat group.) In mid-December 2003 a group of militants entered Dagestan, reportedly from Chechnya, killing a unit of border guards and fleeing with a number of hostages. A state of emergency was declared and élite troops were dispatched to the region. Although the armed group fled after releasing the hostages, at the end of the month it was reported that the majority of the militants had been killed and the remainder taken prisoner.

Instability in the Republic heightened markedly in the mid-2000s, with political opposition to Magomedov's administration increasingly being voiced by a so-called 'Northern Alliance' formed in 2003 that included a number of prominent politicians in Khasyavurt, but which was also reportedly supported by elements close to the controversial First Deputy Prime Minister of Chechnya, Ramzan Kadyrov. Assassinations and attempted assassinations of law enforcement officers and regional government officials in Dagestan continued in 2004–05 (according to the republican Ministry of the Interior, there were an estimated 68 militant attacks in Dagestan in the first half of 2005, the majority of which took place in Makhachkala; at least 28 police officers were reported to have been killed during the same period). In early July the leader of Shariat Dzhamaat, Rasul Makshapirov, was killed by republican security forces. Tensions were also raised on several occasions in 2005 by incursions into Dagestan, particularly the Khasyavurt region, by security forces associated with the Chechen authorities (most notably those answerable to Ramzan Kadyrov) seemingly without the agreement or prior knowledge of the Dagestani authorities and allegedly in response to Chechen rebels taking refuge in the region. Relations with Chechnya were further strained after 11 villagers were abducted during a 'cleansing' operation in Borozdinovskaya, Chechnya, in early June; some 400 people, principally ethnic Avars, subsequently fled to Dagestan and remained there, living in tents, for several weeks; the operation that provoked this exodus was subsequently condemned by both the Chechen and federal authorities. In late July a new exodus of villagers to Dagestan was reported, and in early August clashes broke out between Avars and ethnic Chechens from neighbouring villages near Khasyavurt.

Clashes between Islamist insurgents and security forces continued into late 2005. In separate incidents in early October law-enforcement agencies in Dagestan killed three rebel leaders. None the less, rebel activity in the Republic showed no signs of abating. In November police officers in the Levashi district discovered five large explosive devices at a house reportedly owned by Ismail Omarov, a member of Shariat Dzhamaat. Meanwhile, Shariat Dzhamaat launched a media offensive against both the republican Government and Dagestan's Muslim clergy, whom, it declared, it now regarded as a legitimate target of attack.

Economy

In 2002 gross regional product in Dagestan amounted to 42,443.9m. roubles, or 16,473.3 roubles per head. The economic situation in the Republic was severely affected by the wars in Chechnya. The Republic's major industrial centres are at Makhachkala, Derbent, Kaspiisk and Khasavyurt. In 2002 there were 516 km of railways and 7,385 km of paved roads in the Republic. There are fishing and trading ports in Makhachkala, which is a major junction for trading routes by rail, land and sea. The major railway line between Rostov-on-Don and Baku, Azerbaijan, runs across the territory, as does the Caucasus highway. There is an airport at Makhachkala.

Owing to its mountainous terrain, Dagestan's economy is largely based on animal husbandry, particularly sheep-breeding. Its agriculture also consists of grain production, viniculture, horticulture and fishing. The agricultural sector generated 19,207m. roubles and employed around 31.7% of the Republic's work-force in 2003; only in the Ust-Orda Buryat Autonomous Okrug in Siberia were a higher proportion of the workforce engaged in agriculture. Dagestan's main industries are petroleum and natural gas production, electricity generation, mechanical engineering, metalworking and food-processing. In 2002 industry engaged 11.6% of the work-force and generated 8,046m. roubles.

Dagestan's economically active population comprised 861,000 inhabitants in 2003, when 20.1% of the Republic's labour force were unemployed, a rate considerably in excess of the federal average. The average monthly wage was 2,409.2 roubles, the lowest recorded in the Federation. There was a budgetary deficit of 292.2m. roubles in 2003. External trade amounted to US $64.2m. in exports and $73.4m. in imports in 2003. Foreign investment in the territory was minimal, amounting to just US $53,000 in 1998. There were 1,500 small businesses registered in Dagestan at the end of 2003.

Directory

Chairman of the State Council (Head of the Republic): MAGOMEDALI M. MAGOMEDOV (indirectly elected 26 July 1994, 26 June 1998 and 25 June 2002), 367005 Dagestan, Makhachkala, pl. Lenina 1; tel. (8722) 67-30-59; fax (8722) 67-30-60; e-mail info@dagestan.ru; internet www.magomedov.ru.

Chairman of the Cabinet of Ministers (Head of Government): ATAI B. ALIYEV, 367005 Dagestan, Makhachkala, pl. Lenina; tel. (8722) 67-20-17; internet www.diap.ru.

Chairman of the People's Assembly: MUKHU G. ALIYEV, 367005 Dagestan, Makhachkala, pl. Lenina; tel. (8722) 67-30-55; fax (8722) 67-30-66; internet rd.dgu.ru.

Chief Representative of the Republic of Dagestan in the Russian Federation: RAMAZAN SH. MAMEDOV, 105062 Moscow, ul. Pokrovka 28, POB 116; tel. (495) 916-15-36; fax (495) 928-41-12.

Head of Makhachkala City Administration: SAID D. AMIROV, 367012 Dagestan, Makhachkala, pl. Lenina 2; tel. (8722) 67-21-09; e-mail z999@km.ru; internet www.makhachkala.dgu.ru.

Republic of Ingushetiya

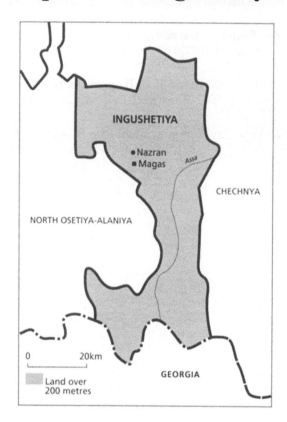

The Republic of Ingushetiya is situated on the northern slopes of the Greater Caucasus, in the centre of the Northern Caucasus mountain ridge. It forms part of the Southern Federal Okrug and the North Caucasus Economic Area. The Chechen (Nokchi) Republic lies to the east and north (although the border has not been exactly determined) and North Osetiya—Alaniya to the west. (The boundary between these two Republics was partially disputed.) In the southern mountains there is an international border with Georgia. The Terek and the Assa are the territory's main rivers. The Republic is extremely mountainous, with some peaks over 3,000 m high. The Republic occupies about 3,600 sq km (1,400 sq miles). According to the census of 9–16 October 2002, the population of the Republic was 467,294 and the population density 129.8 per sq km. 42.8% of the population lived in urban areas. 77.3% of the population were ethnically Ingush, 20.4% were Chechen and 1.2% were ethnically Russian. The Ingush are a Muslim people closely related to the Chechens (collectively they are known as Vainakhs). They are indigenous to the Caucasus Mountains and have been known historically as Galgai, Lamur, Mountain-eers and Kist. Like the Chechen language, their native tongue is a dialect of the Nakh group of the Caucasian language family. Ingushetiya's administrative centre is at Magas, a new city, opened officially in 1998, which was named after the medieval

Alanic capital believed to have been situated thereabouts. Initially the city consisted solely of a gold-domed presidential palace and government buildings, and by October 2002 its population was only about 100. The former capital of Nazran remained the largest city in the Republic, with a population of 126,700, according the provisional results of the 2002 census. The Republic of Ingushetiya is included in the time zone GMT+3.

History

The Ingush are descended from the western Nakh people, whose different reaction to Russian colonization of the Caucasus region in the 1860s distinguished them from their eastern counterparts (subsequently known as the Chechens). The Chechens resisted the invaders violently and were driven into the mountains, while the Ingush reacted more passively and settled on the plains. Despite this, the Ingush suffered severely under Soviet rule. In 1920 their territory was temporarily integrated into the Mountain (Gorskaya) People's Republic, but became the Ingush Autonomous Oblast on 7 July 1924. In 1934 the region was joined to the Chechen Autonomous Oblast to form the Checheno-Ingush Autonomous Oblast, which was upgraded to the status of a Republic in 1936. At that time, many leading Ingush intellectuals became victims of 'purges' and the Ingush literary language was banned. In February 1944 the entire Ingush population (74,000, according to the 1939 census) was deported to Soviet Central Asia, owing to its alleged collaboration with Nazi Germany. The territory was subsequently handed over to the Osetiyans. On their return after rehabilitation in 1957 the Ingush were forced to purchase the property from Osetiyan settlers.

With the ascendancy in the ASSR of the All-National Congress of the Chechen People in 1991, a *de facto* separation between Chechen and Ingush territories was achieved. In June 1992 the federal Supreme Soviet confirmed Ingushetiya's status as a separate republic, although the borders between the two new units were not delineated. In addition, Ingushetiya claimed the eastern regions of North Osetiya and part of the North Osetiyan capital, Vladikavkaz (which had been shared until the 1930s). Prigorodnyi raion (district), with a majority of Ingush inhabitants, was at the centre of the dispute. (The federal Law on the Rehabilitation of Repressed Peoples, approved in April 1991, established the right for deported peoples to repossess their territory.) Armed hostilities between the two Republics ensued from October 1992, until a peace agreement was signed in 1994, although subsequent relations remained strained.

On 27 February 1994, alongside simultaneous parliamentary and presidential elections in the Republic, 97% of the electorate voted in favour of a draft republican constitution, which took immediate effect. At the republican presidential election, held in March 1998, Ruslan Aushev (who had headed the Republic since November 1992) was re-elected. His popular mandate emboldened him to seek to amend republican laws to conform more closely to what he termed 'national traditions', but which also incorporated aspects of *Shari'a* Islamic law. Following a declaration by federal President Boris Yeltsin that a planned referendum, which sought, in particular, to pardon those charged with crimes such as revenge killings, was unconstitutional, in February 1999 Aushev signed a power-sharing agreement with the federal Government. In July Aushev issued a decree permitting men up to four wives, in breach of the Russian Federation's family code.

The population of Ingushetiya remained generally supportive of the federal authorities, but strongly opposed federal military intervention in Chechnya. This apparent inconsistency was reflected in the outcome of the federal presidential election of 26 March 2000; despite his leading role in recommencing armed hostilities in Chechnya, Ingushetiya awarded Vladimir Putin a larger proportion of the votes cast (85.4%) than in any other federal subject. The successful implementation of a settlement between Ingushetiya and North Osetiya, signed in March 2001, according to which the Ingush could return to their former homes in Prigorodnyi and Vladikavkaz, was inhibited by logistical difficulties and protests. In late December 2001 Aushev resigned. Following two rounds of voting, in April 2002 Murat Zyazikov, the Deputy Presidential Representative in the Southern Federal Okrug (and a general in the Federal Security Service—FSB) was elected President. In late September up to 70 deaths were reported near the village of Galashki, as Chechen rebels, who were reported to have entered the territory from the Pankisi Gorge in Georgia, clashed with federal forces; notably, rebels shot down a helicopter gunship, killing two people. In October Ingushetiya and North Osetiya signed an 'Agreement on the Development of Co-operation and Good Neighbourly Relations', which committed both sides to adopting measures to resolve their remaining differences. On 2 June 2003 Zyazikov dismissed the republican Government, and on 19 June the hitherto Deputy Chairman of the republican Government and a petroleum-industry business executive, Timur Mogushkov, was appointed premier. At the end of July five federal troops died after their vehicles struck a landmine near Galashki. In September an explosive device, assembled outside the residence of Zyazikov, was successfully disabled. Later in the month three people were killed and another 31 injured when a truck bomb was detonated by two suicide bombers outside the offices of the FSB in Magas. At the end of September renewed clashes, apparently involving several hundred rebel fighters, in which at least 17 deaths were reported, broke out between Chechen rebels and troops and police near Galashki, although the rebels subsequently fled.

In the March 2004 elections to the federal presidency, Ingushetiya again recorded the highest proportion of support of any federal subject for Putin (98.2%, according to the Central Election Commission). On 6 April Zyazikov was briefly hospitalized following an apparent attempt on his life by a suicide bomber. In June the final camp in Ingushetiya for persons displaced by the war in Chechnya was closed, despite widespread concern that the refugees were being forced to return to Chechnya against their will. (In 1999–2000 the camps had accommodated some 200,000 persons.) Meanwhile, according to human rights organizations, there were over 40 instances of kidnapping in the Republic in the first half of 2004. On 21–22 June, a series of raids took place on interior ministry targets in the Republic, variously attributed to Chechen, Ingush, and international Islamist militants; more than 90 people were killed. On 5 July Ingushetiya's mufti, Magomed haji Albogachiyev, resigned in protest at what he termed Zyazikov's 'anti-Islamic' policies. In June 2005 Zyazikov resigned as republican President to seek a demonstration of confidence from Putin; Putin duly nominated Zyazikov to a further term of office, which was confirmed by voting in the republican legislature on 14 June. In September Putin proposed a revision to the 1991 Law on the Rehabilitation of Repressed Peoples that would prevent the restoration of the internal borders between the Republics of the North Caucasus that existed prior to 1943–44, and thus impede the return of the disputed Prigorodnyi raion to Ingushetiya; the move was vehemently opposed by the republican People's Assembly. Between mid-August and mid-October more than 20 operations were carried out against security officials in the Republic by rebel insurgents; these attacks continued throughout November.

Economy

In 2002 the gross regional product of the Republic totalled 3,842.1m. roubles, or 8,222.0 roubles per head, the lowest figure recorded in any federal subject no figures were available for Chechnya. In 2002 there were 39 km of railways and 816 km of paved roads in the Republic.

By the early 2000s the role of agriculture in Ingushetiya's economy had considerably declined (the sector employed 16.4% of the Republic's work-force in 2003, compared with 28.5% in 1995), its primary activity being cattle-breeding. In 2003 the sector generated 1,800m. roubles. Ingushetiya's industry, which employed 9.4% of the working population and generated 880m. roubles in 2003, consists of electricity production, petroleum-refining and food-processing. The major petroleum company, LUKoil, was a participant in the construction of the Caspian pipeline running through the territory. From the mid-1990s the services sector had also made a contribution to the economy, with the local economy receiving substantial benefits from registration fees paid by companies operating in the so-called 'offshore' zone that was in operation in 1994–97. At that time, the resources of this zone accounted for some 70% of the Republic's capital investments, but it was terminated following criticism by the IMF. In 2001 the economic sectors providing the largest share of employment in Ingushetiya were trade and commerce (21.0% of the total) and construction (15.9%).

In 2003 the economically active population of Ingushetiya numbered 143,000, when 53.1% of the Republic's labour force were unemployed—by far the highest level of any federal subject, excluding Chechnya—compared with 34.9% in 2001. In 2003 the average monthly wage in the Republic was 3,576.0 roubles. In 2003 the republican budget showed a surplus of 6.5m. roubles. In 2003 the Republic's foreign trade amounted to US $14.7m. in exports and $0.3m. in imports. At the end of 2003 there were around 1,000 small businesses registered in the Republic.

Directory

President: MURAT M. ZYAZIKOV (elected 28 April 2002; appointment confirmed 14 June 2005), 366720 Ingushetiya, Magas, Dom Pravitelstva; tel. and fax (8734) 55-11-55; e-mail murad@ingushetia.ru; internet ingushetia.ru.

Chairman of the Government (Prime Minister): IBRAGIM MALSAGOV, 366720 Ingushetiya, Magas, Dom Pravitelstva; tel. (8734) 55-11-05.

Chairman of the People's Assembly: MAKHMUD S. SAKALOV, 366720 Ingushetiya, Magas, Narodnoye Sobraniye; tel. (8734) 55-12-00; fax (87322) 2-56-80.

Chief Representative of the Republic of Ingushetiya in the Russian Federation: KHAMZAT M. BELKHAROYEV, 109044 Moscow, ul. Vorontsovskaya 22/2; tel. (495) 912-93-09; fax (495) 912-92-75.

Head of Magas City Administration: VAKHA U. MERZHOYEV, tel. (8734) 55-12-33.

Kabardino-Balkar Republic

The Kabardino-Balkar Republic is situated on the northern slopes of the Greater Caucasus and on the Kabardin Flatlands. It forms part of the Southern Federal Okrug and the North Caucasus Economic Area. North Osetiya—Alaniya (Ossetia) lies to the east and there is an international border with Georgia in the south-west. Stavropol lies to the north, with the Karachai-Cherkess Republic to the west. The Republic's major rivers are the Terek and the Baskan. The Republic occupies 12,500 sq km (4,800 sq miles), of which one-half is mountainous. The highest peak in Europe, twin-peaked Elbrus, at a height of 5,642 m (18,517 feet), is situated in the Republic. According to the census of 9–16 October 2002, the population of the Republic was 901,494 and the population density 72.1 per sq km; 56.6% of the population lived in urban areas. 55.3% of the population were Kabardin, 25.1% were ethnically Russian, 11.6% were Balkar, 1.1% Osetiyan, 1.0% Turkish and 0.8% Ukrainian. Both the Kabardins and the Balkars are Sunni Muslims. The Kabardins' native language belongs to the Abkhazo-Adyge group of Caucasian languages. The Balkars speak a language closely related to Karachai, part of the Kipchak group of the Turkic branch of the Uralo-Altaic family. Both peoples almost exclusively speak their native tongue as a first language, but many are fluent in the official language, Russian. The capital of the Republic is at Nalchik, which had a population of 273,900 in 2002, according to provisional census results. The Kabardino-Balkar Republic is included in the time zone GMT+3.

History

The Turkic Kabardins, a Muslim people of the North Caucasus, are believed to be descended from the Adyges. They settled on the banks of the Terek river, mixed with the local Alan people, and became a distinct ethnic group in the 15th century. They were converted to Islam by the Khanate of Crimea in the early 16th century, but in 1561 appealed to Tsar Ivan IV for protection against Tatar rule. The Ottoman Turks and the Persians (Iranians) also had interests in the region, and in 1739 Kabardiya was established as a neutral state between the Ottoman and Russian Empires. In

1774, however, the region once again became Russian territory under the terms of the Treaty of Kuçuk Kainavci. Although the Kabardins were not openly hostile to the Russian authorities, in the 1860s many of them migrated to the Ottoman Empire. The Balkars were pastoral nomads until the mid-18th century, when they were forced to retreat further into the Northern Caucasus Mountains, where they settled as farmers and livestock breeders. They were converted to Islam by Crimean Tatars, followed by the Nogai from the Kuban basin, although their faith retained strong elements of their animist traditions. Balkariya came under Russian control in 1827, when it was dominated by the Kabardins. Many ethnic Russians migrated to the region during the 19th century. In 1921 autonomous Balkar and Kabardin Okrugs were created within the Mountain (Gorskaya) People's Republic. In January 1922 the two former Okrugs (which had been recently separated from the Mountain Republic and reconstituted as Autonomous Oblasts) were merged into a Kabardino-Balkar Autonomous Okrug (which became an ASSR on 5 December 1936), although the process of integrating the two polities was achieved in defiance of widespread hostility from both peoples. In 1943 the Balkars were deported to Kazakhstan and Central Asia, in response to their alleged collaboration with German forces during the Second World War, and the territory thereby became the Kabardin ASSR. Following the rehabilitation of the Balkars in 1956, in the following year the Republic reverted to its previous name.

Thus, although greatly outnumbered by Kabardins and Russians, the Balkars had developed a strong sense of ethnic identity. In 1991 they joined the Assembly of Turkic Peoples and on 18 November 1996 the first congress of the National Council of the Balkar People declared the formation of a 'Republic of Balkariya' within the Russian Federation; this declaration, which had little support among the Balkar population, was rescinded later in the month. Meanwhile, the Kabardino-Balkar Republic declared its sovereignty on 31 December 1991, and signed a bilateral treaty with the federal authorities during 1995. Kokov was elected to a second term of office in January 1997.

In the 1990s the republican leadership took a pragmatic approach to reform and encouraged foreign investment. A new republican Constitution was adopted in July 2001, which prevented the Republic from existing independently of the Russian Federation. In August it was reported that an attempt to stage a *coup d'état* in the Republic, and in the neighbouring Karachai-Cherkess Republic, had been prevented, and that the alleged leaders of the plot had been arrested. On 13 January 2002 Kokov was elected to serve a third term as republican President, receiving 87.2% of the votes cast. Republican legislative elections to a new, unicameral, legislature (replacing a bicameral parliament), took place on 7 December 2003, concurrently with elections to the federal State Duma. According to Central Election Commission figures for the March 2004 federal presidential elections, Kabardino-Balkariya achieved the second highest voter turnout (98%) and the second highest proportion of support for the victorious incumbent, Vladimir Putin (96.5%), of any subject in the Federation. Observers and opposition activists, however, disputed the veracity of these figures.

From mid-2004 increasing concern was expressed at an apparent increase in support for militant Islamist groups in the Republic, in particularly among the Balkar population. Militant Islamists associated with the Yarmuk Dzhamaat group, aligned with the Chechen rebel leader, Shamil Basayev, claimed responsibility for an attack, in December, on the offices of the Federal Anti-narcotics Service in Nalchik, in which four people were killed; a significant number of weapons and quantity of ammunition were also stolen in the attack; members of Yarmuk had also been implicated in the killing of two police officers in August, when eight militants had reportedly escaped capture by up to 400 heavily armed members of the security forces. The leader of Yarmuk, Muslim Atayev, was shot dead in Nalchik in January 2005, while his presumed successor, Rusam Bekanov, was also killed in a gun-fight in April. Meanwhile, the abolition of the separate administrative status of a number of ethnically Balkar villages, and their absorption into the municipality of Nalchik in February was a further source of discontent. Tensions in the Republic were heightened further following reports, in late April, that nine female students at the Kabardino-Balkar State University in Nalchik had been detained, threatened with expulsion from the University, and questioned by police for meeting regularly to recite the Islamic scriptures and wearing the Islamic veil, activities which were deemed to violate university regulations. In late August the Nalchik authorities prohibited public rallies in the city, following the assassinations of a total of six police officers on two occasions over the previous month. On 16 September Kokov submitted his resignation, on grounds of ill-health. (He died the following month.) On 28 September the republican legislature approved Putin's nominee, a former Gosudarstvennaya Duma (State Duma) deputy, Arsen Kanokov, as President. On 13 October up to 100 militants staged a series of co-ordinated attacks against government, police, and commercial buildings across Nalchik. In the fighting that ensued between rebels and members of the security forces some 130 people were killed, including 93 militants and 12 civilians, according to official reports. Basayev, subsequently claimed responsibility for the organization of the attacks; Yarmuk also claimed to have participated in the attacks as part of a 'Caucasus Front' of militants, the formation of which had been announced earlier in the year. Many of the bodies of those killed in the clashes were held by police, under the 2002 federal law on terrorism. This gave rise to demonstrations by their relatives and a subsequent appeal to the European Court of Human Rights. Amid accusations of police brutality, a massive security operation was launched in October against suspected participants in the raids. In the same month the republican legislature adopted a resolution appealing to the federal authorities to impose temporary travel restrictions between the federal republics of the North Caucasus and to take measures to combat the widespread poverty and unemployment across the region. In addition to adopting measures intended to improve the Republic's economy, Kanokov pledged in the weeks following the attacks to reopen all unofficial mosques closed during Kokov's administration, and announced other attempts to reach out to disaffected Muslims, although the apparent disappearance in November 2005 of Ruslan Nakhushev, a leading Muslim scholar in the Republic, who had not been seen after leaving the republican headquarters of the Federal Security Service, where he had been summoned in connection with the recent violence, was regarded as representing a significant setback to these proposals.

Economy

Gross regional product in the Kabardino-Balkar Republic amounted to 23,518.8m. roubles in 2002, equivalent to 26,088.7 roubles per head. The Republic's main industrial centres are at Nalchik, Tyrnauz and Prokhladnyi. In 2002 there were 133 km of railways and 2,918 km of roads in the Republic. Prokhladnyi is an important junction on the North Caucasus Railway. There is an international airport at Nalchik, from which there are regular flights to the Middle East, as well as to other cities within the Russian Federation.

The Republic's main agricultural activities are the production of grain, fruit and vegetables, and animal husbandry. In 2003 agriculture engaged 24.2% of the work-force and generated 13,049m. roubles. The Republic is rich in minerals, with reserves of petroleum, natural gas, gold, iron ore, garnet, talc and barytes. The industrial sector, which employed 20.8% of the work-force and generated 9,116m. roubles in 2003, chiefly comprises mechanical engineering, metal-working, non-ferrous metallurgy, food-processing, the production of electricity, and the production and processing of tungsten-molybdenum ores.

In 2003 the economically active population numbered 332,000, when 22.0% of the labour force were unemployed. The average monthly wage was 2,877.1 roubles. In 2003 there was a budgetary deficit of 259.7m. roubles. External trade amounted to US $12.1m. in exports and $8.2m. in imports in 2003. Most of the Republic's exports (of which raw materials comprise some 70%) are to Finland, Germany, the Netherlands, Turkey and the USA. Some four-fifths of its imports are from Europe. Foreign investment in the Republic in 2000 amounted to just $244,000. At the end of 2003 there were 2,300 small businesses registered in the Republic.

Directory

President: ARSEN B. KANOKOV (appointment confirmed 28 September 2005), 360028 Kabardino-Balkar Rep., Nalchik, pr. Lenina 27; tel. (8662) 40-41-42; fax (8662) 47-61-74; internet www.prezident-kbr.ru.

Prime Minister: GENNADII S. GUBIN, 360028 Kabardino-Balkar Rep., Nalchik, pr. Lenina 27; tel. (8662) 40-29-70; fax (8662) 47-61-83.

Chairman of Parliament: ILYAS B. BECHELOV, 360028 Kabardino-Balkar Rep., Nalchik, pr. Lenina 55; tel. (8662) 47-13-65; fax (8662) 47-27-13.

Chief Representative of the Kabardino-Balkar Republic in the Russian Federation: MUKHAMED M. SHOGENOV, 109004 Moscow, ul. B. Kommunisticheskaya 4; tel. (495) 911-18-52; fax (495) 912-40-53.

Head of Nalchik City Administration: KHAZRETALI BERDOV, 360000 Kabardino-Balkar Rep., Nalchik, ul. Sovetskaya 70; tel. (86622) 2-20-04.

Republic of Kalmykiya

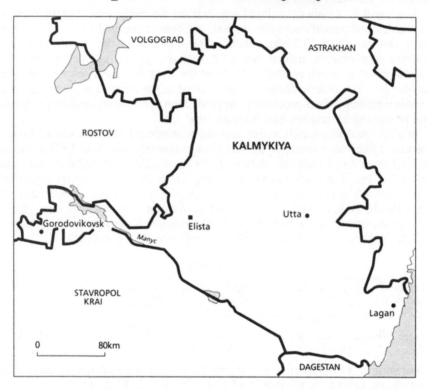

The Republic of Kalmykiya is situated in the north-western part of the Caspian Sea lowlands. It forms part of the Southern Federal Okrug and the Volga Economic Area. The south-eastern part of the Republic lies on the Caspian Sea. It borders Dagestan in the south, Stavropol Krai in the south-west, while Rostov, Volgograd and Astrakhan Oblasts lie to the west, north-west and north-east, respectively. The Republic occupies 75,900 sq km (29,300 sq miles), one-half of which is desert. According to the census of 9–16 October 2002, it had a population of 292,410 and a population density of 3.8 per sq km. Some 44.3% of the Republic's population lived in urban areas. 53.3% of the population were Kalmyk, 33.6% ethnically Russian, 2.5% Dargin, 2.0% Chechen, 1.7% Kazakh, 1.1% Turkish, 0.9% Ukrainian and 0.8% Avar. Uniquely for Europe, the dominant religion among the Kalmyks is Lamaism (Tibetan Buddhism). Some 90% of the indigenous population speak the Kalmyk language, which is from the Mongol division of the Uralo-Altaic family. The republican capital is at Elista, which had 104,300 inhabitants in 2002, according to provisional census results. Kalmykiya is included in the time zone GMT+3.

History

The Kalmyks (also known as the Kalmuks, Kalmucks, and Khalmgs) originated in Eastern Turkestan (Dzungaria or Sungaria, mostly in the People's Republic of China) and were a semi-nomadic Mongol-speaking people. Displaced by the Han

Chinese, some 100,000 Kalmyks migrated westwards, in 1608 reaching the Volga basin, which had been under Russian control since the subjugation of the Astrakhan Khanate in 1556. The region became the Kalmyk Khanate, which was dissolved by Russia in 1771. By this time the Kalmyk community was severely depleted, the majority having been slaughtered during a mass migration eastwards to protect the Oirots from persecution by the Chinese. Those that remained were dispersed: some settled along the Ural, Terek and Kuma rivers, some were moved to Siberia, while others became Don Cossacks. Many ethnic Russians and Germans settled in Kalmykiya during the 18th century. A Kalmyk Autonomous Oblast was established on 4 November 1920 and the Kalmyks living in other regions of Russia were resettled there. Its status was upgraded to that of an ASSR in 1935. In 1943 the Republic was dissolved as retribution for the Kalmyks' alleged collaboration with German forces in the Second World War. The Kalmyks were deported to Central Asia, where they lived until the reconstitution of a Kalmyk Autonomous Oblast in 1957, which was restored to the status of an ASSR in 1958. (The Kalmyks were not, however, formally rehabilitated until 1993.) In the late 1990s territorial disputes between Kalmykiya and Astrakhan Oblast over a particularly fertile area known as the 'Black Lands' resurfaced, with Kalmykiya claiming three districts that had been part of the pre-1943 Kalmyk ASSR. These territories were of particular significance, because they stood on the route of a pipeline being constructed from Tengiz, Kazakhstan, to Novorossiisk, in Krasnodar Krai.

During the late 1980s a growing Kalmyk nationalist movement began protesting against the treatment of the Kalmyks under Stalin (Iosif Dzhugashvili) and demanding local control of the region's mineral resources. A declaration of sovereignty by the Republic was adopted on 18 October 1990. The Republic was known as the Republic of Kalmykiya—Khalmg Tangch in 1992–96. In April 1993 a business executive, Kirsan Ilyumzhinov, was elected as President of Kalmykiya. A new republican Constitution, known as the Steppe Legislation, was adopted on 5 April 1994. The new Constitution provided for a presidential form of government, with a presidential term of seven years, and for a unicameral legislature, the People's Khural, to which deputies were to be elected for terms of four years.

In October 1995 Ilyumzhinov (who was also elected head of the International Chess Federation—FIDE in that year) was the sole, unopposed candidate in the presidential election, in contravention of federal legislation. There was little serious challenge to his rule in the second half of the decade, although he attracted increasing controversy. Reforms to the republican Constitution, approved in mid-2002, appeared to place greater restrictions on the Kalmyk authorities than had hitherto existed; notably, elected local councils were to be established, and heads of local and city administrations to be reinstated. Following two rounds of polling, Ilyumzhinov was re-elected President on 27 October, receiving around 57% of the votes cast in the 'run-off' election. In January 2003 Ilyumzhinov dismissed the Prime Minister since 1999, Aleksandr Dorzhdeyev, and assumed the responsibilities of premier. Republican legislative elections took place on 7 December 2003, concurrently with elections to the federal State Duma. Suspicion that the vote-counting had been influenced in favour of a candidate in the federal elections supported by Ilyumzhinov precipitated two days of protest by opposition groups outside the President's office in Elista. Later in December Ilyumzhinov announced the appointment of a premier, Anatolii Kozachko. Further anti-Ilyumzhinov demonstrations took place in Elista in February 2004; another peaceful demonstration in Elista in September was violently dissolved, resulting in the hospitalization of at least 11 demonstrators. In November of that year the Tibetan Buddhist leader, the Dalai Lama (Tenzin Gyatso), visited the Republic, a measure that precipitated criticism from the authorities of the People's Republic of China, although the Russian Government emphasized that they regarded the trip as purely religious in nature, and unrelated to the status of Tibet (Xizang).

In October 2005, more than two years before the expiry of his mandate, Ilyumzhinov requested an expression of confidence in his administration (which would thereby result in his nomination to a further term as President) from the federal President, Vladimir Putin. Later that month Putin submitted Ilyumzhinov's name for confirmation by the republican legislature, which duly occurred on 24 October. Ilyumzhinov's move was thought to have come at a time when he was in favour with both Putin and the People's Khural.

Economy

In 2002 Kalmykiya's gross regional product amounted to 13,476.2m. roubles, or 46,086.7 roubles per head. Kalmykiya is primarily an agricultural territory. In the 1990s much of its agricultural land suffered from desertification, a consequence of its over-exploitation by the Soviet authorities during the 1950s. Kalmykiya's major industrial centres are at Elista and Kaspiiskii. At the end of 2002 there were 165 km of railway lines and 2,751 km of paved roads in the Republic. The Republic is intersected by the Astrakhan–Kizlyar railway line. The Republic has serious problems with its water supply, with a deficit of fresh water affecting almost all regions.

Although agricultural output declined sharply, in real terms, throughout much of the 1990s, in 2003 the sector employed 26.9% of the work-force, and generated 2,207m. roubles. Kalmykiya's agriculture consists mainly of animal husbandry. Industry, which engaged 7.7% of the working population and generated 1,722m. roubles in 2003, consists mainly of electricity production, the manufacture of building materials, and the production of petroleum and natural gas. The Republic has major hydrocarbons reserves, which, however, remain largely unexploited, and Kalmykiya remains a net importer of energy.

The economically active population in the Republic amounted to 142,000 in 2003, when 17.9% of the Republic's labour force were unemployed. The average monthly wage was 2,960.8 roubles. In December 2003 the cost of a 'minimum consumer basket' in Kalmykiya was 890.2 roubles, the third lowest of any federal subject. There was a budgetary surplus of 181.2m. roubles in 2003, when external trade comprised US $49.1m. in exports and $44.8m. in imports. In 1995 there was some US $1.64m. of foreign investment in the Republic (no more recent figures were available). At the end of 2003 around 600 small businesses were registered in the Republic.

Directory

President: KIRSAN N. ILYUMZHINOV (elected 11 April 1993, re-elected unopposed 15 October 1995, re-elected 27 October 2002; appointment confirmed 24 October 2005), 358000 Kalmykiya, Elista, pl. Lenina, Dom Pravitelstva; tel. (84722) 6-13-88; fax (84722) 6-28-80; e-mail kalmykia@data.ru; internet www.president.kalm.ru.

Chairman of the Government (Prime Minister): ANATOLII V. KOZACHKO, 358000 Kalmykiya, Elista, pl. Lenina, Dom Pravitelstva; tel. (84722) 6-13-88; fax (84722) 6-28-80; e-mail kalmykia@data.ru; internet kalm.ru.

Chairman of the People's Khural (Parliament): IGOR V. KICHIKOV, 358000 Kalmykiya, Elista, pl. Lenina, Dom Pravitelstva; tel. (84722) 5-27-35; fax (84722) 5-03-02.

Chief Representative of the Republic of Kalmykiya in the Russian Federation: ALEKSEI M. ORLOV, 121170 Moscow, ul. Poklonnaya 12/2; tel. (495) 249-87-47; fax (495) 249-87-41; e-mail kalmykia@data.ru; internet www.kalmykiaembassy.ru.

Head of Elista City Administration (Mayor): RADII N. BURULOV, 358000 Kalmykiya, Elista, ul. Lenina 249; tel. (84722) 5-35-81; fax (84722) 5-42-56.

Karachai-Cherkess Republic

The Karachai-Cherkess Republic is situated on the northern slopes of the Greater Caucasus. It forms part of the Southern Federal Okrug and the North Caucasus Economic Area. There are borders with Krasnodar to the north-west, Stavropol to the north-east and the Kabardino-Balkar Republic to the east. There is an international boundary with Georgia (mainly Abkhazia) to the south. Its major river is the Kuban. The Republic occupies 14,100 sq km (5,440 sq miles). According to the census of 9–16 October 2002, it had a population of 439,470 and a population density of 31.2 per sq km. 44.1% of the Republic's population inhabited urban areas. The capital city, Cherkessk, had a population of 116,400. Some 38.5% of the population were Karachai, 33.6% ethnically Russian, 11.3% Cherkess, 7.4% Abazin, 3.4% Nogai, 0.8% Osetiyan and 0.8% Ukrainian. Both the Karachai and the Cherkess are Sunni Muslims of the Hanafi school. The Cherkess speak a language close to Kabardin, from the Abkhazo-Adyge group of Caucasian languages, while the Karachais' native tongue, from the Kipchak group, is the same as that of the Balkars. The Karachai-Cherkess Republic is included in the time zone GMT+3.

History

The Karachai, a transhumant group descended from Kipchak tribes, were driven into the highlands of the North Caucasus by Mongol tribes in the 13th century. Their territory was annexed by the Russian Empire in 1828 and they continued to resist Russian rule throughout the 19th century. In the 1860s and 1870s many Karachai migrated to the Ottoman Empire to escape oppression by the tsarist regime, as did many Cherkess, a Circassian people descended from the Adyges who inhabited the region between the lower Don and Kuban rivers. They had come under Russian control in the 1550s, having sought protection from the Crimean Tatars and some Turkic tribes, including the Karachai. Relations between the Cherkess and Russia deteriorated as many Russians began to settle in Cherkess territory. Following the Treaty of Adrianople in 1829, by which the Ottomans abandoned their claim to the Caucasus region, a series of rebellions by the Circassians and reprisals by the

Russian authorities occurred. In 1864 Russia completed its conquest of the region and many Cherkess fled.

The Cherkess Autonomous Oblast was established in 1928 and was subsequently merged with the Karachai Autonomous Oblast to form the Karachai-Cherkess Autonomous Oblast. Following the deportation of the Karachai to Central Asia in late 1943, the region was renamed the Cherkess Autonomous Oblast, until the Karachai were rehabilitated and permitted to return in 1957. In February 1992 the President of the Russian Federation, Boris Yeltsin, presented draft legislation to the federal Supreme Council (Supreme Soviet) that provided for formation of a Karachai Republic within the Federation. However, a referendum held in the Oblast in March 1992 demonstrated widespread opposition to the division of the territory, which was upgraded to the status of a Republic, separate from Stavropol Krai, under the terms of the Federation Treaty, in the same month.

In 1995 the Republic signed a power-sharing treaty with the federal authorities. On 6 March 1996 a new constitutional system was adopted in the Republic, based on the results of a referendum on a republican presidency. The Communist Party of the Russian Federation remained the predominant party in the region. The Republic's first presidential election, in 1999, provoked violence and ethnic unrest, when a second round of voting, in May, reversed the positions achieved by the 'run-off' candidates, Stanislav Derev, an ethnic Cherkess (who secured 40% of the votes in the first round and 12% in the second), and Gen. Vladimir Semonov, an ethnic Karachai and a former Commander-in-Chief of the Russian Ground Troops (who secured 18% of the votes in the first round and 85% in the second). Semonov was confirmed as the winning candidate in August and sworn in on 14 September. In August 2001 it was reported that an attempt to stage a *coup d'état* in the Republic, and in neighbouring Kabardino-Balkar Republic, had been prevented. Following two rounds of voting in August 2003 (in the first round of which all five candidates were Karachai), Mustafa Batdyyev, hitherto director of the republican bank, was elected President, narrowly defeating Semonov.

Further unrest occured in late 2004. In late October Ansar Tipuyev, a deputy chairman of the Government, who in his previous post of first deputy interior minister had taken an uncompromising stance against militant Islamists, was assassinated in Cherkessk. The killing, in early November, of seven shareholders (all of whom were Karachai) in a cement company controlled by Ali Kaitov, Batdyyev's son-in-law, following a meeting at Kaitov's home, resulted in organized demonstrations against the republican authorities. Some 400 people demonstrated outside the presidential offices and demanded Batdyyev's resignation, ransacking the building and occupying it for two days. Kaitov and 12 other men were subsequently arrested on charges related to the killings, and the resignation of the republican prosecutor, later in the month, was regarded as a significant concession to the wishes of the demonstrators. In mid-May 2005 six militants, whom, the authorities stated, were associated with the radical Islamist Chechen rebel, Shamil Basayev, were killed in an operation by security forces in Cherkessk. In late June some 200 members of the Abazin population in the Republic broke into the republican parliamentary building in order to protest at recent changes to the structures of local government which, it was claimed, discriminated against the ethnic group. In early July the republican legislature approved legislation creating new national districts for the Abazin and Nogai groups, while the re-districting that had prompted the recent protests was suspended; the creation of a new Abazin district was approved by referendum on 25 December.

Economy

In 2002 gross regional product in the Karachai-Cherkess Republic totalled 10,539.2m. roubles, or 23,981.6 roubles per head. The Republic's major industrial centres are at Cherkessk and Karachayevsk. In 2002 it contained 51 km of railway track and 1,889 km of paved roads, including the Stavropol–Sukhumi (Abkhazia, Georgia) highway.

Agriculture employed some 19.7% of the working population and generated 4,905m. roubles in 2003 The principal crops include grain, sunflower seeds, sugar beet and vegetables, while animal husbandry is also significant. The Republic's main industries are petrochemicals, chemicals, mechanical engineering and metal-working, although the manufacture of building materials, food-processing and coal production are also important. In 2003 industry employed 18.5% of the work-force and generated 6,562m. roubles.

In 2003 the economically active population of the Republic numbered 185,000, and 19.0% of the Republic's labour force were unemployed. The average monthly wage was 3,080.9 roubles. In 2003 the republican budget recorded a deficit of 211.2m. roubles. International trade was minimal, amounting to US $7.9m. in exports, and $11.5m. in imports in 2003, and foreign investment in the Republic in 2001 amounted to less than $500. At the end of 2003 there were 1,200 small businesses registered in the Republic.

Directory

President and Head of the Republic: MUSTAFA A-A. BATDYYEV (elected 31 August 2003), 357100 Karachai-Cherkess Rep., Cherkessk, ul. Krasnoarmeiskaya 54; tel. (87822) 5-40-11; fax (87822) 5-29-80; e-mail info@kchr.info; internet www.kchr .info/?page=president.

Chairman of the Government: ALIK KH. KARDANOV, 357100 Karachai-Cherkess Rep., Cherkess, ul. Krasnoarmeiskaya 54; tel. (87822) 5-40-08; fax (87822) 5-40-20; e-mail info@kchr.info; internet www.kchr.info/government/index .php?section=premier.

Chairman of the People's Assembly: SERGEI A. SMORODIN, 357100 Karachai-Cherkess Rep., Cherkess, ul. Krasnoarmeiskaya 54; e-mail info@kchr.info; internet www.kchr.info/parlament/index.php?section=speeker.

Chief Representative of the Republic of the Karachai-Cherkess Republic in the Russian Federation: EMMA M. KARDANOVA, 119333 Moscow, ul. D. Ulyanova 4/2/2; tel. (495) 137-65-40.

Head of Cherkessk City Administration (Mayor): MIKHAIL M. YAKUSH, 357100 Karachai-Cherkess Rep., Cherkessk, pr. Lenina 54A; tel. (87822) 5-37-23; fax (87822) 5-78-43.

Republic of North Osetiya—Alaniya

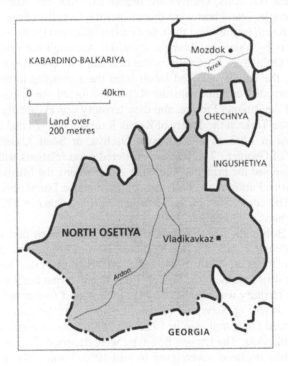

The Republic of North Osetiya—Alaniya, is situated on the northern slopes of the Greater Caucasus and forms part of the Southern Federal Okrug and the North Caucasus Economic Area. Of the other federal subjects, the Kabardino-Balkar Republic lies to the west, Stavropol Krai to the north, and Chechnya and Ingushetiya to the east. There is an international boundary with Georgia (the territories of the former South Ossetian Autonomous Oblast) in the south. Its major river is the Terek. In the north of the Republic are the steppelands of the Mozdok and Osetiyan Plains, while further south in the foothills are mixed pasture and beechwood forest (about one-fifth of the territory of the Republic is forested). Narrow river valleys lie in the southernmost, mountainous region. The territory of North Osetiya covers 8,000 sq km (3,090 sq miles). According to the census of 9–16 October 2002, it had a population of 710,275 and a population density of 88.8 per sq km. 65.4% of the Republic's population inhabited urban areas. 62.7% of the population were Osetiyan, 23.2% ethnically Russian, 3.0% Ingush, 2.4% Armenian, 1.8% Kumyk and 1.5% Georgian. Around one-quarter of Russians resident in the Republic were thought to have left North Osetiya between 1989 and 1999, largely owing to the decline of the military-industrial complex in the Republic, which had been their major employer. The Osetiyans speak an Indo-European language of the Persian (Iranian) group. According to provisional census results, in 2002 some 315,100 people lived in the capital, Vladikavkaz, situated in the east of the Republic. The Republic is included in the time zone GMT+3.

History

The Osetiyans (Ossetins, Oselty) are descended from the Alans, a tribe of the Samartian people. The Alans were driven into the foothills of the Caucasus by the Huns in the fourth century and their descendants (Ossetes) were forced further into the mountains by Tatar and Mongol invaders. Although the Osetiyans had been converted to Orthodox Christianity in the 12th and 13th centuries by the Georgians, a sub-group, the Digors, adopted Islam from the Kabardins in the 17th and 18th centuries. Perpetual conflict with the Kabardins forced the Osetiyans to seek the protection of the Russian Empire, and their territory was eventually ceded to Russia by the Ottoman Turks at the Treaty of Kuçuk Kainavci in 1774 and confirmed by the Treaty of Iaşi in 1792. (Transcaucasian Osetiya, or South Ossetia, subsequently became part of Georgia.) The Russians fostered good relations with the Osetiyans, as they represented the principal Christian group among the Muslim peoples of the North Caucasus. Furthermore, both ends of the strategic Darial pass were situated in the region. The completion of the Georgian Military Road in 1799 facilitated the Russian conquest of Georgia in 1801.

After the Bolshevik Revolution, and having briefly been part of the Mountain (Gorskaya) People's Autonomous Republic, North Osetiya was established as an Autonomous Oblast on 7 July 1924, and as an ASSR in 1936. The Osetiyans were rewarded for their loyalty to the Soviet Government during the Second World War: in 1944 their territory was expanded by the inclusion of former Ingush territories to the east and of part of Stavropol Krai to the north. Furthermore, for 10 years the capital, renamed Ordzhonikidze in 1932, was known as Dzaudzhikau, the Osetian form of Vladikavkaz. The Digors, however, were deported to Central Asia in 1944.

The Republic declared sovereignty in mid-1990. From 1991 there was considerable debate about some form of unification with South Ossetia (which had, however, been deprived of its autonomous status and merged with adjoining regions by the Georgian Supreme Soviet in December 1990). This resulted in armed hostilities between the South Ossetians and Georgian troops, during which thousands of refugees fled to North Osetiya. Meanwhile, the Republic's administration refused to recognize claims by the Ingush to the territory they were deprived of in 1944 (the Prigorodnyi raion—district), which led to the onset of violence in October 1992 and the imposition of a state of emergency in the affected areas (see Ingushetiya). Despite a peace settlement in 1994, the region remained unstable. (In late 1999 there were approximately 37,000 registered refugees from the armed hostilities in South Ossetia in the Republic, while at that time about 35,000 Ingush were still displaced from the Prigorodnyi raion, most of whom were living in Ingushetiya.) Under the terms of its Constitution, adopted on 7 December 1994, the Republic's name was amended to North Osetiya—Alaniya. A power-sharing agreement was signed with the federal authorities in 1995.

The territory was a redoubt of the Communist Party of the Russian Federation during the late 1990s, although in the 2000 presidential election Vladimir Putin received the highest share of the votes cast for any candidate in the region. In January 1998 Aleksandr Dzasokhov, a former member of the Communist Party of the Soviet Union Politburo, and the chairman of the Russian delegation to the Parliamentary Assembly of the Council of Europe, was elected as republican President, with 75% of the votes cast.

Instability in North Osetiya, as elsewhere in the North Caucasus, increased from 1999, as insurgency became increasingly widespread. A bomb exploded in Vladikavkaz in March, killing 42. In March 2001 three simultaneous explosions in the republic killed over 20. (The trial of two Ingush residents of Prigorodnyi, on charges of perpetrating bombings in Vladikavkaz in 1999–2002, and of maintaining contacts with Chechen rebels commenced at the Supreme Court of North Osetiya—Alaniya in April 2003.) On 27 January 2002 Dzasokhov was re-elected President, receiving 56.0% of the votes cast. In September the power-sharing agreement of 1995 was dissolved, and in October North Osetiya and Ingushetiya signed an 'Agreement on the Development of Co-operation and Good Neighbourly Relations', which committed both sides to adopting measures to resolve remaining differences. Following republican legislative elections held in May–June 2003, supporters of the pro-Government Unity and Fatherland-United Russia party were reported to have a working majority in the chamber. In early June a suicide bomber detonated explosives close to a bus carrying federal air-force personnel near Mozdok, killing 17 people; later in the month 13 police officers were killed when their vehicle hit a landmine in the Republic. On 1 August more than 50 people were killed, and at least 100 others injured, following a suicide bombing outside a military hospital at Mozdok, near one of the principal bases for federal troops fighting in Chechnya.

On 1 September 2004, the first day of the school year, around 30 armed militants seized control of a school in the city of Beslan, taking at least 1,100 pupils, parents and teachers hostage. Federal special-forces officers stormed the school on 3 September, following a series of explosions. Official figures claimed that some 331 hostages were killed, including 186 children, although some independent estimates placed the number of fatalities at closer to 600. The siege was characterized by conflicting information and uncertainty regarding the number of hostages and casualties, the cause of the storming of the school, and the number and ethnicity of the hostage takers. The demands of the hostage-takers were variously reported as the withdrawal of Russian troops from Chechnya and the release of militants captured in the raids in Ingushetiya in mid-June. Accusations of deliberate obfuscation and incompetence were levelled at the regional and federal authorities; the regional FSB chief and Minister of Internal Affairs both resigned, and after a crowd of some 3,500 gathered in Vladikavkaz on 8 September to demand the resignation of President Dzasokhov, the entire republican Government of Mikhail Shatalov was dismissed. Alan Boradzov was appointed Chairman of the Government on 10 September. On 31 May Dzasokhov resigned as President; his departure followed several months of demands that he leave office issued by relatives of those killed in Beslan. The nomination by the federal President, Vladimir Putin, of Taimuraz Mamsurov, hitherto Chairman of the republican legislature, was approved by voting in that body on 7 June. A new Chairman of the Government, Aleksandr Merkulov (hitherto First Deputy Chairman), was approved by the republican legislature several days later. Meanwhile, in May 2005 the trial of Nurpasha Kulayev, a Chechen militant who was reported to be the sole survivor of the 32 instigators of the hostage-taking at Beslan, commenced in Vladikavaz; Kulayev was charged with eight offences including murder, terrorism and hostage-taking. The trial became a focus of attention for demonstrators, led by the relations, and particularly the mothers, of those killed in Beslan. Although Mamsurov was a native of Beslan, and the father of two children injured in the siege in September 2004, his appointment failed to satisfy protestors, who continued to demand the resignation of all those who had held office under

Dzasokhov, and that the leaders of both the republican and federal authorities be held responsible for the deaths at Beslan. In August Mamsurov publicly appealed to Putin to end the moratorium on the death penalty, while in the following month Mamsurov and Stanislav Kesayev, head of the republic's parliamentary commission investigating the Beslan tragedy, were criticized by the Deputy Prosecutor-General for being unwilling to co-operate with federal investigators.

Economy

In 2002 gross regional product in North Osetiya—Alaniya totalled 16,757.3m. roubles, equivalent to 23,592.7 roubles per head. Its major industrial centres are at Vladikavkaz, Mozdok and Beslan. In 2002 the Republic contained 144 km of railway track. There were 2,288 km of paved roads, and one of the two principal road routes from Russia to the Transcaucasus, the Transcaucasian Highway. There is an international airport at Vladikavkaz.

Agriculture in North Osetiya, which employed 16.1% of the labour force and generated 5,738m. roubles in 2003, consists mainly of vegetable and grain production, horticulture, viniculture and animal husbandry. In the same year industry employed 17.3% of the work-force and generated 11,446m. roubles. The Republic's main industries are radio-electronics, non-ferrous metallurgy and food-processing. There are also five hydroelectric power stations, with an average capacity of around 80 MWh.

The economically active population totalled 330,000 in 2003, when 10.1% of the labour force were unemployed, compared with 28.5% in 2000. Those in employment earned an average wage of 2,792.6 roubles per month in 2003. The republican budget showed a deficit of 35.8m. roubles in 2003. In that year external trade comprised US $47.1m. in exports and $84.1m. in imports. At the end of 2003 there were 1,300 small businesses registered in the Republic.

Directory

Head of the Republic: TAIMURAZ D. MAMSUROV (appointment confirmed 7 June 2005), 362038 North Osetiya—Alaniya, Vladikavkaz, pl. Svobody 1, Dom Pravitelstva; tel. (8672) 53-35-24; fax (8672) 74-92-48.

Chairman of the Government: ALEKSANDR MERKULOV, 362038 North Osetiya—Alaniya, Vladikavkaz, pl. Svobody 1, Dom Pravitelstva; tel. (8672) 53-35-56; fax (8672) 75-87-30.

Chairman of the Parliament: LARISA B. KHABITSOVA, 362038 North Osetiya—Alaniya, Vladikavkaz, pl. Svobody 1, Parlament; tel. (8672) 53-81-01; fax (8672) 53-93-46; e-mail parliament@rno-a.ru; internet parliament.rno-a.ru.

Chief Representative of the Republic of North Osetiya—Alaniya in the Russian Federation: VLADIMIR Z. GUGKAYEV, 109028 Moscow, per. Durasovskii 1/9; tel. (495) 916-21-47; fax (495) 916-25-22.

Head of Vladikavkaz City Administration (Mayor): KAZBEK PAGIYEV, 362040 North Osetiya—Alaniya, Vladikavkaz, pl. Shtyba 1; fax (8672) 75-34-35.

Krasnodar Krai

Krasnodar Krai, often known as the Kuban, is situated in the south of European Russia, in the north-western region of the Greater Caucasus and in the Kuban-Azov lowlands. The Krai forms part of the Southern Federal Okrug and the North Caucasus Economic Area. It has a short international border with Georgia (Abkhazia) in the south, while the Karachai-Cherkess Republic and Stavropol Krai lie to the east and Rostov Oblast to the north-east. The Krai's territory encloses the Republic of Adygeya (formerly an Autonomous Oblast within the Krai). The Krai lies on the Black Sea in the south-west and on the Sea of Azov in the north-west. The narrow Kerch Gulf, in places only 10 km (six miles) wide, separates the western tip of the province from Crimea (Ukraine). Its major river is the Kuban. The Krai covers 76,000 sq km (29,340 sq miles). According to the census of 9–16 October 2002, the territory had a population of 5,125,221, compared with 4,621,000 in 1989; this increase chiefly reflecting migration into the region from the unstable regions of the North Caucasus. The province's population density in 2002 was 67.4 per sq km, a considerably higher figure than the national average. Some 53.5% of the population lived in urban areas. 86.6% of the population were ethnically Russian, 5.4% Armenian and 2.6% Ukrainian. Krasnodar, the Krai's administrative centre, had a population of 644,800, according to provisional census figures. Other important cities included the resort town of Sochi (328,800) and Novorossiisk (231,900). Krasnodar Krai is included in the time zone GMT+3.

History

Krasnodar city (known as Yekaterinodar until 1920) was founded as a military base in 1793, during the campaign of Catherine (Yekaterina) II—'the Great' to win control of the Black Sea region for the Russian Empire, which was eventually achieved in 1796. Dominated by the 'Whites' in the civil wars that followed the collapse of the tsarist regime, the Krai, which then included the territory which now forms the Republic of Adygeya, was formed on 13 September 1937. In post-Soviet Russia the area became a stronghold of the Communist Party of the Russian Federation (CPRF). In September 1993 the Krai Soviet (Council) condemned President Boris Yeltsin's dissolution of the federal legislature. In October the Soviet refused to dissolve itself, but announced that elections would be held to a new, 32-member, provincial legislative assembly in March 1994, although this poll was subsequently postponed. CPRF leadership of the new Provincial Legislative Assembly was not seriously challenged by other forces, and the party also fared well in federal parliamentary and presidential elections in the province in 1995–96.

During 1996 attempts by the incumbent Governor, Nikolai Yegorov, to postpone the gubernatorial election scheduled for December failed, however, and Nikolai Kondratenko, a communist and the former Chairman of the Provincial Soviet, was elected Governor by a large majority. Supporters of Kondratenko retained control of the provincial legislative assembly at elections held in November 1998. Kondratenko attracted national notoriety for his promotion of hostility towards minority groups, particularly Jews and Armenians, while a voluntary Cossack militia in the region, established in the late 1990s, was also accused of persecuting members of ethnic minorities. Following a gubernatorial election, held on 3 December 2000, Kondratenko was replaced as Governor by Aleksandr Tkachev, who obtained 82% of the votes cast. Kondratenko did not stand as a candidate in the election, citing ill health. (However, in advance of elections to the federal State Duma in December 2003, the CPRF chose Kondratenko as its second-placed candidate on its federal party list.) Tkachev also became noted for his xenophobic remarks, on occasion urging various groups of non-ethnic Russians to leave the region. At the provincial legislative election, held on 24 November, Kondratenko's chauvinist 'Fatherland' movement (unconnected with the pro-Government Unity and Fatherland-United Russia party) won 32 of the 50 seats. Tkachev won a second term in the gubernatorial election on 14 March 2004, receiving 84% of the votes cast.

From the late 1990s the presence of some 21,000 Meshketian Turks—who had been exiled to the region from Georgia under Stalin (Iosif Dzhugashvili—Soviet leader 1924–53), or who sought refuge in the Krai following the outbreak of inter-ethnic violence in the Fergana valley (in Kyrgyzstan, Tajikistan and Uzbekistan) in 1989 (the majority of whom were stateless) in the Krai, was exploited by the Fatherland movement. In 2002 the Krai implemented legislation that restricted the granting of permanent residency permits to migrants, and limited access to housing and education for those without permanent residency. In October the US mission to the Organization for Security and Co-operation in Europe (OSCE) issued a statement which, *inter alia*, criticized the treatment of Meshketian Turks by the provincial authorities, and which urged the federal authorities to intervene to ensure that full civil rights were granted to them. By mid-2004 almost 5,000 Meshketian Turks had received Russian citizenship. A large proportion of the remainder, however, accepted an offer to emigrate to the USA, with the first emigrants departing in July. In November 2005 it was reported that more that 5,000 Meshketian Turks had resettled in the USA, with a further 4,400 preparing to leave Krasnodar Krai for that country. An additional 7,000 were reported to have filed applications for resettlement with US officials. In the same month, and amid reports of violence by Cossacks against the Meshketian Turks, a law was passed by the Gosudarstvennaya Duma (State Duma) allowing Cossacks to serve in special units in the military, and to work with police and border-control authorities.

Meanwhile, in September 2003 work commenced to construct a causeway across the Kerch Strait, which separates the Crimea region of Ukraine from the Taman peninsula, between the Black Sea and the Sea of Azov. The regional authorities stated that the causeway was required to protect part of the Krai from environmental erosion; however, Ukraine argued that the causeway would encroach on its territory and dispatched border troops to the nearby island of Tuzla, of which it claimed ownership. In late October, following talks between the leaders of the Russian and Ukrainian Governments, Russia agreed to halt work on the causeway's construction, provided that Ukraine withdrew its troops from Tuzla. On 24 December federal President Vladimir Putin signed an agreement with the President of Ukraine, Leonid Kuchma, recognising the status of the Sea of Azov and the Kerch Strait as inland waters of both Russia and Ukraine, granting freedom of navigation to vessels of both countries in those waters (but excluding the military vessels of other countries without invitation), and pledging to co-operate in clearly defining the border between the two states in the area.

Economy

In 2002 gross regional product in Krasnodar Krai amounted to 234,503.7m. roubles, or 45,754.8 roubles per head. Krasnodar is one of the Krai's main industrial centres, as are Armavir, Novorossiisk and Kropotkin. Novorossiisk is one of the largest seaports in Russia, while Tuapse, Yeisk and Temryuk are also important seaports. In 2002 the Krai had 2,126 km of railway track and 10,785 km of paved roads.

The Krai's principal crops are grain, sugar beet, rice, tobacco, essential-oil plants, tea and hemp. Horticulture, viniculture and animal husbandry are also important. Agricultural output was worth 71,450m. roubles in 2003, the highest agricultural output of any federal subject), when 19.7% of the work-force were engaged in agriculture. There are important reserves of petroleum and natural gas in Krasnodar Krai, and petroleum is refined in the territory. The Krai's main industries are food-processing (which comprised 45.7% of industrial output in 2002), electricity generation, fuel extraction, mechanical engineering and metal-working, and building materials. In 2003 industry employed 15.6% of the work-force and generated 111,174m. roubles. The tourism sector is also important: the region's climate, scenery and mineral and mud springs attracted around 6m. visitors annually in the mid-1990s, when some 400,000 people were employed in tourism. The Krai contains the resort towns of Sochi, Anapa and Tuapse. The transportation and refinery of Caspian Sea hydrocarbons reserves brought economic benefits to the region, and particularly Novorossiisk, the terminus of major petroleum pipelines from Baku, Azerbaijan and Tengiz, Kazakhstan, which opened in 1997 and 2001, respectively.

In 2003 the economically active population numbered 2,252,000, and 10.1% of the labour force were unemployed. The average monthly wage was 4,033.1 roubles.

In 2003 there was a budgetary deficit of 1,403.9m. roubles. International trade comprised US $1,494.2m of exports and $834.1m. of imports. The recommencement, in January 2003, of passenger rail services between Sochi and Sukhumi, in Abkhazia, for the first time since the initiation of the Abkhaz–Georgian conflict in 1992, was expected to facilitate increased international trade with the separatist region. (The railway line was closed briefly by the Russian authorities in December 2004, following a disputed presidential election in Abkhazia, but subsequently reopened.) Foreign investment amounted to $325.7m. in 2003. At the end of that year 29,600 small businesses were registered in the Krai.

Directory

Head of the Provincial Administration: ALEKSANDR N. TKACHEV (elected 3 December 2000, re-elected 14 March 2004), 350014 Krasnodar, ul. Krasnaya 35; tel. (861) 262-57-16; fax (861) 268-35-42; e-mail registry@kuban.ru; internet admkrai .kuban.ru.

Chairman of the Legislative Assembly: VLADIMIR A. BEKETOV, 350014 Krasnodar, ul. Krasnaya 3; tel. (861) 268-50-07; fax (861) 268-37-41; internet www.kubzsk.ru.

Chief Representative of Krasnodar Krai in the Russian Federation: DMITRII L. MIKHEYEV, 119180 Moscow, per. 2-i Kazachii 6; tel. (495) 238-20-28.

Head of Krasnodar City Administration (Mayor): VLADIMIR L. YEVLANOV, 350000 Krasnodar, ul. Krasnaya 122; tel. (861) 255-43-48; fax (861) 255-01-56; e-mail post@krd.ru; internet www.krd.ru.

Stavropol Krai

Stavropol Krai is situated in the central Caucasus region and extends from the Caspian lowlands in the east to the foothills of the Greater Caucasus Mountains in the south-west. It is part of the Southern Federal Okrug and the North Caucasus Economic Area. It borders Krasnodar Krai to the west, Rostov Oblast to the north-west, Kalmykiya to the north and north-east, Dagestan to the east, and there are borders to the south with (from east to west): the Chechen (Nokchi) Republic, North Osetiya—Alaniya, the Kabardino-Balkar Republic and the Karachai-Cherkess Republic. Much of the territory is steppe. Its total area is 66,500 sq km (25,670 sq miles). According to the census of 9–16 October 2002, the population numbered 2,735,139 and the population density 41.1 per sq km; 55.9% of the population lived in urban areas. 81.6% of the population were ethnically Russian, 5.5% Armenian, 1.7% Ukrainian, 1.5% Dargin, 1.2% Greek and 0.8% Nogai. The Krai's administrative centre is at Stavropol, which had a population of 354,600 in 2002, according to provisional census results. Other major cities are Pyatigorsk (140,300), Nevinnomyssk (132,100) and Kislovodsk (129,800). Stavropol Krai is included in the time zone GMT+3.

History

Stavropol city was founded in 1777 as part of the consolidation of Russian rule in the Caucasus. The territory was created on 13 February 1924, although it was originally known as South-Eastern Oblast (when it also incorporated territories of Krasnodar Krai) and, subsequently, North Caucasus Krai. It was named Ordzhonikidze Krai in 1937–43, before adopting its current title. The former Karachai and Cherkess Autonomous Oblasts, which were reconstituted as the Karachai-Cherkess Republic upon the adoption of the 1992 Federation Treaty, previously formed part of the Krai.

In March 1994 elections were held to a new representative body, the Provincial State Duma. In June 1995 the town of Budennovsk, situated about 150 km north of the Chechen border, was the scene of a large-scale hostage-taking operation at a hospital by rebel Chechen forces led by Shamil Basayev; over 1,000 civilians were seized, and more than 100 people were killed during the siege. In the gubernatorial elections of November 1996 the Communist Party of the Russian Federation candidate, Aleksandr Chernogorov, defeated the government-supported incumbent. Chernogorov was re-elected for a further term as Governor in December 2000. In June 2002, following a similar development in neighbouring Krasnodar Krai, the regional legislature approved legislation, which, in contravention of federal requirements, sought to place restrictions on the number of immigrants permitted to settle in specific regions of the Krai. There was a series of bomb attacks in the Krai during 2000–03, which official sources attributed to Chechen separatists, and in which more than 75 people died. These included a bomb attack on a train near the town of Yessentuki, in the south of the Krai, in December 2003, which killed at least 45 people and injured about 170.

In September 2005 Chernogorov sought an expression of confidence from federal President Vladimir Putin (which would thereby result in his being appointed to a further term of office), three months before the expiry of his mandate. During a subsequent radio broadcast Putin stated that Chernogorov's reappointment would be conditional on the resolution of a particular local issue, namely that of running water in Degtyarevskii village; on the same day the Governor allocated 80m. roubles for the repair of the village's water system. He was duly nominated for a third term, and on 31 October the Krai's legislature approved his appointment.

Economy

In 2002 Stavropol Krai's gross regional product was 85,482.3m. roubles, or 31,253.4 roubles per head. Its main industrial centres are at Stavropol, Nevinnomyssk and Budennovsk. In 2002 there were 937 km of railway lines and 7,580 km of paved roads in the Krai.

The Krai contains extremely fertile soil. Agriculture, which employed 21.5% of the work-force and generated 31,490m. roubles in 2003, consists mainly of grain, sunflower seeds and sugar beet and vegetables. Horticulture, viniculture, bee-keeping and animal husbandry are also important. The Krai's main industries are food-processing, mechanical engineering, production of building materials, chemicals and petrochemicals and the production of natural gas, petroleum, non-ferrous metal ores and coal, and electrical energy. In 2003 industry employed 15.1% of the labour force and generated 54,118m. roubles in 2003.

The economically active population of Stavropol Krai numbered 1,226,000 in 2003, when 10.3% of the region's labour force were unemployed. The average monthly wage was 3,512.2 roubles. In 2003 there was a budgetary surplus of 690.4m. roubles. In that year the value of exports from the Krai amounted to US $344.6m., and imports were worth $198.1m. Foreign investment in the territory amounted to $13.8m. At the end of 2003 there were some 12,700 small businesses registered in the Krai.

Directory

Head of the Provincial Administration (Governor): ALEKSANDR L. CHERNOGOROV (elected 17 November 1996, re-elected 17 December 2000; appointment confirmed

31 October 2005), 355025 Stavropol, pl. Lenina 1; tel. (8652) 35-22-52; fax (8652) 35-03-30; e-mail stavadm@stavropol.net; internet gubernator.stavkray.ru.

Chairman of the Provincial State Duma: YURII A. GONTAR, 355025 Stavropol, pl. Lenina 1; tel. (8652) 34-82-55; fax (8652) 35-14-55; internet www.dumask.ru.

Chief Representative of Stavropol Krai in the Russian Federation: ANATOLII L. KOLIYEV, 119034 Moscow, ul. Prichistenka 40/2/1; tel. (495) 708-33-66; fax (495) 203-55-39.

Head of Stavropol City Administration (Mayor): DMITRII S. KUZMIN, 355000 Stavropol, pr. K. Marksa 96/307; tel. (8652) 26-78-06; fax (8652) 26-28-23; e-mail goradm@smtn.stavropol.ru; internet www.stavropol.stavkray.ru.

Astrakhan Oblast

Astrakhan Oblast is situated in the Caspian lowlands and forms part of the Southern Federal Okrug and the Volga Economic Area. Lying between the Russian federal subject of Kalmykiya to the south and the former Soviet state of Kazakhstan to the east, Astrakhan is a long, relatively thin territory, which flanks the River Volga as it flows out of Volgograd Oblast in the north-west towards the Caspian Sea to the south-east, via a delta at Astrakhan. The delta is one of the largest in the world and occupies more than 24,000 sq km (9,260 sq miles) of the Caspian lowlands. The Oblast has some 200 km (over 120 miles) of coastline and occupies 44,100 sq km (17,000 sq miles). According to the census of 9–16 October 2002, its population was 1,005,276 and its population density 22.8 per sq km. 67.9% of the population lived in urban areas. 69.7% of the population were ethnically Russian, 14.2% Kazakh, 7.0% Tatar, 1.3% Ukrainian, 1.0% Chechen and 0.8% Azeri. The Oblast's administrative centre is at Astrakhan (formerly Khadzhi-Tarkhan), which had a population of 506,400, according to provisional census results. The city lies at 22 m (72 feet) below sea level and is protected from the waters of the Volga delta by 75 km of dykes. Astrakhan Oblast is included in the time zone GMT+3.

www.europaworld.com

History

The Khanate of Astrakhan, which was formed in 1446, following the dissolution of the Golden Horde, was conquered by the Russians in 1556. The region subsequently became an important centre for trading in timber, grain, fish and petroleum. Astrakhan Oblast was founded on 27 December 1943. (The region had briefly formed part of the Kazakh SSR in the early 1920s.)

There was considerable hardship in the region following the dissolution of the USSR and the economic reforms of the early 1990s. Dissatisfaction was indicated by the continued pre-eminence of the Communist Party of the Russian Federation in the Oblast. The Governor, Anatolii Guzhvin, initially a federal appointee, retained his post at elections in 1997, and was re-elected for a further term of office in December 2000, receiving 81% of the votes cast. Elections to the regional legislature, the Representative Assembly, were held on 28 October 2001; in the following month the Assembly voted to rename itself the State Duma. The region continued to suffer from severe social difficulties in the early 2000s; it was reported that the operations of the Oblast's police force had been subject to criticism in a document commissioned in late 2002 by the federal Ministry of Internal Affairs. On 17 August 2004 Guzhvin died, following a heart attack. The hitherto First Deputy Governor, Aleksandr Zhilkin, assumed gubernatorial responsibilities, on an acting basis, pending elections. On 5 December Zhilkin was elected Governor, having received the support of the pro-Government Unity and Fatherland-United Russia party. He obtained 65.3% of the votes cast in an election contested by seven candidates. The rate of participation in the election was 48.5%.

Economy

Astrakhan Oblast's gross regional product was 44,807.2m. roubles in 2002, equivalent to 44,572.0 roubles per head. The Oblast's main industrial centres are at Astrakhan and Akhtubinsk. In 2002 there were 556 km of railways and 2,703 km of paved roads on the Oblast's territory. In October 2003 Russia's first container terminal on the Caspian Sea opened at the port of Olya, as part of work towards the construction of a 6,500 km north–south transport corridor to connect India with northern Europe, via Iran and Russia. The rise in the level of the Caspian Sea (by some 2.6 m between the late 1970s and the late 1990s) and the resulting erosion of the Volga delta caused serious environmental problems in the region. These were exacerbated by the pollution of the water by petroleum products, copper, nitrates and other substances, which frequently contributed to the death of a significant proportion of fish reserves.

The Oblast remains a major producer of vegetables and cucurbits (gourds and melons). Grain production and animal husbandry are also important. Agriculture engaged 15.3% of the work-force and generated 4,975m. roubles in 2003. The Oblast is rich in natural resources, including gas and gas condensate, sulphur, petroleum and salt. Its main industries are the production of petroleum and natural gas, food-processing (particularly fish products), mechanical engineering, ship-building and electricity production. It was anticipated that the extraction of petroleum and natural gas would improve the economic fortunes of the region from the mid-2000s. In 2003 industry employed 14.9% of the labour force and generated 28,097m. roubles. Regional trade was also important to the economy of Astrakhan. The Lakor freight company established important shipping links with Iran, handling around 940,000 metric tons of cargo in 1996, and in early 2000 announced plans to develop a trade route with India. Astrakhan's exports to Iran mainly comprised paper, metals, timber, mechanical equipment, fertilizers and chemical products.

Astrakhan Oblast's economically active population numbered 521,000 in 2003, when 10.1% of the region's labour force were unemployed. The average monthly wage was 4,431.6 roubles. In 2003 there was a budgetary deficit of 522.0m. roubles. In that year export trade totalled US $334.7m., and the value of imports amounted to $126.5m, while foreign investment in the territory amounted to $56.1m. At the end of 2003 some 3,600 small businesses were registered in the Oblast.

Directory

Head of the Regional Administration (Governor): ANATOLII GUZHVIN (elected 5 December 2004), 414000 Astrakhan, ul. Sovetskaya 14–15; tel. (8512) 22-85-19; fax (8512) 22-95-14; e-mail ves@astrakhan.ru; internet www.gubernator .astrakhan-region.ru.

Chairman of the Regional Government (Vice-Governor and Prime Minister): KONSTANTIN A. MARKELOV, 414000 Astrakhan, ul. Sovetskaya 14–15; tel. (8512) 22-85-19; fax (8512) 22-95-14; e-mail adm@astranet.ru; internet www.astrobl.ru.

Chairman of the State Duma of Astrakhan Oblast: PAVEL P. ANISIMOV, 414000 Astrakhan, ul. Volodarskogo 15; tel. (8512) 22-96-44; fax (8512) 22-22-48; e-mail ootsops@astranet.ru; internet duma.astranet.ru.

Chief Representative of Astrakhan Oblast in the Russian Federation: ANATOLII A. VOLODIN, 129090 Moscow, pr. Mira 3/1; tel. (495) 251-07-19; fax (495) 251-06-96.

Head of Astrakhan City Administration (Mayor): SERGEI A. BOZHENKOV, 414000 Astrakhan, ul. Chernyshevskogo 6; tel. (8512) 22-55-88; fax (8512) 24-71-76; e-mail admin@astrgorod.ru; internet www.astrgorod.ru.

Rostov Oblast

Rostov Oblast is situated in the south of the Eastern European Plain, in the Southern Federal Okrug and the North Caucasus Economic Area. It lies on the Taganrog Gulf of the Sea of Azov. It borders: Krasnodar and Stavropol Krais in the south; Kalmykiya in the south and east; Volgograd in the north-east and Voronezh in the north-west. There is an international border with Ukraine to the west. Its major rivers are the Don and the Severnyi Donets. The Volga–Don Canal runs through the region. The Oblast covers 100,800 sq km (38,910 sq miles). According to the census of 9–16 October 2002, there were 4,404,013 inhabitants and a population density of 43.7 per sq km. 67.6% of the region's inhabitants resided in urban areas. 89.3% of the population were ethnically Russian (including 2.0% of the total that defined their ethnic identity as Cossack), 2.7% Ukrainian and 2.5% Armenian. The administrative centre is at Rostov-on-Don (Rostov-na-Donu), which had a population of 1,070,200 in 2002, according to provisional census results. Other major cities are Taganrog (with a population of 282,300), Shakhty (220,400), Novocherkassk (170,900), Volgodonsk (166,500), Bataisk (107,300) and Novoshakhtinsk (101,200). Rostov Oblast is included in the time zone GMT+3.

History

The city of Rostov-on-Don was established as a Cossack outpost in 1796. It became an important grain-exporting centre in the 19th century, and increased in economic importance after the completion of the Volga–Don Canal. Rostov Oblast was formed in September 1937. The region became heavily industrialized after 1946 and, therefore, considerably increased in population.

In the mid-1990s the liberal Yabloko party enjoyed its highest level of support outside the two federal cities and Kamchatka Oblast in Rostov. The regional

Government signed a power-sharing treaty with the federal authorities in June 1996. The incumbent Governor (appointed in October 1991), Vladimir Chub, was elected to that post in September 1996. He was re-elected on 23 September 2001, as the candidate of the pro-Government Unity bloc, receiving 78.1% of the votes cast. On 29 March 2003, one day before the holding of regional legislative elections, Chub was elected to the Supreme Council of the pro-Government Unity and Fatherland-United Russia (UF-UR) party. In these elections, supporters of UF-UR were successful in 39 (of a total of 45) districts, although it was reported that many of these candidates had, in fact, concealed their party allegiance. Commentators observed that regional media legislation had resulted in severe restrictions being placed on coverage of candidates' campaigns.

In mid-2004 considerable social tension was reported in Rostov Oblast as workers from several sectors, particularly coal miners, staged strikes and protests. The main source of complaint was non-payment of back wages: reports estimated the total wage arrears for the Oblast at 500m. roubles. In early June 2005 Chub submitted his resignation as Governor to federal President Vladimir Putin, in order to seek confirmation that the President intended to nominate him to serve a further term of office. Putin duly nominated Chub, and his reappointment was confirmed by the regional legislature on 14 June.

In late June 2005 a private aeroplane carrying Garry Kasparov, the former world chess champion, and, as leader of the United Civil Front (UCF), a prominent opponent of President Putin, was refused permission to land at the airports at both Rostov and Taganrog. The subsequent cancellation of a proposed press conference in a state-owned building in Rostov, at which Kasparov had intended to promote the opposition 'Committee 2008' grouping, was similarly attributed to the reluctance of the regional authorities to permit the expression of viewpoints hostile to the federal authorities. Meanwhile, it was announced that mounted Cossack patrols, comprising volunteers, were to be established in rural areas across the Oblast in order to assist the law-enforcement agencies. In November legislation was passed by the Gosudarstvennaya Duma (State Duma) that set out the legal and organizational foundations for such units. In the same month, the UCF regional co-ordinator, Roman Motunov, was attacked in Rostov.

Economy

In 2002 Rostov Oblast's gross regional product amounted to 147,157.5m. roubles, or 33,414.4 roubles per head. The Oblast's main industrial centres are at Rostov-on-Don, Taganrog, Novocherkassk, Shakhty, Novoshakhtinsk and Volgodonsk. In 2002 there were 1,849 km of railways and 12,139 km of paved roads in the Oblast. Its ports are both river-ports, at Rostov-on-Don and Ust-Donetskii.

The Oblast is one of the major grain-producing regions in Russia, with agricultural land comprising some 85% of its territory. Agriculture employed 17.2% of the workforce and generated 42,934m. roubles in 2003. The production of sunflower seeds, coriander, mustard, vegetables and cucurbits (gourds and melons) is also important, as are viniculture and horticulture. The Oblast is situated in the eastern Donbass coal-mining region. Some 8.4m. metric tons on coal were mined in the Oblast in 2002, when it was the eighth-largest producer of coal of any federal subject. It is also rich in natural gas. Its other principal industries are food-processing, ferrous metallurgy, electricity generation, metal-working and mechanical engineering: Rostov-on-Don contained some 50 machine-building plants. In 2003 industry engaged 18.3% of the

Oblast's work-force and generated 119,882m. roubles. The largest industrial concern in the oblast is the Taganrog Metallurgical Plant (TagMet).

The economically active population numbered 2,043,000 in 2003, when 12.3% of the labour force were unemployed. Those in employment earned an average monthly wage of 3,989.3 roubles. The 2003 budget showed a surplus of 344.9m. roubles. In that year external trade amounted to US \$1,320.1m. in exports and \$926.1m. in imports; total foreign investment in the region amounted to \$223.5m. At the end of 2003 there were some 24,200 small businesses registered in the Oblast.

Directory

Head of the Regional Administration (Governor): VLADIMIR F. CHUB (appointed 8 October 1991, elected 29 September 1996, re-elected 23 September 2001; appointment confirmed 14 June 2005), 344050 Rostov-on-Don, ul. Sotsialistiche-skaya 112; tel. (863) 244-18-10; fax (8632) 44-15-59; e-mail rra@donpac.ru; internet www.donland.ru.

Chairman of the Legislative Assembly: ALEKSANDR V. POPOV, 344050 Rostov-on-Don, ul. Sotsialisticheskaya 112; tel. (863) 240-14-47; fax (8632) 40-55-82; e-mail zsrnd@donpac.ru; internet www.zsro.ru.

Chief Representative of Rostov Oblast in the Russian Federation: VIKTOR P. VODOLATSKII, 115184 Moscow, ul. Novyi Arbat 19/1909–13; tel. (495) 953-90-01; fax (495) 953-89-80; e-mail info@rostovregion.ru; internet www.rostovregion.ru.

Head of Rostov-on-Don City Administration (Mayor): MIKHAIL A. CHERNYSHEV, 344007 Rostov-on-Don, ul. B. Sadovaya 47; tel. (863) 244-15-05; fax (8632) 66-62-62; e-mail meria@rostov-gorod.ru; internet www.rostov-gorod.ru.

Volgograd Oblast

Volgograd Oblast is situated in the south-east of the Eastern European Plain. It forms part of the Southern Federal Okrug and the Volga Economic Area. The Oblast has an international border with Kazakhstan to its east. Astrakhan and Kalmykiya lie to the south-east, Rostov to the south-west, Voronezh to the north-west and Saratov to the north. The Oblast's main rivers are the Volga and the Don. Its terrain varies from fertile black earth (*chernozem*) to semi-desert. The region occupies an area of 113,900 sq km (43,980 sq miles). According to the census of 9–16 October 2002, the Oblast had a total of 2,699,223 inhabitants, and a population density of 23.7 per sq km. 75.2% of the population lived in urban areas. 88.9% of the population were ethnically Russian (including the 0.8% of the oblast population that defined their ethnic identity as Cossack), 2.1% Ukrainian, 1.7% Kazakh, 1.1% Tatar, 1.0% Armenian. The Oblast's administrative centre is at Volgograd, which had a population of 1,012,800 in 2002, according to provisional census results. Other major cities include Volzhskii (310,700). Volgograd Oblast is included in the time zone GMT+3.

History

The city of Volgograd (known as Tsaritsyn until 1925 and Stalingrad in 1925–61) was founded in the 16th century, to protect the Volga trade route. It was built on the River Volga, at the point where it flows nearest to the Don (the two river systems were later connected by a canal at this point). The Oblast was formed on 10 January 1934. In 1942–43 the city was the scene of a decisive battle between the forces of the USSR and Nazi Germany.

In October 1993 the Volgograd Oblast Soviet (Council) agreed to reform the system of regional government. It decided to hold elections to a new, 30-seat Oblast Duma, which took place the following year. The Communist Party of the Russian Federation (CPRF) was the largest single party. The December 1996 gubernatorial election was won by Nikolai Maksyuta, a member of the CPRF and a former Chairman of the regional assembly. Maksyuta was re-elected for a second term as Governor on 24 December 2000. In September 1998 the regional Duma, dominated by the CPRF, had voted for the principle of restoring the Oblast's previous name of Stalingrad, and this notion remained popular, both among members of the oblast legislature and the broader populace, although federal President Vladimir Putin expressed his opposition to the proposal in December 2002. Prior to the first round of gubernatorial elections, held on 5 December 2004, the candidacy of Maksyuta's principal opponent had been declared invalid. Maksyuta and a member of the oblast assembly, Nikolai Volkov, proceeded to a second round of polling, held on 26 December, when Maksyuta was elected to a further term of office, receiving around 51.1% of votes cast, compared with the 38.6% obtained by Volkov.

Economy

In 2002 Volgograd Oblast's gross regional product amounted to 112,241.0m. roubles, or 41,582.7 roubles per head. Its main industrial centres are at Volgograd, Volzhskii and Kamyshin. In 2002 there were 1,618 km of railways and 8,828 km of paved roads. In 1996 construction of a road bridge across the Volga river into Volgograd began; completion of the bridge was scheduled for 2007.

The region's principal agricultural products are grain, sunflower seeds, vegetables and cucurbits (gourds and melons). Horticulture, bee-keeping and animal husbandry are also important. In 2003 agriculture engaged 16.8% of the work-force and generated 30,021m. roubles. The Oblast's mineral reserves include petroleum, natural gas and phosphorites. The main industries in the Oblast are petroleum-refining, chemicals and petrochemicals, mechanical engineering, metal-working, ferrous metallurgy, the production of electricity, food-processing and the production of petroleum and natural gas. Industry employed 21.0% of the working population and generated 101,332m. roubles in 2003.

The economically active population of the Oblast numbered 1,267,000 in 2003, when 10.9% of the labour force were unemployed. The average monthly wage was 3,866.1 roubles in 2003. In 2003 there was a budgetary deficit of 723.1m. roubles. In that year external trade constituted US $1,639.9m. in exports and $374.5m. in imports; total foreign investment amounted to $44.6m., compared with $178.6m. in the previous year. At the end of 2003 some 13,800 small businesses were registered in the Oblast.

Directory

Head of the Regional Administration (Governor): Nikolai K. Maksyuta (elected 29 December 1996, re-elected 24 December 2000 and 26 December 2004), 400098 Volgograd, pr. Lenina 9; tel. (8442) 33-66-88; fax (8442) 93-62-12; e-mail glava@volganet.ru; internet www.volganet.ru.

Chairman of the Regional Duma: Roman G. Grebennikov, 400098 Volgograd, pr. Lenina 9; tel. (8442) 30-90-00; fax (8422) 36-44-03; internet duma.volganet.ru.

Chief Representative of Volgograd Oblast in the Russian Federation: Tatyana Ye. Trubitsyna, 119121 Moscow, Smolenskaya-Sennaya pl. 6; tel. (495) 241-52-02.

Head of Volgograd City Administration (Mayor): Yevgenii P. Ishchenko, 400131 Volgograd, ul. Volodarskogo 5; tel. (8442) 33-16-82; fax (8442) 38-54-66; e-mail kancelyaria@volgadmin.ru; internet www.volgadmin.ru.

VOLGA FEDERAL OKRUG

Republic of Bashkortostan

The Republic of Bashkortostan is situated on the slopes of the Southern Urals. It forms part of the Volga Federal Okrug and the Urals Economic Area. There are borders with Perm Krai to the north, the Udmurt Republic in the north-west, Tatarstan in the west, and with the oblasts of Orenburg in the south-west and south, Chelyabinsk in the east, and Sverdlovsk to the north. The north of the Republic is forested, while the southern part is steppe. The Republic occupies 143,600 sq km (55,440 sq miles). According to the census of 9–16 October 2002, Bashkortostan had a total population of 4,104,336 and a population density of 30.0 per sq km. Some 64.1% of the Republic's population inhabited urban areas. 36.3% of the population were ethnically Russian, 29.8% Bashkir, 24.1% Tatar, 2.9% Chuvash, 2.6% Mari and 1.3% Ukrainian. (According to the 1989 census, which recorded ethnicity on the basis of official declaration of nationality, rather than self-definition, Tatars out-numbered Bashkirs in the Republic, representing 28% and 22% of the population respectively.) Bashkir, spoken by the majority of ethnic Bashkirs, is a Kipchak language closely related to that spoken by the Tatars, and has two distinct dialects:

Kuvakan, spoken in the north of the Republic; and Yurmatin, current in the south. The majority of Bashkirs and Tatars are Sunni Muslims of the Hanafi school, although some Bashkirs, the Nagaibak, were converted to Orthodox Christianity. The Republic's administrative centre is at Ufa, which had a population of 1,042,400 in 2002, according to provisional census results. Its other major cities include Sterlitamak (264,400), Salavat (158,500), Neftekamsk (122,300) and Oktyabrskii (108,700). Bashkortostan is included in the time zone GMT+5.

History

The Bashkirs were thought to have originated as a distinct ethnic group during the 16th century, out of the Tatar, Mongol, Volga, Bulgar, Oguz, Pecheneg and Kipchak peoples. They were traditionally a pastoral people renowned for their bee-keeping abilities. The territory was annexed by Russia in 1557, during the reign of Ivan IV ('the Terrible'), and many Bashkirs subsequently lost their land and wealth and were forced into servitude. Rebellions against Russian control, most notably that led by Salavat Yulai in 1773, were unsuccessful, and the identity and survival of the Bashkir community came under increasing threat. A large migration of ethnic Russians to the region in the late 19th century resulted in their outnumbering the Bashkir population. A Bashkir ASSR was formed on 23 March 1919. Bashkir resistance to the collectivization policy of Stalin (Iosif Dzhugashvili) caused many to be relocated to other regions in the USSR.

The Bashkir Autonomous Republic declared its sovereignty on 11 October 1990. On 12 December 1993, when Murtaza Rakhimov (hitherto President of the republican Supreme Soviet—Council) was elected to the new post of President, a republican majority voted against acceptance of the new federal Constitution. On 24 December the republican Supreme Soviet adopted a new Constitution, which stated that its own laws had supremacy over federal laws. The name of Bashkortostan was adopted, and a bicameral legislature, the Kurultai, established. The Republic's constitutional position was regularized and further autonomy granted under treaties signed in 1994 and in 1995. The administration of the Republic, meanwhile, remained highly centralized, with the executive retaining extensive controls over both local government and industry, particularly the petroleum sector. Rakhimov was re-elected as President in June 1998, having received the endorsement of the federal President, Boris Yeltsin. In the State Duma elections of December 1999, the candidates of Rakhimov's favoured grouping, Fatherland-All Russia, were successful in the Republic; prior to the election Rakhimov was rebuked by the federal Prime Minister, Vladimir Putin, for blocking the transmission of two television channels opposed to the grouping. Commentators also observed the absence of any opposition press in Bashkortostan, and the removal from electoral lists of most of Rakhimov's opponents, owing to alleged electoral violations.

In May 2000 President Putin ordered that Bashkortostan's Constitution be altered to conform with Russia's basic law. A new republican Constitution was introduced in November. In January 2001 one of the most significant contradictions, the statement in the new document that republican legislation should take precedence over federal law, was rescinded. In June 2002 the federal Supreme Court ruled that some 37 articles of Bashkortostan's new Constitution failed to comply with federal law, and the redaction of a further new Constitution commenced.

On 3 December 2002 a further new republican Constitution was adopted, which, notably, transferred several powers from the Prime Minister to the President. The new document removed all references to the 'sovereignty' of Bashkortostan, although reference was made to the 'statehood' of the Republic. None the less, the text was widely regarded as broadly conforming with federal laws, and the power-sharing treaties signed between the republican and federal authorities were annulled. The Kurultai was, meanwhile, reformed as a unicameral body.

At elections to the new Kurultai, held on 16 March 2003, the pro-Government Unity and Fatherland-United Russia (UF-UR) party obtained control of 91 of the 120 seats. In the first round of the republican presidential election, held on 7 December, no candidate received an absolute majority of the votes cast. Rakhimov (who received 42.6% of the votes cast) and the second-placed candidate, who had been initially favoured by the federal authorities, Sergei Veremeyenko (with 23.0%), duly proceeded to a second round of voting on 21 December. Prior to the 'run-off' election, Veremeyenko announced that he had ceased campaigning, although his name remained on the ballot. This effective lack of opposition, now combined with public support from Putin, enabled Rakhimov to secure re-election to a third term, with some 78.0% of the votes cast. Putin's change of position was seen partly as the result of Rakhimov's highly effective campaigning on behalf of UF-UR in the federal legislative elections, also held on 7 December. On 15 January 2004 Rakhimov re-appointed Rafael Baidavletov (who had held that position since 1999) as republican premier, following the unanimous approval of his nomination by the Kurultai.

Rakhimov's re-election was not without controversy: prior to the poll there had once again been claims that the independent media in the Republic had been subject to intimidation by the authorities. Furthermore, a large number of false ballot papers were discovered at a printing house controlled by the republican presidential administration, resulting in a criminal investigation overseen by Bashkortostan's Prosecutor-General, who resigned later in the month, apparently on grounds of ill health.

Widespread controversy arose nationally following an incident in the city of Blagoveshchensk, north-east of Ufa, in December 2004, in which republican police officers were reported to have seized up to 1,000 men over a period of five days, and beaten at least several dozen of them severely, apparently in revenge for an attack against a police patrol; according to official statistics, more than 340 people were illegally arrested, of whom 40 sustained serious injuries. In March 2005 some 20,000 people were reported to have participated in a demonstration, organized by the republican branches of eight political parties, including the Communist Party of the Russian Federation, the Liberal Democratic Party of Russia, Motherland and Yabloko, in Ufa against human rights abuses in Bashkortostan. The demonstrators demanded Rakhimov's resignation and the payment of compensation to those beaten in Blagoveshchensk. In late May, following further protests it was announced that at least nine police officers were to be charged with exceeding their authority or abuse of office. In late July, however, the republican prosecutor announced that a criminal case was to be opened against Airat Dilmukhametov, one of the leaders of the protests that took place earlier in the year, on charges of promulgating extremism. In early August the Supreme Court of Bashkortostan sentenced nine members of the prohibited transnational militant Islamist group, Hizb-ut-Tahrir al-Islami (Party of Islamic Liberation), to custodial sentences of up to six years, representing the first use of federal anti-terrorist legislation approved in 2003. In September the first police officer to be convicted in connection with the police-abuse scandal of

December 2004 was given a three-year suspended sentence. In the same month the Kurultai made an official appeal to Putin to restore the power-sharing treaties between the republican and the federal authorities that had been annulled in 2002.

Economy

Bashkortostan's economy is dominated by its fuel and energy and agro-industrial complexes. The Republic is one of Russia's key petroleum-producing areas and the centre of its petroleum-refining industry. It produced 11.4m. metric tons of petroleum, 3.0% of Russia's total output in 2002, and accounted for around 15% of its petroleum-refining in 2000. The quantity of petroleum produced and refined in the Republic declined significantly during the 1990s. In 2002 the territory's gross regional product stood at 214,822.2m. roubles, or 52,340.3 roubles per head. Amid concerns that the federal Government was seeking to gain increased control over the natural resources of the Republic, at the expense of the republican authorities, republican President Rakhimov announced, in mid-2002, that several of the republican petroleum companies were to be transferred to private ownership. (Subsequently, Rakhimov's son, Ural, obtained control of significant energy assets in the Republic.) However, in an apparent attempt to gain support from the federal authorities prior to the presidential election of late 2003, Rakhimov ceded management of the Republic's largest petrochemical plant, Salavatnefteorgsintez, to the state-controlled corporation, Gazprom, which announced proposals to privatize the plant in 2008. Bashkortostan's major industrial centres are at Ufa, Sterlitamak, Salavat and Ishimbai. At the end of 2002 there were 1,462 km of railways on its territory, and 22,037 km of paved roads. There is an international airport at Ufa.

Bashkortostan's agriculture employed 16.5% of the work-force and generated 50,769m. roubles in 2003; the only federal subject with higher agricultural output in that year was Krasnodar Krai. The main agricultural activities are animal husbandry, bee-keeping and grain and vegetable production. As well as its petroleum resources (of which the deposits amount to 400m. metric tons), Bashkortostan contains deposits of natural gas (55m. tons), brown coal—lignite (250m. tons), iron ore, copper, gold (with reserves amounting to 32 tons in 1997, sufficient for 19 years of production), zinc, aluminium, chromium, salt (2,270m. tons), manganese, gypsum and limestone. The Republic's other industries include mechanical engineering, metal-working, electricity generation, and chemicals and petrochemicals. In 2003 industry employed 22.3% of the Republic's working population, and generated 197,163m. roubles.

In 2003 the economically active population of the Republic numbered 1,968,000, and 8.2% of the labour force were unemployed. The average monthly wage was 4,449.4 roubles. There was a budgetary surplus of 2,158.4m. roubles. In the same year the Republic's external trade comprised US $2,775.5m. in exports and $266.7m. in imports. In 2003 foreign investment in the Republic amounted to some $40.2m. At the end of 2003 some 18,200 small businesses were registered in the Republic.

Directory

President: MURTAZA G. RAKHIMOV (elected 12 December 1993, re-elected 14 June 1998 and 21 December 2003), 450101 Bashkortostan, Ufa, ul. Tukayeva 46; tel. (3472) 50-27-24; fax (3472) 50-02-81; e-mail aprbinfo@admbashkortostan.ru; internet www.bashkortostan.ru.

Prime Minister: RAFAEL I. BAIDAVLETOV, 450101 Bashkortostan, Ufa, ul. Tukayeva 46, Dom Respubliki; tel. (3472) 50-27-24; fax (3472) 50-02-81.

Chairman of the State Assembly (Kurultai): KONSTANTIN B. TOLKACHEV, 450101 Bashkortostan, Ufa, ul. Tukayeva 46; tel. (3472) 50-19-15; fax (3472) 50-08-86; e-mail pred@kurultai.rb.ru.

Chief Representative of the Republic of Bashkortostan in the Russian Federation: ALBERT M. KHARISOV, 105066 Moscow, ul. Dobroslobodskaya 6/2; tel. (495) 933-90-00; e-mail bashpred-la@umail.ru; internet www.bashpred.ru.

Head of Ufa City Administration (Mayor): PAVEL R. KACHKAYEV, 450098 Bashkortostan, Ufa, pr. Oktyabrya 120; tel. (3472) 79-05-79; fax (3472) 33-18-73; e-mail cityadmin@ufacity.info; internet www.ufacity.info.

Chuvash Republic

The Chuvash Republic is situated in the north-west of European Russia. It forms part of the Volga Federal Okrug and the Volga-Vyatka Economic Area. The Republic lies on the Eastern European Plain, on the middle reaches of the Volga. Ulyanovsk neighbours it to the south, Mordoviya to the south-west, Nizhnii Novgorod to the west and Marii-El and Tatarstan to the north and the east, respectively. The Republic's major rivers are the Volga and the Sura, and one-third of its territory is covered by forest. It occupies 18,300 sq km (7,070 sq miles). According to the census of 9–16 October 2002, the Republic had a total population of 1,313,754 and a population density of 71.8 per sq km. Some 60.6% of the population lived in urban areas. 67.7% of the population were ethnically Chuvash, 26.5% Russian, 2.8% Tatar and 1.2% Mordovian. An estimated 76.5% of the ethnically Chuvash population speak Chuvash, which has its origins in the Bulgar group of the Western Hunnic group of Turkic languages, as a first language. The dominant religions in the Republic are Islam and Orthodox Christianity. The Republic's capital is at Cheboksary (Shupashkar—with a population of 440,800 in 2002, according to provisional census results). Its other major town is nearby Novocheboksarsk (125,900). The Republic is included in the time zone GMT+3.

History

The Chuvash, traditionally a semi-nomadic people, were conquered by the Mongol-Tatars in the 13th century. Their territory subsequently became part of the dominion of the Golden Horde and many were converted to Islam. From the late 1430s the Chuvash were ruled by the Kazan Khanate. In 1551 the region became a part of the

Russian Empire. Despite intense Christianization and 'russification' on the part of the Russian state, the Chuvash acquired their own national and cultural identity, which had Suvar-Bulgar and Finno-Ugric components, by the end of the 15th century. The Chuvash capital was founded at Cheboksary in 1551, at the site of a settlement first mentioned in Russian chronicles in 1469. The construction of other towns and forts, intended to encourage migration into the area, followed. After 1917 the Chuvash people made vociferous demands for autonomy to the Soviet Government. A Chuvash Autonomous Oblast was established in June 1920, which was upgraded to the status of an ASSR on 21 April 1925.

Chuvash nationalism re-emerged in the early 1990s: the Chuvash ASSR declared its sovereignty on 27 October 1990 and adopted the name of the Chuvash (Chavash) Republic in March 1992. In December 1993 the Republic voted against acceptance of the federal Constitution. In that month Nikolai Fedorov, a supporter of economic reform and former Minister of Justice in the federal Government, was elected republican President. In May 1996 the republican Government signed a treaty with the federal President, Boris Yeltsin, on the delimitation of powers between the federal and republican authorties. Fedorov was elected to a further term of office on 28 December 1997, receiving 56.5% of the votes cast. In October 2001 the Chairman of the republican Council of Ministers (Prime Minister), Enver Ablyakimov, resigned; Fedorov appointed himself to the position, announcing that combining the roles of republican president and prime minister would increase the Government's accountability. Fedorov was re-elected with some 41% of the votes in an election held on 16 December. Immediately following his re-election as Governor, Fedorov announced that he was to rescind his position as Prime Minister. In August 2005 federal President Vladimir Putin nominated Fedorov to serve a further term of office; this nomination was approved by the republican legislature on 29 August.

Economy

In 2002 the Republic's gross regional product amounted to 39,845.7m. roubles, equivalent to 30,329.7 roubles per head. The major industrial centres are at Cheboksary, Novocheboksarsk and Kanash. At the end of 2002 there were 396 km of railways and 4,629 km of paved roads in the Republic.

Agriculture, which employed 18.1% of the work-force and generated 11,617m. roubles in 2003, consists mainly of animal husbandry and of grain, potato and hop production. The Republic contains deposits of peat, sand, limestone and dolomite. Its main industries are mechanical engineering, metal-working, electricity generation, production of chemicals and petrochemicals, light industry and food-processing. The industrial sector employed 25.1% of the working population in 2003, and generated 39,664m. roubles.

The economically active population in the Chuvash Republic amounted to 674,000 in 2003; 8.6% of the Republic's labour force were unemployed. The average monthly wage in the territory was 3,215.0 roubles. In that year there was a budgetary deficit of 245.4m. roubles. Exports from the Republic amounted to US $107.0m., and imports to the Republic to $55.3m. Foreign investment in 2003 amounted to just $4.0m. At the end of 2003 some 4,000 small businesses were registered in the Republic.

Directory

President: NIKOLAI V. FEDOROV (elected 12 December 1993, re-elected 28 December 1997 and 16 December 2001; appointment confirmed 29 August 2005), 428004 Chuvash Rep., Cheboksary, pl. Respubliki 1; tel. (8352) 39-33-01; fax (8352) 62-17-99; e-mail president@cap.ru; internet www.cap.ru.

Chairman of the Cabinet of Ministers (Prime Minister): SERGEI A. GAPLIKOV, 428004 Chuvash Rep., Cheboksary, pl. Respubliki 1; tel. (8352) 62-01-76; fax (8352) 62-31-84; e-mail km@cap.ru; internet gov.cap.ru/main.asp?govid=17.

Chairman of the State Council (Parliament): MIKHAIL A. MIKHAILOVSKII, 428004 Chuvash Rep., Cheboksary, pl. Respubliki 1; tel. (8352) 62-22-72; fax (8352) 62-23-15; e-mail gs@cap.ru; internet www.gs.chuvashia.com.

Chief Representative of the Chuvash Republic in the Russian Federation: GENNADII S. FEDOROV, 109017 Moscow, ul. B. Ordynka 46/1; tel. and fax (495) 953-21-59; e-mail polprcheb@cap.ru; internet gov.cap.ru/main.asp?govid=100.

Head of Cheboksary City Administration (Mayor): NIKOLAI I. YEMELYANOV, 428000 Chuvash Rep., Cheboksary, ul. K. Marksa 36; tel. (8352) 62-35-76; fax (8352) 62-40-50; e-mail gcheb@cap.ru; internet www.gcheb.cap.ru.

Republic of Marii-El

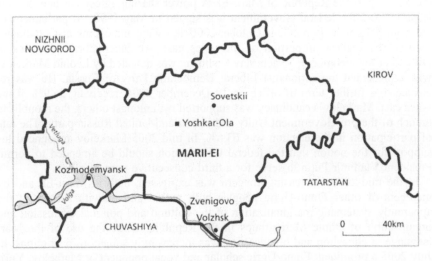

The Republic of Marii-El is situated in the east of the Eastern European Plain in the middle reaches of the River Volga. It forms part of the Volga Federal Okrug and the Volga-Vyatka Economic Area. Tatarstan and the Chuvash Republic neighbour it to the south-east and to the south, respectively. Nizhnii Novgorod lies to the west and Kirov to the north and north-east. Marii-El occupies 23,200 sq km (9,000 sq miles). According to the census of 9–16 October 2002, the total population was 727,979, and the population density 31.4 per sq km. Some 63.2% of the population inhabited urban areas. 47.5% of the population were ethnically Russian; 42.9% were Mari (Cheremiss), including 7.2% of the total population who described themselves as Lugovo-Vostochnye Mari and 2.4% of the total who described themselves as Mountain Mari; 6.0% were Tatar; and 1.0% were Chuvash. Orthodox Christianity is the predominant religion in Marii-El, although many Mari have remained faithful to aspects of their traditional animistic religion. Their native language belongs to the Finnic branch of the Uralo-Altaic family. The capital of the Republic is at Yoshkar-Ola, with a population of 256,800 in 2002, according to provisional census results. Marii-El is included in the time zone GMT+3.

History

The Mari emerged as a distinct ethnic group in the sixth century. In the eighth century they came under the influence of the Khazar empire, but from the mid-ninth to the mid-12th century they were ruled by the Volga Bulgars. In the 1230s Mari territory was conquered by the Mongol Tatars and remained under the control of the Khazar Khanate until its annexation by Russia in 1552. Nationalist feeling on the part of the Mari did not become evident until the 1870s, when a religious movement, the Kugu Sorta (Great Candle), attacked the authority of the Orthodox Church in the region. A Mari Autonomous Oblast was established in 1920. On 5 December 1936 the territory became the Mari ASSR.

The Republic declared its sovereignty on 22 October 1990. A presidential election was held on 14 December 1991. In December 1993 elections were held to a new 300-

seat parliament, the State Assembly, which was dominated by the Communist Party. The new legislature adopted a republican Constitution in June 1995 that designated the territory as the Republic of Marii-El. A power-sharing agreement between the Republic and the federal Government was signed in May 1998. At parliamentary elections held in the Republic in October 2000, left-wing and communist candidates secured the highest proportion of the votes cast. At gubernatorial elections in December the incumbent, Vyacheslav Kislitsyn, was defeated by Leonid Markelov, who represented the nationalist Liberal Democratic Party of Russia. He was re-elected to a further term of office on 19 December 2004, receiving 56.9% of the votes cast. Markelov's candidacy was supported by, amongst others, the republican branch of the pro-Government Unity and Fatherland-United Russia party. The rate of participation in the election was 63.6%. In mid-2005 Markelov announced his support for the notion that the federal Constitution should be amended to permit President Vladimir Putin to serve for a third consecutive term of office.

In the mid-2000s increasing concern was expressed, both in Marii-El, and by members of other Finno-Ugric peoples both within and outwith Russia, at the apparently systematic marginalization of the cultural and political expression and organization of ethnic Mari groups in the Republic, while the use of the Mari language in education and broadcasting was increasingly subject to restrictions. In July 2005 a prominent Finno-Ugric scholar and vocal opponent of Markelov, Yurii Anduganov (who had ceased to reside in the Republic, apparently as a result of political pressures against him), died in a road accident, in circumstances that remained unexplained, and at least two prominent Mari leaders were assaulted in the Republic during the first half of 2005.

Economy

In 2002 the Republic's gross regional product amounted to 18,887.6m. roubles, equivalent to 25,945.3 roubles per head. Its major industrial centres are at Yoshkar-Ola and Volzhsk. At the end of 2002 there were 195 km of railway lines and 3,251 km of paved roads on the Republic's territory.

Marii-El's agriculture, which in 2003 employed 17.4% of the work-force and generated 8,011m. roubles, consists mainly of animal husbandry and the production of flax, vegetables, potatoes and grain. The Republic's main industries are mechanical engineering, metal-working, electricity production and the processing of forestry and food products. In 2003 industry employed 21.9% of the work-force and generated 16,817m. roubles.

In 2003 the economically active population in the Republic numbered 369,000, and 12.2% of the labour force were unemployed; the average monthly wage was 3,105.8 roubles. In 2003 there was a budgetary deficit of 119.1m. roubles. In that year external trade comprised US $ 83.4m. in exports and $18.1m. in imports. Exports primarily comprised raw materials (peat), machine parts and medical supplies. Foreign investment in Marii-El was minimal, amounting to $4.4m. in 2003. At the end of 2003 some 3,400 small businesses were registered in the Republic.

Directory

President and Head of the Government: LEONID I. MARKELOV (elected 17 December 2000, re-elected 19 December 2004), 424001 Marii-El, Yoshkar-Ola, Leninskii pr. 29; tel. (8362) 64-15-25; fax (8362) 64-19-21; e-mail president@gov .mari.ru; internet gov.mari.ru.

Chairman of the State Assembly: YURII A. MINAKOV, 424001 Marii-El, Yoshkar-Ola, Leninskii pr. 29; tel. (8362) 64-14-13; e-mail info@parliament.mari.ru; internet parlament.mari.ru.

Chief Representative of the Republic of Marii-El in the Russian Federation: SERGEI V. SEMKIN, 121019 Moscow, ul. Novyi Arbat 21; tel. (495) 291-48-38; fax (495) 291-46-32.

Head of Yoshkar-Ola City Administration (Mayor): OLEG P. VOINOV, 424001 Marii-El, Yoshkar-Ola, Leninskii pr. 27; tel. (8362) 11-44-89; fax (8362) 63-03-71; internet capital.mari-el.ru.

Republic of Mordoviya

The Republic of Mordoviya is situated in the Eastern European Plain, in the Volga river basin. The north-west of the Republic occupies a section of the Oka-Don plain and the south-east lies in the Volga Highlands. The region forms part of the Volga Federal Okrug and the Volga-Vyatka Economic Area. The Chuvash Republic lies to the north-east, the Oblasts of Ulyanovsk to the east, Penza to the south, Ryazan to the west and Nizhnii Novgorod to the north. The major rivers in Mordoviya are the Moksha, the Sura and the Insar. Mordoviya occupies 26,200 sq km (10,110 sq miles). According to the census of 9–16 October 2002, the Republic had a population of 888,766 and a population density of 33.9 per sq km. Some 59.8% of the Republic's population inhabited urban areas. 60.8% of the population were ethnically Russian; 31.9% were Mordovian (Mordvinian), including 8.9% of the total population who described themselves as Erzya-Mordovian and 5.3% of the total who described themselves as Moksha-Mordovian; and 5.2% were Tatar. The majority of Mordovians inhabited the agricultural regions of the west and north-east. The dominant religion is Orthodox Christianity. The native tongue of the Mordovians belongs to the Finnic group of the Uralo-Altaic family. Mordoviya's capital is at Saransk, which had a population of 304,900 in 2002, according to provisional census results. The Republic is included in the time zone GMT+3.

History

The Mordovians first appear in historical records of the sixth century, when they inhabited the area between the Oka and the middle Volga rivers. In the late 12th and early 13th centuries a feudal society began to form in Mordoviya. One of its most famous fiefdoms was that headed by Prince Purgas. The Mordovians came under the control of the Mongols and Tatars between the 13th and the 15th centuries and, at the fall of the Khanate of Kazan in 1552, were voluntarily incorporated into the Russian state. Many thousands of Mordovians fled Russian rule in the late 16th and early 17th centuries to settle in the Ural Mountains and in southern Siberia, while

www.europaworld.com

those that remained were outnumbered by ethnic Russian settlers. The region was predominantly agricultural until the completion of the Moscow–Kazan railway in the 1890s, when it became more commercial and its industry developed.

Although Mordovians had become increasingly assimilated into Russian life from the late 19th century, a Mordovian Autonomous Okrug was created in 1928, which was upgraded to an Autonomous Oblast in 1930, and to an ASSR in 1934. It declared its sovereignty on 8 December 1990 and was renamed the Republic of Mordoviya in January 1994. A Constitution was adopted on 21 September 1995, establishing an executive presidency and a legislative State Assembly. Nikolai Merkushkin, Chairman of the republican legislature since January, became President. In February 1998 Merkushkin was elected President, with 96.6% of the votes cast, owing to a legislative device that disqualified all opponents other than the director of a local pasta factory, who had frequently announced his support for Merkushkin's policies. On 16 February 2003 Merkushkin was re-elected to a further term of office, receiving 87.3% of the votes cast in an election contested by five candidates; the rate of participation by the registered electorate was measured at 83.2%. Merkushkin was subsequently appointed to the Supreme Council of the pro-Government Unity and Fatherland–United Russia party; the party performed strongly in Mordoviya at elections to the federal State Duma on 7 December, held concurrently with elections to the republican legislature. In early November 2005, some three years ahead of the expiry of his term of office, Merkushkin was nominated by federal President Vladimir Putin to serve a further term; on 10 November this appointment was confirmed by the republican parliament.

Economy

In 2002 the gross regional product of Mordoviya was 24,332.4m. roubles, or 27,377.7 roubles per head. The territory's major industrial centres are at Saransk and Ruzayevka. At the end of 2002 there were 546 km of railway lines and 4,287 km of paved roads on the Republic's territory.

The principal crops in Mordoviya are grain, sugar beet, potatoes and vegetables. Animal husbandry (especially cattle) and bee-keeping are also important. Agriculture employed 17.5% of the working population and generated 11,958m. roubles in 2003, when total agricultural production was worth 11,958m. roubles. In that year industry employed 24.4% of the labour force and generated 28,629m. roubles. The main industries are mechanical engineering and metal-working. There is also some production of electricity, production of chemicals and petrochemicals, and food-processing. Mordoviya is the centre of the Russian lighting-equipment industry and contains the Rossiiskii Svet (Russian Light) association. As regional President, Nikolai Merkushkin established close trading relationships with Moscow City.

In 2003 the economically active population was 431,000, and 7.4% of the labour force were unemployed. The average monthly wage in the Republic was 3,251.6 roubles in that year. In 2003 there was a budgetary surplus of 89.7m. roubles. External trade amounted to US $32.0m. in exports and $40.8m. in imports in that year. In 2003 foreign investment in the Republic amounted to $23.2m. At the end of 2003 some 2,100 small businesses were registered in the Republic.

Directory

President: NIKOLAI I. MERKUSHKIN (assumed office 22 September 1995, elected 15 February 1998, re-elected 16 February 2003; appointment confirmed 10 November

2005), 430002 Mordoviya, Saransk, ul. Sovetskaya 35; tel. (8342) 17-54-71; fax (8342) 17-45-26; e-mail radm@whrm.moris.ru; internet whrm.moris.ru.

Chairman of the Government (Prime Minister): VLADIMIR D. VOLKOV, 430002 Mordoviya, Saransk, ul. Sovetskaya 35; tel. (8342) 32-74-69; fax (8342) 17-36-28; e-mail pred@whrm.moris.ru.

Chairman of the State Assembly: VALERII A. KECHKIN, 430002 Mordoviya, Saransk, ul. Sovetskaya 26; tel. (8342) 32-79-50; fax (8342) 17-04-95; e-mail gsprot@whrm.moris.ru.

Chief Representative of the Republic of Mordoviya in the Russian Federation: VIKTOR I. CHINDYASKIN, 127018 Moscow, ul. Obraztsova 29; tel. (495) 219-40-49; fax (495) 218-01-42.

Head of Saransk City Administration: VLADIMIR SUSHKOV, 430002 Mordoviya, Saransk, ul. Sovetskaya 34; tel. (8342) 17-64-16; fax (8342) 17-67-70; e-mail saransk@moris.ru.

Republic of Tatarstan

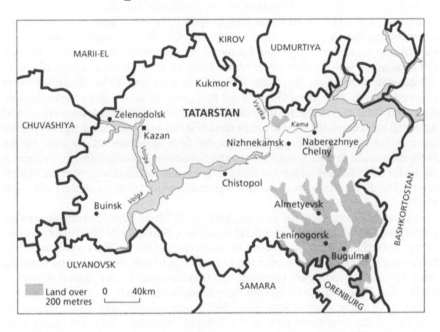

The Republic of Tatarstan is situated in the east of European Russia and forms part of the Volga Federal Okrug and the Volga Economic Area. Bashkortostan lies to the east; the Udmurt Republic to the north; Marii-El to the north-west; and the Chuvash Republic to the west. The Oblasts of Ulyanovsk, Samara and Orenburg lie to the south, and Kirov to the north. The Republic's major rivers are the Volga and the Kama. According to the census of 9–16 October 2002, it had an estimated population of 3,779,265 and a population density of 55.6 per sq km. 73.8% of the Republic's population inhabited urban areas. 52.9% of the population were Tatar, 39.5% ethnically Russian and 3.3% Chuvash. Although figures on ethnicity in the 2002 census are not directly comparable with those in previous censuses, they suggested an increase of around one-tenth in the proportion of the population accounted for by Tatars since 1989, and a similar decline in the proportion of Russians. Tatarstan's capital is Kazan, which lies on the River Volga and had a population of 1,105,300 in 2002, according to preliminary census results. Other major cities include Naberezhnye Chelny (formerly Brezhnev—with a population of 510,000), Nizhne-kamsk (225,500), Almetyevsk (140,500) and Zelenodolsk (100,100). The Republic is included in the time zone GMT+3.

History

After the dissolution of the Mongol Empire the region became the Khanate of Kazan, the territory of the Golden Horde. The city of Kazan was founded in 1005. Kazan was conquered by Russian troops, led by Tsar Ivan IV ('the Terrible') in 1552. Some of the Muslim Tatars succumbed to Russian pressures to convert to Orthodox Christianity (becoming known as Kryashens), but most did not. A modernist school of thought in Islam, Jadidism, originated among the Volga Tatars in the 19th century. A Tatar ASSR was established on 27 May 1920.

On 31 August 1990 the Chairman of the republican Supreme Soviet, Mintimer Shaimiyev, declared Tatarstan a sovereign republic. In 1991 Shaimiyev was elected as republican President. Apart from secessionist Chechnya, Tatarstan was the only Republic to reject the Federation Treaty of the following year, adopting its own Constitution on 6 November 1992, which provided for a presidential republic with a bicameral legislature, the State Council. In February 1994 Shaimiyev won concessions from the federal Government by signing an accord that ceded extensive powers to Tatarstan, including full ownership rights over its petroleum reserves and industrial companies, the right to retain most of its tax revenue and the right to pursue its own foreign-trade policy. This was the first agreement of its kind in the Federation and, despite significant contradictions and weaknesses, it became a model for other federal subjects seeking to determine their relations with the federal centre. The division of responsibilities was confirmed by treaty with the Federation in 1995.

In a republican presidential election, held on 24 March 1996, Shaimiyev was re-elected unopposed, in breach of federal legislation. During 1999 Shaimiyev was one of the regional governors most active in the creation of the All Russia political bloc. Shaimiyev was elected to a further term of office in March 2001, when he obtained some 80% of the votes cast, becoming the first Governor of any federal subject in the Russian Federation to be elected three times to that post.

As Putin's administration, from mid-2000, sought to harmonize federal legislation with that of the constituent units of the Russian Federation, Tatarstan (along with neighbouring Bashkortostan) became one of the principal regions in which the republican authorities demonstrated sustained resistance to these measures. In May 2001 the federal Supreme Court declared that some 42 articles of the Republic's Constitution were at variance with federal law (a ruling by the republican Supreme Court confirmed these findings in October). The text of a new Constitution, which was intended to comply with federal law, was approved by the republican State Council in February 2002 and took effect from 19 April. Although the new document referred to Tatarstan being subject to the Constitution and laws of the Russian Federation, it continued to declare the 'limited' and 'residual' sovereignty of the Republic of Tatarstan and preserved the notion of Tatar citizenship. Consequently, in June the office of the federal Prosecutor-General demanded that several articles of the Constitution be amended, issuing a complaint to both the republican legislature and republican Supreme Court. However, in September the State Council rejected any notion that the constitutional text was in breach of federal law, and instead referred the matter to both the republican and federal Constitutional Courts. In July 2003 the federal Constitutional Court ruled that it was the sole body with the authority to determine whether the constitutions of federal subjects were in conformity with federal law; one consequence of this ruling appeared to be that a number of challenges to the Constitution of Tatarstan from other bodies (including the federal Supreme Court) were declared invalid. Meanwhile, tensions between the federal and republican authorities were further heightened by federal legislation, approved in November 2002, that demanded that all state languages of federal subjects be written in Cyrillic on official documents—the republican authorities had, in September 1999, begun to implement a programme to re-introduce the Latin script (previously used in the 1920s–30s) for the Tatar language. In February 2004 the

State Council appealed to the federal Constitutional Court to review the law on Cyrillic-based alphabets on grounds that Russia's constituent Republics were entitled to adopt their own state languages. In November the Court rejected the State Council's appeal; this ruling was upheld by the federal Supreme Court in the following month.

In March 2005, following the introduction of a system of presidential appointment for regional Governors and Presidents, and the amendment of the republican Constitution to that end, Shaimiyev (who was by now regarded as an important ally of the federal President, Vladimir Putin) requested that Putin nominate him to serve a further term as President of Tatarstan. Shaimiyev was duly nominated, and his appointment to a further five-year term of office was confirmed by the republican State Council on 25 March. On 28 October the republican legislature approved a new draft power-sharing treaty between Tatarstan and the federal authorities, the first such agreement to take effect for several years; however, it was thought that under the new agreement the Republic had lost some of the special status it had enjoyed under the administration of Putin's predecessor, Boris Yeltsin.

Economy

In 2002 the Republic's gross regional product totalled 261,843.9m. roubles, or 69,284.3 roubles per head. The territory is one of the most developed economic regions of the Russian Federation and has vast agricultural and industrial potential. Its main industrial centres are Kazan, Naberezhnye Chelny, Zelenodolsk, Nizhnekamsk and Almetyevsk. Kazan is the most important port on the Volga and a junction in the national rail, road and air transport systems. Russia's second primary petroleum export pipeline to Europe starts in Almetyevsk. At the end of 2002 there were 865 km of railway lines and 12,742 km of paved roads on the Republic's territory.

Agriculture which employed 12.7% of the work-force and generated 46,449m. roubles in 2003 (the third-highest output of any federal subject) in 2003, consists mainly of grain production, animal husbandry, horticulture and bee-keeping. The Republic has significant reserves of hydrocarbons reserves. In 2003 industry accounted for 23.2% of employment in 2003 and generated 281,547m. roubles. Kazan, Zelenodolsk and Vasilyevo are centres for light industry, the manufacture of petrochemicals and building materials, and mechanical engineering. The automobile and petroleum industries are major employers in the region. The petrochemicals company Kazanorgsintez is the largest polyethylene producer in Russia. Output of petroleum in the region in 2002 amounted to 28.7m. metric tons, a figure surpassed among federal subjects only by the Khanty-Mansii and Yamalo-Nenets AOks in Tyumen Oblast. Industries connected with the extraction, processing and use of petroleum typically represent around 40% of the Republic's total industrial production. In the mid-1990s the US automobile company, General Motors, signed a contract to manufacture automobiles at the Yelabuga plant, which later became the centre of a zone offering special tax incentives. In 2002 some 38,700 automobiles were manufactured in the Republic.

The economically active population in the Republic amounted to 1,865,000 in 2003, when 6.7% of the labour force were unemployed. The average monthly wage was 4,530.0 roubles in 2003. The 2003 budget recorded a deficit of 1,430.3m. roubles. The value of exports amounted to US $3,676.5m. in 2003, and imports to $384.7m. In the same year foreign investment in the Republic amounted to

$176.1m., compared with $642.5m. in the previous year. At the end of 2003 some 16,900 small businesses were registered in the Republic.

Directory

President: MINTIMER SH. SHAIMIYEV (elected 12 June 1991, re-elected unopposed 24 March 1996, re-elected 25 March 2001; appointment confirmed 25 March 2005), 420014 Tatarstan, Kazan, Kreml; tel. (843) 292-74-66; fax (843) 291-78-66; e-mail secretariat@tatar.ru; internet www.tatar.ru.

Prime Minister: RUSTAM N. MINNIKHANOV, 420060 Tatarstan, Kazan, pl. Svobody 1; tel. (843) 264-15-51; fax (843) 236-28-24; e-mail premier@kabmin.tatarstan.ru; internet kabmin.tatar.ru.

Chairman of the State Council: FARID KH. MUKHAMETSHIN, 420060 Tatarstan, Kazan, pl. Svobody 1; tel. (843) 267-63-00; fax (843) 267-64-89; e-mail gossov@gossov.tatarstan.ru; internet www.gossov.tatarstan.ru.

Chief Representative of the Republic of Tatarstan in the Russian Federation: NAZIF M. MIRIKHANOV, 115172 Moscow, per. 3-i Kotelnicheskii 13/15/1; tel. (495) 915-58-02; fax (495) 915-06-10; e-mail adm@msk.tatarstan.ru.

Head of Kazan City Administration: IRSHAT MINKIN, 420014 Tatarstan, Kazan, ul. Kremlevskaya 1; tel. (843) 299-16-60; fax (843) 299-16-61; e-mail kazan@kabmin.gov.tatarstan.ru; internet www.kazan.org.ru.

Udmurt Republic

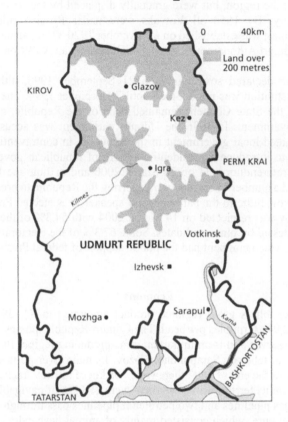

The Udmurt Republic occupies part of the Upper Kama Highlands. It forms part of the Volga Federal Okrug and the Urals Economic Area. Tatarstan lies to the south, Bashkortostan to the south-east, Perm Krai to the east and Kirov Oblast to the north and west. Its major river is the Kama. About one-half of its territory is forested. The Republic covers 42,100 sq km (16,250 sq miles). According to the census of 9–16 October 2002, the Republic had a population of 1,570,316, and a population density of 37.3 per sq km. Some 69.7% of the population inhabited urban areas. 60.1% of the population were ethnically Russian, 29.3% were Udmurt and 7.0% were Tatar. The dominant religion in the Republic is Orthodox Christianity. The 1989 census showed that some 70% of Udmurts spoke their native tongue, from the Permian group of the Finnic branch of the Uralo-Altaic family, as their first language. The capital of the Udmurt Republic is at Izhevsk (formerly Ustinov), which had a population of 632,100 in 2002, according to preliminary census results. Other major towns in the region are Sarapul (103,200) and Glazov (100,900). The Republic is included in the time zone GMT+4.

History

The first appearance of the Votyaks (the former name for Udmurts) as a distinct ethnic group occurred in the sixth century. The territories inhabited by Votyaks were conquered by the Khazars in the eighth century, although Khazar influence gave way to that of the Volga Bulgars in the mid-ninth century. In the 13th century the Mongol Tatars occupied the region, but were gradually displaced by the Russians from the mid-15th century. By 1558 all Votyaks were under Russian rule. A Votyak Autonomous Oblast was established on 4 November 1920. On 1 January 1932 it was renamed the Udmurt Autonomous Oblast, which became an ASSR on 28 December 1934.

The Republic declared sovereignty on 21 September 1990, although a new republican Constitution was not adopted until 7 December 1994. The Chairman of the legislature, the State Council, remained head of the Republic, and a premier chaired the Government. In 1996 the Udmurt parliament was accused of having virtually eliminated local government in the Republic, in contravention of federal law. Measures to introduce a presidential system of republican government were endorsed by a referendum held on 26 March 2000 and in June the Udmurt State Council adopted a number of draft laws transferring the Republic to presidential rule. Aleksandr Volkov, hitherto the parliamentary speaker, was elected President on 15 October. Volkov was re-elected on 14 March 2004 with 54.3% of the votes cast in an election contested by nine candidates. Some 67.3% of the electorate participated in the elections. The incumbent had the public support of federal President Vladimir Putin.

Economy

In 2002 the Republic's gross regional product amounted to 83,139.7m. roubles, equivalent to 52,944.6 roubles per head. The Udmurt Republic possesses significant hydrocarbons reserves and is an important arms-producing region. Its major industrial centres are at Izhevsk, Sarapul and Glazov. Its main river-ports are at Sarapul and Kambarka. At the end of 2002 there were 768 km of railway track and 5,668 km of paved roads on its territory. In 1998 there were 178 km of navigable waterways. Twelve major gas pipelines and two petroleum pipelines pass through the Republic.

In 2003 agriculture, which consisted mainly of animal husbandry and grain and potato production, employed 11.9% of the work-force and generated 14,999m. roubles. There are substantial reserves of coal and of petroleum. In 2003 industry employed 28.4% of the labour force and generated 85,030m. roubles. The main industries, apart from the manufacture of weapons, are mechanical engineering (in 2002 some 65,800 automobiles were produced in the Republic, a figure exceeded among federal subjects only by Samara Oblast), metal-working, metallurgy, food-processing, petroleum production and the production of peat. From the 1990s the disposal of chemical weapons on the territory of the Republic proved to be a serious social and ecological problem—the Republic was thought to contain around one-quarter of Russia's entire arsenal of such weapons.

In 2003 the economically active population amounted to 830,000, and 6.7% of the labour force were unemployed; in 2003 the average monthly wage was 4,349.9 roubles. The republican budget recorded a deficit of 552.5m. roubles in 2003, when there was foreign investment in the Republic of US $21.6m., compared to $156.7m. in the previous year. Export trade in 2003 comprised $660.4m. in exports, and $79.9m. in imports. The principal exports are metallurgical products, engines and machinery, and rifles. At the end of 2003 some 8,800 small businesses were registered in the Republic.

Directory

President: ALEKSANDR A. VOLKOV (elected 15 October 2000), 426074 Udmurt Rep., Izhevsk, pl. 50 let Oktyabrya 15; tel. and fax (3412) 49-70-10; e-mail president@udmurt.ru; internet www.udmurt.ru/ru/president.

Chairman of the Government: YURII S. PITKEYVICH, 426007 Udmurt Rep., Izhevsk, ul. Pushkinskaya 214; tel. (3412) 25-50-89; fax (3412) 25-50-17; e-mail premier@udmurt.ru; internet www.udmurt.ru.

Chairman of the State Council (Legislature): IGOR N. SEMENOV, 426074 Udmurt Rep., Izhevsk, ul. 50 let Oktyabrya 15; tel. (3412) 75-34-98; fax (3412) 75-29-87; e-mail webadmin@gossovet.udm.ru; internet www.udmgossovet.ru.

Chief Representative of the Udmurt Republic in the Russian Federation: ANDREI V. SAKOVICH, 103025 Moscow, Oktyabrskii per. 9; tel. (495) 734-60-78; fax (495) 203-91-47.

Head of Izhevsk City Administration (Mayor): VIKTOR V. BALAKIN, 426070 Udmurt Rep., Izhevsk, ul. Pushkinskaya 276; tel. (3412) 22-45-90; fax (3412) 22-84-94; e-mail izhevsk@izh.ru; internet www.izh.ru.

Perm Krai

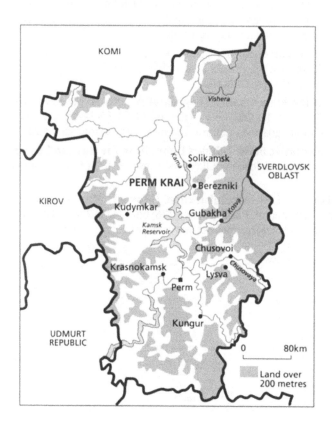

Perm Krai (formed in 2005 by the merger of Perm Oblast and the Komi-Permyak Autonomous Okrug, the latter of which was located in the north-western part of the territory) is situated on the western slopes of the Central and Northern Urals and the eastern edge of the Eastern European Plain. It forms part of the Volga Federal Okrug and the Urals Economic Area. The Republic of Komi lies to the north, Kirov Oblast and the Udmurt Republic lie to the west, Bashkortostan to the south and Sverdlovsk Oblast to the east. The major rivers are the Kama, the Chusovaya and the Kosva. The Kamsk reservoir lies in the centre of the region. The Krai occupies 160,600 sq km (61,990 sq miles). According to the census of 9–16 October 2002, the region's total population was 2,819,421, giving a population density of 17.6 per sq km. Some 75.2% of the population inhabited urban areas. 85.2% of the population were ethnically Russian, 4.8% Tatar, 3.7% Komi-Permyak, 0.9% Udmurt and 0.9% Ukrainian. The Oblast's administrative centre is at Perm, which had a population of 1,000,100 in 2002, according to provisional census results. Other major cities include Berezniki (with a population of 173,500) and Solikamsk (102,800). Perm Krai is included in the time zone GMT+5.

History

Perm city was founded in 1723, with the construction of a copper foundry. Industrial development was such that by the latter part of the 20th century the city extended for some 80 km along the banks of the Kama. Perm Oblast was formed on 3 October 1938. The Komi-Permyak National Okrug was established on 26 February 1925. In 1977 the Okrug received the nominal status of an Autonomous Okrug (AOk). Perm city was called Molotov in 1940–57 and entry was forbidden to foreigners until 1989.

In December 1993 there were regional elections for a new parliament, the Legislative Assembly. In May 1996 the regional administrations of both Perm Oblast and the Komi-Permyak AOk signed separate power-sharing treaties with the federal President, Boris Yeltsin. (In the early 1990s the AOk, in common with the other territories of that status across the Russian Federation, had become a subject of the Federation in its own right, as well as an integral part of the territory within which it was contained, and the constitutional relationship between the entities remained obscure.) In December the Governor appointed earlier that year, Gennadii Igumnov, retained his post in direct elections, and pro-reform candidates loyal to Igumnov were successful in securing an absolute majority of seats in elections to the regional legislature in December 1997. Meanwhile, the incumbent governor of the Komi-Permyak AOk, Nikolai Poluyanov (appointed in December 1991), retained his position following a gubernatorial election held in November 1996; Poluyanov was, however, defeated by the deputy president of the audit chamber of Perm Oblast, Gennadii Savelyev, in the gubernatorial election held in the AOk in December 2000. Following the gubernatorial election held in Perm Oblast in the same month, Igumnov was replaced by Yurii Trutnev, hitherto the Mayor of Perm City. Elections to the Legislative Assemblies in both entities were held in December 2001.

In July 2002, following visits by the Chairman of the Federation Council, Sergei Mironov, and the Presidential Representative in the Volga Federal Okrug, Sergei Kiriyenko, to the territorial capitals, Trutnev announced that measures to merge the two federal subjects would be initiated in the near future. In February 2003 the legislative organs of both territories voted in favour of a merger, and in March the Governors of the two regions met federal President Vladimir Putin, who expressed support for the proposal. In May the oblast parliament approved legislation to permit the holding of a plebiscite on the merger, and further laws pertaining to the measure were approved by the parliaments of both administrative entities in June. On 7 December a referendum was held (concurrently with elections to the federal State Duma) to seek approval for the merger. Some 83% of the participating electorate supported the unification of the two territories to form a new federal subject, to be known as Perm Krai. On 26 March 2004, following the acceptance of the measures by the federal legislature, Putin signed legislation approving the formation of the Krai, which came into existence on 1 December 2005. He also confirmed Oleg Chirkunov as acting Governor of Perm Oblast. (Chirkunov had been nominated by the outgoing Governor, Yurii Trutnev, following the latter's appointment as the Minister of National Resources in the federal Government in March 2004.) Chirkunov's nomination as Governor was confirmed by the legislatures of the two territories on 10 October 2005. The legislature of Perm Krai was to be elected in December 2006 and the establishment of a common budget was to take place the following year.

Economy

All figures in this survey pertain to the former Perm Oblast, including the Komi-Permyak Autonomous Okrug (AOk). In 2002 Perm Oblast's gross regional product amounted to 194,355.1m. roubles, or 68,934.4 roubles per head—the highest level in the Volga Federal Okrug. The Krai's industrial centres are at Perm, Berezniki, Chusovoi and Krasnokamsk. At the end of 2002 there were 1,493 km of railways and 10,593 km of paved roads on the Oblast's territory.

Agriculture in the territory, which in 2003 employed 7.7% of the working population in the Oblast as a whole and generated 17,454m. roubles, consists mainly of grain and vegetable production, bee-keeping and animal husbandry. Some 27.7% of the working population were engaged in industry in Perm Oblast in 2003, when industrial output amounted to 199,365m. roubles. The main industries of the territory are coal, petroleum, natural gas, potash and salt production, mechanical engineering, chemicals and petrochemicals, petroleum-refining and electricity generation. There is also a significant defence sector.

The economically active population numbered 1,469,000 in 2003, when 6.9% of the labour force were unemployed. The average wage represented the highest rate in the Volga Federal Okrug, amounting to 5,283.5 roubles per month in 2003. The economic situation in the Komi-Permyak AOk was far harsher than in the region as a whole, and the territory was one of the most underdeveloped and deprived regions of European Russia. In 2003 there was a budgetary surplus of 922.3m. roubles in Perm Oblast. In that year external trade amounted to a value of US $2,359.5m. in exports and $323.6m. in imports. Foreign investment in 2003 amounted to $35.9m. At the end of 2003 some 8,700 small businesses were registered in Perm Oblast.

Directory

Governor: OLEG A. CHIRKUNOV (assumed office 1 December 2005), 614006 Perm, ul. Kuibysheva 14; tel. (3422) 58-70-75; fax (3422) 34-89-52; e-mail webmaster@ perm.ru; internet www.perm.ru.

Chairman of the Legislative Assembly: NIKOLAI A. DEVYATKIN, 614006 Perm, ul. Lenina 51; tel. (3422) 58-75-55; fax (3422) 34-27-47; e-mail parliament@perm.ru; internet www.parliament.perm.ru.

Chief Representative of Perm Krai in the Russian Federation: ALEKSANDR A. POTEKHIN, 121151 Moscow, nab. T. Shevchenko 23A; tel. (495) 299-48-36; fax (495) 209-08-97.

Head of Perm City Administration: ARKADII L. KAMENEV, 614000 Perm, ul. Lenina 15; tel. (3422) 34-33-02; fax (3422) 34-94-11; e-mail info@perm.permregion.ru; internet www.gorodperm.ru.

Kirov Oblast

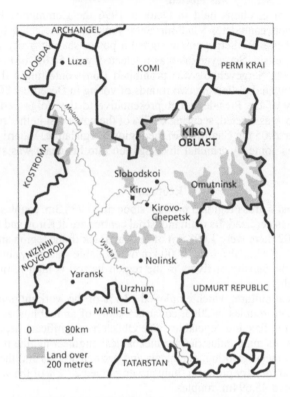

Kirov Oblast is situated in the east of the Eastern European Plain. It forms part of the Volga Federal Okrug and the Volga-Vyatka Economic Area. It is bordered by Archangel and Komi to the north, Perm Krai and the Udmurt Republic to the east, Tatarstan and Marii-El to the south, and Nizhnii Novgorod, Kostroma and Vologda to the west. Its main rivers are the Kama and the Vyatka. The Oblast occupies 120,800 sq km (46,640 sq miles). According to the census of 9–16 October 2002, the Oblast's population numbered 1,503,529 and the population density was 12.5 per sq km. Around 71.8% of the population inhabited urban areas. 90.8% of the population were ethnically Russian, 2.9% Tatar, 2.6% Mari, 1.2% Udmurt and 0.8% Ukrainian. The Oblast's administrative centre is at Kirov, a river-port, which had 457,400 inhabitants in 2002, according to provisional census results. The territory is included in the time zone GMT+3.

History

The city of Khlynov was founded in 1181 as an outpost of Novgorod, and came under Muscovite rule in 1489. The city was renamed Vyatka in 1781, and Kirov in 1934, in which year Kirov Oblast was formed. In September 1993 a draft constitution for Kirov Oblast was prepared, which referred to the Oblast as Vyatka Krai and provided for a popularly elected governor and a new legislature, a provincial duma. On 18 October the Kirov Oblast Soviet (Council) voted to disband itself. The federal authorities refused to acknowledge the area's redesignation and during 1994 an oblast legislative assembly was elected.

At gubernatorial elections held in October 1996 the Communist Party of the Russian Federation candidate, Vladimir Sergeyenkov, was elected by a narrow margin. In October 1997 Sergeyenkov signed a power-sharing treaty with federal President Boris Yeltsin. Sergeyenkov was re-elected, with 58.0% of the votes cast, on 26 March 2000. Sergeyenkov was prohibited from contesting a third term of office by local law, and, following two rounds of voting in December 2003, Nikolai Shaklein, an ally of the Presidential Representative to the Volga Federal Okrug, Sergei Kiriyenko, was elected, securing 62.7% of the votes cast in the 'run-off' poll. On 25 September 2005 the Chairman of the regional legislature, Valerii Kaisin, was found dead at his home. A criminal investigation into his death was subsequently opened.

Economy

In 2002 the Oblast's gross regional product stood at 53,738.3m. roubles, equivalent to 35,741.4 roubles per head. Its main industrial centres are at Kirov and Slobodskoi. At the end of 2002 there were 1,098 km of railway track in the region and 9,043 km of paved roads. There are also over 2,000 km of navigable waterways on the Vyatka river. Owing to the density of rivers in the region its soil is high in mineral salts, reducing its fertility.

The Oblast's agriculture, which employed 13.1% of the working population and generated 15,492m. roubles in 2003, consists mainly of animal husbandry and the production of grain, flax and vegetables. The Oblast has significant deposits of peat and phosphorites. Its main industries are mechanical engineering, the production of electrical energy, metal-working, chemicals and petrochemicals and the processing of agricultural and forestry products. Industry employed 27.2% of the work-force in 2003 and generated 45,694m. roubles.

The economically active population numbered 828,000 in 2003, when 7.4% of the Oblast's labour force were unemployed. The average monthly wage was 3,640.9 roubles in 2003. In 2003 the Oblast recorded a budgetary deficit of 666.8m. roubles. External trade comprised US $299.6m. in exports and $40.3m. in imports. In 2003 foreign investment amounted to just $2.1m. At the end of 2003 some 5,300 small businesses were registered in the Oblast.

Directory

Head of the Regional Administration (Governor): NIKOLAI I. SHAKLEIN (elected 21 December 2003), 610019 Kirov, ul. K. Libknekhta 69; tel. (8332) 62-95-64; fax (8332) 62-89-58; e-mail region@ako.kirov.ru; internet ako.kirov.ru.

Chairman of the Legislative Assembly: VLADIMIR A. VASILYEV, 610019 Kirov, ul. K. Libknekhta 69; tel. and fax (8332) 62-48-00; e-mail assembly@ako.kirov.ru; internet ako.kirov.ru.

Chief Representative of Kirov Oblast in the Russian Federation: ALEKSANDR L. ZIMENKOV, 121248 Moscow, Kutuzovskii pr. 12/7; tel. (495) 243-23-59; e-mail kirov-pred@mail.ru.

Head of Kirov City Administration (Mayor): VASILII A. KISELEV, 610000 Kirov, ul. Vorovskogo 39; tel. (8332) 62-89-40; fax (8332) 67-69-91.

Nizhnii Novgorod Oblast

Nizhnii Novgorod Oblast is situated on the middle reaches of the Volga river. It forms part of the Volga Federal Okrug and the Volga-Vyatka Economic Area. Mordoviya and Ryazan lie to the south, Vladimir and Ivanovo to the west, Kostroma to the north-west, Kirov to the north-east and Marii-El and the Chuvash Republic to the east. Its major rivers are the Volga, the Oka, the Sura and the Vetluga. The terrain in the north of the Oblast is mainly low lying, with numerous forests and extensive swampland. The southern part is characterized by fertile black soil (*chernozem*). The Oblast occupies a total area of 76,900 sq km (29,690 sq miles). According to the census of 9–16 October 2002, the Oblast had a population of 3,524,028 and a population density of 45.8 per sq km. Some 78.2% of the Oblast's inhabitants resided in urban areas. 95.0% of the population were ethnically Russian; 1.4% were Tatar. Its administrative centre is at Nizhnii Novgorod (formerly Gorkii), which lies at the confluence of the Volga and Oka rivers. The city is Russia's fourth largest, with a population of 1,311,200 in 2002, according to provisional census results. Other major cities include Dzerzhinsk (formerly Chernorech—with a population of 261,400) and Arzamas (109,500). The territory is included in the time zone GMT+3.

History

Nizhnii Novgorod city was founded in 1221 on the borders of the Russian principalities. With the decline of Tatar power the city was absorbed by the Muscovite state. Industrialization took place in the late tsarist period. In 1905 mass unrest occurred in the region, which in late 1917 was one of the first areas of Russia to be seized by the Bolsheviks. Nizhnii Novgorod Oblast was formed on 14 January

1929. In 1932–90 the city and region were named Gorkii, and for much of the time the city was 'closed', owing to the importance of the defence industry.

In 1991 the Russian President, Boris Yeltsin, appointed a leading local reformer, Boris Nemtsov, as regional Governor. Nemtsov instituted a wide-ranging programme of economic reform, which was widely praised by liberals and by the federal Government. Nemtsov secured popular election in December 1995, and was a prominent advocate of democratization and decentralization in the Federation. In June 1996 Nemtsov signed a treaty on the delimitation of powers with the federal Government, giving the Oblast greater budgetary independence. In April 1997 Nemtsov was appointed to the federal Government; gubernatorial elections were subsequently held, in which the pro-Government candidate, Ivan Sklyarov (hitherto Mayor of Nizhnii Novgorod), defeated Gennadii Khodyrev (who was supported both by the Communist Party of the Russian Federation—CPRF and the nationalist Liberal Democratic Party of Russia). The Oblast's economic situation subsequently deteriorated somewhat, and the federal Government withheld funds for the continuing conversion of the Oblast's defence industry. At the second round of gubernatorial elections held in July 2001, Khodyrev, by this time a CPRF deputy in the State Duma, was elected Governor, obtaining almost 60% of the votes cast. Following his election, Khodyrev suspended his membership of the CPRF. (He resigned from the party in May 2002 and by late 2003 was associated with the pro-Government Unity and Fatherland-United Russia party—UF-UR.) In September 2001 the regional legislature voted in favour of a proposal made by Khodyrev that he act both as Governor and as Prime Minister of the Oblast. Elections to the regional Legislative Assembly in March 2002 resulted in the formation of a centre-right majority in the new chamber, with UF-UR becoming the single largest party grouping. In the following month the power-sharing treaty agreed in 1996 was annulled. In March 2005, in association with the recently introduced system whereby regional Governors were to be appointed, Khodyrev was reported to have asked the federal President, Vladimir Putin, for an expression of his trust (which would have therefore resulted in Khodyrev's nomination for a further term as Governor). However, despite legislation requiring that such a request be responded to within the period of one week, no response was forthcoming until July, shortly before the expiry of Khodyrev's mandate. In the event Putin did not nominate Khodyrev, instead selecting the hitherto deputy Mayor of Moscow City, Valerii Shantsev (who was regarded as a technocrat, and had no previous connection with the Nizhnii Novgorod region), as his nominee; this appointment was confirmed by vote of the regional legislature on 8 August.

Economy

In 2002 the Oblast's gross regional product amounted to 196,901.4m. roubles, or 55,874.0 roubles per head. Its principal industrial centres are at Nizhnii Novgorod, Dzerzhinsk and Arzamas. Nizhnii Novgorod contains a major river-port, from which it is possible to reach the Baltic, Black, White and Caspian Seas. At the end of 2002 there were 13,350 km of paved roads and 1,214 km of railway track in the region. In 1985 an underground railway system opened in Nizhnii Novgorod and in 1994 an international airport was opened, from which regular flights to the German city of Frankfurt operate.

Agriculture, which employed 8.1% of the working population and generated 21,249m. roubles in 2003, consists mainly of animal husbandry and the production of grain, sugar beet, flax and onions and other vegetables. The sector was subject to extensive privatization and restructuring in the 1990s. It is the Oblast's industry that dominates the regional economy, however; in 2002 the sector generated 196,365m. roubles and employed 30.3% of the labour force. The principal industries of the Oblast include mechanical engineering and metal-working, ferrous metallurgy, chemicals, petrochemicals and the processing of agricultural and forestry products. During the Soviet period the region was developed as a major military-industrial centre, with the defence sector accounting for around three-quarters of the regional economy. In the 1990s the Oblast was among those territories of the Federation that dealt most successfully with the transition from military to civilian industry.

The economically active population numbered 1,846,000 in 2003, when 6.1% of the labour force were unemployed and the average monthly wage was 4,205.9 roubles. The budget in that year recorded a deficit of 1,807.9m. roubles. In 2003 external trade in the Oblast comprised US 1,831.5m. in exports and $679.7m. in imports. In 1997 the Oblast became the third Russian federal subject, after the cities of federal status, to issue Eurobonds. In 2003 foreign investment in the region totalled $124.2m. At the end of 2003 some 18,400 small businesses were registered in the Oblast.

Directory

Head of the Regional Administration (Governor and Prime Minister): VALERII SHANTSEV (appointment confirmed 8 August 2005), 603082 Nizhnii Novgorod, Kreml, kor. 1; tel. (8312) 39-13-30; fax (8312) 39-00-48; e-mail official@kreml .nnov.ru; internet www.government.nnov.ru.

Chairman of the Legislative Assembly: YEVGENII B. LYULIN, 603082 Nizhnii Novgorod, Kreml, kor. 2; tel. (8312) 39-05-38; fax (8312) 39-06-29; e-mail nnovg@ duma.gov.ru; internet www.zsno.ru.

Chief Representation of Nizhnii Novgorod Oblast in the Russian Federation: VIKTOR A. GULYASHKO, 127006 Moscow, Nastasyinskii per. 5/3; tel. (495) 956-92-48.

Head of Nizhnii Novgorod City Administration (Mayor): VADIM YE. BULAVINOV, 603082 Nizhnii Novgorod, Kreml, kor. 5; tel. (8312) 39-15-06; fax (8312) 39-13-02; internet www.admgor.nnov.ru.

Orenburg Oblast

Orenburg Oblast is situated in the foothills of the Southern Urals. It forms part of the Volga Federal Okrug and the Urals Economic Area. An international border with Kazakhstan lies to the south and east, and there are borders with Samara Oblast to the west, Bashkortostan and Chelyabinsk to the north and a short border with Tatarstan in the north-west. The region occupies 124,000 sq km (47,860 sq miles). According to the census of 9–16 October 2002, the total population of the Oblast was 2,179,551 and the population density 17.6 per sq km. Some 57.8% of the population lived in urban areas. 73.9% of the population were ethnically Russian, 7.6% Tatar, 5.8% Kazakh, 3.5% Ukrainian, 2.4% Bashkir, 2.4% Mordovian, 0.8% German and 0.8% Chuvash. The Oblast's administrative centre is at Orenburg, which had 548,800 inhabitants in 2002, according to provisional census results. Other major cities are Orsk (250,600) and Novotroitsk (106,200). Orenburg is included in the time zone GMT+5.

History

The city of Orenburg originated as a fortress in 1743. During the revolutionary period Orenburg was a headquarters of 'White' forces and possession of it was fiercely contested with the Bolsheviks. The city was also a centre of Kazakh (then erroneously known to the Russians as Kyrgyz) nationalists and was the capital of the Kyrgyz ASSR in 1920–25. The region was then separated from the renamed Kazakh ASSR. Orenburg Oblast was formed on 7 December 1934.

Gubernatorial elections, held concurrently with elections to the federal State Duma in December 1995, were won by the incumbent appointed in October 1991, Vladimir Yelagin. A power-sharing treaty was agreed between the regional and federal authorities in early 1996. (The treaty was annulled in April 2002.) Yelagin was defeated in the gubernatorial elections of December 1999 by the former Chairman of the State Duma Committee on Agrarian Issues, Aleksei Chernyshev. In regional legislative elections held in March 2002 the representation of left-wing deputies declined to just four seats. On 7 December Chernyshev was re-elected to the governorship, securing 65.2% of the votes cast. 54.3% of the registered electorate participated in the elections. In early June 2005 Chernyshev announced his resignation, in order to request that federal President Vladimir Putin nominate him to a further term of office. Putin duly nominated Chernyshev, and his appointment was confirmed by the regional Legislative Assembly on 15 June.

Economy

The Oblast's gross regional product was 102,995.0m. roubles in 2002, or 47,255.1 roubles per head. At the end of 2002 there were 1,652 km of railways and 13,219 km of paved roads on the Oblast's territory. Its principal industrial centres are at Orenburg, Orsk and Novotroisk. There is a high level of atmospheric pollution in the region, while the intensive exploitation of petroleum and gas deposits have caused serious damage to arable land.

Agriculture which employed 18.6% of the work-force and generated 25,557m. roubles in 2003, consists mainly of grain, vegetable and sunflower production and animal husbandry. The Oblast's major industries are ferrous and non-ferrous metallurgy, mechanical engineering, metal-working, natural gas production, electrical energy and the production of petroleum, ores, asbestos and salt. In 2002 production of petroleum in the Oblast amounted to 11.5m. metric tons, a figure exceeded among federal subjects only by Tatarstan and the two AOks (Khanty-Mansii and Yamalo-Nenets) within Tyumen Oblast. In that year the Oblast was also the second largest producer of natural gas, with output of some 23,769m. cu m, less only than the Khanty-Mansii AOk. In 2003 industry engaged 19.8% of the working population and generated a total of 103,299m. roubles.

The economically active population numbered 1,037,000 in 2003, when 11.3% of the labour force were unemployed. The regional average monthly wage was 3,898.1 roubles. The Oblast's budget for 2003 showed a deficit of 499.7m. roubles. In 2003 external trade comprised US $2,266.2m. in exports and $458.8m. in imports. Total foreign investment in the region in that year amounted to $60.0m. At the end of 2003 some 7,700 small businesses were registered in the Oblast.

Directory

Head of the Regional Administration (Governor): ANDREI A. CHERNYSHEV (elected 26 December 1999, re-elected 7 December 2003; appointment confirmed 15 June 2005), 460015 Orenburg, Dom Sovetov; tel. (3532) 77-69-31; fax (3532) 77-38-02; e-mail office@gov.orb.ru; internet www.orb.ru.

Chairman of the Legislative Assembly: YURII V. TROFIMOV, 460015 Orenburg, Dom Sovetov; tel. (3532) 77-33-20; fax (3532) 77-42-12; e-mail parlament@gov .orb.ru; internet www.parlament.orb.ru.

Chief Representative of Orenburg Oblast in the Russian Federation: VYACHE-SLAV S. RYABOV, 127025 Moscow, ul. Novyi Arbat 19/2014; tel. (495) 203-85-32; fax (495) 203-59-76.

Head of Orenburg City Administration (Mayor): YURII N. MISCHERYAKOV, 461300 Orenburg, ul. Sovetskaya 60; tel. (3532) 98-70-10; fax (3532) 77-60-58; e-mail glava@admin.orenburg.ru; internet www.admin.orenburg.ru.

Penza Oblast

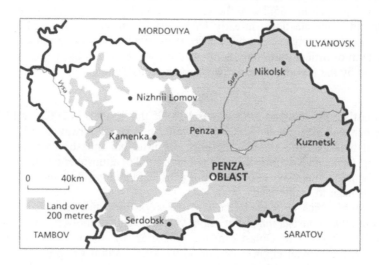

Penza Oblast is situated in the Volga Highlands. It forms part of the Volga Federal Okrug and the Volga Economic Area and borders Mordoviya to the north, Ulyanovsk to the east, Saratov to the south, Tambov to the south-west and Ryazan to the north-west. The Oblast covers 43,200 sq km (16,750 sq miles). According to the census of 9–16 October 2002, the population of the Oblast was 1,452,941 and the population density 33.6 per sq km. Some 65.1% of the population inhabited urban areas. 86.4% of the population were ethnically Russian, 6.0% Tatar, 4.9% Mordovian and 0.9% Ukrainian. The Oblast's administrative centre, Penza, had a population of 518,200 in 2002, according to provisional census results. The territory is included in the time zone GMT+3.

History

The city of Penza was founded in 1663 as an outpost on the south-eastern border of the Russian Empire. The region was annexed by Bolshevik forces in late 1917 and remained under the control of the Red Army throughout the period of civil war. Penza Oblast was formed on 4 February 1939.

In April 1993 the Communist Party candidate, Anatolii Kovlyagin, defeated the pro-Governmental incumbent appointed in 1991, Aleksandr Kondratyev, in elections to head the regional administration. On 12 April 1998 Vasilii Bochkarev, an independent regarded as a technocrat, was elected as Governor. He was re-elected on 14 April 2002, with the support of the pro-Government Unity and Fatherland-United Russia party. The adoption, in 2002, of a new oblast flag, depicting an image based upon a Russian Orthodox icon, resulted in protests in the region, particularly by representatives of the estimated 100,000-strong (principally Tatar) Muslim population of the region and communists; concern was expressed that the design could breach the separation of religion and state guaranteed by the federal Constitution. In May 2005 Bochkarev resigned, in order to seek nomination by federal President Vladimir Putin to a further term of office. Putin duly nominated Bochkarev, and his reappointment was confirmed by the regional Legislative Assembly on 14 May.

Economy

In 2002 Penza's gross regional product was 44,860.3m. roubles, or 30,875.5 roubles per head. The Oblast's principal industrial centres are at Penza and Kuznetsk. Several major railway routes pass through the Oblast; at the end of 2002 there were 827 km of railway track in the region. Some 6,524 km of paved roads included several major highways.

Around three-quarters of the agricultural land in the Oblast consists of fertile black earth (*chernozem*). Agriculture, which employed 17.8% of the work-force and generated 11,661m. roubles in 2003, consists mainly of the production of grain and vegetables and animal husbandry. Almost 400,000 ha of arable land were thought to be lying fallow in late 2003: at this time a British company secured a lease on 1,000 ha of land in the Oblast, becoming the first foreign business to purchase a lease on agricultural land in Russia. The Oblast's main industries are mechanical engineering, the processing of timber and agricultural products, chemicals and petrochemicals and light manufacturing. Industry employed some 21.3% of the working population in 2003, and generated 29,439m. roubles.

The economically active population in Penza Oblast numbered 712,000 in 2003, when 9.1% of the labour force were unemployed. Those in employment earned an average of 3,474.4 roubles per month in 2002. The 2003 regional budget showed a deficit of 166.3m. roubles. The external trade of the Oblast was relatively low, amounting to US $73.2m. in exports and $70.3m. in imports in 2003. Foreign investment in the Oblast in that year amounted to just $0.3m. At the end of 2003 some 5,800 small businesses were registered in the Oblast.

Directory

Head of the Regional Administration (Governor): VASILII K. BOCHKAREV (elected 12 April 1998, re-elected 14 April 2002; appointment confirmed 14 May 2005), 440025 Penza, ul. Moskovskaya 75; tel. (8412) 55-04-11; fax (8412) 63-35-75; e-mail pravobl@sura.com.ru; internet www.penza.ru.

Chairman of the Regional Legislative Assembly: VIKTOR A. CHERUSHOV, 440025 Penza, pl. Lenina, Dom Sovetov; tel. (8412) 52-22-66; fax (8412) 55-25-95; e-mail zsobl@sura.ru.

Chief Representative of Penza Oblast in the Russian Federation: ALEKSANDR A. RODIONOV, 127025 Moscow, ul. Novyi Arbat 19/1914; tel. (495) 203-10-75; fax (495) 203-48-93.

Head of Penza City Administration: ALEKSANDR V. PASHKOV, 440064 Penza, pl. Marshala Zhukova 4, Gorodskaya Duma; tel. (8412) 63-14-63; fax (8412) 6-65-88; internet www.penza-gorod.ru.

Samara Oblast

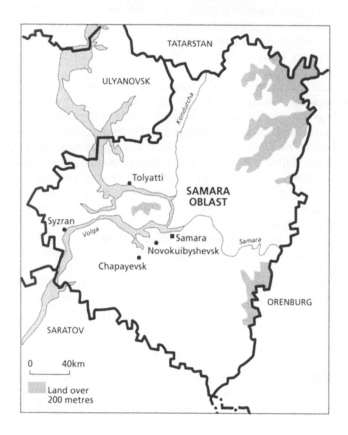

Samara Oblast is situated in the south-east of the Eastern European Plain on the middle reaches of the Volga river. It forms part of the Volga Federal Okrug and the Volga Economic Area. Its southernmost tip lies on the border with Kazakhstan. Saratov lies to the south-west, Ulyanovsk to the west, Tatarstan to the north and Orenburg to the east. The Volga snakes through the west of the territory. The region occupies 53,600 sq km (20,690 sq miles). Owing to its proximity to the Kazakhstan desert, the southernmost part of the Oblast is prone to drought. According to the census of 9–16 October 2002, the region had a total population of 3,239,737, and a population density of 60.4 per sq km. Some 80.6% of the population inhabited urban areas. 83.6% of the population were ethnically Russian, 3.9% Tatar, 3.1% Chuvash, 2.7% Mordovian and 1.9% Ukrainian. The administrative centre is at Samara, which had 1,158,100 inhabitants in 2002, according to preliminary census results. The region's second city is Tolyatti (701,900), and other major cities include Syzran (187,800) and Novokuibyshevsk (113,000). The Oblast is included in the time zone GMT+4.

History

Samara city was founded in 1586 as a fortress. It became rich from the Volga grain trade and further increased in prosperity after the construction of the railways in the late 19th century. A Middle Volga Oblast was formed on 14 May 1928. In 1929 it was upgraded to the status of a krai, which was renamed Kuibyshev Krai in 1935 (Samara city was similarly renamed.). On 5 December 1936 the Krai reverted to oblast status. Kuibyshev was the headquarters of the Soviet Government between 1941 and 1943, when Moscow was threatened by the German invasion. Both the city and oblast assumed their current names in 1991.

The local legislature defied President Boris Yeltsin in the constitutional crisis of 1993, and was dissolved in October and replaced by a Regional Duma. The head of the regional administration, Konstantin Titov, who had been appointed to that position by Yeltsin in August 1991 was regarded as a strong proponent of economic reform. On 1 December 1996 Titov was elected Governor. Titov sought to protect the power and relative independence of governors from the federal authorities and strongly urged the Regional Duma to approve legislation on land ownership, which was achieved in June 1998. Titov attempted to gain a higher profile in national politics by standing for the presidency of the Russian Federation at the elections of March 2000. However, his performance, even in Samara Oblast, where he obtained only 20% of the votes cast and came third, was disappointing. Consequently, he resigned from the post of Governor in April, but stood as a candidate for re-election in July, in an attempt to confirm his legitimacy; he was re-elected with 53% of the votes cast. In November 2001 Titov, who had hitherto led a small social-democratic party, was elected as co-chairman of the recently formed Social Democratic Party of Russia, alongside the former executive President of the USSR, Mikhail Gorbachev. (However, in May 2004 Gorbachev resigned his post, and Titov resigned his chairmanship of the party later in the year.) In April 2005 Putin nominated Titov to serve for a further term as Governor, following the recent abolition of regional gubernatorial elections; this nomination was confirmed by the regional Duma on 26 April by a unanimous vote of those deputies present. In November of that year Titov announced his membership of the pro-Government Unity and Fatherland-United Russia party.

Economy

In 2002 Samara Oblast's gross regional product amounted to 238,056.4m. roubles, or 73,480.2 roubles per head. The Oblast's major industrial centres are at Samara, Tolyatti and Syzran. At the end of 2002 there were 1,377 km of railways and 7,518 km of paved roads in the region.

Agriculture in the Oblast, which employed 7.0% of the working population and generated 22,181m. roubles in 2003, consists mainly of the production of grain, sugar beet and sunflower seeds and of animal husbandry and bee-keeping. Total agricultural production in 2003 was worth 22,181m. roubles. There are some reserves of petroleum and natural gas in the Oblast. Its main industries are mechanical engineering, metal-working, petroleum-production and -refining, food-processing, and chemicals and petrochemicals. The Oblast's principal company is AvtoVAZ (Volga Automobile Plant), manufacturer of the Lada automobile, accounting for over 40% of industrial output in the region, and the largest automobile manufacturer in Russia. In 2002, as part of a joint venture with the US corporation, General Motors, AvtoVAZ also began to manufacture Chevrolet Niva automobiles and sports-utility vehicles. (In 2002, some 76.1% of automobiles manufactured in Russia were produced in Samara Oblast.) In 2003 industry employed 26.8% of the work-force and generated 297,551m. roubles.

The economically active population of Samara Oblast numbered 1,690,000 in 2003, when just 4.4% of the labour force were unemployed, representing one of the lowest rates of unemployment in the Federation. Those in employment earned an average wage of 5,138.9 roubles per month. In 2003 the regional budget recorded a deficit of 2,001.8m. roubles. In 2003 total foreign investment in the region amounted to US $414.3m—around 44% of all foreign investment in the Volga Federal Okrug in that year. By 1998 some 300 foreign companies, including some of the world's largest, such as Coca-Cola and General Motors of the USA and Nestlé of Switzerland, had invested in the region, attracted by its technologically advanced industrial base and well-educated, urbanized labour force. In 2003 the external trade of the region amounted to some $5,070.6m. in exports and $865.5m. in imports, representing one of the highest levels of trade in any federal subject. At the end of 2003 some 30,800 small businesses were registered in the Oblast.

Directory

Governor: KONSTANTIN A. TITOV (appointed 31 August 1991, elected 1 December 1996, resigned 6 April 2000, re-elected 2 July 2000; appointment confirmed 26 April 2005), 443006 Samara, ul. Molodogvardeiskaya 210; tel. (8462) 32-22-68; fax (8462) 32-13-40; e-mail governor@samara.ru; internet www.adm.samara.ru.

Chairman of the Regional Duma: VIKTOR F. SAZANOV, 443110 Samara, ul. Molodogvardeiskaya 187; tel. (8462) 32-75-06; fax (8462) 42-38-08; e-mail samgd@duma.sam-reg.ru; internet www.duma.sam-reg.ru.

Chief Representative of Samara Oblast in the Russian Federation: ALEKSANDR BARANOVSKII, 103030 Moscow, per. Veskovskii 2; tel. (495) 973-19-95; fax (495) 973-05-54; e-mail tradoc@samarapostpred.ru.

Head of Samara City Administration (Mayor): GEORGII S. LIMANSKII, 443010 Samara, ul. Kuibysheva 135/137; tel. (8462) 32-20-68; fax (8462) 33-67-41; e-mail city@vis.infotel.ru; internet city.samara.ru.

Saratov Oblast

Saratov Oblast is situated in the south-east of the Eastern European Plain. It forms part of the Volga Federal Okrug and the Volga Economic Area. Saratov Oblast has an international border with Kazakhstan (to the south-east), and borders with the Oblasts of Volgograd (to the south), Voronezh and Tambov (west), and Penza, Ulyanovsk and Samara (north). Its main river is the Volga. Those regions of the Oblast on the west bank of the Volga are is mountainous, those to the east are low-lying. The region occupies 100,200 sq km (38,680 sq miles). According to the census of 9–16 October 2002, Saratov Oblast had 2,668,310 inhabitants, and a population density of 26.6 per sq km. Some 73.6% of the Oblast's population inhabited urban areas. 85.9% of the population were ethnically Russian, 2.9% Kazakh, 2.5% Ukrainian, 2.2% Tatar and 0.9% Armenian. Its administrative centre is at Saratov, a major river-port on the Volga, with a population of 873,500 in 2002, according to preliminary census results. Other major cities are Balakovo (200,600) and Engels (formerly Pokrovsk—193,800). The region is included in the time zone GMT+3.

History

Saratov was founded in 1590 as a fortress, to protect against nomad raids on the Volga trade route. In the mid-18th century the area was colonized by some 30,000 settlers, mainly from the Hesse and Palatinate regions of present-day Germany. Strategically placed on the Trans-Siberian Railway, Saratov city was seized by Bolshevik forces in late 1917 and remained under communist control, despite attacks by the 'White' forces under Adm. Aleksandr Kolchak in 1918–19. The Autonomous Commune of Volga German Workers was established in the region in 1918 and renamed the Volga German ASSR in 1924. (The ASSR had its capital at Pokrovsk—renamed Engels in 1931, on the opposite bank of the Volga from Saratov city.) Saratov Oblast was formed in 1936, having been part of a Saratov Krai from 1934. The region became heavily industrialized in the Soviet period, before the Second World War. In 1941 the Volga German ASSR was abolished and its inhabitants deported to Siberia, Central Asia and the North Caucasus. In 1972 they were permitted to return to the region, although from the mid-1980s many German-Russians were allowed to emigrate to Germany, and at the 2002 census only 0.5% of the Oblast's population described their ethnicity as German.

In September 1996 Dmitrii Ayatskov, who had been appointed as head of the regional administration by federal President Boris Yeltsin in April, was elected as Governor, receiving 81.4% of the popular vote. Ayatskov carried out extensive reform to the region's agro-industrial sector, which culminated, in November 1997, in the passing in the Oblast of the first law in Russia to provide for the purchase and sale of agricultural land. The law greatly diminished the power base of communists and nationalists in the region, as well as generating a significant income for the regional economy. (A series of bilateral trade agreements signed with the Mayor of Moscow, Yurii Luzhkov, in August 1996, also had beneficial effects for Saratov Oblast.) Ayatskov was re-elected for a further term in March 2000, amid accusations of electoral manipulation, which removed all other serious candidates from the contest, and press censorship.

In February 2003 the former oblast Minister of Culture, Yurii Grishchenko, was sentenced to two years' imprisonment by the regional court, on charges of accepting bribes during his tenure as minister, becoming one of the highest-ranking state officials to be subject to such punishment. In May 2004 the federal Government filed corruption charges against Ayatskov. These related to the alleged misuse of 70m. roubles (US $2.4m.) in budgetary funds, which had allegedly been used to pay import duties on behalf of a state-owned company. The charges were subsequently dropped, although investigations continued. In mid-June, however, the federal Supreme Court ordered the reopening of a court case against Sergei Shuvalov, a former deputy governor of the Oblast. Shuvalov had originally been charged in January 2002 over the same affair. In September 2004 Shuvalov was elected to the regional legislature (of which he subsequently became Chairman), thereby obtaining immunity from prosecution. Several months before the expiry of Ayatskov's term of office in early 2005, the federal President, Vladimir Putin announced that henceforth, regional governors would be subject to presidential appointment, rather than direct election. Ayatskov became the first incumbent Governor not to be re-appointed under these arrangements; on 3 March 2005 the regional Duma approved Putin's nomination of Pavel Ipatov, the former director of a nuclear power station, who was regarded as a neutral, 'technocratic', figure, as the new Governor; Ipatov took office on 5 April, following the expiry of Ayatskov's term as Governor. (The appointment of Ayatskov as Ambassador to Belarus, announced later in the year, was subsequently withdrawn after Ayatskov made a speech that included several controversial remarks about Russian-Belarusian relations.)

Economy

In 2002 Saratov Oblast's gross regional product totalled 104,666.2m. roubles, equivalent to 39,225.7 roubles per head. The region's major industrial centres are at Saratov, Engels and Balakovo. At the end of 2002 there were 2,288 km of railways and 10,303 km of paved roads on the Oblast's territory. The river port at Saratov is an important transshipment point on routes between Moscow and Central Asia, Siberia, and Southern Russia. The major Soviet/Russian arsenal for chemical weapons was located in the Oblast, although in January 1996 it was announced that chemical weapons stored locally were to be destroyed, in accordance with international agreements. A new processing plant to facilitate this commenced operations at Gornyi in late 2002.

The Oblast's agriculture, which employed some 14.3% of the working population and generated 30,537m. roubles in 2003, consists primarily of the production of grain (the Oblast is one of Russia's major producers of wheat) and sunflower seeds. Animal husbandry is also significant. The Oblast's main industries are mechanical engineering and metal-working, the production of electricity, petroleum-refining, chemicals and petrochemicals, food-processing and the production of petroleum and natural gas. Significant quantities of cement and mineral fertilizer are also produced in the Oblast. Industry employed 19.3% of the work-force and generated 95,034m. roubles in 2003.

The region's economically active population numbered 1,288,000 in 2003, when 10.5% of the labour force were unemployed. The average wage in the Oblast was 3,456.2 roubles per month. The regional budget for 2003 showed a surplus of 477.0m. roubles. In that year the value of external trade amounted to US $1,139.0m. in exports and $190.8m. in imports. Foreign investment amounted to $14.9m. in 2003. At the end of 2003 some 13,400 small businesses were registered in the Oblast.

Directory

Head of the Regional Administration (Governor): PAVEL L. IPATOV (appointment confirmed 3 March 2005), 410042 Saratov, ul. Moskovskaya 72; tel. (8452) 27-20-86; fax (8452) 72-52-54; e-mail governor@gov.saratov.ru; internet www.gov.saratov.ru.

Chairman of the Regional Duma: PAVEL V. BOLSHEDANOV , 410031 Saratov, ul. Radishcheva 24A; tel. (8452) 27-99-80; fax (8452) 27-53-31; e-mail post@srd.ru; internet www.srd.ru.

Chief Representative of Saratov Oblast in the Russian Federation: SERGEI V. KHRISTOLYUBOV, 109028 Moscow, per. Podkopayevskii 7/3; tel. and fax (495) 917-05-19.

Head of Saratov City Administration (Mayor): YURII N. AKSENENKO, 410031 Saratov, ul. Pervomaiskaya 78; tel. (8452) 23-77-78; fax (8452) 27-84-44; e-mail mayor@admsaratov.ru; internet www.saratovmer.ru.

Ulyanovsk Oblast

Ulyanovsk Oblast is situated in the Volga Highlands. It forms part of the Volga Federal Okrug and the Volga Economic Area. Mordoviya, the Chuvash Republic and Tatarstan lie to the north-west and to the north. There are also borders with Samara in the south-east, Saratov in the south and Penza in the south-west. The region's major river is the Volga. The region occupies 7,300 sq km (14,400 sq miles). According to the census of 9–16 October 2002, the total population of the Oblast was 1,382,811, and the population density was 37.1 per sq km. Some 73.2% of the population inhabited urban areas. 72.6% of the population were ethnically Russian, 12.2% Tatar, 8.0% Chuvash, 3.6% Mordovian and 1.1% Ukrainian. The administrative centre at Ulyanovsk had a population of 635,600 in 2002, according to provisional census results. The other major city in the region is Dimitrovgrad (130,900). The Oblast is included in the time zone GMT+3.

History

Simbirsk city was founded in 1648. Lenin (Vladimir Ulyanov) was born there in 1870, and it was his home until 1887. The city assumed his family name following his death in 1924. Ulyanovsk Oblast, which was formed on 19 January 1943, was regarded as part of the 'red belt' of communist support in post-Soviet Russia. Thus, it refused to revert to its pre-Soviet name, while in December 1996 the Communist Party of the Russian Federation-backed candidate, Yurii Goryachev (who had, nonetheless, been appointed to the position in 1992), won the election to the governorship of the Oblast.

Goryachev banned local privatization and collective-farm reforms, imposed restrictions on imports and exports, and subsidized bread prices until early 1997. Goryachev was defeated in the gubernatorial elections held in December 2000, and replaced by Lt-Gen. Vladimir Shamanov, who was regarded as an ally of the federal authorities and who had received several military decorations for his conduct in the conflicts in Chechnya in 1994–96 and after 1999. By mid-2004 Shamanov was widely regarded as one of several regional leaders from military or security backgrounds who had failed to meet prior expectations, in particular as a result of continued difficulties experienced in the Oblast's housing and utilities sectors, and in October the pro-Government Unity and Fatherland-United Russia (UF-UR) party announced that it would not support Shamanov's candidacy at the forthcoming gubernatorial election. UF-UR instead announced its support for another candidate, Sergei Morozov, hitherto Mayor of Dmitrovgrad. At the first round of voting, held on 5 December, Morozov received 27.8% of the votes cast and was to progress to a 'run off', against a local dairy farmer, Sergei Gerasimov, with 20.9%. However, Gerasimov's candidacy was subsequently disqualified by the oblast electoral commission, following allegations of electoral malpractice, and the third-placed candidate (with 14.6%), Margarita Barzhanova, a State Duma deputy of UF-UR and an ally of Morozov, instead contested the second round. On 26 December Morozov was elected Governor, with 52.8% of the votes cast. The option to vote against all candidates received 25.2% of the votes cast, and Barzhanova obtained 20.6%. The rate of participation in the second round of polling was 38.8%.

Economy

In 2002 Ulyanovsk Oblast's gross regional product amounted to 48,735.7m. roubles, or 35,243.9 roubles per head. The Oblast's major industrial centres are at Ulyanovsk and Melekess. At the end of 2002 there were 716 km of railway lines and 4,372 km of paved roads on the Oblast's territory.

Around 1.5m. ha of its territory is used for agricultural purposes, of which over four-fifths is arable land. Agriculture in the region, which employed some 14.8% of the working population and generated 10,072m. roubles in 2003, consists primarily of animal husbandry and the production of grain, sunflower seeds and sugar beet. The Oblast's main industries are mechanical engineering (which accounted for over 56% of industrial output in 2002), food-processing and electrical energy. Industry employed 28.2% of the working population and generated 47,784m. roubles in 2003. The region's major companies included the UAZ automobile plant and the Aviastar aeroplane manufacturer (both of which were operating at 50% capacity in the late 1990s). In late 2002 Aviastar signed a contract, apparently worth US $335m., to construct 25 TU-204-120 jets, following the acquisition of a 25% stake (less one share) in the firm by the Egyptian concern Sirocco Aerospace International; Sirocco expressed the intention of further developing the capacities of the Aviastar plant.

The economically active population numbered 684,000 in 2003, when 7.4% of the labour force were unemployed. Those in employment earned an average of 3,621.4 roubles per month. There was a budgetary deficit of 1,031.4m. roubles in 2003. In that year external trade constituted US $189.6m. in exports and $76.0m. in imports; total foreign investment in the Oblast amounted to $23.5m. At the end of 2003 some 4,900 small businesses were registered in the Oblast.

Directory

Head of the Regional Administration (Governor): SERGEI I. MOROZOV (elected 26 December 2004), 432970 Ulyanovsk, pl. Lenina 1; tel. (8422) 41-20-78; fax (8422) 41-48-12; e-mail admobl@mv.ru; internet www.ulgov.ru.

Chairman of the Legislative Assembly: BORIS I. ZOTOV, 432700 Ulyanovsk, ul. Radishcheva 1; tel. and fax (8422) 41-34-52; internet zsuo.ru.

Chief Representative of Ulyanovsk Oblast in the Russian Federation: ALEKSANDR F. KOTELEVSKII, 121002 Moscow, per. Denezhnyi 12; tel. (495) 241-11-00; fax (495) 241-38-99.

Head of Ulyanovsk City Administration (Mayor): SERGEI N. YERMAKOV, 432700 Ulyanovsk, ul. Kuznetsova 7; tel. (8422) 41-45-08; fax (8422) 41-40-20; e-mail meria@mv.ru; internet www.ulmeria.ru.

URALS FEDERAL OKRUG

Chelyabinsk Oblast

Chelyabinsk Oblast is situated in the Southern Urals, with much of the region lying on the eastern slopes of the Southern Ural Mountains. It forms part of the Urals Federal Okrug and the Urals Economic Area. Orenburg Oblast lies to the south, the Republic of Bashkortostan to the west, Sverdlovsk Oblast to the north and Kurgan Oblast to the east. There is an international border with Kazakhstan in the south-east. The major rivers in the Oblast are the Ural and the Miass. It has over 1,000 lakes, the largest of which are the Uvildy and the Turgoyak. The Oblast covers an area of 87,900 sq km (34,940 sq miles). According to the census of 9–16 October 2002, Chelyabinsk Oblast had a population of 3,603,339, giving a population density of 41.0 per sq km. At that time some 81.8% of the population inhabited urban areas. 82.3% of the population were ethnically Russian, 5.7% Tatar, 4.6% Bashkir, 2.1% Ukrainian, 1.0% Kazakh and 0.8% German. The Oblast's administrative centre is at Chelyabinsk, a city with a population of 1,078,300. Other major cities are Magnitogorsk (419,100), Zlatoust (194,800) and Miass (158,500). Chelyabinsk Oblast is included in the time zone GMT+5.

History

Chelyabinsk city was established as a Russian frontier post in 1736, but was deep within Russian territory by the 19th century. The Oblast was created on 17 January 1934. The region was heavily industrialized during the Soviet period and remained dominated by communist cadres following the disintegration of the USSR.

Following the attempted coup by conservative communists in August 1991, the head of Chelyabinsk oblast administration, Petr Sumin, who had expressed sympathy for the rebels, was dismissed, and replaced by Vadim Solovyev. Sumin subsequently became the Chairman of the oblast legislature, which in January 1993 announced its intention of holding elections for a regional governor. Solovyev announced his intention of challenging this decision at the oblast court, and on 25 March the federal Supreme Court overturned the ruling of the oblast legislature, prohibiting the holding of gubernatorial elections in Chelyabinsk. Nonetheless, at elections held in the Oblast on 11 April, Sumin obtained some 60% of votes cast (although the rate of participation was low, at around 30% of the electorate), and won a second round of polling, held on 25 April. However, the federal President, Boris Yeltsin expressed his support for Solovyev, and the federal Constitutional Court subsequently declared that the elections had been unlawful. Yeltsin re-established his authority in late 1993 and required the election of a Duma during 1994. Both in this body, and in the local results of the general election of 1995, pro-Yeltsin and reformist forces obtained significant levels of support. In the gubernatorial election of late 1996, however, Sumin was returned to power. Sumin's pro-communist movement also won an absolute majority of seats in the regional legislature at elections held in December 1997. Sumin was re-elected Governor in December 2000. In April 2005 the federal President, Vladimir Putin, nominated Sumin to serve a further term of office; this nomination was confirmed by vote of the regional legislature on 18 April.

Economy

In 2002 the gross regional product of the Oblast amounted to 183,386.3m. roubles, equivalent to 50,893.4 roubles per head. The region's major industrial centres are at Chelyabinsk, Magnitogorsk, Miass and Zlatoust. Although steel output in the Oblast declined by around one-third between 1990 and 2002 (even taking into account a marked recovery from 1999), it remained the dominant steel-producing region of Russia. At the end of 2002 there were 1,793 km of railway track in the Oblast and 8,767 km of paved roads.

The Oblast's agriculture, which employed just 8.9% of the working population in 2003, and generated 22,487m. roubles, consists mainly of animal husbandry, horticulture and the production of grain. Chelyabinsk Oblast was one of seven federal subjects to be subject to an outbreak of avian influenza in mid-2005. The Oblast is one of the most polluted in the Federation; in particular, high rates of disease and environmental despoliation resulted from the Kyshtym nuclear accident of 1957, in the north of the region, when up to three times the levels of radiation emitted at the Chornobyl (Chernobyl) disaster in Ukraine in 1986 were released into the surrounding area. Chelyabinsk Oblast became one of the most industrialized territories of the Russian Federation, following the reconstruction of plants moved there from further west during the Second World War. In 2003 industry employed some 31.0% of the economically active population, and generated 264,139m. roubles. The Oblast's main industries are ferrous metallurgy (which accounted for a total of 53.4% of industrial activity in 2002), non-ferrous metallurgy, ore-mining, mechanical engineering, metal-working, and fuel and energy production. In the north-west, the closed city of Ozersk (formerly Chelyabinsk-40) is a major pluto-nium-processing and -storage site, while in the west are located centres for weapons manufacturing and space technology, although several former military plants in the Oblast were converted to civilian use in the 1990s.

The economically active population numbered 1,830,000 in 2003, when 5.9% of the labour force were unemployed. Those in employment earned an average wage of 4,838.5 roubles per month. The 2003 budget recorded a surplus of 4,412.7m. roubles. Export trade amounted to US $2,584.8m. in 2003, when imports were worth $890.8m. Attempts to attract foreign investment in the Oblast from the mid-1990s were largely successful: foreign capital amounted to $1,029.8m. in 2003. At the end of that year some 19,400 small businesses were registered in the Oblast.

Directory

Governor: Petr I. Sumin (elected 22 December 1996, re-elected 24 December 2000; appointment confirmed 18 April 2005), 454089 Chelyabinsk, ul. Tsvillinga 27; tel. (3512) 63-92-41; fax (3512) 63-12-83; e-mail gubernator@chel.surnet.ru; internet www.ural-chel.ru.

Chairman of the Legislative Assembly: Vladimir Myakush, 454009 Chelyabinsk, ul. Kirova 114; tel. (3512) 65-78-26; fax (3512) 63-63-79; e-mail zscr@chel.surnet .ru.

Chief Representative of Chelyabinsk Oblast in the Russian Federation: Valerii A. Shubin, 127422 Moscow, Dmitrovskii pr. 4a; tel. (495) 210-88-59; fax (495) 977-08-35.

Head of Chelyabinsk City Administration (Mayor): Mikhail Yurevich, 454113 Chelyabinsk, pl. Revolyutsii 2; tel. (3512) 33-38-05; fax (3512) 33-38-55.

Kurgan Oblast

Kurgan Oblast is situated in the south of the Western Siberian Plain. It forms part of the Urals Federal District and the Urals Economic Area. Chelyabinsk Oblast lies to the west, Sverdlovsk Oblast to the north and Tyumen Oblast to the north-east. There is an international border with Kazakhstan to the south. The main rivers flowing through Kurgan Oblast are the Tobol and the Iset and there are more than 2,500 lakes in the south-east of the region. The Oblast occupies 71,000 sq km (27,400 sq miles) and had a total population of 1,019,532 in mid-October 2002, according to census results, giving a population density of 14.4 per sq km. At that time some 56.3% of the population inhabited urban areas. 91.5% of the population were ethnically Russian, 2.0% Tatar, 1.5% Bashkir, 1.5% Kazakh and 1.1% Ukrainian. The administrative centre is at Kurgan, which had a population of 345,700, according to the provisional results of the census. Kurgan Oblast is included in the time zone GMT+6.

History

The city of Kurgan was founded as a tax-exempt settlement in 1553, on the edge of Russian territory. Kurgan Oblast was formed on 6 February 1943. The Communist Party of the Russian Federation (CPRF) was the largest party in the Regional Duma elected on 12 December 1993, and remained the most popular party in the Oblast at elections to the State Duma in 1995. The CPRF candidate, Oleg Bogomolov, hitherto speaker of the Regional Duma, was elected Governor in late 1996, running unopposed in the second round of the election after his opponent stood down. Bogomolov was re-elected in December 2000. On 19 December 2004, following two rounds of voting, Bogomolov was again re-elected Governor, having received the support of the pro-Government Unity and Fatherland-United Russia (UF-UR) party and obtaining 49.2% of the votes cast, compared with the 40.1% obtained by his rival, Yevgenii Sobakin. (The candidacy of a business executive, Sergei Kapchuk, who had been regarded as one of Bogomolov's principal challengers in the election, had been disallowed by the oblast court, several days before the first round of voting on 28 November.) UF-UR were the most successful party in elections to the regional legislature held concurrently with the second round of gubernatorial elections.

Economy

In 2002 the gross regional product of Kurgan Oblast amounted to 32,081.1m. roubles, equivalent to 31,466.5 roubles per head, the lowest figure in the Urals Federal Okrug. The Oblast's main industrial centres are at Kurgan, a river-port in the south-east of the region, and Shadrinsk, on the Iset. At the end of 2002 there were 748 km of railways and 6,455 km of paved roads on the Oblast's territory. The Trans-Siberian Railway passes through the Oblast, as do several major petroleum and natural gas pipelines.

The Oblast's important agricultural sector employed 24.0% of the work-force in 2003 and consists mainly of grain production and animal husbandry. Total agricultural production in the region was worth 10,350m. roubles in 2002. The Oblast was one of seven federal subjects in which an outbreak of avian influenza in August 2005 was reported. The Oblast's main industries are mechanical engineering, metal-working, electricity production and food-processing. The industrial sector employed 18.0% of the working population and generated 21,705m. roubles in 2003.

The economically active population numbered 516,000 in 2003. The rate of unemployment was 9.6% in 2003, the highest level recorded in any federal subject in the Urals Federal Okrug in that year. Those in employment earned, on average, 3,664.6 roubles per month, significantly less than the national average. There was a budgetary surplus of 32.9m. roubles in 2003, when foreign investment totalled just US $400,000. In 2003 exports amounted to a value of $101.0m., while imports totalled $76.9m. The economic situation of the region deteriorated markedly from the late 1990s, and in mid-2002 it was reported that up to 60% of the Oblast's budget comprised transfers from the federal Government. At the end of 2003 some 2,800 small businesses were registered in the Oblast.

Directory

Head of the Regional Administration (Governor): OLEG A. BOGOMOLOV (elected 8 December 1996, re-elected 10 December 2000 and 19 December 2004), 640024 Kurgan, ul. Gogolya 56; tel. (3522) 41-70-30; fax (3522) 41-71-32; e-mail kurgan@ kurganobl.ru; internet www.admobl.kurgan.ru.

Chairman of the Regional Duma: MURAT N. ISLAMOV, 640024 Kurgan, ul. Gogolya 56; tel. (3522) 41-72-17; fax (3522) 41-88-91.

Chief Representative of Kurgan Oblast in the Russian Federation: SERGEI N. YAGOVITIN, 103006 Moscow, ul. M. Dmitrovka 3/10/313; tel. (495) 200-39-78; fax (495) 299-33-67.

Head of Kurgan City Administration (Mayor): ANATOLII F. YELCHANINOV, 640000 Kurgan, pl. Lenina; tel. (3522) 6-22-25; fax (3522) 41-70-40; e-mail inform@munic .kurgan.ru; internet www.munic.kurgan.ru.

Sverdlovsk Oblast

Sverdlovsk Oblast is situated on the eastern, and partly on the western, slopes of the Central and Northern Urals and in the Western Siberian Plain. It forms part of the Urals Federal Okrug and the Urals Economic Area. Tyumen Oblast lies to the east (with its constituent Khanty-Mansii AOk to the north-east); there is a short border with the Republic of Komi in the north-west and Perm Krai lies to the west. To the south are Bashkortostan, Chelyabinsk and Kurgan. The region's major rivers are those of the Ob and Kama basins. The west of the region is mountainous, while much of the eastern part is taiga (forested marshland). The Oblast covers an area of 194,800 sq km (75,190 sq miles). According to the census of 9–16 October 2002, the population totalled 4,486,214, and the population density was 23.0 per sq km. 87.9% of the region's inhabitants lived in urban areas at that time. 89.2% of the population were ethnically Russian, 3.7% Tatar, 1.2% Ukrainian and 0.8% Bashkir. The Oblast's administrative centre is at Yekaterinburg, which had a population of 1,293,000, according to provisional census results. Other major cities are Nizhnii Tagil (390,600), Kamensk-Uralskii (186,300) and Pervouralsk (132,800). The territory is included in the time zone GMT+5.

History

Yekaterinburg city was founded in 1821 as a military stronghold and trading centre. Like the Oblast (formed on 17 January 1934) it was named Sverdlovsk in 1924 but, unlike the Oblast, reverted to the name of Yekaterinburg in 1991. The city was infamous as the location where the last Tsar, Nicholas II, and his family were assassinated in 1918. The region became a major industrial centre after the Second World War.

Following the disintegration of the USSR, Sverdlovsk Oblast was among the most forthright regions to demand the devolution of powers from the centre. In September 1993 the Regional Soviet adopted a draft constitution for a 'Ural Republic', which was officially proclaimed on 27 October by the Regional Soviet and the head of the regional administration, Eduard Rossel. The 'Ural Republic' was dissolved by presidential decree, however, and Rossel was dismissed on 9 November, and replaced by Aleksei Strakhov. In 1994 elections were held to a Regional Duma. In August 1995 Rossel was reinstated as Governor, having won a direct election to head the regional administration.

As Governor, Rossel continued to strive for more autonomy for the Oblast, and in January 1996 he signed an agreement on the division of powers and spheres of competence between federal and regional institutions, the first such accord to be signed with a federal territory that did not have republican status. In April elections were held to the bicameral oblast Legislative Assembly: 28 deputies were elected to the Regional Duma, the lower chamber, for a term of four years from party lists on the basis of proportional representation, whereas the 21 members of the House of Representatives were elected on the basis of majoritarian voting within electoral districts for a period of two years. Less than one-third of the electorate participated, but some 35% voted for Rossel's Transformation of the Urals bloc, which had also obtained greater support than any of the national parties in the region at elections to the federal legislature in December 1995. Subsequently, however, Rossel's popularity began to decline: in April 1998 the Transformation bloc won just 9.3% of the votes to the regional legislature and claimed just two seats in the Regional Duma (where it had previously held a majority). Nevertheless, Rossel was re-elected as Governor on 12 September 1999.

It was suggested that the Urals Federal Okrug, formed in mid-2000 by President Vladimir Putin, incorporated several regions traditionally regarded as part of Siberia, while excluding other regions that were included in the Urals Economic Area, so as to inhibit any revival of an appeal for a 'Ural Republic'. Rossel subsequently adopted a less oppositional stance towards the federal authorities, becoming a senior member of the pro-Government Unity and Fatherland-United Russia party. On 21 September Rossel won a third term as Governor, receiving 55.5% of the votes cast in a 'run-off' election. In late 2003 Rossel instigated a proposal to merge Sverdlovsk Oblast with Chelyabinsk and Kurgan Oblasts: this, however, met with opposition from both territorial administrations and in April 2004 the Governor retracted his proposal. Rossel continued to express support for radical reforms to the administrative structure of the Russian Federation, declaring in mid-2005 that the ethnically defined Republics should be abolished and replaced by entities defined in purely territorial terms, so as to ensure equal rights for citizens of all ethnic groups and to lessen the possibility of the Federation disintegrating. On 21 November 2005 the regional legislature voted unanimously to confirm Rossel in his fourth term of office, following his nomination by Putin four days earlier.

Economy

Sverdlovsk Oblast is a leading territory of the Russian Federation in terms of industry. In 2002 the territory's gross regional product amounted to 246,059.5m. roubles, equivalent to 54,847.9 roubles per head. Its most important industrial centres are at Yekaterinburg, Nizhnii Tagil, Pervouralsk, Krasnouralsk, Serov and Kamensk-Uralskii. At the end of 2002 there were 3,569 km of railway lines and 10,762 km of paved roads on the Oblast's territory. There is an international airport, Koltsovo, outside Yekaterinburg.

The Oblast's agriculture, which employed just 5.6% of its work-force in 2003, consists mainly of animal husbandry and grain production. Total agricultural output in 2003 was worth 24,354m. roubles. There is some extraction of gold and platinum in the Oblast. Its main industries are ferrous and non-ferrous metallurgy, the production of electrical energy, mechanical engineering, food-processing and the production of copper and other ores, bauxite, asbestos, petroleum, peat and coal. There is also a significant defence sector. Industry employed some 31.5% of the working population in 2003 and generated 309,489m. roubles.

Sverdlovsk's economically active population numbered 2,394,000 in 2003, when 7.6% of the labour force were unemployed. The average monthly wage in the region was 5,607.0 roubles. The 2003 budget showed a deficit of 1,305.6m. roubles, and total foreign investment in that year was US $1,314.6m.; international trade amounted to some $3,305.1m. in exports and $900.6m. in imports. At the end of 2003 there were 25,100 small businesses registered in the Oblast.

Directory

Chairman of the Administration (Governor): EDUARD E. ROSSEL (elected 20 August 1995, re-elected 12 September 1999 and 21 September 2003; appointment confirmed 21 November 2005), 620031 Sverdlovsk obl., Yekaterinburg, pl. Oktyabrskaya 1; tel. (343) 217-86-24; fax (343) 217-87-79; e-mail press-center@ midural.ru; internet www.rossel.ru.

Chairman of the Government: ALEKSEI P. VOROBYEV, 620031 Sverdlovsk obl., Yekaterinburg, pl. Oktyabrskaya 1; tel. (343) 271-79-20; fax (343) 277-17-00; e-mail webmaster@midural.ru; internet www.midural.ru.

Chairman of the Regional Duma of the Legislative Assembly: NIKOLAI A. VORONIN, 620031 Sverdlovsk obl., Yekaterinburg, pl. Oktyabrskaya 1; tel. (343) 278-91-08; fax (343) 271-80-48; e-mail duma@midural.ru; internet www.duma .midural.ru.

Chairman of the House of Representatives of the Legislative Assembly: YURII V. OSINTSEV, 620031 Sverdlovsk obl., Yekaterinburg, pl. Oktyabrskaya 1; tel. (343) 278-91-08; fax (343) 271-80-48; e-mail duma@midural.ru; internet www.duma .midural.ru.

Chief Representative of Sverdlovsk Oblast in the Russian Federation: VLADIMIR S. MELENTYEV, 121019 Moscow, ul. Novyi Arbat 21; tel. and fax (495) 291-90-72.

Head of Yekaterinburg City Administration (Mayor): ARKADII M. CHERNETSKII, 620014 Sverdlovsk obl., Yekaterinburg, pr. Lenina 24; tel. (343) 256-29-90; fax (343) 271-79-26; e-mail glava@sov.mplik.ru.

Tyumen Oblast

Tyumen Oblast is situated in the Western Siberian Plain, extending from the Kara Sea in the north to the border with Kazakhstan in the south. It forms part of the Urals Federal Okrug and the Western Siberian Economic Area. Much of its territory comprises the Khanty-Mansii—Yugra and Yamalo-Nenets Autonomous Okrugs (AOks). To the west (going south to north) lie Kurgan, Sverdlovsk, Komi and the Nenets AOk—part of Archangel Oblast; to the east lie Omsk, Tomsk and Krasnoyarsk—in the far north the border is with Krasnoyarsk's Taimyr AOk. The region has numerous rivers, its major ones being the Ob, the Taz, the Pur and the Nadym. Much of its territory is taiga (forested marshland). The territory of the Oblast, including that of the AOks, occupies an area of 1,435,200 sq km (554,130 sq miles). The Oblast is a sparsely populated region: according to the census of 9–16 October 2002, the total population was 3,264,841, and the population density was 2.3 per sq km. Some 77.4% of the Oblast's inhabitants lived in urban areas. 71.6% of the population were ethnically Russian, 7.4% Tatar, 6.5% Ukrainian, 1.4% Bashkir, 1.3% Azeri, 1.1% Belarusian, 0.9% Chuvash, 0.9% Nenets, 0.8% German and 0.8% Khant. The Oblast's administrative centre is at Tyumen, which had a population of 510,700, according to provisional census results. The territory is included in the time zone GMT+5.

History

Tyumen city was founded in 1585 on the site of a Tatar settlement. It subsequently became an important centre for trade with the Chinese Empire. Tyumen Oblast was formed on 14 August 1944. The region became industrialized after the Second World War.

On 21 October 1993 the Regional Soviet in Tyumen Oblast repealed its earlier condemnation of government action against the federal parliament but refused to disband itself. Legislative elections were held in the Oblast in March 1994, but the results in several constituencies were declared invalid, owing to a low level of participation. Eventually a new assembly, the Regional Duma, which remained communist-led, was elected.

From the mid-1990s the exact nature of the relationship between Tyumen Oblast proper and the two AOks, which wished to retain a greater share of the income from their wealth of natural resources, became a source of intra-élite contention, despite the establishment of a co-ordinating administrative council between the three entities in 1995. In 1997 the two AOks (which between them accounted for over 90% of the output and profits in the Oblast) had boycotted the regional gubernatorial elections, while a subsequent Constitutional Court ruling failed to clarify the status of the autonomies in relation to the Oblast. However, the AOks did participate in elections to the Regional Duma later in 1997. In 1998 Sergei Korepanov, the former Chairman of the Yamalo-Nenets legislature, was elected Chairman of the legislature of Tyumen Oblast. This was widely considered to form part of a plan by representatives of the AOks (who together constituted a majority of seats in the oblast legislature) to remove the Governor of Tyumen, Leonid Roketskii. At the gubernatorial election held on 14 January 2001, Sergei Sobyanin, a former speaker in the legislature of the Khanty-Mansii AOk and the First Deputy Presidential Representative in the Urals Federal Okrug, defeated Roketskii, obtaining more than 51% of the votes cast. Sobyanin initially stated his opposition to any reabsorption of the two AOks into Tyumen Oblast. None the less, relations between the Oblast and the autonomies deteriorated in the early 2000s, owing to the amendment of federal legislation pertaining to regional political institutions. The legislation, which took effect in 2005, granted responsibility for the spending of all federal subsidies to the oblast authorities, unless a special treaty with the authorities of the autonomous okrugs provided for alternative arrangements. In February 2004 a meeting was held between Sobyanin and the Governor of Yamalo-Nenets AOk and protocols of intention relating to an eventual merger of the three entities were signed. However, in July representatives of the three administrations signed a power-sharing agreement, subsequently ratified by the three regional legislatures, which would have the effect of delaying any such unification until after the end of 2010. In January 2005 Sobyanin resigned as Governor, requesting a declaration of confidence from the federal President, Vladimir Putin, following the recent abolition of elections for regional heads. Putin subsequently confirmed his nomination of Sobyanin for a further term, which was approved by the oblast legislature on 17 February, when Sobyanin became the second regional leader to assume office under the new procedure. On 14 November Sobyanin was appointed head of the federal presidential administration; he was replaced as Governor by the hitherto Mayor of Tyumen, Vladimir Yakushev, whose appointment was confirmed by the regional legislature on 24 November.

Economy

All figures in this survey include data for the two AOks, which are also treated separately (see below). Tyumen Oblast was considered to have great economic potential, owing to its vast hydrocarbons and timber reserves (mainly located in the Khanty-Mansii—Yugra and Yamalo-Nenets AOks). In 2002 its gross regional product amounted to 960,045.5m. roubles, equivalent to 294,055.8 roubles per head (by far the highest figure in the Russian Federation, excluding several resource-rich AOks, including the two contained within Tyumen Oblast). Its main industrial centres are at Tyumen, Tobolsk, Surgut, Nizhnevartovsk (the last two in the Khanty-Mansii AOk—Yugra) and Nadym (Yamalo-Nenets AOk). At the end of 2002 there were 2,451 km of railway lines and 10,022 km of paved roads on the Oblast's territory.

The Oblast's agriculture, which employed just 4.9% of its work-force in 2003 and generated 18,913m. roubles, consists mainly of animal husbandry (livestock- and reindeer-breeding and fur-farming), and the production of grain, potatoes and vegetables. The Oblast was one of seven federal subjects to be subject to an outbreak of avian influenza in mid-2005. The production of alcoholic beverages, particularly vodka, increased markedly in the early 2000s, and by 2003 the region was one of the principal regions active in the sector. In the late 1990s the Oblast's reserves of petroleum, natural gas and peat were estimated at 60%, 90% and 36%, respectively, of Russia's total supply. The Tyumen Oil Company (TNK), formed in 1995 from nine other companies, was among the largest petroleum companies in Russia. From 1997, when the state's share in the company was reduced to less than one-half, TNK became increasingly market-driven. In 2003 TNK merged with Sidanco and the Russian interests of BP (of the United Kingdom—formerly British Petroleum), and was renamed TNK-BP. Overall petroleum output in the region totalled 254.2m. metric tons in 2002. In that year output of natural gas amounted to 539,916m. cubic metres. The Oblast's other major industry is the production of electrical energy; in 2002 the Oblast's output amounted to 65,500m. kwH, of which 55,800m. kwH was produced within the Khanty-Mansii AOk—Yugra. Industry employed some 21.2% of the Oblast's working population in 2003 and generated a total of 833,785m. roubles, by far the highest level of any federal subject (The overwhelming majority of this output was produced within the Khanty-Mansii AOk—Yugra).

The economically active population totalled 1,782,000 in 2003, when 8.3% of the work-force were unemployed. The average monthly wage was 14,584.1 roubles in 2003, among the highest in the Federation. The budget for 2003 recorded a surplus of 210.3m. roubles. In 2003 the external trade of the Oblast comprised US $22,877.2m. in exports and $684.6m. of imports. Total foreign investment in the Oblast (which, like the Oblast's export trade, was particularly concentrated within the Khanty-Mansii AOk—Yugra, q.v.) amounted to some $3,216.9m. in that year. At the end of 2003 some 10,300 small businesses were registered in the Oblast.

Directory

Governor: Vladimir V. Yakushev, 625004 Tyumen, ul. Volodarskogo 45; tel. (3452) 46-35-36; fax (3452) 46-55-42; e-mail kancelaria@mail.ru; internet admtyumen.ru.

Chairman of the Regional Duma: Sergei Ye. Korepanov, 625018 Tyumen, ul. Respubliki 52, Dom Sovetov; tel. (3452) 45-50-81; e-mail tyumduma@tmn.ru; internet www.tmn.ru/~tyumduma.

Chief Representative of Tyumen Oblast in the Russian Federation: Vladimir M. Goryunov, 119017 Moscow, ul. Pyatnitskaya 47/2; e-mail pr_tumen@insar.ru; tel. and fax (495) 953-06-22.

Head of Tyumen City Administration: Sergei Smetanyuk, 625036 Tyumen, ul. Pervomaiskaya 20; tel. (3452) 46-42-72; fax (3452) 24-33-64.

Khanty-Mansii Autonomous Okrug— Yugra

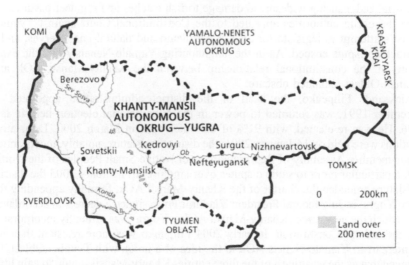

The Khanty-Mansii Autonomous Okrug (AOk)—Yugra is situated in the Western Siberian Plain and the Ob-Irtysh river basin. The district forms part of the Urals Federal Okrug and the Western Siberian Economic Area, and lies within the territory of Tyumen Oblast. The other autonomous okrug within Tyumen Oblast, the Yamalo-Nenets AOk, lies to the north, while to the south of the district's centre lies the 'core' area of Tyumen Oblast. The Republic of Komi is to the west and Sverdlovsk to the south-west; to the south-east lies Tomsk and to the east Krasnoyarsk Krai. The district has numerous lakes, and much of its territory is Arctic tundra (frozen steppe) and taiga (forested marshland). The AOk occupies a total of 523,100 sq km (201,970 sq miles). According to the census of 9–16 October 2002, the AOk had a total of 1,432,817 inhabitants, giving a population density of 2.7 per sq km. Some 90.9% of the population lived in urban areas. Ethnic Khants and Mansi are greatly out-numbered by ethnic Russians in the district: in 2002 some 66.1% of the population were ethnically Russian, 8.6% were Ukrainian, 7.5% Tatar, 2.5% Bashkir, 1.8% Azeri, 1.4% Belarusian, 1.2% Khant, 1.1% Chuvash, 0.8% Moldovan and only 0.7% Mansi. The Khanty and the Mansii languages are grouped together as an Ob-Ugrian sub-division of the Ugrian division of the Finno-Ugrian group. The AOk's admin-istrative centre is at the town of Khanty-Mansiisk, which had 41,300 inhabitants, according to provisional results of the 2002 census. Other major, and larger, cities in the Okrug include Surgut (285,500), Nizhnevartovsk (239,000) and Nefteyugansk (107,800). Khanty Mansii AOk is included in the time zone GMT+5.

History

The Khanty-Mansii region, known as Yugra in the 11th–15th centuries, came under Russian control in the late 16th and early 17th centuries, as Russian fur traders established themselves in western Siberia. Attempts were made to assimilate the Khants and Mansi into Russian culture, and many were forcibly converted to

Orthodox Christianity. The modern territory was created in December 1930, as the East Vogul (Ostyako-Vogulskii) National Autonomous Okrug (becoming known as Khanty-Mansii Autonomous Okrug in 1943).

From about the time of the Second World War the district became heavily industrialized, causing widespread damage to fish catches and reindeer pastures. In 1996 the okrug authorities appealed to the Constitutional Court against Tyumen Oblast's attempt to legislate for district petroleum and natural gas reserves, and a protracted dispute ensued. As in the neighbouring Yamalo-Nenets AOk, the exact nature of the constitutional relationship between the Khanty-Mansii AOk and Tyumen Oblast remained obscure.

Aleksandr Filipenko, the head of the district administration appointed in December 1991, was returned to power in the gubernatorial election held in late 1996. He was re-elected, with 91% of the votes cast, in March 2000. Legislative elections were held on 14 January 2001; the district legislature, notably, incorporated a four-member Assembly of Representatives of Native Small Peoples of the North, with a particular remit to settle disputes over land use. In February 2003 the district legislature amended the charter of the Khanty-Mansii AOk, formally appending the name Yugra; in July federal President Vladimir Putin signed a decree, in accordance with which the new name (Khanty-Mansii AOk—Yugra) was officially incorporated into the federal Constitution. In early 2004 Filipenko was more resistant than his counterpart in Yamalo-Nenets AOk to the idea of a union with Tyumen Oblast: he believed that as the wealthiest of the three entities Khanty-Mansii sought to gain little from a such a merger, and also warned of its potential threat to the rights of the territory's indigenous population. A power-sharing treaty, signed by representatives of the three entities in July and subsequently ratified by the three regional legislatures, *inter alia*, delayed any possible unification until after the end of 2010. In February 2005 the federal President, Vladimir Putin, nominated Filipenko to serve a further term of office, in accordance with recently introduced procedures providing for the appointment, rather than election, of regional Governors; this nomination was approved by a unanimous vote of the district Duma on 24 February.

Economy

The AOk's economy is based on industry, particularly on the extraction and refining of petroleum. In the early 2000s it produced around 5% of Russia's entire industrial output and over 50% of its petroleum. In 2002 the territory's gross regional product amounted to 581,777.0m. roubles, equivalent to some 406,037.2 roubles per head. The AOk's main industrial centre is at the petroleum-producing town of Surgut. Its major river-port is at Nizhnevartovsk. At the end of 2002 there were 1,073 km of railway track and 2,023 km of paved roads, many of which were constructed during the 1990s and early 2000s.

Agriculture in the AOk, which employed just 1.2% of the work-force in 2003 and generated 2,645m. roubles, consists mainly of vegetable production and fishing, reindeer-breeding, fur-farming, hunting and vegetable production. In that year industry employed 24.6% of the work-force and generated 611,904m. roubles. The extraction of petroleum and natural gas and the production of electricity are the principal areas of industrial activity. In 2002 some 55 companies in the Khanty-Mansii AOk—Yugra accounted for 57.3% of the petroleum produced in Russia. The most significant producers of petroleum in the region were Surgutneftegaz (SNG), LUKoil-Western Siberia and Yuganskneftegaz, a subsidiary of Yukos Oil Co until late 2004, when it became a subsidiary of the state-controlled firm, Rosneft. Yukos assisted in the construction of housing and leisure facilities and in the operation of educational establishments during the early 2000s. Overall petroleum output in the region totalled 209.9m. metric tons in 2002. In that year the AOk's production of electrical energy amounted to 55,800m. kwH, and output of natural gas amounted to 20,844m. cubic metres.

The economically active population of the okrug numbered 820,000 in 2003, when 9.4% of the labour force were unemployed. The average monthly wage was some 17,209.3 roubles. In 2003 the local budget recorded a surplus of 210.3m. roubles. There was considerable foreign investment in the okrug from the late 1990s, and it totalled some US $3,143.6m. in 2003, compared with 232.7m. in 2002. The external trade of the AOk constitutes a substantial proportion of that attributed to Tyumen Oblast as a whole; in 2003 the external trade of the AOk comprised $18,718.8m of exports and $355.7m of imports, amounting to 81.0% of the total trade of the Oblast in that year. At the end of 2003 some 4,100 small businesses were registered in the AOk.

Directory

Governor (Chairman of the Government): ALEKSANDR V. FILIPENKO (appointed 18 December 1991, elected 27 October 1996, re-elected 26 March 2000; appointment confirmed 24 February 2005), 628006 Tyumen obl., Khanty-Mansii AOk, Khanty-Mansiisk, ul. Mira 5; tel. (34671) 3-20-95; fax (34671) 3-34-60; e-mail kominf@ hmansy.wsnet.ru; internet www.hmao.wsnet.ru.

Chairman of the District Duma: VASILII S. SONDYKOV, 628007 Tyumen obl., Khanty-Mansii AOk, Khanty-Mansiisk, ul. Mira 5; tel. (34671) 3-06-01; fax (34671) 3-16-84; e-mail dumahmao@hmansy.wsnet.ru; internet www.hmao.wsnet.ru/ power/duma/index.htm.

Chief Representative of the Khanty-Mansii Autonomous Okrug—Yugra in Tyumen Oblast: NIKOLAI M. DOBRYNIN, 626002 Tyumen, ul. Komsomolskaya 37; tel. (3452) 46-67-79; fax (3452) 46-00-91; e-mail hmaoda@tmn.ru.

Chief Representative of the Khanty-Mansii Autonomous Okrug—Yugra in the Russian Federation: VLADIMIR A. KHARITON, 119002 Moscow, Starokonyushennyi per. 10/10/2; tel. (495) 920-42-38; fax (495) 291-17-62; e-mail ugra_msk@dial.cnt .ru.

Head of Khanty-Mansiisk City Administration (Mayor): VALERII M. SUDEIKIN, 626200 Tyumen obl., Khanty-Mansii AOk, Khanty-Mansiisk, ul. Dzerzhinskogo 6; tel. (34671) 5-23-01; fax (34671) 3-21-74; e-mail ugo@admhmansy.ru; internet www.admhmansy.ru.

Yamalo-Nenets Autonomous Okrug

The Yamalo-Nenets Autonomous Okrug (AOk) is situated on the Western Siberian Plain on the lower reaches of the Ob river. It forms part of Tyumen Oblast and, therefore, the Urals Federal Okrug and the Western Siberian Economic Area. The territory lies on the Asian side of the Ural Mountains and has a deeply indented northern coastline; the western section, the Yamal Peninsula, being separated from the eastern section by the Gulf of Ob. The rest of Tyumen Oblast, including the Khanty-Mansii AOk—Yugra, lies to the south. To the west lie the Nenets AOk (within Archangel Oblast) and the Republic of Komi, to the east Krasnoyarsk Krai (including the Taimyr AOk in the north-east). The territory of the AOk occupies 750,300 sq km (289,690 sq miles). According to the census of 9–16 October 2002, it had a total population of 507,006 inhabitants, and a population density of 0.7 per sq km. At that time some 83.4% of the population inhabited urban areas. 58.8% of the population were ethnically Russian, 13.0% Ukrainian, 5.5% Tatar, 5.2% Nenets, 1.8% Belarusian, 1.7% Khant, 1.6% Azeri, 1.6% Bashkir, 1.2% Komi and 1.1% Moldovan. The district administrative centre is at Salekhard, which had a population of 37,000, according to preliminary results of the 2002 census. Larger cities in the AOk included Noyarbsk (96,700) and Novyi Urengoi (94,600). The Yamalo-Nenets AOk is included in the time zone GMT+5.

History

The Nenets were traditionally a nomadic people, who were totally dominated by Russia from the early 17th century. The Yamalo-Nenets AOk was formed within Tyumen Oblast on 10 December 1930. Environmental concerns provoked protests in the 1980s and 1990s, and prompted the local authorities (comprising an administration and, from 1994, an elected Duma) to seek greater control over natural resources and their exploitation. The main dispute was with the central Tyumen Oblast authorities (more pro-communist than the AOk's own), and the AOk's rejection of oblast legislation on petroleum and natural gas exploitation first reached the Constitutional Court during 1996.

The economic importance of the fuel industry in the Yamalo-Nenets AOk was reflected in its political situation. Viktor Chernomyrdin, the former Chairman of the federal Government, was elected to the State Duma as a representative of the Yamalo-Nenets AOk in 1998, and he retained his seat until his appointment as Ambassador to Ukraine in May 2001. At the gubernatorial election of 26 March 2000 the incumbent, Yurii Neyelov, who was regarded as sympathetic to the interests of the domestic gas monopoly Gazprom (the largest employer in the AOk, of which Chernomyrdin had previously served as head), was re-elected, securing some 90% of the votes cast. In early 2004 Neyelov, who had initially expressed opposition to such a measure, participated in several meetings with Sergei Sobyanin, Governor of Tyumen Oblast, to discuss proposals for the formal merger of Tyumen Oblast with its two constituent AOks. A power-sharing treaty, signed by representatives of the three entities in July and subsequently ratified by the three regional legislatures, *inter alia*, delayed any possible unification until after the end of 2010. In early March 2005 the federal President, Vladimir Putin, nominated Neyelov to serve for a further term as Governor; this nomination was confirmed by a unanimous vote of the district State Duma on 11 March. The pro-Government Unity and Fatherland-United Russia party achieved an overwhelming victory in elections to the district legislature in elections held on 27 March, obtaining some 60.2% of the votes cast; the option to vote 'against all candidates' received a greater share of votes cast (14.2%) than any other party. (Notably, the nationalist Liberal Democratic Party of Russia, which had obtained some 15% of votes cast at the previous elections to the district legislature, had not been permitted to contest the elections, as a result of irregularities in registration documents for the party's proposed candidates.)

Economy

In 2002 the territory's gross regional product amounted to 279,355.6m. roubles, equivalent to some 550,990.7 roubles per head. At the end of 2002 there were 495 km of railway track and 939 km of paved roads, many of which were constructed during the 1990s and early 2000s. The major industrial centres include Noyabrsk (a 'closed' city), Novyi Urengoi and Urengoi.

Agriculture, which employed just 1.3% of the work-force in 2003 and generated 541m. roubles, consists mainly of fishing, reindeer-breeding (reindeer pasture occupies just under one-third of its territory), fur-farming and fur-animal hunting. In 2002 17.8% of agricultural output was contributed by crop sales, and 82.2% by animal husbandry. The AOk's main industries are the extraction of natural gas and, to a lesser extent, of petroleum and the production of electricity. In 2003 the industrial sector employed 22.9% of the work-force and generated a total of some 188,699m. roubles. The potential wealth of the district generated foreign interest. In January 1997 a loan of US $2,500m. to Gazprom was agreed by the Dresdner Bank group (of Germany), to support construction of a 4,200-km (2,610-mile) pipeline to transport natural gas from the AOk to Frankfurt-an-der-Oder on the German–Polish border. This was to be the world's largest gas-transport project and was expected to be fully operational by 2005. Output of natural gas amounted to 519,916m. cubic metres in 2002; in that year 43.4m. tons of petroleum were extracted in the AOk.

The economically active population numbered 303,000 in 2003, when just 5.5% of the labour force were unemployed. In 2003 the district government budget showed a surplus of 28.4m. roubles. These statistics, like the high average monthly wage of 20,027.2 roubles (the highest in the Russian Federation) in 2003, have far more in common with those of the Khanty-Mansii AOk than those of those parts of Tyumen Oblast outwith the AOks. The Yamalo-Nenets AOk has been successful in attracting foreign investment, receiving US $58.2m. in 2003. The external trade of the Yamalo-Nenets AOk is, however, substantially smaller than that of the neighbouring AOk; in 2003 exports amounted to US $2,885.5m. and imports to $235.5m.; none the less, this was equivalent to 13.3% of the total external trade of Tyumen Oblast in that year, and greater than the amount of trade generated by those regions of the oblast not contained within the two AOks. At the end of 2003 some 1,800 small businesses were registered in the AOk.

Directory

Governor: YURII V. NEYELOV (appointed 4 August 1994, elected 13 October 1996, re-elected 26 March 2000; appointment confirmed 11 March 2005), 626608 Tyumen obl., Yamalo-Nenets AOk, Salekhard, ul. Respubliki 72; tel. (34922) 4-46-02; fax (34922) 4-52-89; e-mail yanao@salekhard.ru; internet www.yamal.ru.

Chairman of the District State Duma: SERGEI N. KHARYUCHI, 629008 Tyumen obl., Yamalo-Nenets AOk, Salekhard, ul. Respublika 72, POB 14; tel. and fax (34922) 4-51-51; e-mail gdyanao@salekhard.ru; internet www.gdyanao.ru.

Chief Representative of Yamalo-Nenets Autonomous Okrug in Tyumen Oblast: FUAT G. SAIFITDINOV, 625048 Tyumen, ul. Kholodilnaya 136/1; tel. (3422) 27-32-11; fax (3422) 40-24-80.

Chief Representative of Yamalo-Nenets Autonomous Okrug in the Russian Federation: NIKOLAI A. BORODULIN, 101000 Moscow, per. Arkhangelskii 15/3; tel. (495) 924-67-89; fax (495) 925-83-38.

Head of Salekhard City Administration: ALEKSANDR M. SPIRIN, 629000 Tyumen obl., Yamalo-Nenets AOk, Salekhard, ul. Respubliki 72; tel. (34922) 4-50-67; fax (34922) 4-01-82; e-mail press@ytc.ru.

SIBERIAN FEDERAL OKRUG

Altai Republic

The Altai Republic is situated in the Altai Mountains, in the basin of the Ob river. The Republic forms part of the Siberian Federal Okrug and the West Siberian Economic Area. It has international borders with Kazakhstan in the south-west, a short border with the People's Republic of China to the south, and with Mongolia to the south-east. Kemerovo lies to the north, Khakasiya and Tyva to the north-east, and Altai Krai to the north-west. The Republic includes the highest peak in Siberia, Belukha, at 4,506 m (14,783 feet), and about one-quarter of its territory is forested. It contains one of Russia's major national parks, Altai State National Park, covering an area of some 9,000 sq km (3,475 sq miles). The Republic occupies 92,600 sq km. According to the census of 9–16 October 2002, the Republic had a population of 202,947 and a population density of only 2.2 per sq km. Of its inhabitants, only 26.4% resided in urban areas. 57.4% of the population were ethnically Russian, 30.6% Altai, 6.0% Kazakh, 1.2% Telengit and 0.8% Tubalar. The Altai people can be divided into two distinct groups: the Northern Altai, or Chernnevye Tatars, consisting of the Tubalars, the Chelkans or Leberdin and the Kumandins; and the Southern Altai, comprising the Altai Kizhi, the Telengit, the Telesy and the Teleut. The language spoken by both groups is from the Turkish branch of the Uralo-Altaic family: that of the Northern Altais is from the Old Uigur group, while the language of the Southern Altais is close to the Kyrgyz language and is part of the Kipchak group. In 1989 over 84% of Altais spoke one or other language as their native tongue, and some 62% of the Altai population was fluent in Russian. Although the traditional religion of the Altai was animist or Lamaist, many were converted to Christianity, so the dominant religion in the Republic is Russian Orthodoxy. The Republic's administrative centre is at Gorno-Altaisk (known as Ulala until 1932, then as Oirot-Tura until 1948), which had a population of 53,500, according to preliminary results of the 2002 census. The Republic is included in the time zone GMT+6.

History

From the 11th century the Altai peoples inhabited Dzungaria (Sungaria—now mainly in the north-west of the People's Republic of China). The region was under Mongol control until 1389, when it was conquered by the Tatar forces of Timur or Tamerlane ('the Great'); it subsequently became a Kalmyk confederation. In the first half of the 18th century many Altais moved westwards, invading Kazakh territory and progressing almost as far as the Urals. In 1758, however, most of Dzungaria was incorporated into Xinjiang (Sinkiang), a province of the Chinese Empire. China embarked on a war aimed at exterminating the Altai peoples. Only a few thousand survived, finding refuge in the Altai Mountains or in Russian territory. In the 19th century Russia began to assert its control over the region, which was finally annexed in 1866. In the early 1900s Burkhanism or Ak Jang (White Faith), a nationalist religious movement, emerged. The movement was led by Oirot Khan, who claimed to be a descendant of Chinghiz (Genghis) Khan and promised to liberate the Altais from Russian control. However, in February 1918 it was a secular nationalist leader, V. I. Anuchin, who convened a Constituent Congress of the High Altai and demanded the establishment of an Oirot Republic—to include the Altai, the Khakassians and the Tyvans. In partial recognition of such demands, in July 1922 the Soviet Government established an Oirot Autonomous Oblast in as part of an Altai Krai (province). In 1948 the Oblast was renamed the Gorno-Altai (Mountainous Altai) Autonomous Oblast, in an effort to suppress nationalist sentiment.

In the late 1980s nationalism re-emerged in response to Mikhail Gorbachev's policy of *glasnost* (openness). The region became the Altai Republic, separate from Altai Krai, at the signing of the Russian Federation Treaty in March 1992, having adopted a declaration of sovereignty on 25 October 1990. A resolution adopted on 14 October 1993 provided for the establishment of an El Kurultai (State Assembly), which was to be the highest body of power in the Republic. A reform of the republican Government, implemented in August 1997, introduced the position of Head of the Republic, Chairman of the Government; this position was assumed by Vladilen Volkov, who had become Chairman of the El Kurultai in February of that year. In December 1997 Semen Zubakin was elected as Chairman of the Government in direct elections. The Republic was one of only four subjects of the Russian Federation to award the communist candidate, Gennadii Zyuganov, a higher proportion of the votes than Vladimir Putin in the presidential election of 2000. In February 2001 several amendments to the republican Constitution were approved by the El Kurultai, to bring them into conformity with the fundamental laws of the Russian Federation, including the removal of a provision that had forbidden persons of the same ethnicity from simultaneously occupying the posts of chairman of the republican government and parliamentary speaker.

In a second round of polling to the post of Head of the republican Government, held on 20 January 2002, Mikhail Lapshin, the leader of the Agrarian Party of Russia (APR), decisively defeated Zubakin. Notably, Lapshin received the support of the pro-Government Unity and Fatherland-United Russia party in the second round, in addition to that of the Communist Party of the Russian Federation. Legislative elections were held in the Republic in December. In the early 2000s there was a strong movement within Altai Krai for its reunification with the Republic. In mid-2004, however, Lapshin (who was removed as leader of the APR in April of that year) continued to oppose any merger, on grounds that such a move would fail to benefit the economy of either territory. In late March 2005 a vote of 'no confidence' in Lapshin was defeated when it failed to obtain the support of the required two-thirds majority of deputies in the El Kurultai; discontent at the republican Government's management of the consequences of an earthquake in late 2003, in which some 900 homes were destroyed, was cited as the principal factor in bringing about the vote. In October 2005 it was announced that Lapshin would not be nominated to serve a further term following the expiry of his term in January 2006, apparently in consequence of the Republic's poor economic performance. On 22 December the El Kurultai overwhelmingly voted in favour of the gubernatorial candidate proposed by Putin, Aleksandr Berdnikov, a former republican Minister of Internal Affairs. Berdnikov was due to assume office on 20 January 2006. Legislative elections in the Republic were scheduled to be held on 12 March 2006.

Economy

The Altai Republic is predominantly an agricultural region. Its gross regional product amounted to 6,349.4m. roubles in 2002, or 31,286.0 roubles per head. The main industrial centre in the Republic is at its capital, Gorno-Altaisk. At the end of 2002 the Republic contained 2,872 km of paved roads. There are no railways or airports. In March 1996 the Russian Government allocated some 1,800m. old roubles to alleviate the effects in the Republic of the nuclear tests conducted at Semipalatinsk, Kazakhstan, in 1949–62. However, in the early 2000s further concern was expressed about the negative effect of frequent rocket launches from the Baikonur Cosmodrome in Kazakhstan on both the health of the residents of the Republic and the surrounding environment.

Agriculture in the Republic, which employed 23.6% of the working population and generated 2,772m. roubles in 2003, consists mainly of livestock-breeding (largely horses, deer, sheep and goats). The export of the antlers of Siberian maral and sika deer, primarily to South-East Asia, is an important source of convertible currency to the Republic. The Republic's mountainous terrain often prevents the easy extraction or transport of minerals, but there are important reserves of manganese, iron, silver, lead and wolfram (tungsten), as well as timber. Stone, lime, salt, sandstone, gold, mercury and non-ferrous metals are also produced. There are also food-processing and construction materials industries. Industry employed just 7.6% of the working population and generated only 814m. roubles in 2003.

In 2003 the economically active population of the Republic numbered 90,000, and 10.2% of the labour force were unemployed. The average monthly wage was just 3,816.7 roubles in 2003. There was a budgetary surplus of 169.4m. roubles in 2003. In that year the value of the Republic's exports was US $20.2m., and its imports were equivalent to around $119.6m. The level of foreign investment was very low, amounting to just $100,000 in 2000, the most recent year for which figures were available. At the end of 2003 around 800 small businesses were registered in the Republic.

Directory

Head of the Republic, Chairman of the Government: MIKHAIL I. LAPSHIN (elected 20 January 2002), 659700 Altai Rep., Gorno-Altaisk, ul. Kirova 16; tel. (38822) 2-26-30; e-mail altai-republic@altai-republic.com; internet www.altai-republic.com; Note: ALEKSANDR BERDNIKOV, whose nomination had been approved by the republican legislature on 22 December 2005, was due to assume office as Head of the Republic, Chairman of the Government, on 20 January 2006.

Chairman of the El Kurultai (State Assembly): IGOR E. YAIMOV, 649000 Altai Rep., Gorno-Altaisk, ul. Erkemena Palkina 1; tel. (38822) 2-26-18; fax (38822) 9-51-65; e-mail tvr@altek.gorny.ru; internet kurultai.altai-republic.ru.

Chief Representative of the Altai Republic in the Russian Federation: NADEZHDA CH. MANZYROVA, 103006 Moscow, ul. M. Dmitrovka 3/10; tel. (495) 299-81-97; fax (495) 299-81-97.

Head of Gorno-Altaisk City Administration: VIKTOR A. OBLOGIN, 659700 Altai Rep., Gorno-Altaisk, pr. Kommunisticheskii 18; tel. (38822) 2-23-40; fax (38822) 2-25-59.

Republic of Buryatiya

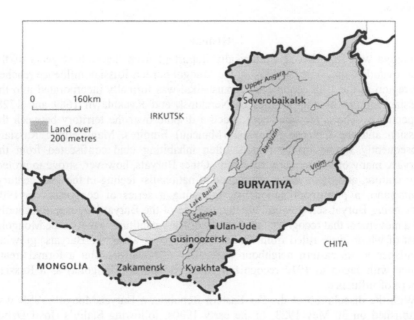

The Republic of Buryatiya is situated in the Eastern Sayan Mountains of southern Siberia and forms part of the Siberian Federal Okrug and the Eastern Siberian Economic Area. It lies mainly in the Transbaikal region to the east of Lake Baikal, although it also extends westwards along the international boundary with Mongolia in the south, to create a short border with the Russian federal subject of Tyva in the extreme west. Irkutsk Oblast lies to the north and west, and Chita Oblast to the east. Buryatiya's rivers mainly drain into Lake Baikal, the largest being the Selenga, the Barguzin and the Upper Angara, but some, such as the Vitim, flow northwards into the Siberian plains. Lake Baikal, the oldest and deepest lake in the world, possessing over 80% of Russia's surface freshwater resources and 20% of the world's total, forms part of the western border of the Republic. Intensive industrialization along its shores threatened Baikal's environment, and only in the 1990s were serious efforts made to safeguard the lake. Some 70% of Buryatiya's territory, including its low mountains, is forested, and its valleys are open steppe. The Republic covers 351,300 sq km (135,640 sq miles). The winter is protracted but sees little snow, with the average temperature in January falling to –27.1°C; the average temperature in July is 16.0°C. According to the census of 9–16 October 2002, Buryatiya had a population of 981,238, and a population density of 2.8 per sq km. Around 59.6% of the population inhabited urban areas. 67.8% of the population were ethnically Russian, 27.8% Buryat, 1.0% Ukrainian and 0.8% Tatar. The industrialized areas of the Republic are mainly inhabited by ethnic Russians. The Buryats are a native Siberian people of Mongol descent. The Buryats' native tongue is a Mongol dialect. Some Buryats are Orthodox Christians, but others practise Lamaism (Tibetan Buddhism), which has been syncretized with the region's traditional animistic shamanism. The Pandito Hambo Lama, a Buddhist spiritual leader, resides in

Buryatiya's capital, Ulan-Ude, which had a population of 359,400 in October 2002, according to provisional census results. The Republic is included in the time zone GMT+8.

History

Buryatiya was regarded as strategically important from the earliest years of the Muscovite Russian state, as it lay on the Mongol border. Russian influence reached the region in the 17th century and Transbaikal was formally incorporated into the Russian Empire by the Treaties of Nerchinsk and Kyakhta in 1689 and 1728, respectively. The latter agreement ended a dispute over the territory between the Russian and the Chinese Manzhou (Manchu) Empires. Many ethnic Russians subsequently settled in the region, often inhabiting land confiscated from the Buryats, many of whom were 'russified'. Other Buryats, however, strove to protect their culture, and there was a resurgence of nationalist feeling in the 19th century. Jamtsarano, a prominent nationalist, following a series of congresses in 1905 demanding Buryat self-government and the use of the Buryat language in schools, led a movement that recognized the affinity of Buryat culture to that of the Mongols, most of whom were ruled from China. Russia's fears about the Buryats' growing allegiance to its eastern neighbour were allayed, however, after a formal treaty signed with Japan in 1912 recognized Outer Mongolia (Mongolia) as a Russian sphere of influence.

With the dissolution of the Far Eastern Republic, a Buryat-Mongol ASSR was established on 30 May 1923. In the early 1930s, following Stalin's (Iosif Dzhugashvili's) policy of collectivization, many Buryats fled the country or were found guilty of treason and executed. In 1937 the Soviet Government considerably reduced the territory of the Republic, transferring the eastern section to Chita Oblast and a westerly region to Irkutsk Oblast. Furthermore, the Buryat language's Mongolian script was replaced with a Cyrillic one. In 1958 the Buryat-Mongol ASSR was renamed the Buryat ASSR, amid suspicions of increasing co-operation between the Mongolian People's Republic (Mongolia) and the People's Republic of China. The territory declared its sovereignty on 10 October 1990, and was renamed the Republic of Buryatiya in 1992.

In March 1994 the republican legislature, the Supreme Soviet (Supreme Council), adopted a Constitution, providing for an executive presidency. The hitherto Chairman of the Supreme Soviet, Leonid Potapov, became the Republic's first President, following elections on 30 June, and the legislature was redesignated the People's Khural. A bilateral treaty on the division of powers was signed with the Federation Government in 1995. On 21 June 1998 presidential and legislative elections were held in the Republic, and Potapov was re-elected President. In October 2000 the People's Khural approved several amendments to Buryatiya's Constitution, but rejected the implementation of several proposed amendments required by federal legislation, including, notably, the abolition of the requirement that presidential candidates know both state languages, Russian and Buryat. In early 2002 Potapov resigned from the Communist Party of the Russian Federation, and in April oversaw the rescission of the declaration of sovereignty issued in 1990. In June 2002 Potapov was re-elected for a third term as President of the Republic, receiving 68% of the votes cast, having obtained the support of the pro-Government Unity and Fatherland-United Russia party. In the period preceding the election three of the four independent radio stations in Ulan-Ude had their operations suspended by the republican State Communications Inspectorate.

Economy

In 2002 Buryatiya's gross regional product amounted to 39,065.5m. roubles, equivalent to 39,812.5 roubles per head. Its major industrial centre is at Ulan-Ude, which is situated on the Trans-Siberian Railway. At the end of 2002 there were 1,199 km of railways on Buryatiya's territory, and 6,259 km of paved roads.

The Republic's agriculture, which employed around 10.4% of the work-force and generated 6,955m. roubles in 2003, consists mainly of animal husbandry (livestock and fur-animal breeding) and the production of grain, vegetables and potatoes. Buryatiya is rich in mineral resources, including gold, uranium, coal, wolfram (tungsten), molybdenum, brown coal, graphite and apatites. In 1996 its gold reserves were estimated at 3.2m. troy ounces (almost 100 metric tons). Apart from ore-mining and the extraction of minerals, its main industries are mechanical engineering, metal-working, food-processing, timber production and wood-working. The Republic is also a major producer of electrical energy. The industrial sector employed 18.2% of the Republic's work-force and generated 26,170m. roubles in 2003. The services sector with the most potential is tourism, owing to the attractions of Lake Baikal.

Buryatiya's economically active population numbered 471,000 in 2002, when 16.8% of the Republic's labour force were unemployed. The average monthly wage in the Republic was 5,011.2 roubles. In 2003 there was a budgetary surplus of 53.3m. roubles. Foreign trade in that year comprised US $340.2m. in exports and $29.4m. in imports. It was hoped that Buryatiya's economy might be buoyed by the construction of the Angarsk–Nakhodka petroleum pipeline through its territory; in mid-2004 it was reported that the borders of the Republic's national park had been adjusted to accommodate the project. Foreign investment in Buryatiya amounted to just $1.2m. in 2003. At the end of that year some 2,900 small businesses were registered in the Republic.

Directory

President and Chairman of the Government: LEONID V. POTAPOV (elected 30 June 1994, re-elected 21 June 1998 and 23 June 2002), 670001 Buryatiya, Ulan-Ude, ul. Sukhe-Batora 9; tel. (3012) 21-51-86; fax (3012) 21-28-22; e-mail pres_rb@icm .buryatia.ru; internet president.buryatia.ru.

Chairman of the People's Khural: ALEKSANDR G. LUBSANOV, 670001 Buratiya, Ulan-Ude, ul. Sukhe-Batora 9; tel. (3012) 21-31-57; fax (3012) 21-49-61; e-mail kontup01@icm.buryatia.ru; internet chairman.buryatia.ru.

Chief Representative of the Republic of Buryatiya in the Russian Federation: BAIR G. BALZHIROV, 107078 Moscow, ul. Myasnitskaya 43/2; tel. (495) 925-88-61; fax (495) 923-60-46.

Head of Ulan-Ude City Administration (Mayor): GENNADII A. AIDAYEV, 670000 Buryatiya, Ulan-Ude, ul. Lenina 54; tel. (3012) 21-57-05; fax (3012) 26-32-44.

Republic of Khakasiya

The Republic of Khakasiya is situated in the western area of the Minusinsk hollow, on the left bank of the River Yenisei, which flows northwards towards, ultimately, the Arctic Ocean. It lies on the eastern slopes of the Kuznetsk Alatau and the northern slopes of the Western Sayan Mountains. It comprises part of the Siberian Federal Okrug and the Eastern Siberian Economic Area. Tyva lies to the south-east, the Altai Republic to the south-west, Kemerovo to the west, and Krasnoyarsk Krai to the north and east. Khakasiya occupies 61,900 sq km (23,900 sq miles). According to the census of 9–16 October 2002, the Republic had a population of 546,072 and a population density of 8.8 per sq km. 70.8% of the population lived in urban areas. 80.3% of the population were ethnically Russian, 12.0% Khakass, 1.7% German and 1.5% Ukrainian. In 1989 over 76% of the Khakass spoke the national language—primarily derived from the Uigur group of Eastern Hunnic languages of the Turkic family—as their native tongue. Khakasiya's capital is at Abakan, which had 165,200 inhabitants in 2002, according to provisional census results. The Republic is included in the time zone GMT+7.

History

The Khakass or Khakasiyans were traditionally known as the Minusinsk (Minusa), the Turki, the Yenisei Tatars or the Abakan Tatars. They were semi-nomadic hunters, fishermen and livestock-breeders. Khakasiya was a powerful state in Siberia, owing to its trading links with Central Asia and the Chinese Empire. Russian settlers began to arrive in the region in the 17th century and their presence was perceived as valuable protection against Mongol invasion. The annexation of Khakasiyan territory by the Russians was eventually completed during the reign of Peter (Petr) I—'the Great', with the construction of a fort on the River Abakan. The Russians subsequently imposed heavy taxes, seized the best land and imposed Orthodox Christianity on the Khakass. After the construction of the Trans-Siberian Railway in the 1890s the Khakass were heavily outnumbered. Following the Bolshevik Revolution a Khakass National Uezd (district) was established in 1923, becoming an okrug in 1925, and the Khakass Autonomous Oblast on 20 October 1930, within Krasnoyarsk Krai. In 1992 it was upgraded to the status of a Republic under the terms of the Federation Treaty, having declared its sovereignty on 3 July 1991.

The Communist Party remained the most popular political grouping in the Republic in the early 1990s, and the nationalist Liberal Democratic Party of Russia also enjoyed significant support. On 25 May 1995 the Republic adopted its Constitution. Aleksei Lebed, an independent candidate and younger brother of the politician and former general, Aleksandr Lebed (Governor of Krasnoyarsk Krai from May 1998 until his death in 2002), was elected to the presidency of the Republic in December 1996, when elections were also held for a new republican legislature. A former representative of the Republic in the Gosudarstvennaya Duma (State Duma), Aleksei Lebed had based his electoral campaign on the issues of administrative, budgetary, social and economic reform. Lebed was re-elected as Chairman of the Government, receiving 72% of the votes cast, in December 2000. In early 2004 the republican authorities were involved in a dispute with the electricity monopoly Unified Energy System of Russia (RAO EES Rossii) concerning the fate of the Sayano-Shushenskaya hydroelectric plant, situated on the border with Krasnoyarsk Krai. The plant had been privatized in 1993 and was subsequently 79% owned by RAO EES Rossii. When Aleksei Lebed's application to have extended a deal that had hitherto offered the territory preferential rates for electricity was rejected by RAO EES Rossii he applied to have the plant re-nationalized. The Republic eventually won its case on appeal in March 2004, but in June Lebed agreed to drop all demands for the re-nationalization of the installation in return for RAO EES Rossii abandoning plans to re-register the plant in Krasnoyarsk Krai. Lebed was re-elected to a further term of office on 26 December 2004, receiving 59.2% of the votes cast. In concurrent elections to the republican legislature the pro-Government Unity and Fatherland-United Russia was the most successful grouping, closely followed by the regional Khakasiya bloc. The rate of participation in both elections was around 30%.

Economy

Khakasiya's gross regional product amounted to 24,509.9m. roubles in 2002, or 44,884.0 roubles per head. Khakasiya's major industrial centres are at Abakan, Sorsk, Sayanogorsk, Chernogorsk and Balyksa. At the end of 2002 there were 642 km of railway lines and 2,538 km of paved roads in the Republic.

The Republic's agriculture, which employed around 10.1% of the working population and generated 3,833m. roubles in 2003, consists mainly of animal husbandry and potato and vegetable production. The Republic's main industries are ore-mining and non-ferrous metallurgy. Electricity generation is also important; the Sayano-Shushenskaya plant is the fourth largest hydroelectric power station in the world, producing around 245,000m. kWh per year. The territory is also renowned for its handicrafts (wood-carving and embroidery). There are significant reserves of coal and iron ore. Other mineral reserves included molybdenum, lead, zinc, barytes, aluminium and clay. There was also the potential for extraction of petroleum and natural gas. In 2003 industry employed 22.7% of the work-force and generated 20,728m. roubles.

The Republic's economically active population numbered 283,000 in 2003, when 10.5% of the labour force were unemployed. The average monthly wage stood at 5,054.1 roubles. The republican budget for 2003 showed a surplus of 12.3m. roubles. Foreign investment in Khakasiya was minimal: the highest level recorded was US $2.3m., in 1996, and such investment totalled just $28,000 in 2002. However, external trade was somewhat more substantial; in 2003 exports amounted to a value of $465.3m. and imports amounted to $195.6m. At the end of 2003 some 1,200 small businesses were registered in the Republic.

Directory

Chairman of the Government: ALEKSEI I. LEBED (elected 22 December 1996, re-elected 24 December 2000 and 26 December 2004), 655019 Khakasiya, Abakan, pr. Lenina 67; tel. (39022) 9-91-02; fax (39022) 2-50-91; e-mail pressa@khakasnet.ru; internet www.gov.khakassia.ru.

Chairman of the Supreme Council: VLADIMIR N. SHTYGASHEV, 655019 Khakasiya, pr. Lenina 67; tel. (39022) 2-53-35; e-mail info@vskhakasia.ru; internet www .vskhakasia.ru.

Chief Representative of the Republic of Khakasiya in the Russian Federation: MONYA M. BERGMAN, 127025 Moscow, ul. Novyi Arbat 19/1820; tel. (495) 203-57-32; fax (495) 203-83-45.

Head of Abakan City Administration: NIKOLAI G. BULAKIN, 655000 Khakasiya, Abakan, ul. Shchetinkina 10A/6, POB 6; tel. and fax (39022) 6-37-91; internet meria .abakan.ru.

Republic of Tyva

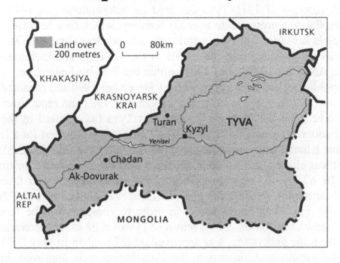

The Republic of Tyva is situated in the south of eastern Siberia in the Sayan Mountains. It forms part of the Siberian Federal Okrug and the Eastern Siberian Economic Area. Tyva has an international border with Mongolia to the south and east. The Republic of Altai lies to the west, the Republic of Khakasiya to the north-west and Krasnoyarsk Krai to the north. Irkutsk Oblast lies to the north-east and the Buryatiya forms part of the eastern border. Tyva's major river is the Yenisei, which rises in the Eastern Sayan range. The territory of the Republic consists of a series of high mountain valleys. The Republic has over 12,000 rivers and 8,400 freshwater lakes. Tyva occupies 170,500 sq km (65,830 sq miles). According to the census of 9–16 October 2002, Tyva had a population of 305,510 and a population density of only 1.8 per sq km. Some 51.7% of the population lived in urban areas. Some 77.0% of the population were Tyvan (Tuvinians), including 1.5% of the total population who categorized themselves as Tuvan-Todzhin, and 20.1% were ethnically Russian. (In the 1989 census, when ethnicity had been determined on the basis of official declaration of nationality, rather than self-definition, some 64.3% of inhabitants were Tyvans and 32.0% Russians.) Lamaism (Tibetan Buddhism) is the predominant religion in the Republic. The Tyvan language belongs to the Old Uigur group of the Turkic branch of the Uralo-Altaic linguistic family. The capital of Tyva is at Kyzyl, which had a population of 104,100 in mid-October 2002, according to provisional census results. The Republic is included in the time zone GMT+7.

History
The Tyvans (known at various times as Soyons, Soyots and Uriankhais) emerged as an identifiable ethnic group in the early 18th century. The territory of what is now Tyva was occupied in turn between the sixth and the ninth centuries by the Turkish Khanate, the Chinese, the Uigurs and the Yenisei Kyrgyz. The Mongols controlled the region from 1207 to 1368. In the second half of the 17th century the Dzungarians (Sungarians) seized the area from the Altyn Khans. In 1758 the Manzhous (Manchus) annexed Dzungaria and the territory thus became part of the Chinese Empire.

Russian influence dates from the Treaty of Peking (Beijing) of 1860, after which trade links were developed and a number of Russians settled there. One year after the Chinese Revolution of 1911 Tyva declared its independence. In 1914, however, Russia established a protectorate over the territory, which then became the Tannu-Tuva People's Republic. This was a nominally independent state until October 1944, when it was incorporated into the USSR as the Tuvinian Autonomous Oblast. It became an ASSR on 10 October 1961, within the Russian Federation.

The Republic declared sovereignty on 11 December 1990 and renamed itself the Republic of Tuva in August 1991. On 21 October 1993 the republican Supreme Soviet resolved that the Republic's name was Tyva (as opposed to the russified Tuva) and adopted a new Constitution. The Constitution provided for a legislature, the Supreme Khural, and a supreme constitutional body, the Grand Khural. The new parliament was elected on 12 December, when the new republican Constitution was approved by 62.2% of votes cast. Only 32.7%, however, voted in favour of the Russian Constitution. In 2000 the Grand Khural was obliged to make 26 amendments to the republican Constitution, in order to comply with the federal Constitution. A new Constitution, which removed Tyva's right to self-determination and to secede from the Federation, was approved by referendum in May 2001. In early March 2002 various amendments to the Constitution were approved, in order to bring it more closely into compliance with federal norms. The Supreme Khural was reconstituted as a bicameral legislature, comprising an upper chamber, the 130-member Chamber of Representatives, and a lower chamber, the 32-member Legislative Chamber. On 17 March the incumbent President (previously elected in 1992 and 1997), Sherig-ool Oorzhak, was elected to serve a third term of office, receiving 53% of the votes cast. Elections to the bicameral legislature were held on 2 June.

Economy

Tyva's economy is largely agriculture-based and is relatively underdeveloped. In 2002 its gross regional product stood at 6,749.3m. roubles, or 22,091.9 roubles per head. The Republic's main industrial centres are at Kyzyl and Ak-Dovurak. At the end of 2002 there were 2,519 km of paved roads in the Republic.

Tyva's agriculture, which employed 12.3% of the work-force and generated 1,973m. roubles in 2003, consists mainly of animal husbandry, although forestry and hunting are also important. Gold extraction was developed from the mid-1990s; in 1996 it amounted to almost one metric ton. Tyva's main industries were ore-mining (asbestos, coal, cobalt and mercury), production of electricity, food-processing and non-ferrous metallurgy. In 2003 industry employed 8.8% of the working population and generated 1,523m. roubles.

The economically active population of Tyva totalled 133,000 in 2002, when 20.7% of the labour force were unemployed—the highest rate of unemployment of any territory outwith the Southern Federal Okrug. In 2003 the average monthly wage in the Republic was 4,698.1 roubles, somewhat lower than the national average. The 2003 budget showed a deficit of 169.2m. roubles. Foreign investment in the Republic was minimal, and amounted to just US $381,000 in 2000. External trade was also minimal, amounting to $4.5m. in exports and $2.9m. in imports in 2003. At the end of that year around 600 small businesses were registered in the Republic.

Directory

President (Chairman of the Government): SHERIG-OOL D. OORZHAK (elected 15 March 1992, re-elected 16 March 1997 and 17 March 2002), 667000 Tyva, Kyzyl, ul. Chulduma 18, Dom Pravitelstva; tel. (39422) 1-12-77; fax (39422) 3-74-59; e-mail tuva@tuva.ru; internet gov.tuva.ru.

President of the Chamber of Representatives of the Supreme Khural: DANDAR-OOL K.-KH. OORZHAK, 667000 Tyva, Kyzyl, ul. Lenina 32; tel. (39422) 1-31-79; fax (39422) 3-33-71; e-mail parliament@tuva.ru; internet gov.tuva.ru/gosvo/predct_p .htm.

President of the Legislative Chamber of the Supreme Khural: VASILII M. OYUN, 667000 Tyva, Kyzyl, ul. Lenina 32; tel. (39422) 3-74-78; fax (39422) 1-16-32; e-mail parliament@tuva.ru; internet gov.tuva.ru/gosvo/zakdat_p.htm.

Chief Representative of the Republic of Tyva in the Russian Federation: ORLAN O. CHOLBENEI, 119049 Moscow, ul. Donskaya 8/2; tel. (495) 236-48-01; fax (495) 236-45-53.

Head of Kyzyl City Administration (Mayor): DMITRII K. DONGAK, 667000 Tyva, Kyzyl, ul. Lenina 32; tel. (39422) 3-50-55.

Altai Krai

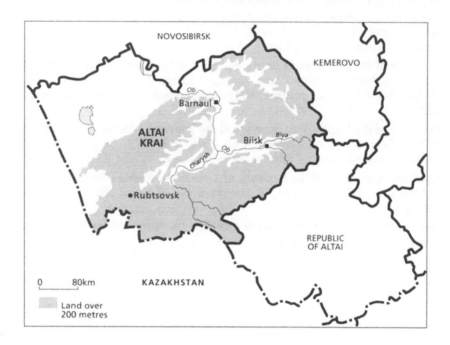

Most of Altai Krai lies within the Western Siberian Plain. Part of the Siberian Federal Okrug and the Western Siberian Economic Area, it has an international boundary to the south with Kazakhstan. Novosibirsk lies to the north, Kemerovo to the north-east and the Altai Republic to the south-east. Its major river is the Ob. There are many thousands of lakes, about one-half of which are fresh water. About one-third of its total area is forested. In the east of the Krai are mountains, in the west steppe. The Krai occupies 169,100 sq km (65,290 sq miles). According to the census of 9–16 October 2002, it had a total population of 2,607,426, and a population density of 15.4 per sq km. At that time 53.2% of the population lived in urban areas. 92.0% of the population were ethnically Russian, 3.0% German, 2.0% Ukrainian and only 0.1% Altai. The Krai's administrative centre is at Barnaul, which had a population of 603,500, according to the provisional results of the 2002 census. Other major cities are Biisk (218,600) and Rubtsovsk (163,100). Altai Krai is included in the time zone GMT+6.

History

The territory of Altai Krai was annexed by Russia in 1738 (for more on the Altais, see the Republic of Altai). The region was heavily industrialized during the Soviet period, particularly in 1926–40. Altai Krai was formed on 28 September 1937, at which time it included the territory of what is now the Altai Republic. This territory, then known as the Gorno-Altai (Mountainous Altai) Autonomous Oblast, declared its sovereignty in 1990 and its secession from the Krai was formally recognized in 1992.

On 13 March 1994, in accordance with a federal presidential decree of October 1993, a new provincial legislature, the Legislative Assembly, was elected to replace the provincial Soviet. The new legislature was bicameral, comprising a lower chamber of 25 deputies and an upper chamber of 72 deputies. The Chairman of the provincial Council of People's Deputies (the lower chamber), Aleksandr Surikov, a communist, defeated the incumbent Governor, Lev Korshunov, in the gubernatorial election of November 1996. Surikov retained his post in the election of 26 March 2000, obtaining 77% of the votes cast. Later that year legislation was approved reforming the provincial legislature on a unicameral basis. In the gubernatorial election of 2004 Surikov was unexpectedly defeated in a second round of voting on 4 April by a former television comedian and the marketing director for a local coal company, Mikhail Yevdokhimov, who was regarded as a populist. Surikov won 46.3% of votes cast, compared to Yevdokhimov's 49.5%. The incumbent, who had allied himself with the pro-Government Unity and Fatherland-United Russia (UF-UR) party and still had the support of local communists, had generally been perceived as a competent economic manager of the region and had been widely expected to obtain re-election. The victory of Yevdokhimov was regarded as indicating widespread dissatisfaction at the consequences of the ambitious privatization programme implemented in the region in the early 1990s. However, Yevdokhimov failed to bring about an improvement in the economic situation in the Krai, and significant increases in costs of housing and communal services were imposed under his leadership, while the industrial sector reportedly stagnated. In March 2005 the leaders of the provincial branches of 21 political organizations, including UF-UR, the Communist Party of the Russian Federation, the Agrarian Party of Russia and the pro-market Union of Rightist Forces wrote a letter to the federal President, Vladimir Putin, urging him to dismiss Yevdokhimov. Later in March a similar petition was filed by a majority of the municipal agencies in the Krai, and at the end of the month the provincial legislature overwhelmingly approved a vote of 'no confidence' in the Governor's leadership. A further vote of 'no confidence' in Yevdokhimov was approved, again by an overwhelming majority, at the end of April, although the Governor stated that he would not resign, despite continuing demands for his dismissal. On 7 August Yevdokhimov was killed as a result of an automobile accident in the Krai; his hitherto deputy, Mikhail Kozlov, was appointed as Governor in an acting capacity. Later in the month Putin nominated Aleksandr Karlin, a former deputy Minister of Justice in the federal Government and hitherto Chairman of the presidential administration's Civil Service Directorate (who was also native to the Krai), as Governor; this nomination was confirmed by vote of the provincial legislature on 25 August.

Economy

Altai Krai's gross regional product totalled 75,629.8m. roubles in 2002, equivalent to 29,005.5 roubles per head. Its main industrial centres are at Barnaul, Biisk, Rubtsovsk and Novoaltaisk. There are major river-ports at Barnaul and Biisk. The Krai has well-developed transport networks—1,803 km of railway lines at the end of 2002, and 14,476 km of paved roads. About one-quarter of its territory is served by water transport, which operates along a network of some 1,000 km of navigable waterways. There are five airports, including an international airport at Barnaul, with a service to Düsseldorf, Germany. The Krai is bisected by the main natural gas pipeline running from Tyumen to Barnaul via Novosibirsk.

The Krai's principal crops are grain, flax, sunflowers and sugar beet. Animal husbandry, including fur-farming and bee-keeping, is also important. In 2003 agriculture engaged 21.1% of the work-force and generated 37,054m. roubles. The Krai was one of seven federal subjects to experience an outbreak of avian influenza in mid-2005. The Krai contains substantial mineral resources, including salt, iron ore, soda and precious stones, most of which are not industrially exploited. Its main industries are mechanical engineering (including tractor-manufacturing), food-processing (the Krai's agro-industrial complex is one of the largest in the country), metal-working, electricity production, and chemicals and petrochemicals. In addition, Barnaul contains one of the largest textiles enterprises in Russia, producing cotton fibre and yarn for cloth. Industry employed 18.4% of the work-force and generated 60,340m. roubles in 2003.

In 2003 the economically active population of Altai Krai totalled 1,270,000, and 12.1% of the Krai's labour force were unemployed. The average monthly wage was 3,147.5 roubles in 2003, substantially lower than the federal average. Living costs are, however, low in the region. In 2003 the provincial budget showed a deficit of 497.6m. roubles. External trade amounted to a value of US $402.5m. in exports and $135.0m. in imports. Foreign investment in the territory totalled $2.0m in 2003. At the end of that year some 13,200 small businesses were registered in the Krai.

Directory

Head of the Provincial Administration (Governor): ALEKSANDR KARLIN (appointment confirmed 25 August 2005), 656035 Altai Krai, Barnaul, pr. Lenina 59; tel. (3852) 35-69-35; e-mail glava@alregn.ru; internet www.altairegion.ru.

Chairman of the Provincial Council of People's Deputies: ALEKSANDR G. NAZARCHUK, 656035 Altai Krai, Barnaul, pr. Lenina 59; tel. (3852) 35-69-86; fax (3852) 36-35-28; e-mail sovet@alregn.ru; internet www.altairegion.ru/rus/gov/leg_assembly.

Chief Representative of Altai Krai in the Russian Federation: ALEKSANDR S. POMENOV, 109017 Moscow, per. B. Tolmachevskii 5/9; tel. (495) 953-36-83; fax (495) 953-01-84; e-mail altay.pred@mail.ru.

Head of Barnaul City Administration: VLADIMIR N. KOLGANOV, 656099 Altai Krai, Barnaul, pr. Lenina 18/16; tel. (3852) 39-32-72; e-mail info@barnaul.org; internet barnaul.altai.ru.

Krasnoyarsk Krai

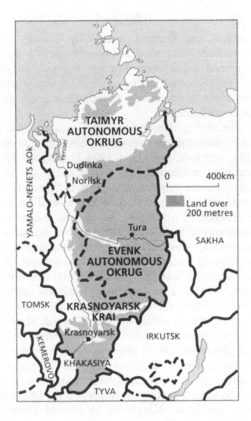

Krasnoyarsk Krai occupies the central part of Siberia and extends from the Arctic Ocean coast in the north to the Western Sayan Mountains in the south. The Krai forms part of the Siberian Federal Okrug and the Eastern Siberian Economic Area. It is bordered by the Sakha (Yakutiya) and Irkutsk to the east and by Tyva to the south. To the west lie Khakasiya, Kemerovo and Tomsk, as well as the Khanty-Mansii—Yugra and Yamalo-Nenets AOks within Tyumen Oblast. Its major river is the Yenisei, one of the longest in Russia, measuring 4,102 km (2,549 miles). Most of its area is covered by taiga (forested marshland). The Krai, including its two autonomous okrugs (Evenk and Taimyr—Dolgano-Nenets), covers a total area of 2,339,700 sq km (903,358 sq miles), the second largest federal unit in Russia. Krasnoyarsk Krai measures almost 3,000 km from south to north. The Krai lies within three climatic zones—arctic, sub-arctic and continental. According to the census of 9–16 October 2002, it had a total population of 2,966,042, and a population density of 1.3 per sq km. Some 75.7% of the population inhabited urban areas. 88.9% of the population were ethnically Russian, 2.3% Ukrainian, 1.5% Tatar and 1.2% German. The Krai's administrative centre is at Krasnoyarsk, which had a population of 911,700 in 2002, according to provisional census results. Other major cities include Norilsk (135,100—which is considered an integral part of the Krai and not part of Taimyr, which surrounds it), Achinsk (118,700) and Kansk (103,100). The territory is included in the time zone GMT+7.

History

The city of Krasnoyarsk was founded in 1628 by Cossack forces as an ostrog (military transit camp) during the period of Russian expansion across Siberia (1582–1639). The region gained importance after the discovery of gold, and with the construction of the Trans-Siberian Railway. The Krai was formed on 7 December 1934. During the Soviet era the region was closed to foreigners, owing to its nuclear-reactor and defence establishments.

A gubernatorial election in December 1992 was won by Valerii Zubov, a supporter of federal President Boris Yeltsin, and elections to a new parliament, the Legislative Assembly, were held on 6 March 1994. In the mid-1990s Zubov's regime proved to be increasingly ineffectual, and a poor record on paying wage arrears contributed to the victory in the gubernatorial election, held on 17 May 1998, of Gen. (retd) Aleksandr Lebed, the former secretary of the National Security Council. Lebed died in a helicopter crash on 28 April 2002. An election to appoint a successor, held on 8 September, and contested by 14 candidates, proved inconclusive; the Chairman of the provincial legislature, Aleksandr Uss, whose campaign was supported by the aluminium company RusAl, received 27.6% of the votes cast, closely followed by the Governor of the Taimyr AOk and the former General Director of Norilsk Nickel, Aleksandr Khlopanin, with 25.2%; these two candidates proceeded to a second round. In the 'run-off' election, held on 22 September 2002, Khlopanin was the first-placed candidate, winning 48.1% of the votes cast, compared with the 41.8% of the votes received by Uss. However, at the end of September the Krai's electoral commission annulled the results of the election, citing irregularities in the conduct of Khlopanin's campaign. On 1 October a court in Krasnoyarsk overturned the decision of the commission, and two days later federal President Vladimir Putin appointed Khlopanin to serve as acting Governor; on the following day the central electoral commission confirmed Khlopanin as elected Governor, and he was inaugurated shortly afterwards. The Supreme Court confirmed the validity of the election results in November. In March 2003 Khlopanin was elected to the Supreme Council of the pro-Government Unity and Fatherland-United Russia party. Following his inauguration as Governor of Krasnoyarsk Krai, Khlopanin was thereby obliged to resign as Governor of the Taimyr AOk. Khlopanin's victory appeared to heighten speculation that Krasnoyarsk Krai and the two AOks contained therein would eventually merge to form a single unit. (A proposed referendum on such a merger had been cancelled in 2002, following the death of Lebed.) A Council of Governors and a council of the legislative assemblies of the three entities were subsequently established. In referendums on the merger of the three polities, held on 17 April 2005, the unification was approved by a clear majority of votes in all three territories, with the vote in favour of the proposal (some 92.4% of the total) in Krasnoyarsk Krai proper being particularly overwhelming; the merger was scheduled to take effect from 1 January 2007, with elections to a unified regional legislature expected to be held on 15 April of that year. In late August 2005 the federal President, Vladimir Putin, submitted draft legislation providing for the merger, and which confirmed that the reunified territory would continue to be known as Krasnoyarsk Krai, to the Gosudarstvennaya Duma (State Duma), both chambers of the federal legislature had approved the legislation by early October.

Economy

Krasnoyarsk Krai is potentially one of Russia's richest regions, containing vast timber reserves and deposits of minerals, gold and petroleum, although, particularly since the late 1990s, it has experienced serious economic problems, many of them typical of northern regions. All of the figures included in this survey include figures for the two autonomous okrugs, which are also considered separately (see below). In 2002 the Krai's gross regional product amounted to 235,988.7m. roubles, equivalent to 79,563.5 roubles per head. The Krai's major industrial centres are at Krasnoyarsk, Norilsk, Achinsk, Kansk and Minusinsk. In 2002 there were 2,069 km of railway track and 12,924 km of paved roads on the Krai's territory.

The principal crops are grain, potatoes and vegetables. Animal husbandry and bee-keeping are also important. The agricultural sector employed 9.6% of the working population and generated 23,919m. roubles in 2003. The Krai's main industries are non-ferrous metallurgy (which accounted for 68.4% of total output in 2002), electricity production (in which it is one of the dominant federal subjects) and ore-mining (particularly bauxite, for aluminium). Industry employed 24.5% of the work-force and generated 231,365m. roubles in 2003. The Krai contains the world's second largest aluminium smelter, Krasnoyarsk Aluminium, which forms part of the Krasnoyarsk Metallurgical Plant (KraMZ).

In 2003 the territory's economically active population totalled 1,566,000, and 11.2% of the labour force were unemployed. The average monthly wage in the Krai was 7,366.8 roubles, somewhat in excess of the national average. In 2003 the local budget showed a deficit of 4,859.5m. roubles. In that year export trade amounted to US $3,999.0m., and imports to $498.5m. Foreign investment totalled $208.9m. in 2003. At the end of that year some 11,100 small businesses were registered in the Krai.

Directory

Head of the Provincial Administration (Governor): ALEKSANDR G. KHLOPANIN (elected 22 September 2002), 660009 Krasnoyarsk, pr. Mira 110; tel. (3912) 22-22-63; fax (3912) 22-11-63; e-mail klimik@krskstate.ru; internet www.krskstate.ru.

Chairman of the Legislative Assembly: ALEKSANDR V. USS, 660009 Krasnoyarsk, pr. Mira 110; tel. (3912) 22-33-87; fax (3912) 22-22-24; internet www.legis.krsn.ru.

Chief Representative of Krasnoyarsk Krai in the Russian Federation: ANATOLII V. TIKHONOV, 107031 Moscow, ul. Zvonarskii per. 9; tel. (495) 517-90-51; fax (495) 284-82-41.

Head of Krasnoyarsk City Administration (Mayor): PETR I. PIMASHKOV, 660049 Krasnoyarsk, ul. K. Marksa 93; tel. (3912) 22-22-31; fax (3912) 22-25-12; e-mail webmaster@admkrsk.ru; internet www.admkrsk.ru.

Chita Oblast

Chita Oblast is situated in Transbaikal, forming part of the Siberian Federal Okrug and the Eastern Siberian Economic Area. Buryatiya lies to the west, Irkutsk to the north, Sakha (Yakutiya) and Amur to the east. To the south there are international borders with the People's Republic of China and Mongolia. The Aga-Buryat Autonomous Okrug (AOk) lies within the Oblast, in the south. The western part of the region is situated in the Yablonovii Khrebet mountain range. The Oblast covers 431,500 sq km (166,600 sq miles). According to the census of 9–16 October 2002, its population, including the Aga-Buryat AOk, was 1,155,346, and its population density 2.7 per sq km. Some 65.9% of the region's inhabitants lived in urban areas. 89.8% of the population were ethnically Russian, 6.1% Buryat and 1.0% Ukrainian. The Oblast's administrative centre is at Chita, which had a population of 317,800, according to provisional census results. The territory is included in the time zone GMT+9.

History

The city of Chita was established by the Cossacks in 1653. The city was pronounced the capital of the independent, pro-Bolshevik Far Eastern Republic upon its establishment in April 1920; the Republic merged with Soviet Russia in November 1922. Chita Oblast was founded on 26 September 1937.

A new Regional Duma was elected in 1994. The Communist Party of the Russian Federation and the nationalist Liberal Democratic Party of Russia were the most popular parties in the mid- and late 1990s. In a gubernatorial election held on 29 October 2000 the incumbent, Ravil Genialutin (who had been elected in October 1996, having been appointed as Governor by President Boris Yeltsin earlier that year) was re-elected. In July 2003 one of the Oblast's vice-governors, Aleksandr Shapnevskii, was murdered, in what was suspected of being a contract killing.

Genialutin won a third term on 14 March 2004, with a comfortable majority, in an election contested by three candidates.

Economy

All figures in this survey incorporate data for the Aga-Buryat AOk, which is also treated separately. Chita Oblast's gross regional product amounted to 45,053.4m. roubles in 2002, or 38,995.6 roubles per head. In 2001 there were some 2,399 km of railway track in the territory, including sections of the Trans-Siberian and the Baikal–Amur Railways. There were also 9,843 km of paved roads, and in 1998 there were 1,000 km of navigable waterways. The Chita–Khabarovsk highway (forming part of a direct route between Moscow and Vladivostok) opened in September 2003.

Chita Oblast's agriculture, which employed some 13.4% of its work-force and generated 7,249m. roubles in 2003, consists mainly of animal husbandry (livestock- and reindeer-breeding) and fur-animal hunting. The region's major industries are non-ferrous metallurgy, electrical energy, fuel extraction (including uranium), food-processing and ore-mining. Industry employed some 14.1% of the work-force and generated 16,530m. roubles in 2003. Coal-mining in the Oblast is centred around the Vostochnaya mine; gold- and tin-mining are based at Sherlovaya Govra; and lead- and zinc-ore mines are situated at Hapcheranga. In 1992 it was revealed that thorium and uranium had been mined until the mid-1970s at locations just outside Balei. The resulting high levels of radiation had serious consequences among the town's population, with abnormally high incidences of miscarriages and congenital defects in children. The regional Government lacked sufficient funds to relocate Balei's inhabitants and reduce radiation in the area. In 1997, however, the Australian mining company, Armada Gold, announced that it planned to seal the abandoned mines and exploit the nearby gold deposits.

The territory had an economically active population of 565,000 in 2003, when 15.3% of the labour force were unemployed; the average monthly wage was 5,442.2 roubles. In 2003 the budget showed a deficit of 459.4m. roubles. In that year the Oblast's exports amounted to US $89.4m., and imports to $106.1m. For much of the 1990s and into the 2000s foreign investment in the Oblast remained low, and it totalled only $100,000 in 2003. At the end of that year some 2,200 small businesses were registered in Chita Oblast.

Directory

Head of the Regional Administration (Governor): Ravil F. Genialutin (appointed 1 February 1996, elected 26 October 1996, re-elected 29 October 2000 and 14 March 2004), 672021 Chita, ul. Chaikovskogo 8; tel. (3022) 23-34-93; fax (3022) 26-33-19; internet obladm.chita.ru.

Chairman of the Regional Duma: Anatolii P. Romanov, 672021 Chita, ul. Chaikovskogo 8; tel. (3022) 23-58-59; e-mail info@oblduma.chita.ru; internet oblduma.chita.ru.

Chief Representative of Chita Oblast in the Russian Federation: Viktor M. Stolyarov, 127025 Moscow, ul. Novyi Arbat 19/2001; tel. (495) 203-33-28; fax (495) 203-45-39.

Head of Chita City Administration (Mayor): Anatolii D. Mikhalev, 672090 Chita, ul. Butina 39; tel. (3022) 23-24-07; fax (3022) 32-06-85; e-mail info@admin .chita.ru.

Irkutsk Oblast

Irkutsk Oblast is situated in eastern Siberia in the south-east of the Central Siberian Plateau. The Oblast forms part of the Siberian Federal Okrug and the Eastern Siberian Economic Area. The Republic of Sakha (Yakutiya) lies to the north-east, Krasnoyarsk Krai (including the Evenk AOk) to the north-west and Tyva to the south-west. Most of the long south-eastern border is with Buryatiya and, in the east, with Chita. Irkutsk Oblast includes the Ust-Orda Buryat Autonomous Okrug (AOk). Lake Baikal (which forms part of the border with Buryatiya) is the deepest in the world, possessing over 80% of Russia's, and 20% of the world's, surface freshwater resources. The Oblast's main rivers include the Angara (the only river to drain Lake Baikal), the Nizhnyaya Tunguska and the Lena. More than four-fifths of the region's territory is covered with forest (mainly coniferous). The total area of the Oblast, including the Ust-Orda Buryat AOk, is 767,900 sq km (296,500 sq miles). According to the census of 9–16 October 2002, the Oblast's total population was 2,581,705, giving a population density of 3.4 per sq km. Some 83.7% of the total population lived in urban areas. 89.9% of the population were ethnically Russian, 3.1% Buryat, 2.1% Ukrainian and 1.2% Tatar. The Oblast's administrative centre is at Irkutsk, which had a population of 593,400 in 2002, according to provisional census results. Other major cities in the region include Bratsk (259,200), Angarsk (247,100) and Ust-Ilimsk (100,600). Irkutsk Oblast is included in the time zone GMT+8.

History

The city of Irkutsk was founded as an ostrog (military transit camp) in 1661, at the confluence of the Irkut and Angara rivers, 66 km to the west of Baikal. Irkutsk became one of the largest economic centres of eastern Siberia. After the collapse of the Russian Empire, the region was part of the independent, pro-Bolshevik Far Eastern Republic based in Chita, which was established in April 1920 and merged with Soviet Russia in November 1922. Irkutsk Oblast was formed on 26 September 1937.

In late 1993 the executive branch of government secured the dissolution of the Regional Soviet, and in 1994 a Legislative Assembly was elected in its place. As a 'donor region' to the Russian Federation, federal-regional relationships in Irkutsk Oblast were frequently strained. In May 1996 the regional and federal authorities signed a power-sharing agreement. Following the resignation of the Governor, Yurii Nozhikov, the government-supported candidate, Boris Govorin, was elected as his successor, on 27 July 1997. At the gubernatorial election held in August 2001 Govorin was re-elected for a further term of office; however, the relatively high proportion of votes awarded to the Communist Party of the Russian Federation candidate, Sergei Levchenko, who received 45.4% (compared with the 47.5% received by Govorin), appeared to reflect increasing dissatisfaction with the economic situation in the region. In August 2005, shortly before the expiry of Govorin's term of office, federal President Putin nominated Aleksandr Tishanin, previously a manager in several business organizations and, most recently, the head of the East Siberian Railway, as Govorin's replacement; Tishanin's nomination was approved by the regional legislature on 26 August.

During the early 2000s proposals to unite the Ust-Orda Buryat AOk and Irkutsk Oblast became increasingly popular and appeared to be supported by the authorities in both territories. In February 2004 it was agreed that referendums on unification would be held in each of the territories, although the process subsequently stalled. Following his appointment as Governor, Tishanin declared his support for the merger, which he hoped would be implemented by the end of 2006.

Economy

Irkutsk Oblast is one of the most economically developed regions in Russia, largely owing to its significant fuel, energy and water resources, minerals and timber, and its location on the Trans-Siberian Railway. All figures in this survey incorporate data for the Ust-Orda Buryat AOk, which is also treated separately. In 2002 the Oblast's gross regional product totalled 149,613.2m. roubles, or 57,951.3 roubles per head. The region's main industrial centres are at Irkutsk, Bratsk, Ust-Ilimsk and Angarsk. The Oblast, which is traversed by the Trans-Siberian and the Far Eastern (Baikal–Amur) Railways, contained 2,478 km of railway track at the end of 2002. There were 12,308 km of paved roads in the region. The Oblast has two international airports, at Irkutsk and Bratsk, from which there are direct and connecting flights to Japan, the People's Republic of China, the Republic of Korea (South Korea), Mongolia and the USA. In the late 1990s approximately one-10th of the region's freight was transported by river—there are two major river-ports on the Lena river, at Kirensk and Osetrovo (Ust-Kut). These are used to transport freight to Sakha (Yakutiya) and the northern seaport of Tiksi.

Agriculture, which employed 8.0% of the work-force and generated 17,607m. roubles in 2003, consists mainly of animal husbandry (fur-animal-, reindeer- and livestock-breeding), hunting and fishing and grain and potato production. The region contains huge energy reserves, including the Kovytkinskoye gas field and the Angarsk petroleum field. Despite a non-binding agreement, signed in 2003 and backed by the petroleum company Yukos, which envisaged building a pipeline from the Angarsk field to Daqing in the People's Republic of China, in February 2004 the federal Government decided in favour of the construction by the state-controlled company Transneft of a 3,900 km pipeline linking Angarsk with the Pacific coast, in particular to facilitate the export of petroleum to Japan. The first stage of the pipeline, which was to link Taishet, in the Angarsk field, with Skovorodino (Amur Oblast), on the Trans-Siberian Railway, was expected to commence operations in late 2005. Industry engaged some 24.6% of the work-force in 2003 and generated some 139,439m. roubles. The main industries are non-ferrous metallurgy, the processing of forestry products, mining (coal, iron ore, gold, muscovite or mica, gypsum, talc and salt), mechanical engineering, metal-working and electricity generation (in which field the Oblast is among Russia's leading producers).

The economically active population in Irkutsk Oblast totalled 1,363,000 in 2003, when 11.7% of the labour force were unemployed. For those in employment, the average wage amounted to 6,137.6 roubles per month. In 2003 there was a budgetary deficit of 1,409.2m. roubles. In that year the value of exports from the Oblast amounted to some US $2,754.1m., while imports were worth $418.8m. Foreign investment in the territory amounted to some $111.2m. in 2003. At the end of that year some 8,300 small businesses were registered in the Oblast.

Directory

Governor: ALEKSANDR G. TISHANIN (appointment confirmed 26 August 2005), 664047 Irkutsk, ul. Lenina 1A; tel. (3952) 20-00-15; fax (3952) 24-33-40; e-mail mail@admirk.ru; internet governor.govirk.ru.

Chairman of the Legislative Assembly: VIKTOR K. KRUGLOV, 664047 Irkutsk, ul. Lenina 1A; tel. (3952) 24-17-60; fax (3952) 20-00-27; internet irk.gov.ru.

Chief Representative of Irkutsk Oblast in the Russian Federation: TATYANA I. RYUTINA, 109028 Moscow, per. Durasovskii 3/2; tel. (495) 916-17-08; fax (495) 915-70-58.

Head of Irkutsk City Administration (Mayor): VLADIMIR V. YAKUBOVSKII, 664025 Irkutsk, ul. Lenina 14; tel. (3952) 24-37-04; internet www1.irkutsk.ru/ru/mer.

Kemerovo Oblast

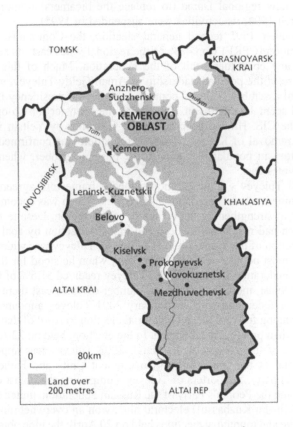

Kemerovo Oblast, known as the Kuzbass, is situated in southern central Russia and forms part of the Siberian Federal Okrug and the Western Siberian Economic Area. Krasnoyarsk Krai and the Khakasiya lie to the east, Tomsk to the north, Novosibirsk to the west and the Altai Krai and the Republic of Altai to the south-west. The region lies in the Kuznetsk basin, the area surrounding its main river, the Tom. The territory of the Oblast occupies 95,500 sq km (36,870 sq miles). According to the census of 9–16 October 2002, the total population numbered 2,899,142 and the population density was 30.4 per sq km. Some 86.7% of the population inhabited urban areas. 91.9% of the population were ethnically Russian, 1.8% Tatar, 1.3% Ukrainian and 1.2% German. The region's administrative centre is at Kemerovo, which had a population of 485,000 in 2002, according to provisional census results. Other major cities include Novokuznetsk (550,100), and Prokopevsk (224,600). Kemerovo Oblast is included in the time zone GMT+7.

History

Kemerovo was founded in 1918 (as Shcheglovsk) and became the administrative centre of the Oblast at its formation on 26 January 1943. The city is at the centre of Russia's principal coal-mining area. In July 1997 the Governor appointed in August 1991, Mikhail Kislyuk, a former head of the Kuzbass coal workers, was dismissed by President Boris Yeltsin, as the result of a dispute over unpaid pensions arrears. Kislyuk had earned criticism, as had the federal authorities, for refusing to schedule elections to a new regional Duma (to replace the bicameral Regional Assembly elected in March 1994; its activities were suspended in 1995).

In the December 1995 federal general election, the Communist Party of the Russian Federation (CPRF) won 48% of the regional votes cast, its second highest proportion in any constituent unit of the Federation. Much of this support was secured because of the popular leadership of Aman-Geldy Tuleyev, speaker of the suspended local assembly. Tuleyev contested the federal presidency in 1991, 1996 and 2000, and spent 11 months in 1996–97 as the Minister for Co-operation with Members of the CIS. Having been appointed Governor by Yeltsin in July 1997, following the removal of Kislyuk, Tuleyev's position was confirmed by an overwhelming victory in popular elections to the post in October, when he received 94.6% of the votes cast.

In mid-1998 Tuleyev's administration signed a framework agreement with the federal Government on the delimitation of powers, which was accompanied by 10 accords aimed at strengthening the economy of the region. Despite the economic situation (which had resulted in widespread industrial action by coal miners, who blockaded a section of the Trans-Siberian Railway), Tuleyev was widely considered to be Russia's most popular regional leader and, when he stood for the presidency of the Russian Federation in March 2000, Tuleyev received 51.6% of the votes cast in Kemerovo Oblast, more than twice the number of votes cast there for Vladimir Putin, the victor federation-wide. In January 2001 Tuleyev announced his resignation, thus bringing forward the gubernatorial election to April of that year, several months earlier than previously scheduled. In the election, held on 22 April, Tuleyev received 93.5% of the votes cast. In March 2003 Tuleyev was appointed to the Supreme Council of the generally pro-Government Unity and Fatherland-United Russia (UF-UR) party. Supporters of Tuleyev, comprising the oblast organizations of the UF-UR and the People's Party of the Russian Federation, united in the I Serve the Kuzbass! (Sluzhu Kuzbassu!) electoral bloc, won an overwhelming majority in oblast legislative and municipal elections held on 20 April; the bloc obtained 34 seats in the 35-member legislature, and obtained control of 11 of 12 municipalities where elections were held. In January 2004 Tuleyev encouraged the CPRF to support Putin in his campaign for re-election to the presidency in March. In April 2005 Putin nominated Tuleyev, who remained extremely popular in the Oblast, to serve a further term of office; this nomination was confirmed by a unanimous vote in the regional legislature on 20 April.

Economy

The economy of Kemerovo Oblast is based on industry. It is rich in mineral resources and contains the Kuzbass basin, one of the major coal reserves of the world. In 2002 Kemerovo's gross regional product amounted to 144,610.9m. roubles, equivalent to 49,880.6 roubles per head. The Oblast's main industrial centres are at Kemerovo, Novokuznetsk, Prokopevsk, Kiselevsk and Leninsk-Kuznetskii. At the end of 2002 the region had 1,728 km of railway track and 5,771 km of paved roads on its territory.

Kemerovo Oblast's agriculture, which employed just 4.2% of the work-force in 2003, consists mainly of potato and grain production, animal husbandry and beekeeping. The value of agricultural output in 2003 was 14,456m. roubles. In the mid-

1990s reserves of coal to a depth of 1,800 m (5,900 feet) were estimated at 733,400m. metric tons. In the same period deposits of iron ore were estimated at 5,250m. tons. In 2002 output of coal amounted to 131.3m. metric tons, equivalent to 51.3% of the coal mined in the Russian Federation in that year, and intensive mining has resulted in severe environmental degradation. Production of complex ores, ferrous metallurgy and electricity generation are also important industries in the region. The industrial sector as a whole employed 31.1% of the working population in 2003 and generated 200,731m. roubles.

The economically active population numbered 1,479,000 in 2003, when 9.7% of the labour force were unemployed. The average monthly wage was 5,263.6 roubles. The 2003 regional budget recorded a surplus of 1,150.0m. roubles. In that year export trade totalled US $2,649.6m., and imports were worth $160.8m. Total foreign investment in the Oblast amounted to $39.4m. in 2003. At the end of 2003 some 13,500 small businesses were registered in the Oblast.

Directory

Head of the Regional Administration (Governor): AMAN-GELDY M. TULEYEV (appointed 1 July 1997, elected 19 October 1997, re-elected 22 April 2001; appointment confirmed 20 April 2005), 650099 Kemerovo, pr. Sovetskii 62; tel. (3842) 36-34-09; fax (3842) 58-31-56; e-mail postmaster@ako.kemerovo.su; internet www.kemerovo.su.

Chairman of the Regional Council of People's Deputies: GENNADII T. DYUDYAYEV, 650099 Kemerovo, pr. Sovetskii 58; tel. (3842) 58-41-42; fax (3842) 58-54-51.

Chief Representative of Kemerovo Oblast in the Russian Federation: NATALYA V. KHAPII, 113184 Moscow, ul. B. Tatarskaya 5/14/9; tel. and fax (495) 953-54-89.

Head of Kemerovo City Administration (Mayor): VLADIMIR V. MIKHAILOV, 650099 Kemerovo, pr. Sovetskii 54; tel. (3842) 23-18-91; fax (3842) 58-18-91; e-mail sityadm@kuzbass.net; internet www.kemerovo.ru.

Novosibirsk Oblast

Novosibirsk Oblast is situated in the south-east of the Western Siberian Plain, at the Ob-Irtysh confluence. The Oblast forms part of the Siberian Federal Okrug and the Western Siberian Economic Area. There is an international border with Kazakhstan in the south-west. The neighbouring federal territories are Altai Krai to the south, and the Oblasts of: Omsk to the west; Tomsk to the north; and Kemerovo to the east. The region's major rivers are the Ob and the Om. About one-third of its territory is swampland. It occupies a total area of 178,200 sq km (68,800 sq miles). According to the census of 9–16 October 2002, the Oblast had a population of 2,692,251, and a population density of 15.1 per sq km. At that time some 75.1% of the population inhabited urban areas. 93.0% of the population were ethnically Russian, 1.8% German, 1.3% Ukrainian and 1.0% Tatar. Just over one-half of the region's inhabitants live in its administrative centre, Novosibirsk, which had a population of 1,425,600 at mid-October 2002, according to provisional census results. The Oblast is included in the time zone GMT+6.

History

The city of Novosibirsk (known as Novonikolayevsk until 1925) was founded in 1893, during the construction of the Trans-Siberian Railway. It became prosperous through its proximity to the Kuznetsk coal basin (see Kemerovo Oblast). The Oblast, which was formed on 28 September 1937, increased in population throughout the Soviet period as it became heavily industrialized, and was a major centre of industrial production during the Second World War.

In October 1993 the federal President, Boris Yeltsin, dismissed the head of the regional administration appointed in November 1991, Vitalii Mukha, and appointed Ivan Indinok in his place. In 1994 elections were held to a new representative body, which was dominated by the Communist Party of the Russian Federation (CPRF), after the elections in both 1994 and 1998; the regional legislature was constantly in dispute with the executive, the head of which was a presidential appointment. In an effort to resolve this power struggle, the President permitted the Oblast a gubernatorial election in December 1995, as a result of which Mukha, as the CPRF candidate, was returned to office. In January 2000 another politician regarded as a left-wing statist, Viktor Tolokonskii, a former Mayor of Novosibirsk, was elected Governor by a narrow margin following two rounds of voting. Support for the CPRF declined somewhat in the regional legislative elections of December 2001, when the party and its ally, the Agrarian Party of Russia, secured just 18 of the 49 seats available, while the remainder were filled by independent candidates. Tolokonskii was re-elected in the gubernatorial election of 7 December 2003, securing 58.3% of the votes cast. The rate of participation in the election was 55.4%.

Economy

In 2002 Novosibirsk Oblast's gross regional product stood at 130,009.6m. roubles, or 48,290.3 roubles per head. Novosibirsk city is a port on the Ob river, and is also the region's principal industrial centre. At the end of 2002 there were 1,528 km of railways and 9,752 km of paved roads on the Oblast's territory. There are 12 airports in the region, including Tolmachevo, an international airport.

The Oblast's agriculture employed 13.4% of its working population and generated 29,485m. roubles in 2003. It consists mainly of the production of grain, vegetables, potatoes and flax and animal husbandry and bee-keeping. In mid-2005 the Oblast was the first of seven federal subjects in which cases of avian influenza were reported, resulting in the slaughter of large numbers of poultry in affected areas. In 2003 the industrial sector employed 18.3% of the labour force and generated 77,787m. roubles. Extraction industries involved the production of coal, petroleum, natural gas, peat, marble, limestone and clay. Manufacturing industry includes non-ferrous metallurgy, mechanical engineering, metal-working, electricity generation and food-processing.

The Oblast's economically active population totalled 1,359,000 in 2003, when 11.0% of the labour force were unemployed. The average monthly wage in the region was 4,623.5 roubles. The 2003 budget showed a deficit of 3,085.2m. roubles. In 2003 the Oblast's external trade comprised US $672.3m. in exports and $447.7m. in imports. In the same year foreign investment in the Oblast totalled $9.2m. At the end of 2003 there were 26,700 small businesses registered in the Oblast.

Directory

Head of the Regional Administration (Governor): Viktor A. Tolokonskii (elected 9 January 2000, re-elected 7 December 2003), 630011 Novosibirsk, Krasnyi pr. 18; tel. (3832) 23-08-62; fax (3832) 23-57-00; e-mail portal@obladm.nso.ru; internet www3.adm.nso.ru.

Chairman of the Regional Council of Deputies: Viktor V. Leonov, 630011 Novosibirsk, ul. Kirova 3; tel. (3832) 23-09-36; fax (3832) 23-23-78; e-mail info@ sovet.nso.ru; internet www.sovet.nso.ru.

Chief Representative of Novosibirsk Oblast in the Russian Federation: Vadim B. Filatov, 101000 Moscow, ul. Myasnitskaya 35; tel. (495) 204-13-00.

Head of Novosibirsk City Administration (Mayor): Vladimir F. Gorodetskii, 630099 Novosibirsk, Krasnyi pr. 34; tel. (3832) 22-49-32; fax (3832) 22-08-58; e-mail cic@admnsk.ru; internet www.novo-sibirsk.ru.

Omsk Oblast

Omsk Oblast is situated in the south of the Western Siberian Plain on the middle reaches of the Irtysh river. Kazakhstan lies to the south. Tyumen lies to the north-west and Tomsk and Novosibirsk to the east. Omsk forms part of the Siberian Federal Okrug and the Western Siberian Economic Area. The major rivers are the Irtysh, the Ishim, the Om and the Tara. The Oblast covers some 139,700 sq km (53,920 sq miles). According to the census of 9–16 October 2002, the region had a population of 2,079,220 and a population density of 14.9 per sq km. Of the Oblast's inhabitants, some 68.7% lived in urban areas. 83.5% of the population were ethnically Russian, 3.9% Kazakh, 3.7% Ukrainian, 3.7% German and 2.3% Tatar. The administrative centre is at Omsk, which lies at the confluence of the Om and Irtysh rivers and had a population of 1,133,900 in 2002, according to provisional census results. The region is included in the time zone GMT+6.

History

The city of Omsk was founded as a fortress in 1716. In 1918 it became the seat of Adm. Aleksandr Kolchak's 'all-Russian Government'. Omsk fell to the Bolsheviks in 1919 and Kolchak 'abdicated' in January 1920. Omsk Oblast was formed on 7 December 1934.

In the 1990s the region was generally supportive of the Communist Party of the Russian Federation (CPRF). The regional Governor, Leonid Polezhayev, although a supporter of the federal state President, Boris Yeltsin, was well respected locally and was elected to that position in December 1995, having been appointed in November 1991. In May 1996 the regional and federal administrations signed a treaty on the delimitation of powers. Polezhayev was re-elected in September 1999, defeating the regional leader of the CPRF. Nevertheless, Omsk was one of only four regions in which the CPRF candidate, Gennadii Zyuganov, received a larger proportion of the votes cast than Vladimir Putin in the federal presidential election of March 2000. The Oblast abolished its power-sharing treaty with the federal Government in mid-2001. At elections to the regional Legislative Assembly on 24 March 2002 supporters of Polezhayev, including, notably, members of the Unity and Fatherland–United Russia party, obtained control of the Assembly. Polezhayev was re-elected Governor on 7 September 2003, receiving 57% of the votes cast.

Economy

In 2002 Omsk Oblast's gross regional product amounted to 90,933.0m. roubles, equivalent to 43,734.2 roubles per head. Omsk is one of the highest-ranking cities in Russia in terms of industrial output. The region lies on the Trans-Siberian Railway and is a major transport junction. At the end of 2002 it contained 775 km of railway track and 7,875 km of paved roads. There are also some 1,250 km of navigable waterways on the Oblast's territory and some 580 km of pipeline, carrying petroleum and petroleum products. There are two airports—a third, international airport was under construction in the early 2000s.

The Oblast's soil is the fertile black earth (*chernozem*) characteristic of the region. Its agriculture, which generated a total of 26,660m. roubles in 2003 and employed some 17.3% of the work-force, consists mainly of animal husbandry (including fur-farming) and hunting and the production of grain. The Oblast was one of seven federal subjects directly affected by an outbreak of avian influenza in mid-2005. The region's mineral reserves include clay, peat and lime. There are also deposits of petroleum and natural gas. Industry employed 17.8% of the work-force and generated 56,964m. roubles in 2003. The Oblast's main industries are electricity generation, fuel, chemical and petrochemical production, mechanical engineering, petroleum-refining and food-processing. There is a petroleum refinery at Omsk, operated by Sibneft. The region's exports primarily comprise chemical, petrochemical and petroleum products. The defence sector is also significant to the economy of the region.

The economically active population numbered 1,006,000 in 2003, when 9.5% of the region's labour force were unemployed. The average wage in the Oblast was 4,426.9 roubles per month. The 2003 budget recorded a deficit of 181.1m. roubles. In that year external trade comprised US $1,312.1m. in exports and $183.2m. in imports. The Oblast's main foreign trading partners include the People's Republic of China, Cyprus, Germany, Kazakhstan, Spain, Switzerland and the United Kingdom. In 2003 foreign investment in the region totalled some $1,716.8m.—more than 80% of the total foreign investment recorded in the Siberian Federal Okrug in that year. At the end of 2003 some 10,900 small businesses were registered in the Oblast.

Directory

Head of the Regional Administration (Governor): Leonid K. Polezhayev (appointed 11 November 1991, elected 17 December 1995, re-elected September 1999 and 7 September 2003), 644002 Omsk, ul. Krasnyi Put 1; tel. (3812) 24-14-15; fax (3812) 24-23-72; e-mail comtv@omsknet.ru; internet www.omskportal.ru.

Chairman of the Regional Legislative Assembly: Vladimir A. Varnavskii, 640002 Omsk, ul. Krasnyi Put 1; tel. (3812) 24-23-33; fax (3812) 23-24-66; e-mail root@topos.omsk.ru.

Chief Representative of Omsk Oblast in the Russian Federation: Boris S. Tsyba, 107078 Moscow, per. B. Kozlovskii 14–15/1; tel. and fax (495) 921-43-16.

Head of Omsk City Administration (Mayor): Viktor Shreider, 644099 Omsk, ul. Gagarina 34; tel. (3812) 24-30-33; fax (3812) 24-49-34; e-mail media@grad.omsk .ru; internet www.omsk.ru.

Tomsk Oblast

Tomsk Oblast is situated in the south-east of the Western Siberian Plain. It forms part of the Siberian Federal Okrug and the Western Siberian Economic Area. Kemerovo and Novosibirsk lie to the south, Omsk to the south-west, the Khanty-Mansii AOk— Yugra (part of Tyumen Oblast) to the north-west and Krasnoyarsk Krai to the east. The major rivers are the Ob, the Tom, the Chulym, the Ket and the Vasyugan. The largest lake is the Mirnoye. Almost all the Oblast's territory is taiga (forested marshland). It occupies 316,900 sq km (122,320 sq miles). According to the census of 9–16 October 2002, the oblast's population was 1,046,039, giving a population density of only 3.3 per sq km. Some 68.4% of the population inhabited urban areas. 90.8% of the population were ethnically Russian, 1.9% Tatar, 1.6% Ukrainian and 1.3% German. The administrative centre of the Oblast is at Tomsk, which had a population of 487,700 in 2002, according to provisional census results. The other major city in the region is Seversk (formerly Tomsk-7—115,700). Tomsk Oblast is included in the time zone GMT+7.

History

Tomsk city was founded as a fortress in 1604. It was a major trading centre until the 1890s, when the construction of the Trans-Siberian Railway promoted other centres. Tomsk Oblast was formed on 13 August 1944.

In 1993 the Regional Soviet was initially critical of President Boris Yeltsin's forcible dissolution of the federal parliament. It too, therefore, was disbanded, and replaced by a Regional State Duma. In a gubernatorial election held in December 1995, the pro-Yeltsin incumbent appointed in October 1991, Viktor Kress, won the popular mandate. Kress, the Chairman of the inter-regional association 'Siberian Accord', and a member of Our Home is Russia, was re-elected with a clear majority at the gubernatorial election of 5 September 1999. Kress was elected to a further term of office on 21 September 2003, obtaining 70.1% of the votes cast; 41.4% of the electorate participated in polling.

Economy

In 2002 the gross regional product of Tomsk Oblast amounted to 80,918.5m. roubles, equivalent to 77,357.1 roubles per head. The industrial sector plays a dominant role in the economy of the Oblast. Its major industrial centres are at Tomsk, Kolpashevo and Asino. At the end of 2002 there were 346 km of railways and 3,602 km of paved roads in the Oblast.

The Oblast's agricultural sector, which generated 7,618m. roubles in 2003 and employed 7.0% of the working population of the region in that year, consists mainly of animal husbandry and the production of grain, vegetables and potatoes. In 2002 crop sales accounted for 38.9% of agricultural output, and animal husbandry for 61.1%. Around 1.4m. ha (3.4m. acres) of the Oblast's territory was used for agricultural purposes, of which one-half was arable land. The Oblast has substantial reserves of coal, as well as of petroleum and natural gas. Its other main industries are mechanical engineering, metal-working, chemicals and petrochemicals, non-ferrous metallurgy and electricity generation. Industry employed 20.3% of the working population and generated 57,636m. roubles in 2003.

The economically active population of the Oblast numbered 526,000 in 2003, when 13.7% of the labour force were unemployed. The average monthly wage was 6,685.4 roubles. There was a budgetary deficit of 571.2m. roubles in 2003. The Oblast's most significant partners in international trade are the USA and the Republic of Korea (South Korea), with the chemicals industry accounting for the majority of this activity. In 2003 the value of external trade amounted to US $572.5m. in exports and $84.8m. in imports. In that year total foreign investment amounted to $49.1m. At the end of 2003 some 7,400 small businesses were registered in the Oblast.

Directory

Head of the Regional Administration (Governor): Viktor M. Kress (appointed 20 October 1991, elected 17 December 1995, re-elected 5 September 1999 and 21 September 2003), 634050 Tomsk, pl. Lenina 6; tel. (3822) 51-05-05; fax (3822) 51-03-23; e-mail ato@tomsk.gov.ru; internet www.tomsk.gov.ru.

Chairman of the Regional State Duma: Boris A. Maltsev, 634050 Tomsk, pl. Lenina 6; tel. (3822) 51-01-47; fax (3822) 51-06-02; e-mail duma@tomsk.gov.ru; internet duma.tomsk.ru.

Chief Representative of Tomsk Oblast in the Russian Federation: Aleksandr N. Cherevko, 123001 Moscow, ul. Spiridonovka 6/1; tel. (495) 290-24-20; fax (495) 299-37-95; e-mail tomskadm@chat.ru.

Head of Tomsk City Administration (Mayor): Aleksandr S. Makarov, 634050 Tomsk, pr. Lenina 73; tel. (3822) 52-68-99; fax (3822) 52-68-60; e-mail pmayor@ admin.tomsk.ru; internet admin.tomsk.ru.

Aga-Buryat Autonomous Okrug

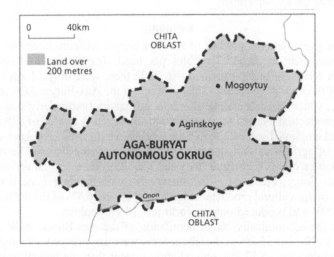

The Aga-Buryat Autonomous Okrug (AOk) is situated within the southern part of Chita Oblast. It forms part of the Siberian Federal Okrug and the East Siberian Economic Area. The Aga-Buryat AOk occupies 19,000 sq km (7,340 sq miles). Its climate is severe and annual precipitation is as little as 250 mm–380 mm (about 100 inches–150 inches) per year. According to the census of 9–16 October 2002, the AOk's population was 72,213, and the population density 3.8 per sq km. 35.3% of the population inhabited urban areas. 62.5% of the population were Buryat and 35.1% ethnically Russian. The Buryats inhabiting the district are Transbaikal Buryats, who are more closely related to their Mongol ancestors than their western counterparts, the Irkutsk Buryats. The administrative centre is at Aginskoye 'urban-type settlement', which had a population of just 11,700, according to preliminary results of the 2002 census. The Aga-Buryat AOk is included in the time zone GMT+9.

History

The Aga-Buryat-Mongol AOk was created on 26 September 1937, as part of Stalin's (Iosif Dzhugashvili's) policy of dispersing the Buryat population, whom he perceived as a threat because of their ethnic and cultural links with the Mongolian People's Republic. Its formation occurred as part of the division of the Eastern Siberian Oblast into Chita and Irkutsk Oblasts (the former of which it became a part). It assumed its current name on 16 September 1958. Under the Federation Treaty of March 1992, the Aga-Buryat AOk was recognized as a constituent units of the Russian Federation.

The district attracted some notoriety in 1997, when Iosif Kobzon, a popular singer frequently referred to as the 'Russian Frank Sinatra', won a by-election for a seat representing the AOk in the federal legislature. Kobzon attracted controversy, owing to his reputedly close connections with organized crime networks. The incumbent head of the okrug administration, Bair Zhamsuyev, elected to that position in February 1997, was re-elected in October 2000, obtaining 89.3% of the votes cast.

In September 2005 federal President Vladimir Putin nominated Zhamsuyev to a further term of office; this appointment was confirmed by a unanimous vote in the district Duma on 15 September.

Economy

In 2002 the gross regional product of the Aga-Buryat AOk amounted to 1,634.7m. roubles, equivalent to 22,637.2 roubles per head. The district's transport infrastructure is relatively unsophisticated—in 2002 there were only 71 km of railway track and 898 km of paved roads. The economy of the Aga-Buryat AOk is based on agriculture, which consists mainly of animal husbandry (particularly sheep-rearing) and grain production. Agricultural production amounted to a value of 875m. roubles in 2003 and employed some 22.4% of the work-force. In 2002 crop sales accounted for 21.0% of agricultural output and animal husbandry for 79.0%. The territory is rich in reserves of wolfram (tungsten) and tantalum. Its main industries are non-ferrous metallurgy, ore-mining, the manufacture of building materials and the processing of agricultural products. Industry employed 16.8% of the district's work-force in 2003, and produced output worth just 106m. roubles.

In 2003 the economically active population of the Aga-Buryat AOk numbered 31,000. In 1998 some 35.2% of the labour force were unemployed, although by 2003 the rate had declined to 12.2%, only slightly greater than the federal average. The average monthly wage was 3,255.9 roubles in 2003. The 2003 district budget showed a surplus of 143.4m. roubles. The external trade of the AOk is minimal, and comprised US $2.5m. in exports and $26.7m. in imports in 2003. The main foreign trading partners are the People's Republic of China and Mongolia. At the end of 2003 around 100 small businesses were registered in the territory.

Directory

Head of the District Administration (Governor): BAIR B. ZHAMSUYEV (elected 23 February 1997, re-elected 29 October 2000; appointment confirmed 15 September 2005), 674460 Chita obl., Aga-Buryat AOk, PGT Aginskoye, ul. Bazara Rinchino 92; tel. (30239) 3-41-52; fax (30239) 3-45-40; e-mail admabao@mail.ru; internet www.aginskoe.ru.

Chairman of the District Duma: DASHI TS. DUGAROV, 674460 Chita obl., Aga-Buryat AOk, PGT Aginskoye, ul. Bazara Rinchino 92; tel. (30239) 3-44-81; fax (30239) 3-45-95; e-mail duma@agatel.ru.

Representation of the Aga-Buryat Autonomous Okrug in Chita Oblast: Chita.

Chief Representative of the Aga-Buryat Autonomous Okrug in the Russian Federation: OCHIP D. DAMDINOV, 127025 Moscow, ul. Novyi Arbat 19/1733; tel. (495) 203-95-09; fax (495) 203-80-14; e-mail postpredstvo@hotmail.ru.

Evenk Autonomous Okrug

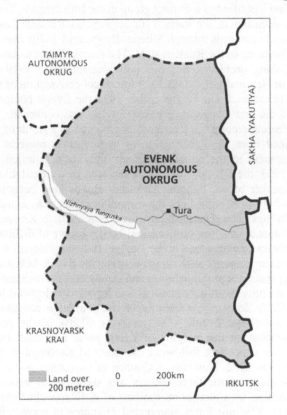

The Evenk Autonomous Okrug (AOk) is a land-locked territory situated on the Central Siberian Plateau. It is part of the Siberian Federal Okrug and the Eastern Siberian Economic Area. The district forms the central-eastern part of Krasnoyarsk Krai, with the core territories of the province lying to the west and south and the other autonomous okrug, the Taimyr (Dolgano-Nenets) AOk, to the north. Sakha (Yakutiya) adjoins to the east, and Irkutsk to the south-east. The district has numerous rivers, the largest being the Nizhnyaya Tunguska, a tributary of the Yenisei. The Evenk AOk occupies 767,600 sq km (296,370 sq miles), of which almost three-quarters is forested. According to the census of 9–16 October 2002, the total population was 17,697. Its population density, of 0.02 per sq km, was the lowest in the Federation. Some 32.8% of the population inhabited urban areas. Some 61.9% of the population were ethnically Russian, 21.5% Evenk (compared with 67.5% and 14.0%, respectively, in 1989, although differences in methodology mean that the two sets of figures are not directly comparable), 5.6% Yakut, 3.1% Ukrainian, 1.2% Ket, 0.9% Tatar and 0.9% Khakass. The Evenks' native tongue is part of the Tungusic group of the Tungusic-Manuchu division of the Uralo-Altaic language family. The region's administrative centre is at Tura 'urban-type settlement', which had just 5,800 inhabitants, according to the preliminary results of the 2002 census. The Evenk AOk is included in the time zone GMT+7.

History

The Evenks, who are thought to be descended from a mixture of Tungus and Yukagir culture, were first identified as a distinct group in the 14th century. Their first contact with Russians occurred in the early 17th century, as Russian Cossacks and fur trappers advanced eastwards through Siberia. By the mid-1620s many Evenks were forced to pay fur taxes to the Russian state. The Evenks' right to land, pasture, and hunting and fishing preserves was officially guaranteed in 1919 by the Soviet Commissariat of Nationalities, but in 1929 forced collectivization of their economic activities was introduced. On 10 December 1930 the Evenk National Okrug was established and the first Congress of Evenk Soviets was convened.

Nationalist feeling among the Evenks later emerged as a result of environmental damage sustained from the construction of hydroelectric projects and extensive mineral development in the region. After the forcible dissolution of the federal parliament in 1993, the District Soviet was replaced by a Legislative Assembly or Suglan. The speaker of the Suglan, Aleksandr Bokovikov, became Governor in March 1997, after an election held three months earlier was annulled, owing to various irregularities. The relationship of the Evenk AOk to Krasnoyarsk Krai, of which it also forms a part, has, on occasion, been a source of difficulties, although to a considerably lesser extent than in the Taimyr (Dolgano-Nenets) AOk. From June 1997 a number of agreements were signed between the Evenk AOk and Krasnoyarsk Krai, regulating specific economic issues and stating that the residents of the district would participate fully in all gubernatorial and legislative elections in the Krai. On 8 April 2001 Boris Zolotarev, a director of the petroleum company Yukos, was elected Governor of the Evenk AOk, receiving 51.8% of the popular vote. A proposed referendum on the merging of Krasnoyarsk Krai with both of its constituent AOks was cancelled, following the death of Krasnoyarsk Krai Governor Aleksandr Lebed in 2002. However, a Council of Governors and a council of the legislative assemblies of the three entities was subsequently established, despite continued opposition to a merger on the part of Zolotarev. In February 2005 the federal President, Vladimir Putin, nominated Zolotarev to serve a further term of office as district Governor; this nomination was approved by vote of the Suglan on 3 March. In referendums on the merger of the three polities within Krasnoyarsk Krai, held on 17 April 2005, the unification was approved by a clear majority of votes in all three territories; 79.9% of the votes cast in the Evenk AOk were in favour of the proposal. The merger was scheduled to take effect from 1 January 2007, with elections to a unified regional legislature expected to be held on 15 April of that year. In late August 2005 the federal President, Vladimir Putin, submitted draft legislation providing for the merger, and confirming that the reunified territory would be known as Krasnoyarsk Krai, to the federal legislature, both chambers of which had approved the legislation by early October 2005.

Economy

Despite its size and, indeed, its potential wealth, the Evenk AOk remains an undeveloped and economically insignificant producer. In 2002 the gross regional product of the AOk amounted to just 870.1m. roubles, equivalent to 21,869.5 roubles per head. In 2003 agriculture engaged 4.9% of the work-force and generated only 92m. roubles. The estimated combined hydroelectric potential of the district's two major rivers is 81,300m. kWh. Its main industries otherwise are the production of petroleum, natural gas, graphite and Iceland spar, and food-processing. In 2003 industry employed 10.5% of the Evenk AOk's work-force, and generated 701m. roubles.

The economically active population of the Evenk AOk numbered 10,000 in 2003, when the rate of unemployment was just 5.0%, although in the previous year only 2.5% of the labour force had been unemployed. External trade was believed to be substantial, but data were aggregated with those of Krasnoyarsk Krai. The average monthly wage was some 9,560.2 roubles in 2003. The 2003 budget showed a deficit of 1,155.3m. roubles. At 31 December 2002 five small businesses were registered in the district.

Directory

Head of the District Administration (Governor): BORIS N. ZOLOTAREV (elected 8 April 2001; appointment confirmed 3 March 2005), 648000 Krasnoyarsk Krai, Evenk AOk, PGT Tura, ul. Sovetskaya 2; tel. (3912) 63-63-55; fax (3912) 63-63-56; e-mail zolotarevbn@tura.evenkya.ru; internet www.evenkya.ru.

Chairman of the District Legislative Assembly (Suglan): ANATOLII YE. AMOSOV, 648000 Krasnoyarsk Krai, Evenk AOk, PGT Tura, ul. Sovetskaya 2; tel. (3912) 63-63-73; fax (3912) 2-26-31; e-mail amosovae@tura.evenkya.ru.

Representation of the Evenk Autonomous Okrug in Krasnoyarsk Krai: 660097 Krasnoyarsk, pr. Mira 36/719; tel. and fax (3912) 26-34-55.

Chief Representative of the Evenk Autonomous Okrug in the Russian Federation: YELENA K. BATYGINA, 115054 Moscow, ul. Dubinskaya 31A/1748; tel. (495) 956-19-00; fax (495) 540-63-96.

Taimyr (Dolgano-Nenets) Autonomous Okrug

Taimyr (Dolgano-Nenets) Autonomous Okrug (AOk) is situated on the Taimyr Peninsula, which abuts into the Arctic Ocean, separating the Kara and Laptev Seas. The district comprises the northern end of Krasnoyarsk Krai and, in common with its south-eastern neighbour, the Evenk AOk, forms part of the Siberian Federal Okrug and the Eastern Siberian Economic Area. The Yamalo-Nenets AOk, in Tyumen Oblast, lies to the west and Sakha (Yakutiya) is located to the south-east. Taimyr district's major rivers are the Yenisei (which drains into the Kara Sea in the west of the region), the Pyasina and the Khatanga. The district is mountainous in the south and in the extreme north, and just under one-half of it is forested. It has numerous lakes, the largest being Lake Taimyr. The territory occupies 862,100 sq km (332,860 sq miles). The climate in Taimyr is severe, with snow for an average of 280 days per year. According to the census of 9–16 October 2002, the Taimyr AOk had a population of 39,786. Its population density was 0.05 per sq km. Some 66.3% of the total population inhabited urban areas. Some 58.6% of the population were ethnically Russian, 13.9% Dolgan, 7.7% Nenets, 6.1% Ukrainian, 1.9% Nganasan, 1.5% German, 1.1% Tatar and 0.8% Evenk. The AOk's administrative centre is at Dudinka, which had a population of 25,200, according to the provisional results of the 2002 census. The city of Norilsk, which had a population of 135,100 at that time, does not form part of the AOk, being considered for administrative purposes a part of Krasnoyarsk Krai proper. Taimyr is included in the time zone GMT+7.

History

The territory of the Taimyr district was first exploited by Russian settlers in the 17th century. An autonomous okrug for the Dolgans and Nenets was founded on 10 December 1930, as part of Krasnoyarsk Krai. In 1993, following Russian President Boris Yeltsin's forcible dissolution of the Russian parliament, on 18 October the Dolgano-Nenets or Taimyr District Soviet voted to disband itself and a new District Duma was subsequently elected.

Tensions arose between Taimyr and Krasnoyarsk Krai over the division of authorities between the two federal subjects, the exact relationship of which remained constitutionally obscure. In October 1997 the federal authorities signed a power-sharing treaty with the leaders of the Taimyr AOk, Krasnoyarsk Krai and the other autonomous okrug within the Krai, the Evenk AOk. The first of its kind, this treaty clearly delineated authority between the federal, krai and okrug authorities, and ensured that some of the wealth generated by the local company, Norilsk Nickel, the world's largest producer of nickel, went to pay salaries and other benefits within Taimyr. None the less, the attitudes of Taimyr leaders towards the Krai were variable; the AOk did not participate in elections to the Krai legislature in 1997 or 2000, although it did participate in the gubernatorial election of the Krai in April 1998. The victor in that election, Gen. (retd) Aleksandr Lebed, unilaterally cancelled the power-sharing agreement in October 1999.

At the gubernatorial election held in the AOk on 28 January 2001, Aleksandr Khlopanin, hitherto the General Director of Norilsk Nickel, the major employer in the region, was elected Governor, with some 63% of the votes cast. However, following Khlopanin's election as Governor of Krasnoyarsk Krai (q.v.) in September 2002, he was obliged to resign as Governor of the AOk. Gubernatorial elections, held on 26 January 2003, were won by Oleg Budargin, hitherto the Mayor of Norilsk and a former senior manager at Norilsk Nickel, with 69.1% of the votes cast.

In February 2003 the governors of Krasnoyarsk Krai and the two autonomies signed a protocol of intent to install a Council of Governors, and a council of the legislative assemblies of the three entities was subsequently established. Elections to the district Duma were held on 23 January 2005. In referendums on the merger of the three polities, held on 17 April 2005, the unification was approved by a clear majority of votes in all three territories, although the proportion of votes in the Taimyr (Dolgano-Nenets AOk) in favour of the proposal (70.0%) was substantially lower than in the other two territories. The merger was scheduled to take effect from 1 January 2007, with elections to a unified regional legislature expected to be held on 15 April of that year. In late August 2005 the federal President, Vladimir Putin, submitted draft legislation providing for the merger, and confirming that the reunified territory would continue to be known as Krasnoyarsk Krai, to the federal legislature, both chambers of which had approved the legislation by early October.

Economy

In 2002 the gross regional product of the Taimyr (Dolgano-Nenets) AOk amounted to 2,863.4m. roubles, equivalent to some 161,801.4 roubles per head. The major ports in the AOk are Dudinka, Dikson and Khatanga. There is limited transport. The district's roads, which totalled 112 km in length at the end of 2002, are concentrated in its more populous areas.

Agricultural production, which employed 9.8% of the territory's labour force, was valued at just 29m. roubles in 2003 and principally comprises fishing, livestock- and reindeer-breeding and fur-animal hunting. There are extensive mineral reserves, including petroleum and natural gas. The main industries are ore-mining (coal, copper and nickel), electricity generation and food-processing (which accounted for 31.5% of the territory's industrial output in 2002). In 2003 industry provided employment to some 19.1% of the work-force and generated 441m. roubles. Norilsk Nickel accounted for some 20% of the world's, and 80% of Russia's, nickel output in the mid-1990s. The plant also produced 19% of the world's cobalt (70% of Russia's), 42% of the world's platinum (100% of Russia's) and 5% of the world's copper (40% of Russia's). Its activity, however, caused vast environmental damage to its surroundings, in the form of sulphur pollution.

The economically active population numbered 27,000 in 2003, when 6.9% of the labour force were unemployed. The average monthly wage in the region was some 14,263.9 roubles in 2003. The district administrative budget for 2003 showed a deficit of 182.8m. roubles. External trade was believed to be substantial, but data were aggregated with those of Krasnoyarsk Krai. Foreign investment in the AOk amounted to around US $100,000 in 2003. At the end of 2002 there were 53 small businesses registered in the AOk.

Directory

Head of the District Administration (Governor): OLEG M. BUDARGIN (elected 26 January 2003), 647000 Krasnoyarsk Krai, Taimyr (Dolgano-Nenets) AOk, Dudinka, ul. Sovetskaya 35; tel. (39111) 2-11-60; fax (39111) 2-33-17; e-mail atao@taimyr .ru; internet www.taimyr.ru.

Chairman of the District Duma: SERGEI V. BATURIN, 647000 Krasnoyarsk Krai, Taimyr (Dolgano-Nenets) AOk, Dudinka, ul. Sovetskaya 35; tel. and fax (39111) 2-29-39; e-mail dudinka@duma.taimyr.ru; internet www.dumatao.ru.

Representation of the Taimyr (Dolgano-Nenets) Autonomous Okrug in Krasnoyarsk Krai: Krasnoyarsk.

Chief Representative of the Taimyr (Dolgano-Nenets) Autonomous Okrug in the Russian Federation: (vacant), Moscow; tel. (495) 120-45-36.

Head of Dudinka City Administration: ANATOLII P. KUZNETSOV, 647000 Krasnoyarsk Krai, Taimyr (Dolgano-Nenets) AOk, Dudinka, ul. Sovetskaya 35; tel. and fax (39111) 2-13-30.

Ust-Orda Buryat Autonomous Okrug

The Ust-Orda Buryat Autonomous Okrug (AOk) is situated in the southern part of the Lena-Angara plateau. The district forms part of Irkutsk Oblast and, hence, the Siberian Federal Okrug and the Eastern Siberian Economic Area. It lies to the north of Irkutsk city, west of Lake Baikal. Its major river is the Angara. The AOk occupies an area of 22,400 sq km (8,650 sq miles). According to the census of 9–16 October 2002, the Ust-Orda Buryat AOk's population was 135,327 and its population density 6.0 per sq km. In 1992 just 18.3% of the population of the district lived in urban areas. According to the 2002 census, 54.4% of the population were ethnically Russian, 39.6% Buryat, 3.0% Tatar and 1.0% Ukrainian. The capital is at Ust-Ordynskii, which had a population of 29,800, according to preliminary results of the 2002 census. The territory is included in the time zone GMT+8.

History

The Buryat-Mongol Autonomous Soviet Socialist Republic (BMASSR), created in 1923, was restructured by Stalin (Iosif Dzhugashvili) in September 1937. Anxious to discourage nationalism and links with Mongolia, Stalin had resolved to divide the Buryat peoples administratively. The Ust-Orda Buryat AOk, which represented the four western counties of the BMASSR, was established within Oblast.

The Communist Party of the Russian Federation remained the most popular party in the Legislative Assembly (which replaced the District Soviet in 1994). In 1996 the federal President, Boris Yeltsin, had signed an agreement with the Ust-Orda Buryat AOk's administration on the delimitation of powers between the federal and district authorities. Later that year an independent candidate, Valerii Maleyev, was elected Governor, and was re-elected on November 2000. He was re-elected to a further term of office on 14 November 2004.

In October 1999 the Governor of Irkutsk Oblast, Boris Govorin, stated that the district (70% of the budget of which comprised federal transfers) should be re-incorporated into the Oblast proper, as the Oblast provided fuel and other resources to the AOk. During the early 2000s proposals to unite the Ust-Orda Buryat AOk and

Irkutsk Oblast became increasingly popular and appeared to be supported by officials in both territories; although the process stalled somewhat in the first half of the 2000s, it was anticipated that the merger would be implemented before the end of 2006, possibly following the holding of referendums in each of the two federal subjects concerned.

Economy

In 2002 the gross regional product of the Ust-Orda Buryat AOk amounted to 3,794.8m. roubles, equivalent to 28,041.7 roubles per head. At the end of 2002 there were 30 km of railways and 2,202 km of paved roads on the AOk's territory.

Agriculture, which consists mainly of animal husbandry and grain and potato production, engaged 44.7% of the work-force (by far the highest proportion of any federal subject) and generated 3,765m. roubles in 2003. The Ust-Orda Buryat AOk's main industries are the processing of agricultural and forestry products and the production of coal and gypsum. Industry generated 255m. roubles in 2003 and employed 7.8% of the work-force.

The economically active population numbered 61,000 in 2003, when 10.9% of the labour force were unemployed. In 2002 the average monthly wage was just 2,754.1 roubles, markedly below the national average. There was a budgetary surplus of 95.9m. roubles in 2003. External trade was extremely small, amounting to only around US $100,000 in exports in 2003; imports were negligiable. Foreign investment in the AOk amounted to less than US $50,000 in 2000. At the end of 2002 some 51 small businesses were registered in the Ust-Orda Buryat AOk.

Directory

Head of the District Administration (Governor): VALERII G. MALEYEV (elected 17 November 1996, re-elected 19 November 2000 and 14 November 2004), 666110 Irkutsk obl., Ust-Orda Buryat AOk, pos. Ust-Ordynskii, ul. Lenina 18; tel. (39541) 2-10-62; fax (39541) 2-25-93; e-mail okrug@irmail.ru; internet www.ust-orda.ru.

Chairman of the District Duma: ALEKSEI P. KHORINOYEV, 669001 Irkutsk obl., Ust-Orda Buryat AOk, pos. Ust-Ordynskii, ul. Lenina 18; tel. (39541) 2-16-87; fax (39541) 2-26-71.

Chief Representative of the Ust-Orda Buryat Autonomous Okrug in Irkutsk Oblast: SERGEI V. DOLGOPOLOV, 626002 Irkutsk, ul. Komsomolskaya 37; tel. (3952) 57-17-14.

Chief Representative of the Ust-Orda Buryat Autonomous Okrug in the Russian Federation: LEONID A. KHUTANOV, 127025 Moscow, ul. Novyi Arbat 19/1730; tel. and fax (495) 203-5256; fax (495) 203-64-04.

FAR EASTERN FEDERAL OKRUG

Republic of Sakha (Yakutiya)

The Republic of Sakha (Yakutiya) is situated in eastern Siberia on the Laptev and Eastern Siberian Seas. Two-fifths of the Republic's territory lies within the Arctic Circle. It forms part of the Far Eastern Federal Okrug and the Far Eastern Economic Area. To the west it borders Krasnoyarsk Krai (the Taimyr and Evenk Autonomous Okrugs—AOks). Irkutsk and Chita Oblasts lie to the south-west, Amur Oblast to the south, Khabarovsk Krai and Magadan Oblast to the south-east, and the Chukot AOk to the north-east. The main river is the Lena, which drains into the Laptev Sea at a large swampy delta. Apart from the Central Yakut Plain, the region's territory is mountainous and four-fifths is taiga (forested marshland). Sakha is the largest federal unit in Russia, occupying an area of 3,103,200 sq km (1,198,150 sq miles), making it larger than Kazakhstan, itself the second largest country, after Russia, in Europe or the former USSR. The north of the Republic lies within the arctic zone whereas the south has a more temperate climate. The average temperature in January is as low as −35.6°C, and the average temperature in July is around 13.3°C. According to the census of 9–16 October 2002, the Republic had a total population of 949,280, and a population density of 0.3 per sq km. Some 64.2% of the population inhabited urban areas. 45.5% of the population were Yakut, 41.2% ethnically Russian, 3.6% Ukrainian, 1.9% Evenk, 1.2% Even, 1.1% Tatar and 0.8% Buryat. In the late 1990s and early 2000s there was a continuous outflow of population from the Republic, particularly of ethnic Russians, who had accounted for an absolute majority (50.3%) of the Republic's population at the 1989 census. (Yakuts accounted for 33.4% of the population at that time, although it should be noted that figures on ethnicity in the 1989 and 2002 censuses are not directly comparable because of methodological differences.) Indeed, by 2002 Yakuts had displaced Russians as the most numerous ethnic group in the Far Eastern Federal Okrug, accounting for 45.5% of the total population. Orthodox Christianity is the dominant religion in the region. The Yakuts' native tongue, spoken as a first language by over 93% of the indigenous population, is part of the North-Eastern branch of the Turkic family, although it is considerably influenced by Mongolian. The capital is at Yakutsk, which had a population of 209,500 in October 2002, according to provisional census results. The Republic of Sakha spans three time zones: GMT+9 (Yakutsk), GMT+10 (Verkhoyansk) and GMT+11 (Cherskii).

History

The Yakuts (Iakuts), also known as the Sakha, were historically known as the Tungus, Jekos and the Urangkhai Sakha. They are believed to be descended from various peoples from the Lake Baikal area, Turkish tribes from the steppe and the Altai Mountains, and indigenous Siberian peoples, including the Evenks. They were traditionally a semi-nomadic people, with those in the north of the region occupied with hunting, fishing and reindeer-breeding, while those in the south were pastoralists who bred horses and cattle and were also skilled blacksmiths. Their territory, briefly united by the toion (chief), Tygyn, came under Russian rule in the 1620s and a fur tax was introduced. This led to violent opposition between 1634 and 1642, although all rebellions were crushed. Increasing numbers of Russians began to settle in the region, as the result of the completion of a mail route to the Far East, the construction of camps for political opponents to the tsars and the discovery of gold in 1846. The territory became commercialized after the construction of the Trans-Siberian Railway in the 1880s and 1890s and the development of commercial shipping on the River Lena. The economic resources of the territory enabled the Yakut to secure a measure of autonomy as an ASSR in 1922. Collectivization and the purges of the 1930s greatly reduced the Yakut population, and the region was rapidly industrialized, largely involving the extraction of gold, coal and timber.

Nationalist feeling re-emerged during the period of *glasnost* (openness) in the late 1980s. Cultural, ecological and economic concerns led to the proclamation of a 'Yakut-Sakha SSR' (Union Republic) on 27 April 1990. The republican Supreme Soviet declared a Yakut Republic on 15 August 1991, and demanded republican control over the reserves of gold, diamonds, timber, coal, petroleum and tin located on its territory. On 22 December elections for an executive presidency were held, and were won by the hitherto Chairman of the republican Supreme Soviet (Supreme

Council), Mikhail Nikolayev. The Republic was renamed the Republic of Sakha (Yakutiya) in March 1992 and a new Constitution was promulgated on 27 April. On 12 October 1993 the Supreme Soviet dissolved itself and set elections to a 60-seat bicameral legislature for 12 December. On 26 January 1994 the new parliament named itself the State Assembly (Il Tumen); it comprised an upper Chamber of the Republic and a lower Chamber of Representatives. Although support for the Communist Party of the Russian Federation was relatively high, the federal Government's willingness to concede a significant degree of local control over natural resources ensured that it too enjoyed some confidence. Native languages were designated official in certain areas and attempts to protect traditional lifestyles even involved the restoration of land. Thus, a Even-Bytantai okrug (district) was established on traditional Even territory in the mid-1990s.

In December 1996 Nikolayev was re-elected President. He continued his efforts to win greater autonomy from the centre, including the maintenance (in breach of federal law) of republican gold and hard-currency reserves and, from August 1998, a ban on the sale of gold outside the republican Government. A power-sharing agreement with the federal Government in June 1995 was followed, in March 1998, by a framework agreement on co-operation for five years, which provided for collaboration on a series of mining and energy projects.

In December 2001 Nikolayev withdrew his candidacy from the forthcoming gubernatorial elections, and urged voters to transfer their support to Vyacheslav Shtyrov, the head of the local diamond-producing joint-stock company, Almazy Rossii-Sakha—Alrosa, who was the candidate of the pro-presidential Unity and Fatherland-United Russia party. Shtyrov was elected, following a second round of voting on 13 January 2002, when he received 59% of the votes cast. The election was characterized by widespread allegations of malpractice.

In 2002 controversy ensued with regard to discrepancies between the republican and federal Constitutions; in March the approval by the republican legislature of amendments to 11 articles of Sakha's Constitution was reportedly considered to be insufficiently rigorous by the federal authorities. Elections to the new, unicameral, 70-member legislature were held on 29 December; some 33 business executives were among the deputies elected, while 14 employees of Alrosa and its subsidiaries were elected.

Economy

Owing to the Republic's wealth of mineral reserves, its gross regional product in 2002 was 114,897.1m. roubles, equivalent to 121,036.0 roubles per head, one of the highest figures in the Federation. The Republic's major industrial centres are at Yakutsk, Mirnyi, Neryungri and Lensk. Its main seaport is at Tiksi. At the end of 2002 there were 165 km (103 miles) of railways in the Republic. In October 2003 the republican Government announced its intention to complete the rail link between Yakutsk and the Baikal-Amur mainline, thus properly linking the Republic to the Russian rail network for the first time and lessening dependency on the River Lena's decreasing water levels. Work on the rail link had commenced in 1985, but stopped after the dissolution of the USSR. During the 1990s the extent of paved roads increased by more than two-fold, reaching some 7,356 km by December 2002.

Sakha's agriculture, which engaged 8.6% of the working population in 2003, and generated 9,221m. roubles, consists mainly of animal husbandry (livestock- and reindeer-breeding), hunting and fishing. Grain and vegetable production tends to be on a small scale. Industry employed 18.3% of the Republic's working population in 2003 and generated 97,363m. roubles: the main industries are non-ferrous metallurgy (which accounted for 71.2% of industrial output in 2002), ore-mining (gold— Sakha produced approximately 25% of the Russian Federation's output in the first half of the 1990s; diamonds; also tin, muscovite—mica, antimony and coal), the production of electricity and natural gas production. Both industrial output and foreign trade in Sakha increased throughout the 1990s. In 1997 Alrosa signed the first of a series of trade accords with the South African diamond producer, De Beers.

The economically active population of the Republic amounted to 514,000 in 2003, and some 9.4% of the labour force were unemployed. The social situation in Sakha from the mid-1990s was typical of the northern regions of the Russian Federation. Growth in the cost of goods and services was compounded by a weak economic structure, poorly developed social services and inappropriate conditions for people to grow their own food. The average monthly wage was 9,697.4 roubles in 2003 (considerably higher than the national average, but offset by the high cost of living). In 2003 the republican budget recorded a deficit of 1,653.5m. roubles. In the same year the value of export trade amounted to some US $1,162.3m., compared with imports of $48.3m. Foreign investment in Sakha amounted to $596.7m. in 2003. At 31 December 2003 there were some 2,500 small businesses registered in the Republic.

Directory

President: VYACHESLAV A. SHTYROV (elected 13 January 2002), 677012 Sakha (Yakutiya), Yakutsk, ul. Kirova 11; tel. (4112) 43-50-50; fax (4112) 24-06-24; e-mail info@gov.sakha.ru; internet www.sakha.gov.ru.

Chairman of the Government: YEGOR A. BORISOV, 677000 Sakha (Yakutiya), Yakutsk, ul. Kirova 11; tel. (4112) 43-55-55; fax (4112) 24-06-07; internet www .sakha.gov.ru/main.asp?c=11.

Chairman of the State Assembly (Il Tumen): NURGUN TIMOFEYEV, 677022 Sakha (Yakutiya), Yakutsk, ul. Yaroslavskogo 24/1; tel. (4112) 43-51-94; fax (4112) 43-53-33; e-mail gs@iltumen.sakha.ru; internet il-tumen.sakha.ru.

Chief Representative of the Republic of Sakha (Yakutiya) in the Russian Federation: SEMEN N. NAZAROV, 107078 Moscow, Myasnitskii pr. 3/26; tel. (495) 928-82-98; fax (495) 923-51-74; e-mail sakhamos@iteranet.ru.

Head of Yakutsk City Administration (Mayor): ILYA F. MIKHALCHUK, 677000 Sakha (Yakutiya), Yakutsk, pr. Lenina 15; tel. (4112) 42-30-20; fax (4112) 42-48-80; e-mail yakutsk@sakha.ru; internet www.yakutsk-city.ru.

Khabarovsk Krai

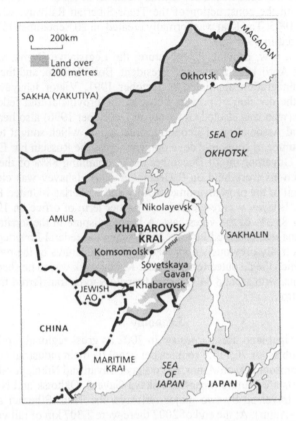

Khabarovsk Krai is situated in the Far East, on the Sea of Okhotsk. The region forms part of the Far Eastern Federal Okrug and the Far Eastern Economic Area. Maritime Krai lies to the south, the Jewish Autonomous Oblast to the south-west, Amur Oblast to the west, the Republic of Sakha (Yakutiya) to the north-west and Magadan Oblast lies to the north-east. The island of Sakhalin (Sakhalin Oblast) lies off shore to the east, across the Tatar Strait. There is a short international border with the People's Republic of China in the south-west. Khabarovsk's main river is the Amur (Heilong Jiang). More than one-half of the Krai's total area of 788,600 sq km (304,400 sq miles) is forested and almost three-quarters comprises mountains or plateaux. The territory, one of the largest in the Federation, has a 2,500-km coastline. The climate is monsoon-like in character, with hot, humid summers. Annual average precipitation in mountain areas can be as much as 1,000 mm (40 inches), while in the north it averages 500 mm. According to the census of 9–16 October 2002, the total population of Khabarovsk Krai was 1,436,570; the population density was 1.8 per sq km. Some 80.6% of the population lived in urban areas. 89.8% of the population were ethnically Russian, 3.4% Ukrainian, 0.8% Nanaits and 0.8% Tatar. The administrative centre is at Khabarovsk, which had a population of 582,700. The Krai's second largest city is Komsomolsk-on-Amur (Komsomolsk-na-Amure— 281,000). Khabarovsk Krai is included in the time zone GMT+10.

History

Khabarovsk city was established as a military outpost in 1858. The region prospered significantly with the construction of the Trans-Siberian Railway, which reached Khabarovsk in 1905. The Krai was formally created on 20 September 1938. The area was industrialized in 1946–80.

Elections to a new, provincial legislature, the Legislative Duma, were held in March 1994. In April 1996 the federal President, Boris Yeltsin, and the head of the provincial administration appointed in October 1991, Viktor Ishayev, signed an agreement on the division of powers between the provincial and federal governments. Ishayev (who was elected Governor in December 1996) also headed the Far East-Transbaikal Association of Economic Interaction, which sought to promote a coherent programme of economic development across the Russian Far East. Ishayev was re-elected Governor on 10 December 2000, obtaining 88% of the votes cast. Legislative elections were held on 9 December 2001. Ishayev was elected to the Supreme Council of the pro-Government Unity and Fatherland-United Russia party in March 2003. Ishayev was re-elected to a further term of office on 19 December 2004, receiving 85.3% of the votes cast. A border dispute in the territory between Russia and China was resolved in June 2005, when the federal President, Vladimir Putin, ratified a treaty previously approved by the legislatures of the two countries, as a result of which the disputed territory near Khabarovsk was to be shared between Russia and China, with around 340 sq km of territory to be transferred from Russian to Chinese control.

Economy

The Krai's principal land use is forestry. In 2002 its gross regional product totalled 101,584.9m. roubles, or 70,713.5 roubles per head. Its main industrial centres are at Khabarovsk, Komsomolsk-on-Amur, Sovetskaya Gavan and Nikolayevsk-on-Amur. Its principal ports are Vanino (near Sovetskaya Gavan), Okhotsk and Nikolayevsk-on-Amur. It is traversed by two major railways, the Trans-Siberian and the Far Eastern (Baikal–Amur). At the end of 2002 there were 2,307 km of railway lines and 4,956 km of paved roads in the territory. The Chita–Khabarovsk highway (forming part of a direct route between Moscow and Vladivostok) opened in September 2003. A ferry service runs between the Krai and Sakhalin Oblast. The Krai is the most important Far Eastern territory in terms of its national and international air services, which connect Moscow and other European cities with Japan.

Agriculture, which employed just 3.6% of the working population in 2003 and generated 6,973m. roubles, consists mainly of the production of grain, soybeans, vegetables and fruit, animal husbandry (including reindeer breeding) and hunting. Of the total value of production in 2002, crop sales generated 62.4% and animal husbandry 37.6%. Hunting is practised on about 97.5% of the Krai's territory. The Krai's main industries are mechanical engineering, electricity production, metalworking, non-ferrous and ferrous metallurgy, food-processing, the processing of forestry products, extraction of coal (2.6m. metric tons of which were mined in 2002), ores and non-ferrous metals, shipbuilding (including oil rigs) and petroleum-refining. Some 21.3% of the territory's work-force were engaged in industry in 2003, when total industrial output amounted to a value of 92,459m. roubles.

Khabarovsk Krai's economically active population numbered 794,000 in 2003, when 6.1% of the labour force were unemployed. The average monthly wage was 7,368.5 roubles. In 2003 the provincial administration recorded a budgetary deficit of 3,047.7m. roubles. In the 1990s the territory began to develop its trade links with 'Pacific Rim' nations apart from Japan (with which it had a long trading history), such as Canada, the People's Republic of China, the Democratic People's Republic of Korea (North Korea) and the Republic of Korea (South Korea), Australia, New Zealand, Singapore and the USA. Its exports largely consisted of raw materials (timber, petroleum products, fish and metals). External trade amounted to a value of some US $1,602.6m. in exports and $274.9m. in imports in 2003. In that year total foreign investment amounted to $27.4m. At the end of 2003 some 6,400 small businesses were registered in the Krai.

Directory

Head of the Provincial Administration (Governor and Chairman of the Provincial Government): VIKTOR I. ISHAYEV (appointed 24 October 1991, elected 8 December 1996, re-elected 10 December 2000 and 19 December 2004), 680000 Khabarovsk, ul. K. Marksa 56; tel. (4212) 32-51-21; fax (4212) 32-87-56; e-mail econ@adm.khv.ru; internet www.adm.khv.ru.

Chairman of the Provincial Legislative Duma: YURII I. ONOPRIYENKO, 680002 Khabarovsk, ul. Muravyeva-Amurskogo 19; tel. (4212) 32-52-19; fax (4212) 32-44-57; e-mail duma@duma.khv.ru; internet www.duma.khv.ru.

Chief Representative of Khabarovsk Krai in the Russian Federation: VALERII F. BELYAYEV (acting), 127025 Moscow, ul. Novyi Arbat 19/2029; tel. (495) 203-41-28; fax (495) 203-83-25; e-mail khab.rep@g23.relcom.ru.

Head of Khabarovsk City Administration (Mayor): ALEKSANDR N. SOKOLOV, 680000 Khabarovsk, ul. K. Marksa 66; tel. (4212) 23-58-67; fax (4212) 33-53-46; internet www.khabarovsk.kht.ru.

Maritime (Primorskii) Krai

Maritime (Primorskii) Krai, Primorye, is situated in the extreme south-east of Russia, on the Sea of Japan. The province is part of the Far Eastern Federal Okrug and the Far Eastern Economic Area. Its only border with another federal subject is with Khabarovsk Krai to the north. There is an international border with the People's Republic of China to the west and a short border with the Democratic People's Republic of Korea (North Korea) in the south-west. The province's major river is the Ussuri. The territory occupies 165,900 sq km (64,060 sq miles), more than two-thirds of which is forested. According to the census of 9–16 October 2002, the total number of inhabitants in the territory was 2,071,210 and the population density was 12.5 per sq km. Some 78.3% of the population lived in urban areas. 89.9% of the population were ethnically Russian, 4.5% Ukrainian and 0.9% Korean. Maritime Krai's administrative centre is at Vladivostok, which had 591,800 inhabitants in 2002. Other major cities are Ussuriisk (formerly Voroshilov—157,800) and Nakhodka (149,300). Maritime Krai is included in the time zone GMT+10.

History

The territories of the Maritime Krai were recognized as Chinese possessions by Russia in the Treaty of Nerchinsk in 1687. They became part of the Russian Empire in 1860, however, being ceded by China under the terms of the Treaty of Peking (Beijing), and the port of Vladivostok was founded. Along with other Transbaikal and Pacific regions of the former Russian Empire, the territory was part of the Far Eastern Republic until its reintegration into Russia under Soviet rule in 1922. Maritime Krai was created on 20 October 1938.

The territory declared itself a republic in mid-1993, but was not recognized as such by the federal authorities. In 28 October 1993 the provincial Governor disbanded the provincial Soviet (Council). Elections for a Governor, set for October

1994, were cancelled by presidential decree, after alleged improprieties by the incumbent, Yevgenii Nazdratenko, during his election campaign. Nazdratenko was elected, however, in December 1995, with 76% of the votes cast, and was re-elected by a similar majority in December 1999. His populist style of government and control of the local media reinforced his position. An ongoing energy crisis, owing to non-payment of bills, finally forced the resignation of Nazdratenko (officially on health grounds) in February 2001. In the gubernatorial election held in May–June 2001, Sergei Darkin, a local businessman, was elected Governor in the second round of voting, with 40% of the votes cast. Viktor Cherepkov, the former Mayor of Vladivostok, who had taken second place in the first round, was barred from standing as a candidate in the second round by the provincial court, which cited irregularities in his campaign. Cherepkov encouraged his supporters to vote against all candidates in the 'run-off' election, and 33.7% of those who voted did so. (The rate of participation in the second round was 36.0%, compared with 42.4% in the first round.) In late January 2005 Darkin resigned from office, in order to request that the federal President, Vladimir Putin, demonstrate his confidence in his leadership by nominating him for a further term of office, becoming the first regional leader to take such a step following the abolition of elections for regional governors. Putin duly nominated Darkin to serve a further term of office, and his appointment was confirmed by a vote of the provincial Duma on 4 February.

Economy

Maritime Krai's gross regional product totalled 100,976.1m. roubles in 2002, equivalent to 48,752.2 roubles per head. Its major industrial centres are at Vladivostok, the terminus of the Trans-Siberian Railway, Ussuriisk, Nakhodka and Dalnegorsk. The Krai's most important ports are at Vladivostok, Nakhodka and Vostochnyi (Vrangel). Vessels based in these ports comprise around four-fifths of maritime transport services in the Far East. During 2004 there were frequent indications that the Russian Government would agree to a Japanese proposal to construct an export pipeline to transport petroleum from the Angarsk oilfield in Siberia (Irkutsk Oblast) to the Pacific coast in Maritime Krai. The construction of a new port at Perevoznaya, near Nakhodka, was underway in 2005, and the first stage of the pipeline, which would link the oilfield with the Trans-Siberian Railway, was expected to commence operations towards the end of that year. Maritime Krai has rail links with Khabarovsk Krai and, hence, other regions, as well as international transport links with North Korea and the Republic of Korea (South Korea). At the end of 2002 there were 1,552 km of railway lines and 7,081 km of paved roads on the Krai's territory.

The Krai's agricultural sector, which employed 7.7% of the labour force in 2003, consists mainly of grain, vegetable and soybean production, animal husbandry (including fur-farming), bee-keeping and fishing. Total agricultural output in 2003 amounted to a value of 8,059m. roubles. in 2002 crop sales accounted for 65.5% of agricultural production, and animal husbandry for 34.5%. The Krai contains substantial reserves of coal and timber. The hydroelectric-energy potential of the region's rivers is estimated at 25,000m. kWh. Its main industries are food-processing (which accounted for 32.8% of industrial production in 2002), fuel and electrical-energy production, ore-mining, the processing of forestry products and mechanical engineering and ship repairs. Total industrial production was worth 57,046m. roubles in 2003, when the sector employed 20.2% of the working population. The territory is ideally placed, in terms of its proximity to the Pacific nations, for international trade, although the perception of widespread corruption and political mismanagement restrained its development. A new railway crossing into the People's Republic of China at Makhalino-Hunchun opened in 1998. The construction of a cross-border trade and economic centre, uniting the city of Pogranichnyi, in the Krai, with Suifenhe, in China, commenced in early 2003, and was due for completion in 2005.

The economically active population of Maritime Krai numbered 1,137,000 in 2003, when 7.9% of the labour force were unemployed. The average monthly wage was 5,793.1 roubles in 2003—the second lowest figure of any territory within the Far Eastern Federal Okrug, after the Jewish Autonomous Oblast. In 2003 there was a budgetary surplus of 8,859.2m. roubles. External export trade amounted to US $759.8m. in that year, when imports totalled $935.9m. Foreign investment totalled $62.7m. in 2003. At the end of 2003 there were some 13,200 small businesses registered in the Krai.

Directory

Head of the Provincial Administration (Governor): SERGEI M. DARKIN (elected 17 June 2001; appointment confirmed 4 February 2005), 690110 Maritime Krai, Vladivostok, ul. Svetlanskaya 22; tel. (4232) 22-38-00; fax (4232) 22-17-69; e-mail gubernator@primorsky.ru; internet www.primorsky.ru.

Chairman of the Provincial Duma: SERGEI A. SOPCHUK, 690110 Maritime Krai, 690110 Vladivostok, ul. Svetlanskaya 22; tel. (4232) 22-35-70; fax (4232) 26-90-23; e-mail predsedatel@duma.primorsky.ru; internet www.zspk.gov.ru.

Chief Representative of Maritime (Primorskii) Krai in the Russian Federation: ALEKSEI V. BESPALOV, 123100 Moscow, 1-i Krasnogvardeiskii proyezd 9; tel. (495) 255-82-13; fax (495) 292-14-83.

Head of the Vladivostok City Administration (Mayor): VLADIMIR V. NIKOLAYEV, 690950 Maritime Krai, Vladivostok, Okeanskii pr. 20; tel. (4232) 22-98-00; fax (4232) 22-31-29; e-mail guestbook@vlc.ru; internet www.vlc.ru.

Amur Oblast

Amur Oblast is situated in the south-east of the Russian Federation, to the west of Khabarovsk Krai. It forms part of the Far Eastern Federal Okrug and the Far Eastern Economic Area. The Jewish Autonomous Oblast lies to the south-east, Chita Oblast to the west and the Republic of Sakha (Yakutiya) to the north. Southwards it has an international border with the People's Republic of China. The Oblast's main river is the Amur (Heilong Jiang), which forms the international border with China. A little under three-quarters of the Oblast's territory is forested. Its total area occupies 363,700 sq km (140,430 sq miles). According to the census of 9–16 October 2002, the territory's inhabitants numbered 902,844, and the population density was 2.5 per sq km. Most people (65.8%) lived in urban areas. 92.0% of the population were ethnically Russian, 3.5% Ukrainian and 0.9% Belarusian. Amur Oblast's administrative centre is at Blagoveshchensk, near the Chinese border, which had a population of 218,800 in 2002, according to provisional census results. Amur Oblast is included in the time zone GMT+9.

History

The Amur region was first discovered by European Russians in 1639 and came under Russian control in the late 1850s. Part of the pro-Bolshevik Far Eastern Republic (based in Chita) until its reintegration into Russia in 1922, Amur Oblast was formed on 20 October 1932.

In the first year of post-Soviet Russian independence, the federal President, Boris Yeltsin, called for a gubernatorial election to be held in the region in December 1992. However, his appointed head of the administration, Albert Krivchenko, was defeated by Aleksandr Surat. In July 1993 Amur Oblast declared itself a republic, a measure that was not recognized by the federal authorities. Surat was subsequently dismissed and the Oblast Soviet dissolved. In January 1996 the oblast administration brought action against the regional Assembly for adopting a Charter, referred to as a republican constitution, some of the clauses of which ran counter to federal laws and presidential decrees. In elections to the new legislature, held in March, Communist Party of the Russian Federation (CPRF) candidates won up to 40% of the votes cast. In June President Yeltsin dismissed the regional Governor appointed in December 1994, Vladimir Dyachenko, and appointed Yurii Lyashko in his place. A gubernatorial election was held on 22 September 1996. The CPRF candidate, Anatolii Belonogov narrowly defeated Lyashko (with 41.0%), but the results were subsequently annulled because of alleged irregularities. Belonogov succeeded in securing a clear majority in the repeat election held in March 1997. In gubernatorial elections held in two rounds in March–April 2001 Belonogov was defeated by Leonid Korotkov. In February 2005 the federal President, Vladimir Putin, nominated Korotkov to serve a further term of office; his appointment was confirmed by a unanimous vote of the regional legislature on 24 February. At elections to the oblast legislature held on 27 March, an alliance of the statist Russian Party of Life and the liberal, pro-market, Yabloko, known as 'We Support the Development of Amur' were the most successful bloc or party, obtaining 17.7% of the votes cast, compared with the 16.3% won by the pro-Government Unity and Fatherland-United Russia (UF-UR) party. However, the legislative Chairman elected following the polling, Oleg Turkov, transferred his allegiance from the alliance to UF-UR several weeks later.

Economy

Amur Oblast's gross regional product (GRP) was 46,606.4m. roubles in 2002, equivalent to 51,621.8 roubles per head. Its main industrial centres are at Blagoveshchensk, Belogorsk, Zeya and Svobodnyi. At the end of 2002 there were 6,980 km of paved roads in the Oblast. There were 2,934 km of railway track, including sections of two major railways, the Trans-Siberian and the Far Eastern (Baikal–Amur). There are five river-ports, at Blagoveshchensk, Svobodnensk, Poyarkovsk, Amursk and Zeisk. There is an international airport at Blagoveshchensk, which serves flights principally to Japan, the Democratic People's Republic of Korea (North Korea) and the Republic of Korea (South Korea).

Agriculture in Amur Oblast, which employed 10.2% of the work-force in 2003, consists mainly of grain and vegetable production, animal husbandry (including reindeer- and fur-animal-breeding) and bee-keeping. The soil in the south of the region is particularly fertile. In 2003 agricultural output amounted to 6,892m. roubles. The region is rich in mineral resources, but by the end of the 1990s it was estimated that only around 5% of these resources were being exploited. None the less, the mining sector produced around 15% of GRP in the late 1990s. At this time around 10–12 metric tons of gold were extracted annually, making the Oblast the third largest producer of gold in Russia. The eventual liberalization of the artisanal sector could be expected to increase the output of gold appreciably. Other raw-material deposits in the Oblast include bituminous coal, lignite (brown coal) and kaolin. There are also substantial reserves of iron, titanium and silver ores. In addition, coal-mining is important, as are mechanical engineering, electricity generation, electro-technical industry and the processing of agricultural and forestry products. In 2003 some 14.4% of the Oblast's work-force were employed in industry, and total output in the sector amounted to a value of 20,447m. roubles. The region contains the Amur Shipbuilding Plant and produces nuclear-powered submarines. There is a hydroelectric power plant at Zeya, with a reservoir of 2,400 sq km. Two units of another power station, at Bureya, commenced operations in 2003; a third unit opened in November 2004.

Amur's economically active population numbered 511,000 in 2003, when 10.1% of the region's labour force were unemployed. Those in employment earned, on average, 5,930.2 roubles per month in 2003. There was a budgetary deficit of 626.5m. roubles in 2003. In that year export trade amounted to a value of US $76.6m., and import trade totalled $37.0m. The Oblast's main trading partners include the People's Republic of China, Japan and North Korea. Foreign investment totalled $16.1m. in 2003. At the end of 2003 there were some 2,600 small businesses registered in the Oblast.

Directory

Head of the Regional Administration: LEONID V. KOROTKOV (elected 8 April 2001; appointment confirmed 24 February 2005), 675023 Amur obl., Blagoveshchensk, ul. Lenina 135; tel. (4162) 59-60-01; fax (4162) 44-62-01; e-mail governor@amurobl .ru; internet www.amurobl.ru.

Chairman of the Regional Council of People's Deputies (Regional Council): OLEG TURKOV, 675023 Amur obl., Blagoveshchensk, ul. Lenina 135; tel. (4162) 44-38-53.

Chief Representative of Amur Oblast in the Russian Federation: SERGEI A. LAVRIKOV, 127006 Moscow, ul. M. Dmitrovka 3/606; tel. (495) 299-46-08; fax (495) 299-42-02.

Head of Blagoveshchensk City Administration (Mayor): ALEKSANDR MIGULYA, 675023 Amur obl., Blagoveshchensk, ul. Lenina 133; tel. (4162) 42-49-85.

Kamchatka Oblast

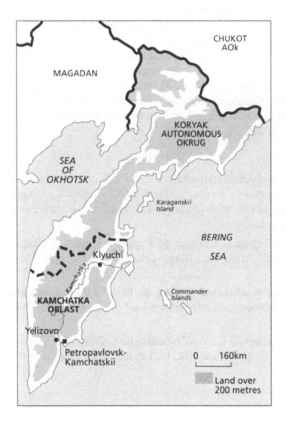

Kamchatka Oblast occupies the Kamchatka Peninsula and forms part of the Far Eastern Federal Okrug and the Far Eastern Economic Area. The Peninsula, some 1,600 km (1,000 miles) in length and 130 km in width, separates the Sea of Okhotsk, in the west, from the Bering Sea, in the east. The Oblast also includes Karaganskii Island and the Komandorskiye (Commander) Islands and the southernmost part of the Chukotka Peninsula. There are land borders with the Chukot Autonomous Okrug (AOk) to the north and Magadan Oblast to the west. This northern part of the Oblast comprises the Koryak AOk. The Oblast is dominated by the Sredinnyi Khrebet mountain range, which is bounded to the west by a broad, poorly drained coastal plain, and to the east by the Kamchatka river valley. Two-thirds of its area is mountainous (including the highest point in the Russian Far East, Mt Klyuchevskaya, at 4,685 m—15,961 feet) and it contains many hot springs. Kamchatka Oblast covers an area of 472,300 sq km (182,350 sq miles), including the AOk. There is a high annual rate of precipitation in the region, sometimes as much as 2,000 mm, and temperatures vary considerably according to region. According to the census of 9–16 October 2002, the total population of the region was 358,801 and the population density was 0.8 per sq km; some 85.2% of the region's population inhabited urban areas. 80.9% of the population were ethnically Russian, 5.8% Ukrainian, 2.0% Koryak, 1.0% Tatar and 1.0% Belarusian. The Oblast's administrative centre is at

Petropavlovsk-Kamchatskii, in the south-east, which was inhabited by 198,200 people in 2002, according to provisional census results. Kamchatka Oblast is included in the time zone GMT+12.

History

The Kamchatka Peninsula was annexed by Russia during the 18th century. Petropavlovsk came under Russian control in 1743. After the Soviet Revolution Kamchatka was part of the short-lived Far Eastern Republic. Kamchatka Oblast was formed on 20 October 1923, but constituted part of Khabarovsk Krai until 23 January 1956.

Following the dissolution of the USSR in 1991, Kamchatka tended to be supportive of the federal Government. In the general election of December 1995, however, the most successful party was the liberal Yabloko, which obtained 20% of the votes cast in the Oblast (a higher proportion than the reformists obtained even in the major cities). However, as the Oblast continued to suffer from economic and social hardship, support for the Communist Party of the Russian Federation (CPRF) increased, and the party's candidate, Mikhail Mashkovtsev, was elected Governor at elections held in December 2000. In March 2004 the oblast prosecutor's office initiated criminal proceedings against Mashkovtsev on charges of having misused 149m. roubles of budgetary heating funds and having illegally permitted unlimited salmon-fishing in the Oblast's rivers. Nonetheless, on 19 December, following two rounds of polling, the first of which had been contested by 15 candidates, Mashkovtsev, again the candidate of the CPRF, was elected to a second term as Governor, receiving 50.0% of the votes cast, compared with the 37.7% received by his opponent, Boris Nevzorov. (The third-placed candidate in the first round, Oleg Kozhemyako, whose candidacy had been supported by the Presidential Representative in the Far Eastern Federal Okrug, Konstantin Pulikovskii, went on to be appointed as Governor of the Koryak AOk in March 2005.) Two further criminal cases were subsequently opened against Mashkovtsev, but in June 2005 all charges against him were dismissed. Meanwhile, in April 2005 the oblast legislature voted to approve a request to the federal President, Vladimir Putin, that a process to merge Kamchatka Oblast with the Koryak AOk be commenced. Shortly afterwards, the Koryak legislature voted to approve an eventual territorial unification. In May the Governors of the two territories signed a protocol on the merger, announcing that referendums on the merger would be held in both territories on 23 October. Mashkovtsev announced that he had no interest in being the Governor of the merged entity, and also stated that he would not seek a further term of office as Governor of Kamchatka Oblast. In the referendum on unification, held as scheduled, 84.9% of the participants in the Oblast voted in favour of the proposal. 52.2% of the electorate participated in the poll.

Economy

The waters around Kamchatka Oblast being extremely rich in marine life, fishing, especially of crabs, is the dominant sector of Kamchatka Oblast's economy. The region's fish stocks comprise around one-half of Russia's total. All figures in this survey incorporate data for the Koryak AOk, which is also treated separately (see below). In 2002 the Oblast's gross regional product amounted to 25,365.7m. roubles, or 70,701.3 roubles per head. Petropavlovsk is one of two main industrial centres and ports in the territory, the other being Ust-Kamchatka. There is an international airport, Yelizovo, near Petropavlovsk-Kamchatskii. There were no railways in the territory, but in 2002 there were 1,355 km of paved roads in the Oblast.

Apart from fishing, agriculture in Kamchatka Oblast consists of vegetable production, animal husbandry (livestock, reindeer, mostly in the Koryak AOk, and fur animals) and hunting. In 2003 agriculture employed 5.1% of the work-force and generated 2,582m. roubles. There are deposits of gold, silver, natural gas, sulphur and other minerals in Kamchatka Oblast, which by the early 2000s had been explored and were in the process of development. The industrial sector, which employed 21.8% of the work-force and generated 26,127m. roubles in 2003, is based on the processing of agricultural products, non-ferrous metallurgy and coal and electricity production. The first geothermal energy plant in Russia, at Mutnovo, commenced operations in 2002; the plant was expected to produce around one-quarter of the Oblast's energy requirements.

The economically active population of Kamchatka Oblast numbered 228,000 in 2003, when 11.4% of the labour force were unemployed. Those in employment earned an average of 10,319.6 roubles per month in 2003, a relatively high wage compared with the rest of the Russian Federation, but one balanced by the high cost of living in the Oblast (in December 2003 the price of a 'consumer basket' of foodstuffs in Kamchatka Oblast was the third most expensive recorded in the Federation). There was a budgetary deficit of 25.7m. roubles in 2003. Foreign investment in the Oblast amounted to US $52.8m. in 2003. In that year international trade amounted to $154.7m. in exports and $41.3m. in imports. With trade dominated by the fishing industry, one of the Oblast's main foreign markets was Japan. In mid-2005 the Minister of Defence, Sergei Ivanov, announced plans to develop military facilities in the Oblast, which remained of strategic importance. At the end of 2003 some 1,700 small businesses were registered in the Oblast.

Directory

Governor: MIKHAIL B. MASHKOVTSEV (elected 17 December 2000, re-elected 19 December 2004), 683040 Kamchatka obl., Petropavlovsk-Kamchatskii, pl. Lenina 1; tel. (4152) 11-20-91; fax (4152) 27-38-43; e-mail kra@svyaz.kamchatka.su.

Chairman of the Council of People's Deputies: NIKOLAI YA. TOKOMANTSEV, 683040 Kamchatka obl., Petropavlovsk-Kamchatskii, pl. Lenina 1; tel. (4152) 11-27-61; fax (4152) 11-26-95; internet www.sovet.kamchatka.ru.

Chief Representative of Kamchatka Oblast in the Russian Federation: DMITRII YU. LATYSHEV, 119002 Moscow, Denezhnyi per. 12/16; tel. (495) 241-03-13; fax (495) 241-35-46.

Head of Petropavlovsk-Kamchatskii City Administration (Mayor): VLADISLAV V. SKVORTSOV, 683040 Kamchatka obl., Petropavlovsk-Kamchatskii, ul. Leninskaya 14; tel. (41522) 2-49-13; e-mail citiadm@svyaz.kamchatka.su.

Magadan Oblast

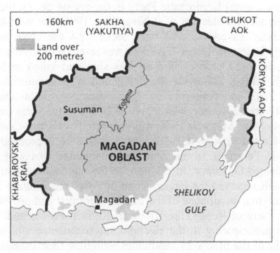

Magadan Oblast is situated in the north-east of Russia and forms part of the Far Eastern Federal Okrug and the Far Eastern Economic Area. To the north-east lies the Chukot Autonomous Okrug (AOk), and there is a border to the east with the Koryak AOk (within Kamchatka Oblast), which lies to the east. Magadan has a coastline on the Sea of Okhotsk in the south-east. Khabarovsk Krai lies to the south-west of the region and Sakha (Yakutiya) to the north-west. Its main river is the Kolyma, which flows northwards and drains into the Arctic Ocean by way of Sakha. A considerable proportion of the territory of the region is mountainous, whereas the south is dominated by larch forests and coastal marshland. Much of the Oblast is tundra or forest-tundra. The Oblast occupies a total area of 461,400 sq km (178,150 sq miles). The climate in the region is severe, with winters lasting from six to over seven months. The average temperature in January is –29.4°C, while that in July is 14.4°C. According to the census of 9–16 October 2002, the Oblast had a total population of 182,726. It is one of the most sparsely populated regions, with a population density of just 0.4 per sq km. 92.3% of the population inhabited urban areas. 80.2% of the population were ethnically Russian, 9.9% Ukrainian, 1.4% Even, 1.2% Belarusian and 1.1% Tatar. The Oblast's administrative centre is at the only large city in the Oblast, Magadan, which had a population of 99,400, according to preliminary results of the 2002 census. Magadan Oblast is included in the time zone GMT+11.

History

Russians first reached the Magadan region in the mid-17th century. Following the Soviet Revolution it was in the Far Eastern Republic, which in 1922 was reintegrated into Russia. The region held many penal establishments of the GULag (State Corrective Camp) system established during the regime of Stalin (Iosif Dzhugashvili, 1924–53). Magadan Oblast was formed on 3 December 1953, after the death of Stalin, although it then included the Chukot National Okrug. The successful rejection of Magadan's jurisdiction over the Chukot AOk (as it had by then become) in 1992 significantly reduced Magadan's territory.

Deteriorating social conditions contributed to local feeling of remoteness and of neglect by the centre in the 1990s, which was exemplified by high levels of support for the nationalist Liberal Democratic Party in the region during the mid- and late 1990s. The gubernatorial election of 3 November 1996 was won by a gold-mine proprietor, Valentin Tsvetkov, who was backed by the communist-dominated People's Patriotic Union of Russia. Tsvetkov was re-elected Governor in November 2000; however, in mid-October 2002 he was shot and killed in Moscow, in an apparent contract killing. Following the first round of gubernatorial elections, held on 2 February 2003 and contested by 12 candidates, Nikolai Dudov, formerly Tsvetkov's First Vice-Governor, who received 26.0% of the votes cast, and Nikolai Karpenko, the Mayor of Magadan (who was supported by the pro-Government Unity and Fatherland-United Russia—UF-UR party), with 37.6%, proceeded to a second round, held on 16 February. In this poll Dudov obtained 50.4% of the votes cast, thereby being elected Governor. In elections to the regional legislature, held on 22 May 2005, UF-UR received the largest share of votes cast (around 29%); notably, Our Home Is Kolyma, an alliance of the liberal, reformist and pro-Western parties, the Democratic Party of Russia, the Union of Rightist Forces and Yabloko, were prohibited from participating in the elections, in accordance with electoral legislation, after eight of the bloc's 24 candidates withdrew their candidacies. (Allegations persisted that various administrative resources had been used to encourage these candidates to withdraw, which would therefore result in the bloc being disqualified from contesting the election.)

Economy

Magadan Oblast is Russia's principal gold-producing region. In 2002 its gross regional product amounted to 20,960.0m. roubles, equivalent to 114,707.3 roubles per head. The Oblast's main industrial centres are at Magadan and Susuman. Magadan and Nagayevo are its most important ports. There are no railways in the territory, but there were 2,231 km of paved roads at the end of 2002. There is an international airport at Magadan.

The region's primary economic activities are fishing, animal husbandry and hunting. These and other agricultural activities, which employed 2.2% of the region's work-force, generated just 834m. roubles in 2003. Ore-mining is important: apart from gold, the region contains considerable reserves of silver, tin and wolfram (tungsten). It is also rich in peat and timber. In early 1998 the regional Government hired a prospecting company to explore offshore petroleum deposits in the Sea of Okhotsk, in a zone thought to hold around 5,000m. metric tons of petroleum and natural gas. The Kolyma river is an important source of hydroelectric energy. In 1997 the Pan American Silver Corporation of Canada purchased a 70% stake in local company Dukat, to reopen a defunct silver mine in the Oblast, which contained an estimated 477m. troy ounces of silver and 1m. troy ounces of gold. However, licensing and other bureaucratic obstacles delayed operations. Other industry includes non-ferrous metallurgy (which accounted for 61.6% of total industrial output in 2002), food-processing, electricity generation, mechanical engineering and metal-working. In 2003 some 24.3% of the working population were engaged in industry, and industrial output amounted to a value of 18,148m. roubles.

The economically active population of the Oblast numbered 138,000 in 2003, when 10.2% of the labour force were unemployed. The average monthly wage was some 9,386.0 roubles in 2003, one of the highest figures in the Federation, although the region was also among those with the highest cost of living: in December 2003 the price of a minimum 'consumer basket' in Magadan Oblast was the second highest in the Federation, after the neighbouring Chukot Autonomous Okrug. In 2003 the budget recorded a surplus of 4.4m. roubles. Throughout the 1990s persistent deficit problems, not helped by high wages, led to continuing problems with payment arrears. The value of external trade was relatively low; in 2003 exports were worth only US $7.7m., while imports amounted to $51.3m. Foreign investment in the Oblast amounted to $7.5m. in that year. At the end of 2003 there were some 1,800 small businesses registered in the Oblast.

Directory

Governor: NIKOLAI N. DUDOV (elected 16 February 2003), 685000 Magadan, ul. Gorkogo 6; tel. (41322) 2-31-34; fax (41322) 2-04-25; e-mail amo@regadm .magadan.ru; internet www.magadan.ru.

Chairman of the Regional Duma: ALEKSANDR P. ALEKSANDROV, 685000 Magadan, ul. Gorkogo 8A; tel. (41322) 2-55-50; fax (41322) 2-55-12; internet www.duma .kolyma.ru.

Chief Representative of Magadan Oblast in the Russian Federation: YURII L. GUTIN, 103025 Moscow, ul. Novyi Arbat 19/2023; tel. (495) 203-92-74.

Head of Magadan City Administration (Mayor): VLADIMIR P. PECHENYI, 685000 Magadan, pl. Gorkogo 1; tel. (41300) 2-50-47; fax (41322) 2-49-40; e-mail admin@ cityadm.magadan.ru; internet www.cityadm.magadan.ru.

Sakhalin Oblast

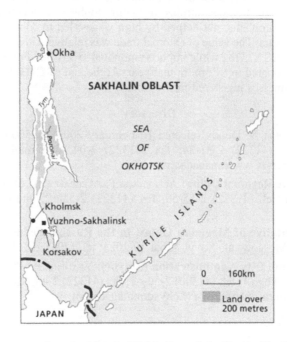

Sakhalin Oblast comprises the island of Sakhalin and the Kurile (Kuril) Islands in the Pacific Ocean. It forms part of the Far Eastern Federal Okrug and the Far Eastern Economic Area. The island of Sakhalin lies off the coast of Khabarovsk Krai, separated from the mainland by the Tatar Strait. Eastward lie the Kurile Islands (annexed by the USSR in 1945, but claimed by Japan), which are an archipelago of some 56 islands extending from the Kamchatka Peninsula in the north-east, to Hokkaido Island (Japan) in the south-west. Sakhalin Island is 942 km (just over 580 miles) in length and contains two parallel mountain ranges running north to south and separated by a central valley. The highest peaks on the island, both belonging to the eastern range of mountains, are Lopatin (1,609 m or 5,281 feet) and Nevelskogo (1,397 m). The north-west coast of the island is marshland, and much of its area is forested. The Kurile Islands are actively volcanic and contain many hot springs. There are some 60,000 rivers on Sakhalin Island, the major ones being the Poronai and the Tym (330 km), both of which are frozen during the winter months (December–April/May). The Kurile Islands contain around 4,000 rivers and streams and the largest waterfall in the Russian Federation, Ilya Muromets. Sakhalin Oblast covers a total area of 87,100 sq km (33,620 sq miles). According to the census of 9–16 October 2002, the Oblast's total population was 546,695, the region's population density being 6.3 per sq km. Some 86.7% of the region's total population resided in urban areas. 84.3% of the population were ethnically Russian, 5.4% Korean, 4.0% Ukrainian, 1.2% Tatar and 1.0% Belarusian. The population of the Oblast declined during the 1990s, largely reflecting migration from the region as a result of the decline of its industrial base. The Oblast's administrative centre is at Yuzhno-

Sakhalinsk, which had 174,700 inhabitants in mid-October 2002, according to provisional census results. Sakhalin Oblast is included in the time zone GMT+12.

History

Sakhalin was traditionally known as a place of exile for political opponents to the tsars. It was originally inhabited by the indigenous Gilyak people. The island was conquered by the Japanese in the late 18th century, but Russia established a military base at Korsakov in 1853. Joint control of the island followed until 1875, when it was granted to Russia in exchange for the Kurile Islands. Karafuto, the southern part of the island, was won by Japan during the Russo–Japanese War (1904–05), but the entire island was ceded to the USSR in 1945. The Kurile Islands were divided between Japan and Russia in the 18th century and ruled jointly until 1875. The USSR occupied the islands in 1945 and assumed full control in 1947. After the disintegration of the USSR in 1991, the southern Kuriles remained disputed between Japan and the Russian Federation. Sakhalin Oblast had been formed on 20 October 1932 as part of Khabarovsk Krai. It became a separate administrative unit in 1947, when the island was united with the Kuriles. The region contained several penal institutions of the GULag (State Corrective Camps) system established during the regime of Stalin (Iosif Dzhugashvili, 1924–53) and remained closed to foreigners until 1990.

On 16 October 1993 the head of the regional administration disbanded the Regional Soviet; a Regional Duma was elected in its place. In May 1995 a major earthquake, one of the largest to occur in Russia, destroyed the settlement of Neftegorsk in the north of the region, and killed an estimated 2,000 people. In May 1996 the federal President, Boris Yeltsin, signed a power-sharing treaty with the regional Government. The gubernatorial elections of October 1996 and October 2000 were won by the incumbent, Igor Farkhutdinov.

In December 1998 the Oblast authorities signed a friendship and economic co-operation accord with the Japanese province of Hokkaido, and a further agreement was signed in January 2000, despite the continuing dispute over the sovereignty of four of the Southern Kuriles (known as the 'Northern Territory' to Japan) between Russia and Japan. Concerns about the high levels of organized crime in the region were believed to have contributed to the introduction by the federal authorities of restrictions on movement on Sakhalin Island (and other border regions of the Russian Federation) from March 2003; henceforth, both foreign citizens and Russian citizens resident outside the Oblast were required to obtain permits before travelling beyond Yuzhno-Sakhalinsk.

On 20 August 2003 Farkhutdinov and several senior oblast officials were killed in a helicopter crash. The first round of voting in a gubernatorial election was held on 7 December (concurrently with elections to the federal State Duma). Acting Governor Ivan Malakhov and the Mayor of Yuzhno-Sakhalinsk, Fedor Sidorenko, proceeded to a second round of voting, held on 21 December, in which Malakhov emerged as the victor, with around 53% of the votes cast. In October 2005, as an indication that Russia had ruled out any immediate resolution to the dispute over the South Kurile Islands, the federal Government approved a 10-year strategy for improving social and economic conditions on the islands, pledging to invest more than 15,000m. roubles in the project. (No progress was seemingly made on resolving the issue at the Russia-Japan summit held in Tokyo, Japan in the following month.)

Economy

In 2002 Sakhalin Oblast's gross regional product amounted to 56,389.7m. roubles, or some 103,146.5 roubles per head. The Oblast's principal industrial centres are at Yuzhno-Sakhalinsk, Kholmsk, Okha (the administrative centre of the petroleum-producing region), Nevelsk, Dolinsk and Poronaisk. At the end of 2002 there were 805 km of railways and 831 km of paved roads in the Oblast. Its ports are Kholmsk (from where the Kholmsk–Vanino ferry connects Sakhalin Island with Khabarovsk Krai and continental Russia) and Korsakov. There are flights to Moscow, Khabarovsk, Vladivostok, Petropavlovsk-Kamchatskii and Novosibirsk, and international services to Alaska, USA, the Republic of Korea (South Korea) and Japan.

Agriculture in the region is minimal, owing to its unfavourable climatic conditions—agricultural land occupies only 1% of its territory. It employed just 4.1% of the working population in 2003, and consists mainly of potato and vegetable production and animal husbandry (largely comprising reindeer-breeding and fur-farming). Total agricultural production amounted to a value of 3,216m. roubles in 2003. In 2002 crop sales generated 62.9% of agricultural production, and animal husbandry 37.1%. Annual catches of fish and other marine life amount to around 400,000 metric tons. Fishing and fish-processing is the major traditional industry. The industrial sector employed some 21.4% of the region's work-force and generated 37,252m. roubles in 2003. There is some extraction of coal and, increasingly, petroleum and natural gas in, and to the north of, Sakhalin Island. Some petroleum is piped for refining to a plant in Komsomolsk-on-Amur (Khabarovsk Krai), although from 1994 the Oblast had its own refinery, with a capacity of some 200,000 tons per year. Coal was the region's primary source of energy, but in the late 1990s a gradual conversion to gas was initiated.

By the end of the 1990s four major consortia had been formed to exploit the natural resources of the region. Sakhalin-1, a project to produce petroleum on the continental shelf of Sakhalin Island comprises ExxonMobil of the USA (30%), Japan's Sodeco consortium (involving Itochi, Japan National Oil Company, Japex and Marubeni, 30%), Rosneft (of which Sakhalinmorneftegaz is a local subsidiary, 20%) and India's Oil and Natural Gas Corporation (20%). Sakhalin-2, two fields containing an estimated 1,000m. barrels of petroleum and 408,000m. cu m of natural gas, was initiated by Sakhalin Energy Investment, comprising Mitsui and Mitsubishi (of Japan), Marathon (of the USA) and RoyalDutch/Shell (Netherlands/United Kingdom). Sakhalin-2 was the largest single foreign direct investment project yet recorded in Russia, worth some US $10,000m; the world's largest liquified natural gas (LNG) plant was to be constructed as a part of the project by 2006. Sakhalin-3, backed by a consortium of Mobil (now ExxonMobil), Texaco (now Chevron-Texaco—of the USA) and the state-owned Russian company Rosneft, was seeking to develop what was potentially the largest field on the Sakhalin shelf, containing an estimated 320m. tons of recoverable reserves. However, in January 2004 federal deputy premier Viktor Khristenko unexpectedly annulled the tender to develop Sakhalin-3 won by the consortium in 1993, while in 2005 it was announced that Sakhalin-3 constituted one of the strategically important deposits of natural resources in which non-Russian companies were henceforth to be prohibited from participating. Meanwhile, in mid-2002 it was announced that Rosneft was to undertake the development of a further project, Sakhalin-5, in association with BP (United Kingdom—the Russian interests of which subsequently were merged into

TNK-BP). In addition, food-processing (largely of fish products) was a significant industrial activity in the Oblast, accounting for 29.9% of industrial output in 2002.

Sakhalin Oblast's economically active population totalled 315,000 in 2003, when 9.1% of the labour force were unemployed. The average monthly wage in the region amounted to some 9,331.0 roubles in that year. The 2003 budget showed a deficit of 523.1m. roubles. In the same year exports from the Oblast were valued at US $646.0m. and imports to the Oblast were worth $364.2m.; total foreign investment in the region amounted to some $2,083.1m. in 2003 (some 73% of all foreign investment in the Far Eastern Federal Okrug in that year), compared with $706.7m in 2002. At the end of 2003 some 4,400 small businesses were registered in the Oblast.

Directory

Governor: IVAN P. MALAKHOV (elected 21 December 2003), 693011 Sakhalin obl., Yuzhno-Sakhalinsk, Kommunisticheskii pr. 39; tel. (4242) 72-19-02; fax (4242) 23-60-81; e-mail webmaster@adm.sakhalin.ru; internet www.adm.sakhalin.ru.

Chairman of the Regional Duma: VLADIMIR I. YEFREMOV, 693000 Sakhalin obl., Yuzhno-Sakhalinsk, ul. Chekhova 37; tel. (4242) 42-14-89; fax (4242) 72-15-46; e-mail chairman@duma.sakhalin.ru; internet www.duma.sakhalin.ru.

Chief Representative of Sakhalin Oblast in the Russian Federation: SERGEI A. OSIPOV, 127025 Moscow, ul. Novyi Arbat 19/1132; tel. (495) 203-78-34; fax (495) 203-84-56; e-mail prsakh2001@mail.ru.

Head of Yuzhno-Sakhalinsk City Administration (Mayor): FEDOR I. SIDORENKO, 693023 Sakhalin obl., Yuzhno-Sakhalinsk, ul. Lenina 173; tel. (4242) 72-25-11; fax (4242) 23-00-06; e-mail ys_mayor@sctel.ru; internet yuzhno.sakh.ru.

Jewish Autonomous Oblast

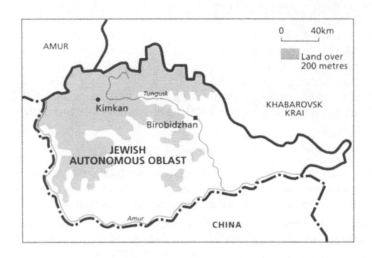

The Jewish Autonomous Oblast (AOb) is part of the Amur river basin, and is included in Russia's Far Eastern Federal Okrug and Far Eastern Economic Area. It is situated to the south-west of Khabarovsk Krai, on the international border with the People's Republic of China. There is a border with Amur Oblast in the north-west. The Amur (Heilong Jiang) and the Tungusk are the region's major rivers. It occupies 36,000 sq km (13,900 sq miles). According to the census of 9–16 October 2002, the Jewish AOb had a population of 190,915, and a population density of 5.3 per sq km. Around 67.3% of its population inhabited urban areas. 89.9% of the population were ethnically Russian, 4.4% Ukrainian; just 1.2% described their ethnicity as Jewish; in the early 1950s Jews were believed to have constituted around one-quarter of the population of the region, and at the 1989 census, 4.2% of the population of the AOb were Jewish according to 'official declaration of nationality' (ethnicity). The subsequent decline was believed to be largely attributable to emigration, particularly to Israel. The regional capital is at Birobidzhan, which had an estimated population of 77,300, according to provisional results of the 2002 census. The Jewish Autonomous Oblast is included in the time zone GMT+10.

History

The majority of Russian Jews came under Russian control following the Partitions of Poland in 1772–95. In Imperial Russia, between 1835 and 1917, Jews were required to receive special permission to live outside the 'Pale of Settlement' in the south-west of the Empire, which constituted territories largely in present-day Belarus, Lithuania, Poland and Ukraine, and were subject to widespread discrimination in the regions that they did inhabit. Attempts by the Soviet authorities in the 1920s to create nominally Jewish regions in Ukraine and Crimea were largely unsuccessful, in part because of hostility from the local population in these regions, although some nominally Jewish administrative sub-districts existed in southern Ukraine prior to the Nazi German invasion of the USSR in 1941. The Soviet regime established a national Jewish district at Birobidzhan in 1928, but it never became the centre of Soviet (or Russian) Jewry, largely because of its remote location and the absence of any prior Jewish settlement there. The district received the status of an Autonomous Oblast in May 1934 and formed part of Khabarovsk Krai until 25 March 1991.

In the early post-Soviet period the region remained a redoubt of communist support. Despite the advice of the Russian President, Boris Yeltsin, at a session on 14 October 1993 the Regional Soviet announced that it would not disband itself. Subsequently, however, the council was replaced by a new body, the Legislative Assembly, elections to which confirmed Communist Party domination. A gubernatorial election held on 20 October 1996 was won by the incumbent, Nikolai Volkov; he was re-elected with 57% of the votes cast on 26 March 2000.

Economy

In 2002 the Jewish AOb's gross regional product stood at 6,649.2m. roubles, equivalent to 34,828.1 roubles per head. Birobidzhan is the region's main industrial centre. At the end of 2002 there were 309 km of railway track, including a section of the Trans-Siberian Railway, and 1,633 km of paved roads on the region's territory. In 2000 the opening of a bridge across the Amur river provided improved road and rail links with the city of Khabarovsk and the People's Republic of China. There are around 600 km of navigable waterways in the south of the Jewish AOb.

Agriculture, which employed 12.8% of the region's work-force in 2003 and generated a total of 1,775m. roubles in that year, consists mainly of grain, soybean, vegetable and potato production, and animal husbandry. (Of the total value of agricultural production in 2002, crop sales accounted for 61.0% and animal husbandry for 39.0%.) From the late 1990s the oblast authorities encouraged Chinese farmers to undertake agricultural activity (both arable and livestock) in the region; greater diversity of crops, as well as an improvement in productivity, resulting in part from a higher level of farming technology, were reported as a result, although concern was expressed in early 2003 about the number of illegal immigrants in the region. There are major deposits of coal, peat, iron ore, manganese, tin, gold, graphite, magnesite and zeolite, although they are largely unexploited. The main industries are mechanical engineering and metal-working, the manufacture of building materials, the production of electricity, wood-working and light manufacturing. Industry employed 14.8% of the Jewish AOb's working population in 2003 and generated 2,383m. roubles. In the mid-2000s the region's foreign economic activity was largely concentrated in the Far East, including the People's Republic of China and Japan.

In 2003 the Jewish AOb's economically active population numbered 93,000. Although more than one-quarter of the labour force were unemployed in 1997, by 2003 the unemployment rate had declined to 6.5%. In 2002 the average monthly wage in the region was 5,409.6 roubles—the lowest figure of any federal subject in the Far Eastern Federal Okrug. The 2003 budget showed a deficit of 66.7m. roubles. In that year external trade amounted to a value of US $8.4m. in exports and $3.8m. in imports. In 2003 foreign investment amounted to just $500,000; five of the seven foreign- or jointly-owned enterprises operating in the territory in 2001 had Chinese partners. At the end of 2003 around 400 small businesses were registered in the region.

Directory

Head of the Regional Administration (Governor and Chairman of the Government): NIKOLAI M. VOLKOV (appointed 14 December 1991, elected 20 October 1996, re-elected 26 March 2000), 679016 Jewish AOb, Birobidzhan, pr. 60-letiya SSSR 18; tel. and fax (42622) 6-04-89; e-mail web@eao.ru; internet www.eao.ru.

Chairman of the Legislative Assembly: ANATOLII F. TIKHOMIROV, 679016 Jewish AOb, Birobidzhan, pr. 60-letiya SSSR 18; tel. (42622) 6-04-72; e-mail press-zs@eao .ru; internet www.eao.ru/?p=22.

Chief Representation of the Jewish Autonomous Oblast in the Russian Federation: (vacant), Moscow.

Head of Birobidzhan City Administration: ALEKSANDR A. VINNIKOV, Jewish AOb, 679016 Birobidzhan, ul. Lenina 29; tel. (42622) 6-22-02; fax (42622) 4-04-93; e-mail goriao@on-line.jar.ru; internet www.eao.ru/?p=746.

Chukot Autonomous Okrug

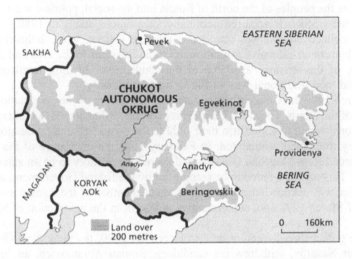

The Chukot Autonomous Okrug (AOk) is situated mostly on the Chukotka Peninsula and forms part of the Far Eastern Federal Okrug and the Far Eastern Economic Area. It is the easternmost part of Russia and faces the Eastern Siberian Sea (Arctic Ocean) to the north and the Bering Sea to the south; the Anadyr Gulf, part of the Bering Sea, cuts into the territory from the south-east. The USA (Alaska) lies eastwards across the Bering Straits. The western end of the district borders the Republic of Sakha (Yakutiya) to the west, and Magadan Oblast to the south. Also to the south lies the Koryak AOk (within Kamchatka Oblast). The district's major river is the Anadyr. The Chukot AOk occupies an area of 737,700 sq km (284,830 sq miles), of which approximately one-half lies within the Arctic Circle. Its climate is severe; the average temperature in January is –29.2°C, and in July it is 9.4°C. According to the census of 9–16 October 2002, it had a total of 53,824 inhabitants, and a population density of 0.07 per sq km. Approximately 66.4% of the territory's population inhabited urban areas. 51.9% of the population were ethnically Russian, 23.5% Chukchi, 9.2% Ukrainian, 2.9% Eskimo (Inuit), 1.8% Chuvanets, 1.0% Tatar and 1.0% Belarusian. Around 80,000 people left the AOk between 1991 and 2002. The Chukchi (who call themselves the Lyg Oravetlyan, and are also known as the Luoravetlan, Chukcha and Chukot) speak the Chukotic language as their native tongue, which belongs to the Paleo-Asiatic linguistic family. Traditionally they were divided into nomadic and semi-nomadic reindeer herders (the Chavchu or Chav-chuven), and coastal dwellers (known as the An Kalyn). The district's administrative centre is at Anadyr, which had a population of 11,100, according to the provisional results of the 2002 census, compared with 17,000 in 1989. The Chukot Autonomous Okrug is included in the time zone GMT+12.

History

Russian settlers first arrived in the territories inhabited by Chukchi tribes in the mid-17th century. Commercial traders, fur trappers and hunters subsequently established contact with the Chukchi, many of whom were forcibly converted to Orthodox

Christianity and enserfed. A Chukot National Okrug was created within Magadan Oblast by the Soviet Government on 10 December 1930, as part of its policy to incorporate the peoples of the north of Russia into the social, political and economic body of the USSR. (It acquired nominally autonomous status in 1980.) Simultaneously, collectivization was introduced into the district, while industrialization resulted both in an extensive migration of ethnic Russians to the area and a drastic reduction of the territory available to the Chukchi for herding reindeer. Many abandoned their traditional way of life to work in industry.

In March 1990 the Chukchi participated in the creation of the Association of the Peoples of the North. They also campaigned for the ratification of two international conventions, which would affirm their right to the ownership and possession of the lands they traditionally inhabited. In February 1991 the legislature of the Chukot AOk seceded from Magadan Oblast and declared the territory to be an autonomous republic. This measure failed to be recognized by the federal Government, although the district was acknowledged as a constituent member of the Federation by the Treaty of March 1992 and, subsequently, as free from the jurisdiction of Magadan Oblast.

At the gubernatorial election held in December 2000, the incumbent Governor, Aleksandr Nazarov, withdrew his candidacy. Roman Abramovich, an 'oligarch' associated with the petroleum company Sibneft, was elected in his place, receiving 91% of the votes cast. Although Abramovich was generally regarded as a popular Governor in the region, owing largely to improvements to public services and utilities implemented in the Okrug after his election, by 2003 he had made it known that he did not intend to seek a further term in office. Meanwhile, Abramovich sought to cultivate closer ties between the region and the nearby US state of Alaska. The first Alaska-Chukotka summit was held in Nome, Alaska, in mid-2001 to that end; it was intended that this summit would henceforth be an annual occurrence. Following the 2002 summit Abramovich and the Governor of Alaska, Tony Knowles, signed a document that provided for the eventual establishment of regular air services between Nome and Anadyr and for the promotion of co-operation in areas including education, health care, economic development and environmental protection.

In early 2004 the Audit Chamber of the State Duma conducted a three-month audit of the finances of the Okrug. The findings, promulgated in May, declared the Okrug to be insolvent, with debts of 9,300m. roubles at the beginning of 2004, compared with revenues of only 3,900m. roubles in 2003. The Chamber also launched an investigation into possible fraud and misuse of public funds committed by Abramovich in connection with the sale of the Maiskoye gold mine. The Chairman of the Audit Chamber, former federal premier Sergei Stepashin, called on Abramovich to resign as Governor, while some commentators suggested the investigations were politically motivated. However, although Abramovich divested much of his financial and business interests in Russia, taking up residence in the United Kingdom, by mid-2005 there was widespread speculation that he would be nominated to serve a further term as Governor of Chukotka, following the abolition of elections to regional gubernatorial posts. In September 2005, despite earlier indications to the contrary, it was reported that Abramovich had agreed to serve a second term; following his nomination by federal President Vladimir Putin, the appointment was confirmed by the District Duma on 21 October.

Economy

In 2002 the Chukot AOk's gross regional product amounted to 11,894.3m. roubles, equivalent to 220,985.1 roubles per head. Although relatively high, this level of regional wealth was highly dependent on federal transfers. At the end of 2001 the territory had 589 km of paved roads and a relatively undeveloped infrastructure. Anadyr is one of the district's major ports, the others being Pevek, Providenya, Egvekinot and Beringovskii.

The AOk's agricultural sector, which employed 9.2% of the work-force in 2003, consists mainly of fishing, animal husbandry (especially reindeer-breeding) and hunting. Total agricultural production was worth 210m. roubles in 2003. In 2002 crop sales accounted for 7.9% of agricultural output, and animal husbandry for 92.1%. In 1992 it was estimated that some 500,000 reindeers were raised in state-controlled breeding areas. The region contains reserves of coal and brown coal (lignite), petroleum and natural gas, as well as gold, tin, wolfram (tungsten), copper and other minerals. It is self-sufficient in energy, containing two coal-mines, six producers of electricity and one nuclear power station. Its main industries are ore-mining, non-ferrous metallurgy (which accounted for 46.1% of total industrial output in 2002), electricity generation and food-processing. Industry employed some 15.9% of the district's working population in 2003 and generated 4,730m. roubles.

The AOk's economically active population numbered 47,000 in 2003. The rate of unemployment has been relatively low; in 2003 only 4.8% of the labour force were unemployed. Those in employment earned an average of 17,270.7 roubles per month, well above the national average and the highest of any federal subject in the Far Eastern Federal Okrug, although this was counterbalanced by some of the highest living costs in the Federation; in December 2003 a minimum 'consumer basket' in the Chukot AOk cost 3,154.9 roubles, almost three times the national average and, indeed, the most expensive in the Federation. The 2003 district government budget showed a deficit of 565.8m. roubles. The external trade of the district is relatively minimal, and in 2003 exports amounted to only US $100,000. and imports to $35.3m. At the end of 2003 there were around 200 small businesses registered in the AOk.

Directory

Head of the District Administration (Governor): Roman A. Abramovich (elected 24 December 2000; appointment confirmed 21 October 2005), 689000 Chukot AOk, Anadyr, ul. Beringa 20; tel. (42722) 2-90-00; fax (42722) 2-27-25; internet www .chukotka.org.

Chairman of the District Duma: Vasilii N. Nazarenko, 689000 Chukot AOk, Anadyr, ul. Otke 29; tel. (42722) 2-93-51; fax (42722) 2-93-73; e-mail dumachao@ mail.ru; internet dumachao.anadyr.ru.

Chief Representative of the Chukot Autonomous Okrug in the Russian Federation: Aleksandr V. Moskalenko, 119034 Moscow, M. Kursovoi per. 4; tel. (495) 502-97-30; fax (495) 925-82-27.

Head of Anadyr City Administration: Andrei G. Shchegolkov, 689000 Chukot AOk, Anadyr, ul. Lenina 45; tel. (41361) 2-21-02; fax (41361) 2-22-16; internet dumachao.anadyr.ru/power/index.htm.

Koryak Autonomous Okrug

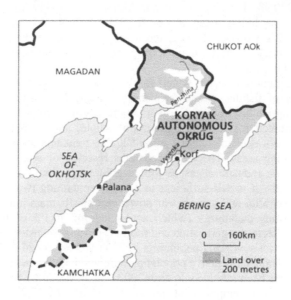

The Koryak Autonomous Okrug (AOk) comprises the northern part of the Kamchatka Peninsula and the adjacent area of mainland. It forms part of the Far Eastern Federal Okrug and the Far Eastern Economic Area, and of Kamchatka Oblast. Its eastern coastline lies on the Bering Sea, and its western shores face the Sea of Okhotsk. South of the district lies the rest of Kamchatka Oblast. In the north it is bordered by the Chukot AOk and Magadan Oblast, to the north and to the west, respectively. The Koryak AOk occupies 301,500 sq km (116,410 sq miles). According to the census of 9–16 October 2002, its total population was 25,157, and its population density stood at just 0.08 per sq km. Just 26.0% of the population inhabited urban areas. 50.6% of the population were ethnically Russian, 26.7% Koryak, 5.6% Chukchi, 4.7% Itelmeni, 4.1% Ukrainian and 0.9% Tatar. The administrative centre of the district is at Palana 'urban-type settlement', which had a population of just 3,900, according to preliminary results of the 2002 census. The Koryak Autonomous Okrug is included in the time zone GMT+12.

History

The area was established as a territorial unit within Kamchatka Oblast on 10 December 1930. Like the Chukchi, the Koryaks comprise nomadic and semi-nomadic hunters and more sedentary coastal dwellers. They first encountered ethnic Russians in the 1640s, when Cossacks, commercial traders and fur trappers arrived in the district. The Soviet Government attempted to collectivize the Koryaks' economic activity, beginning with the fishing industry in 1929 and continuing with reindeer hunting in 1932, a measure that was violently opposed by the Koryak community. After the Second World War large numbers of ethnic Russians moved to the area, which was becoming increasingly industrialized. The resultant threat to the Koryaks' traditional way of life, and environmental deterioration, became a source of contention between the local community and the federal Government during the period of *glasnost* (openness) in the late 1980s. An independent candidate, Valentina Bronevich, was elected Governor in late 1996, the first woman to head the administration of a territorial unit in the Russian Federation. On 5 May 1999 Bronevich signed a co-operation agreement with the Governor of Kamchatka Oblast. On 3 December 2000 a local businessman, Vladimir Loginov, defeated Bronevich in a gubernatorial election, receiving 51% of the votes cast.

Gubernatorial elections held on 14 March 2004 proved inconclusive, necessitating a second round of polling between Loginov and the district Public Prosecutor, Boris Chuyev, whose office had begun investigating Loginov's administration on charges of negligence in the run-up to the election. Loginov was elected to a second term of office on 4 April with 51% of the votes cast. On 9 March 2005 the federal President, Vladimir Putin, dismissed Loginov, expressing dissatisfaction at the provision of heating to housing in the district throughout the preceding winter months. (Loginov thereby became the first regional leader to be formally dismissed by Putin, almost five years after his election to the Presidency). On the same day Oleg Kozhemyako, a business executive and a close associate of the controversial former Governor of Maritime Krai, Yevgenii Nazdratenko, was appointed as Governor in an acting capacity (Kozhemyako had been placed third in gubernatorial elections in Kamchatka Oblast in December 2004.) Meanwhile, on 15 April Kozhemyako's nomination as Governor was approved by the district Duma, under the provisions introduced in late 2004 abolishing the election of regional governors. In late April the district Duma voted, at the second reading, to approve proposals for an eventual merger of the AOk with Kamchatka Oblast (the legislature of which had recently approved a request that Putin approve such a measure.) In early May the Governors of the two territories signed a protocol on the merger, announcing that referendums on the merger would be held in both territories on 23 October. 76.7% of the AOk's electorate participated in the referendum, when some 89.0% voted in support of the unification.

Economy

In 2002 the Koryak AOk's gross regional product amounted to 3,605.6m. roubles, equivalent to 143,323.9 roubles per head. At the end of 2002 the territory had just 65 km of paved roads. Fishing is the most important economic activity in the district, contributing 60% of total industrial output.

The district's agriculture, which employed 11.0% of the work-force in 2003, consists mainly of reindeer-breeding, fur-farming and hunting. Total agricultural output was worth 117m. roubles in that year. In 2002 51.0% of agricultural output was accounted for by crop sales, and 49.0% by animal husbandry. The main industries are food-processing and the production of non-ferrous metals (primarily palladium and platinum, which in 2002 accounted for 47.9% and 42.4% of total output, respectively) and the extraction of brown coal (lignite). Industry employed 22.6% of the work-force and generated a total of 5,378m. roubles in 2003.

The economically active population numbered 16,000 in 2003, when 13.6% of the labour force were unemployed. The average monthly wage was some 11,853.9 roubles in 2003. The budget recorded a deficit of 183.7m. roubles in 2003. By the early 2000s the okrug remained impoverished and dependent on federal subsidies. The external trade of the AOk comprised US $34.3m. of exports and $5.3m. of imports in 2003, when the district attracted foreign investment worth US $2.2m. At the end of 2002 some 36 small businesses were registered in the territory.

Directory

Governor: OLEG KOZHEMYAKO (appointment confirmed 15 April 2005), 684620 Kamchatka obl., Koryak AOk, PGT Palana, ul. Porotova 22; tel. (41543) 3-13-80; fax (41543) 3-13-70.

Chairman of the District Duma: VLADIMIR I. ZUYEV, 684620 Kamchatka obl., Koryak AOk, PGT Palana, ul. Porotova 22; tel. (41543) 3-10-30.

Representation of the Koryak Autonomous Okrug in Kamchatka Oblast: 683000 Kamchatka obl., Petropavlovsk-Kamchatskii, pl. Lenina 1; tel. (41522) 12-51-76; fax (41522) 11-26-95.

Chief Representative of the Koryak Autonomous Okrug in the Russian Federation: VLADIMIR M. SHEVELENKO, 125009 Moscow, ul. B. Dmitrovka 9/7; tel. (495) 229-54-21.

PART THREE
Select Bibliography

Select Bibliography

Bassin, M. *Imperial Visions: Nationalist Imagination and Geographical Expansion in the Russian Far East.* Cambridge, Cambridge Univ. Press, 1999.

Baxendale, J., Dewar, S., and Gowan, D. *The EU and Kaliningrad: Kaliningrad and the Impact of EU Enlargement.* London, Kogan Page, 2000.

Bradshaw, M. J. (Ed.). *The Soviet Union: A New Regional Geography?* London, Belhaven Press, 1991.

The Russian Far East and Pacific Asia. London, RoutledgeCurzon, 2001.

Brunstad, B., Magnus, E., Swanson, P., Hønneland, G., and Øverland, I. (Eds). *Big Oil Playground, Russian Bear Preserve or European Periphery?: The Russian Barents Sea Region Towards 2015.* Delft, Eburon, 2004.

Bukharayev, R. *The Model of Tatarstan: Under Mintimer Shaimiyev.* London, RoutledgeCurzon, 2001.

Chenciner, R. (Ed.). *Daghestan: Tradition and Survival.* London, Curzon, 1997.

Colton, T. *Moscow: Governing the Socialist Metropolis.* Cambridge, MA, Harvard Univ. Press, 1995.

Comité Tchetchenie. *Tchetchenie: Dix Clés pour Comprendre.* Paris, La Découverte, 2003.

Council for Trade and Economic Cooperation USA–CIS (CTEC). *Russia: All 89 Regions Trade & Investment Guide.* New York, CTEC, 2003.

Crosston, M. *Shadow Separatism: Implications for Democratic Consolidation.* Aldershot, Ashgate, 2004.

Dolkinskaya, I. *Transition and Regional Inequality in Russia: Reorganization or Procrastination?* Washington, DC, IMF, 2002.

Dunlop, J. B. *Russia Confronts Chechnya: Roots of a Separatist Conflict.* Cambridge, Cambridge Univ. Press, 1998.

Easter, G. M. *Reconstructing the State: Personal Networks and Elite Identity in Soviet Russia.* Cambridge, Cambridge Univ. Press, 2000.

Evangelista, M. *The Chechen Wars: Will Russia Go the Way of the Soviet Union?* Washington, DC, Brookings Institution Press, 2002.

Evans, A. B., and Gelman, V. (Eds). *The Politics of Local Government in Russia.* Lanham, MD, Rowman & Littlefield, 2004.

Forsyth, J. *A History of the Peoples of Siberia.* Cambridge, Cambridge Univ. Press, 1994.

Freinkman, L. *Subnational Budgeting in Russia.* Washington, DC, World Bank, 2000.

Friedgut, T. H., and Hahn, J. W. (Eds). *Local Power and Post-Soviet Politics.* Armonk, NY, M. E. Sharpe, 1995.

Gall, C., and de Waal, T. *Chechnya: Calamity in the Caucasus.* New York, New York Univ. Press, 1998.

Gelman, V., Ryzhenkov, S., Brie, M., et al. *The Comparative Politics of Russia's Regions.* Lanham, MD, Rowman & Littlefield, 2003.

Gibson, J., and Hanson, P. (Eds). *Transformation from Below: Local Power and the Political Economy of Post-Communist Transitions*. Cheltenham, Edward Elgar, 1996.

Glatter, P. *Tyumen: The West Siberian Oil and Gas Province*. London, Royal Institute of International Affairs, 1997.

Golosov, G. V. *Political Parties in the Regions of Russia: Democracy Unclaimed*. Boulder, CO, Lynne Rienner, 2004.

Gorenburg, D. P. *Minority Ethnic Mobilization in the Russian Federation*. Cambridge, Cambridge Univ. Press, 2003.

Grant, B., and Pika, A. (Ed.). *Neotraditionalism in the Russian North*. Washington, DC, Univ. of Washington Press, 1999.

Hahn, J. (Ed.). *Democratization in Russia: The Development of Legislative Institutions*. Armonk, NY, M. E. Sharpe, 1996.

Regional Russia in Transformation. Washington, DC, Woodrow Wilson Center Press, 2001.

Hanson, P., and Bradshaw, M. J. (Eds). *Regional Economic Change in Russia*. Cheltenham, Edward Elgar, 2000.

Herd, G. P., and Aldis, A. *Russian Regions and Regionalism*. London, RoutledgeCurzon, 2002.

Herspring, D. R. (Ed.). *Putin's Russia: Past Imperfect, Future Uncertain*. 2nd edn, Lanham, MD, Rowman & Littlefield, 2004.

Hill, F. *Russia's Tinderbox: Conflict in the North Caucasus and its Implications for the Future of the Russian Federation*. Cambridge, MA, Harvard Univ. Press, 1995.

Hill, F., and Gaddy, C. G. *The Siberian Curse: How Central Planners Left Russia Out in the Cold*. Washington, DC, Brookings Institution Press, 2003.

Human Rights Watch. *Russia, the Ingush–Ossetian Conflict in the Prigorodnyi Region*. New York, Human Rights Watch, 1996.

Hunter, S. T. *Islam in Russia: The Politics of Identity and Security*. Armonk, NY, M. E. Sharpe, 2004.

Hutcheson, D. *Political Parties in the Russian Regions*. London, RoutledgeCurzon, 2003.

Jacobs, E. M. (Ed.). *Soviet Local Politics and Government*. London, HarperCollins, 1983.

Jaimoukha, A. *The Circassians*. London, RoutledgeCurzon, 2001.

The Chechens: A Handbook. Abingdon, RoutledgeCurzon, 2005.

Kahn, J. *Federalism, Democratization and the Rule of Law In Russia*. Oxford, Oxford Univ. Press, 2002.

Kirkow, P. *Russia's Provinces: Authoritarian Transformation versus Local Autonomy*. London, Macmillan, and New York, St Martin's Press, 1998.

Kondrashev, S. *Nationalism and the Drive for Sovereignty in Tatarstan, 1988–92: Origins and Development (Studies in Diplomacy)*. New York, St Martin's Press, 1999.

Koropeckyi, I. S., and Schroeder, G. E. (Eds). *Economics of Soviet Regions*. New York, Praeger, 1981.

Kotkin, S., and Wolff, D. (Eds). *Rediscovering Russia in Asia: Siberia and the Russian Far East*. New York, M. E. Sharpe, 1995.

Krickus, R. J. *The Kaliningrad Question*. Lanham, MD, Rowman & Littlefield, 2002.

Lankina, T. V. *Governing the Locals: Local Self-Government and Ethnic Mobilization in Russia*. Lanham, MD, Rowman & Littlefield, 2004.

Lavrov, A. M., Makushkin, A. G., et al. *The Fiscal Structure of the Russian Federation: Financial Flows between the Centre and the Regions*. Armonk, NY, M. E. Sharpe, 2001.

Lieven, A. *Chechnya: Tombstone of Russian Power*. New Haven, CT, Yale Univ. Press, 1998.

Lincoln, W. B. *The Conquest of a Continent: Siberia and the Russians*. New York, Random House, 1994.

McAuley, M. *Russia's Politics of Uncertainty*. Cambridge, Cambridge Univ. Press, 1997.

McFaul, M., Petrov, N., and Ryabov, A. *Between Dictatorship and Democracy: Russian Post-Communist Political Reform*. Washington, DC, Carnegie Endowment for International Peace, 2004.

Mandelstam Balzer, M. *The Tenacity of Ethnicity*. Princeton, NJ, Princeton Univ. Press, 1999.

Manezhev, S. A. *Russian Far East*. London, Royal Institute of International Affairs, 1993.

Melvin, N. *Regional Foreign Policies in the Russian Federation*. London, Royal Institute of International Affairs, 1995.

Mote, V. L. *Siberia: Worlds Apart*. Boulder, CO, Westview, 1998.

Nathans, B. *Beyond the Pale: The Jewish Encounter with Late Imperial Russia*. Berkeley, CA, Univ. of California Press, 2002.

Newell, J. *The Russian Far East: A Reference Guide for Conservation and Development*. 2nd edn, McKinleyville, CA, Daniel & Daniel, 2004.

Nivat, A. *La Guerre qui n'aura pas eu lieu*. Paris, Fayard, 2004.

Orttung, R. (Ed.). *The Republics and Regions of the Russian Federation: A Guide to Politics, Policies and Leaders*. 2 vols, Armonk, NY, M. E. Sharpe, 2000 (Vol. 1), 2005 (Vol. 2).

Pascal, E. *Defining Russian Federalism*. New York and London, Praeger, 2003.

Politkovskaya, A. *A Dirty War: A Russian Reporter in Chechnya*. London, Harvill, 2001.

   A Small Corner of Hell: Dispatches from Chechnya. Chicago, IL, Univ. of Chicago Press, 2003.

Pravda, A. (Ed.). *Leading Russia: Putin in Perspective (Essays in Honour of Archie Brown)*. Oxford, Oxford Univ. Press, 2005.

Reddaway, P. and Orttung, R. W. *The Dynamics of Russian Politics: Putin's Reform of Federal-Regional Relations*. 2 vols. Lanham, MD, Rowman & Littlefield, 2004.

Rigby, T. H. *Political Elites in the USSR: Central Leaders and Local Cadres from Lenin to Gorbachev*. Aldershot, Edward Elgar, 1990.

Rorlich, A.-A. *The Volga Tatars: A Profile in National Resilience*. Stanford, CA, Hoover Institution Press, 1986.

Rutland, P. *The Politics of Economic Stagnation in the Soviet Union: The Role of Local Party Organs in Economic Management*. Cambridge, Cambridge Univ. Press, 1993.

Sakwa, R. (Ed.). *Chechnya: From Past to Future*. London, Anthem Press, 2005.

Schiffer, J. R. *Soviet Regional Economic Policy: The East–West Debate over Pacific Siberian Development*. London, Macmillan, 1989.

Seely, R. *The Russo–Chechen Conflict 1800–2000*. London, Frank Cass, 2001.

Segbers, K. *Explaining Post-Soviet Patchworks Vol. 3: The Political Economy of Regions, Regimes and Republics*. Aldershot, Ashgate, 2001.

Smith, G. (Ed.). *The Nationalities Question in the Soviet Union*, 2nd edn. London, Longman, 1996.

Ssorin-Chaikov, N. V. *A Social Life of the State in the Siberian Subarctic*. Stanford, CA, Stanford Univ. Press, 2003.

Stavrakis, P. J., de Bardeleben, J., and Black, L. (Eds). *Beyond the Monolith: The Emergence of Regionalism in Post-Soviet Russia*. Washington, DC, Woodrow Wilson Press Centre and John Hopkins Press, 1997.

Stephan, J. J. *The Russian Far East: A History*. Stanford, CA, Stanford Univ. Press, 1996.

Thornton, J. (Ed.). *Russia's Far East: A Region at Risk*. Seattle, WA, Univ. of Washington Press, 2002.

Thubron, C. *In Siberia*. London, Penguin, 2000.

Tichotsky, J. *Russia's Diamond Colony: The Republic of Sakha*. Reading, Gordon & Breach, 2000.

Tishkov, V. *Chechnya: Life in a War-torn Society*. Berkeley, CA, Univ. of California Press, 2004.

Trenin, D. V. and Malashenko, A. V. *Russia's Restless Frontier: The Chechnya Factor in Post-Soviet Russia*. Washington, DC, Carnegie Endowment for International Peace, 2004.

Twigg, J. L. and Schecter, K. (Eds). *Social Capital and Social Cohesion in Post-Soviet Russia*. Armonk, NY, M. E. Sharpe, 2003.

Wallich, C. I. (Ed.). *Russia and the Challenge of Fiscal Federalism*. Washington, DC, World Bank, 1994.

Weinberg, R. *Stalin's Forgotten Zion: Birobidzhan and the Making of a Soviet Jewish Homeland*. Berkeley, CA, Univ. of California Press, 1998.

Wood, A, and French, R. A. (Eds). *The Development of Siberia: People and Resources*. London, Macmillan, 1989.

Zelkina, A. *The Chechens*. London, RoutledgeCurzon, 2001.

PART FOUR
Indexes

Alphabetic List of Territories

(including a gazetteer of alternative names)

119	Adygeya .	Republic
	Adygheya	*see Adygeya*
265	Aga-Buryat AOk .	Autonomous Okrug
	Alaniya .	*see North Osetiya—Alaniya*
244	Altai Krai	Krai
231	Altai Republic	Republic
285	Amur	Oblast
98	Archangel	Oblast
	Arkhangelsk .	*see Archangel*
	ASSR Nemtsev Povolzhyya/ASSR der	
	Wolgadeutschen (Volga-German ASSR) .	*see Saratov*
162	Astrakhan	Oblast
	Balkariya	*see Kabardino-Balkar Republic*
	Bashkiriya	*see Bashkortostan*
171	Bashkortostan	Republic
54	Belgorod .	Oblast
	Birobidzhan .	*see Jewish AOb*
56	Bryansk .	Oblast
235	Buryatiya	Republic
	Chavash Republic	*see Chuvash Republic*
122	Chechen (Nokchi) Republic	Republic
	Checheno-Ingush ASSR	*see Chechen (Nokchi) Republic and Ingushetiya*
	Checheno-Ingushetiya .	*see Chechen (Nokchi) Republic and Ingushetiya*
	Chechen Republic of Ichkeriya	*see Chechen (Nokchi) Republic*
	Chechnya	*see Chechen (Nokchi) Republic*
213	Chelyabinsk .	Oblast
	Cherkessiya	*see Karachai-Cherkess Republic*
250	Chita	Oblast
	Chkalov .	*see Orenburg*
301	Chukot AOk .	Autonomous Okrug
	Chukotka	*see Chukot AOk*
176	Chuvash Republic	Republic
	Chuvashiya	*see Chuvash Republic*
	Circassia .	*see Karachai-Cherkess Republic*
131	Dagestan .	Republic
	Daghestan	*see Dagestan*
	Dolgano-Nenets AOk .	*see Taimyr (Dolgano-Nenets) AOk*
	East Vogul National Okrug	*see Khanty-Mansii AOk—Yugra*
267	Evenk AOk .	Autonomous Okrug
	Evenkiya .	*see Evenk AOk*
	Far Eastern Republic .	*see Chita Oblast, etc.*
	Gorkii .	*see Nizhnii Novgorod*
	Gorno-Altai AOb .	*see Altai Republic*
	Gornyi Altai .	*see Altai Republic*
	Gorskaya People's Republic	*see Kabardino-Balkariya, etc.*
	Ichkeriya .	*see Chechen (Nokchi) Republic*
136	Ingushetiya	Republic
252	Irkutsk .	Oblast
58	Ivanovo .	Oblast
298	Jewish AOb .	Autonomous Oblast
140	Kabardino-Balkar Republic	Republic
	Kabardino-Balkariya .	*see Kabardino-Balkar Republic*

202	Penza	Oblast
192	Perm.	Krai
	Perm Oblast	*see Perm Krai*
	Petrograd	*see St Petersburg*
	Primorskii Krai	*see Maritime*
	Primorye	*see Maritime*
111	Pskov	Oblast
165	Rostov	Oblast
72	Ryazan	Oblast
89	St Petersburg City	City of Federal Status
275	Sakha (Yakutiya)	Republic
294	Sakhalin	Oblast
204	Samara	Oblast
	Sankt-Peterburg	*see St Petersburg*
207	Saratov	Oblast
	Severnaya Osetiya	*see North Osetiya—Alaniya*
	Severno-Kavkazskii Krai	*see Stavropol*
	Shcheglovsk	*see Kemerovo*
	Simbirsk	*see Ulyanovsk*
74	Smolensk	Oblast
	South-Eastern Oblast	*see Stavropol*
	Sredne-Volzhskaya Oblast	*see Samara*
	Stalingrad	*see Volgograd*
159	Stavropol	Krai
218	Sverdlovsk	Oblast
270	Taimyr (Dolgano-Nenets) AOk	Autonomous Okrug
76	Tambov	Oblast
	Tannu-Tuva	*see Tyva*
185	Tatarstan	Republic
263	Tomsk	Oblast
	Tsaritsyn	*see Volgograd*
78	Tula	Oblast
	Tuva	*see Tyva*
81	Tver	Oblast
221	Tyumen	Oblast
241	Tyva	Republic
189	Udmurt Republic	Republic
	Udmurtiya	*see Udmurt Republic*
210	Ulyanovsk	Oblast
273	Ust-Orda Buryat AOk	Autonomous Okrug
83	Vladimir	Oblast
	Volga-German ASSR	*see Saratov*
168	Volgograd	Oblast
114	Vologda	Oblast
85	Voronezh	Oblast
	Voroshilovsk	*see Stavropol*
	Votyak AOb	*see Udmurt Republic*
	Vyatka	*see Kirov*
	Yakutiya	*see Sakha*
228	Yamalo-Nenets AOk	Autonomous Okrug
87	Yaroslavl	Oblast
	Yekaterinburg	*see Sverdlovsk*
	Yekaterinodar	*see Krasnodar*
	Yevreiskaya AOb	*see Jewish AOb*
	Yugo-Vostochnaya Oblast	*see Samara*
	Yugra	*see Khanty-Mansii AOk—Yugra*

Federal Okrugs

Economic Areas

For Product Safety Concerns and Information please contact our EU representative GPSR@taylorandfrancis.com Taylor & Francis Verlag GmbH, Kaufingerstraße 24, 80331 München, Germany

T - #0016 - 270225 - C0 - 234/156/18 [20] - CB - 9781857433579 - Gloss Lamination